Francisco Sanches: That Nothing Is Known

Francisco Sanches
(Franciscus Sanchez)

That Nothing Is Known
(QVOD NIHIL SCITVR)

Introduction, notes, and bibliography by
ELAINE LIMBRICK
UNIVERSITY OF VICTORIA

Latin text established, annotated, and translated by
DOUGLAS F. S. THOMSON
UNIVERSITY COLLEGE, UNIVERSITY OF TORONTO

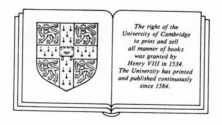

The right of the
University of Cambridge
to print and sell
all manner of books
was granted by
Henry VIII in 1534.
The University has printed
and published continuously
since 1584.

CAMBRIDGE UNIVERSITY PRESS
CAMBRIDGE
NEW YORK   NEW ROCHELLE   MELBOURNE   SYDNEY

Published by the Press Syndicate of the University of Cambridge
The Pitt Building, Trumpington Street, Cambridge CB2 1RP
32 East 57th Street, New York, NY 10022, USA
10 Stamford Road, Oakleigh, Melbourne 3166, Australia

First published 1988

Printed in the United States of America

Library of Congress Cataloging-in-Publication Data
Sánches, Francisco, ca. 1550–ca. 1623.
[Quod nihil scitur. English & Latin]
That nothing is known = (Quod nihil scitur) / Francisco Sanches
(Franciscus Sanchez); introduction, notes, and bibliography by
Elaine Limbrick; Latin text established and translated by Douglas F. S. Thomson
p. cm.
English and Latin.
Bibliography: p.
Includes index.
ISBN 0-521-35077-8
1. Skepticism – Early works to 1800.   I. Limbrick, Elaine.
II. Thomson, Douglas F. S.   III. Title.   IV. Title: Quod nihil
scitur.
B785.S23Q6813   1988
149'.73 – dc19   87–33395

British Library Cataloguing in Publication Data
Sanchez, Franciscus
[Quod nihil scitur. *English and Latin.*]
That nothing is known (Quod nihil scitur).
1. Knowledge.   Scepticism
I. Title   II.   Limbrick, Elaine
III. Thomson, Douglas F.S.
121'.5

ISBN 0 521 35077 8

IN MEMORY OF CHARLES B. SCHMITT

Contents

Preface

I am grateful to the Warden and Fellows of All Souls College, Oxford, for kindly providing a photocopy of the *Quod nihil scitur* (Lugduni: apud Antonium Gryphium, 1581) which has served as a basis for this critical edition and translation. The marginal glosses which appear in the 1581 edition and all subsequent editions have been omitted; the vague references to sources have been incorporated in my notes to the translation. I was obliged to consult the original sources, often unacknowledged in the text, in order to determine the exact references and quotations made by Sanches. As the *Quod nihil scitur* is in the main a running commentary and attack on the works of Aristotle, I have endeavoured to identify as far as possible the major references to individual works of Aristotle, although at times Sanches is as obscure and confused as he states Aristotle is.

The most useful modern edition of the *Quod nihil scitur* is that of Joaquim de Carvalho, included in his Coimbra 1955 edition of Sanches's *Opera philosophica*, republished in 1957 with a different pagination. In my introduction and notes I refer to the 1957 Carvalho edition. The large body of critical studies on Sanches produced by Portuguese scholars has been mainly neglected by North American and European scholars. In order to make these studies known I have listed them in the bibliography. I thank Senhora Pereira for correcting the Portuguese quotations.

The most recent Latin-French critical edition and translation of the *Quod nihil scitur, Il n'est science de rien* (Paris: Klincksieck, 1984) by Andrée Comparot, who generously sent me a copy of her edition, stresses Sanches's indebtedness to the Spanish humanist Vives. Mme Comparot's fine French translation brings out the rhetorical aspects of Sanches's Latin.

For Charles Schmitt, who first encouraged me to publish my

research on Sanches, I mourn: he was a great Renaissance scholar and devoted friend.

My greatest debt is to my colleague, Douglas F. S. Thomson, of the Department of Classics, University of Toronto, who willingly undertook the difficult task of translating the *Quod nihil scitur* in the spring of 1980. Professor Thomson also kindly accepted the laborious task of establishing the Latin text. Without his magnificent contribution this book would not have seen the light of day.

I would like to extend my thanks to friends and colleagues in France for inviting me to Paris to lecture on Sanches in December 1980 and for their many kindnesses in facilitating my research; in particular Robert Aulotte, Claude Blum, Jean Céard, Jean Ecole, Joseph Moreau, and Philippe Sellier.

The research for this critical edition was carried out thanks to the generous support of the University of Victoria and the Social Sciences and Humanities Research Council of Canada. I am grateful to the libraries and librarians of the Bibliothèque Nationale, the Centre Culturel Portugais (Paris), the Institut Catholique de Toulouse, the British Library, the Warburg Institute, and the University of Victoria. Without their courteous help the research for this book would have been even more difficult.

Finally I would like to express my gratitude to Dr Samuel Scully for aiding me with the Greek text of Aristotle; to my colleagues in the Department of French Language and Literature for enabling me to make frequent research trips to Europe; to my typist, Mrs Lucie Miller, for undertaking such a difficult manuscript and never complaining; to my editors, Mary Byers and Louise Calabro Gruendel, for their infinite care and patience; and to my son, David, for understanding long absences from Victoria.

Victoria, British Columbia   Elaine Limbrick

Introduction

I

The fame of Francisco Sanches (1551–1623), the Portuguese philosopher and doctor who held chairs in philosophy and in medicine at the University of Toulouse, rests mainly on the success of one book, the *Quod nihil scitur*, published in Lyons in 1581. His contemporaries considered him to be a great sceptic and he was known widely as "Sanchez le sceptique". In the seventeenth century his advocacy of an extreme form of scepticism prompted a Dutch opponent of Descartes, the Utrecht theologian and philosopher Martin Schoock, and the German theologian Gabriel Wedderkopff, to place Sanches on a long list of the most dangerous enemies of the Christian religion, among whom were included the illustrious Cardinal Nicholas of Cusa and Agrippa von Nettesheim.[1] Wedderkopff went so far as to call Sanches the "most ruinous of the Sceptics". Another German theologian, Daniel Hartnack, thought

---

[1] Martin Schoock (Schoockius), in his *De scepticismo pars prior, sive libri quatuor* (Groningae: ex officina Henrici Lussindi, 1652), examines the history of scepticism as part of his continuing campaign to discredit Descartes. In his review of modern sceptics he writes: "Ulterius ex recentioribus progressus est Cardinalis Crescentius in libro *de docta ignorantia:* ac prae aliis Franciscus Sanchez in opusculo, quod inscripsit *de multum nobili et prima universali scientia, quod nihil scitur*" (p. 69). Sanches is mentioned frequently in the work, as are Agrippa and Gassendi. The Frankfurt 1618 edition of the *Quod nihil scitur* first brought Sanches to the attention of Schoock and Voetius, who had already attacked Descartes in their *Admiranda methodus novae philosophiae Renati Des Cartes* (Ultraiechti: ex officina J. Van Waesbergae, 1643). Gabriel Wedderkopff refers to Schoock's work in his *Dissertationes duae quarum prior de Scepticismo profano et sacro praecipue remonstrantium, posterior de Atheismo praeprimis Socinianorum* (Argentorati: ex officina Josiae Staedelii, 1665) and includes Cardinal Cusa as a member of the Pyrrhonian sect together with "prae caeteris Franciscum Sanchez, cujus opusculum de multum nobili et prima universali scientia, quod nihil scitur, extat, quo in strenuum se collapsi ac iamdudum profligati Scepticismi restauratorem praebet" (p. 7).

1

it necessary to publish an entire refutation of Sanches under the title *Sanchez aliquid sciens* (Stettin, 1665), attacking each paragraph of the *Quod nihil scitur* with copious references and quotations from the works of all the philosophers who had previously examined the possibility and non-possibility of knowledge, and justifying his own position doctrinally by referring to Saint Augustine.[2] Sanches's reputation as a sceptic lingered even as late as the eighteenth century, Pierre Bayle saying of him in his *Dictionnaire historique et critique,* "C'etoit un grand Pyrrhonien".[3]

Although Sanches's treatise on epistemology attacking Aristotle and his adherents was well known in the late Renaissance and the seventeenth century, running into six editions between 1581 and 1665, his fame suffered an eclipse as the debate over Pyrrhonism quietened down. Montaigne, Pascal, and Descartes emerged as the major French thinkers who had written on philosophical scepticism, leaving Sanches in relative obscurity. It was not until the beginning of this century that European scholars began to research extensively the life and works of this most interesting figure of the late French Renaissance whose importance as a precursor of Descartes has yet to be acknowledged fully.[4] With the inclusion

---

[2] Daniel Hartnack's commentary in his *Sanchez aliquid sciens, h.e. in Francisci Sanchez . . .* (Stetini: apud Jeremiam Mamphrasium, 1665) was prompted by his first reading the *Quod nihil scitur* in the 1649 Rotterdam edition.

[3] See the article on Sanchez, François, in the *Dictionnaire historique et critique par Mr Pierre Bayle,* troisième édition (Rotterdam: Michel Bohm, 1720).

[4] Among early studies on Sanches the following are important: Ludwig Gerkrath, *Franz Sanchez. Ein Beitrag zur Geschichte der philosophischen Bewegungen im Anfänge der neueren Zeit* (Vienna: Wilhelm Braumüller, 1860); John Owen, *The Skeptics of the French Renaissance* (London: Swan Sonnenschein, 1893); the many articles of H.P. Cazac in the early part of the century and his extensive documentation on Sanches, which is now housed in the archives of the Institut Catholique de Toulouse; the first full-length study of Sanches by Emilien Senchet in his *Essai sur la méthode de Francisco Sanchez* (Paris: V. Giard & E. Briere, 1904); the lively chapter on Sanches in Fortunat Strowski's *Montaigne* (Paris: Félix Alcan, 1906); the critical essay, "De los Orígenes del Criticismo y del Escepticismo" by Menéndez y Pelayo in his *Ensayos de Crítica Filosófica,* vol. XLIII of *Edición nacional de las obras completas de Menéndez y Pelayo* (Santander: Aldus, S. A. de Artes Gráficas, 1948); finally, the many studies of Portuguese scholars, notably the critical editions of Joaquim de Carvalho, *Francisco Sanches*

of Sanches in Richard Popkin's masterly survey *The History of Scepticism from Erasmus to Spinoza,* interest has grown among English-speaking scholars in the *Quod nihil scitur.* Perhaps Sanches will now be considered a unique representative of the philosopher-physician whose scientific background led him to question the very foundations of the Aristotelian structure of knowledge.[5] A true sceptic in the profoundest sense of the term, that of an enquirer, Sanches preferred to terminate most of his philosophical and medical treatises with the question *"Quid?"* a symbol of his tireless quest for the truth and which his disciple Delassus, in the preface to the 1636 Toulouse edition of the complete works of Sanches, states that he affixed like an obelisk to his treatises.[6] Now, an obelisk indicates in a classical text that a word or passage is totally uncertain or incomprehensible. Sanches questioned not only the works of others but also his own, since he believed that perfect knowledge is impossible and man can only reach an approximation of the truth. As a sceptic he did not believe in mathematical certainty: approximation was the only possible resolution of his particular form of scepticism.

The present critical edition and translation of the text of the *Quod nihil scitur* endeavours to situate Sanches in the history of the revival of Greek scepticism in France during the sixteenth century and to shed light on the close relationship between philosophy and

---

Opera philosophica (1955; Coimbra: Separata da *Revista da Universidade de Coimbra,* vol. XVIII, Imprensa de Coimbra, 1957), and Artur Moreira de Sá, *Francisco Sanches Prefácio e Selecção* (Lisbon: SNI, 1948).

[5] See Richard H. Popkin, *The History of Scepticism from Erasmus to Spinoza* (Berkeley: University of California Press, 1979), which is a revised and expanded edition of *The History of Scepticism from Erasmus to Descartes* (Assen: Van Gorcum, 1960). Popkin's analysis of the *Quod nihil scitur,* pp. 37–41, and the information contained in his notes on Sanches, pp. 259–61, are by far the best materials available in English.

[6] See Francisco Sanchez, *Opera medica. His iuncti sunt tractatus quidam philosophici non insubtiles* (Tolosae tectosagum: apud Petrum Bosc, 1636), p. ẽ 3r. Delassus states: "Nam alieni operis se censorem exhibuit, impulsus sacro veritatis amore, nec plus suis quam aliorum operibus detulit, propriis enim non pepercit, omnibus siquidem tractatibus in umbilico vel extremo apice notam illam Quid? ceu obeliscum affixit".

3

medicine which existed in the universities. No more convincing demonstration of this alliance between philosophy and medicine can be offered than the distinguished career of Sanches himself at the University of Toulouse, where he was renowned for his contributions to both disciplines and enjoyed the honour of serving as regius professor in both faculties.

II

Francisco Sanches (Franciscus Sanchez) was probably born on July 16, 1551, in Túy, a city of northwestern Spain, situated on the right bank of the river Minho, opposite Valença do Minho in Portuguese Galicia.[1] Túy belonged to the Portuguese diocese of Braga and, according to the civil register of Braga, Sanches was

[1] There is much debate among scholars concerning the Portuguese or Spanish origins of Sanches (Sánchez), which reflects, I believe, the indiscriminate use of the adjectives "Lusitanus" and "Hispanus" in the sixteenth and seventeenth centuries. In the life of Sanches, written by his disciple Delassus at the request of Sanches's sons Guillaume and Denys, and which prefaces the 1636 Toulouse edition of his *Opera medica* and the philosophical treatises, it is stated that Sanches was born in Braga: "Bracara Lusitaniae urbs insignis natales nostro praebuit Professori, ..." (p. ẽ r.). Delassus then relates that, because of the uncertainties of the time, Sanches's father, Dr. António Sanches, emigrated to Bordeaux, where Sanches continued his studies, with the result that he was more indebted to France than to Spain: "ut plus Gallico caelo debeat quam Hispano" (p. ẽ r.). A similar confusion exists in the official documents in the archives of the universities of Montpellier and Toulouse. In the archives of the faculty of medicine at Montpellier, Registre des Matricules 1573, 21 octobre, fol. 49, v°, Sanches declared: "Ego Franciscus Sanctius Hispanus natus in civitate tudensi interrogatus fui". Other official documents for the baccalaureate diploma, B.A., and Ph.D. degrees in the Montpellier archives refer to "Franciscus Sanctis, Hispanus, diocensis Bracarensis". See Evaristo de Moraes Filho, *Francisco Sanches Na Renascença Portuguesa* (Lisbon: Ministério da Educação e Saúde, 1953), p. 35, for a complete documentation on this issue. In the archives of Toulouse University, however, he is always described as "Franciscus Sanchez Lusitanus". See Joaquim de Carvalho, *Opera philosophica*, pp. 161–2. According to documents found by Severiano Tavares, Sanches was really born in Valença do Minho. See his article "Francisco Sanches. O homem", *Revista Portuguesa de Filosofia*, 7, fasc. 1 (1951), pp. 118–19. Consequently Sanches's place of birth is given variously as Túy, Braga, and Valença do Minho.

baptised there on July 25, 1551, his parents being named in the register as Dr. António Sanches and Filipa de Souza.[2] The family lived in Braga, where Sanches attended the very old and famous school until the age of eleven.[3] In 1562 his father decided, probably because of the severe economic conditions in Portugal and the uncertain political and religious climate, to move the family to Bordeaux, where his brother Adám-Francisco Sanches was in business and had been granted letters of citizenship. Bordeaux had long been a safe haven for the Spanish and Portuguese Jews who had fled the terrors of the Inquisition. The French kings had followed a policy of encouraging foreigners to settle in Bordeaux, since the city had been greatly depopulated following the expulsion of the English in 1454 and the ravages of the plague of 1473, which had brought about a considerable decline in commerce. By an edict of Louis XI in February 1474, foreigners were granted free disposal of their property and the right to pursue commerce without having to take out citizenship papers. In 1550 Henry II had granted letters-patent to all Portuguese merchants and others who were called "New Christians", enabling them to dwell in any French city they chose and to enjoy all the privileges of French citizens.[4]

It was Guy Patin who started the controversy over Sanches's religious beliefs by stating in his *Patiniana* that Sanches was born of Jewish parents.[5] His father, Dr. António Sanches, was a highly

---

[2] The most conclusive evidence concerning Sanches's date of birth, which is usually given as 1550, or 1551, is the registration of his birth in the civil register of Braga. José Machado describes this discovery in the *Boletim da Biblioteca Pública e Arquivo Distrital de Braga*, 1920, pp. 127–32. Joaquim de Carvalho has pointed out that the ecclesiastical laws of the diocese of Braga required baptism no later than nine days after the birth of a child (*Opera philosophica*, p. 161).

[3] For Braga's reputation see Jean de Launoy, *De scholis celebrioribus*, vol. IV of *Opera omnia* (Lutetiae Parisiorum: typis-viduae E. Martini, 1672).

[4] See Arnaud Detcheverry, *Histoire des Israélites de Bordeaux* (Bordeaux: Imprimerie de Balarac Jeune, 1850), and Francisque Michel, *Histoire du commerce à Bordeaux*, 2 vols. (Bordeaux: Imprimerie de J. Delmas, 1866).

[5] Guy Patin, *Naudaeana et Patiniana ou Singularitez remarquables prises des conversations de Mess. Naudé et Patin* (Paris: Florentin & Pierre Delaulne, 1701), pp. 72–3.

esteemed physician, and medicine was one of the professions in which Jews had excelled in Spain and Portugal, since it was little practised by Christians.[6] According to Henri Cazac, it is likely that the family of Sanches was closely related to the famous "Marranos" (New Christians) of Aragon who had held distinguished offices at the courts of John I of Aragon and Ferdinand the Catholic until the time of the plot of the Judeós conversós against the Holy Office (1484–6).[7] After the Edictogeneral de Expulsión of March 31, 1492, many Jewish families had sought safety in the French provinces of Guyenne, Languedoc, and Provence. Even the Jewish converts to Christianity felt threatened by the zealous preoccupation with the purity of the blood displayed by the members of the Inquisition.[8] Cazac states that the Sanches family first established itself on the border of Spanish and Portuguese Galicia before emigrating to France in the middle of the sixteenth century.[9] An additional factor in persuading many Portuguese in the liberal professions to leave the country, and to seek their fortune in France, may have been the establishment of the Inquisition in Portugal in 1536, allied to the increasing spiritual domination of the Jesuits at court and their monopoly of teaching in the humanities.[10]

In view of these historical and religious circumstances, many scholars have inclined to the opinion that Francisco Sanches was a "New Christian". Yet there are no contemporary references to Sanches as a "New Christian". But, then, neither do Montaigne's contemporaries refer to his Jewish heritage through his mother, Antoinette de Louppes, a rich descendant of Portuguese Jews, the Lopez family. Moreover, as Thomas Platter points out in his *Notes*

---

[6] For a discussion of the importance of the Jews in medicine see Américo Castro, *The Structure of Spanish History,* trans. Edmund L. King (Princeton, N.J.: Princeton University Press, 1954), pp. 491–6.

[7] See Cazac papers, Boîte II, in the archives of the Institut Catholique de Toulouse.

[8] See Américo Castro, *Structure of Spanish History,* pp. 521–44.

[9] See Cazac papers, Boîte II.

[10] For information on the Jesuits' campaign against French humanism in Portugal, see Theophilo Braga, *Renascença,* vol. II of *História da Litteratura Portugueza* (Porto: Livraria Chardron, de Lello & Irmão, 1914), pp. 584–602.

de Voyage, the name of "Marrans" was regarded as an insult and one could be fined for using the term in Montpellier.[11] Sanches himself went to great pains to assure his readers of his orthodox Catholic beliefs and habitually ended his philosophical and medical treatises, written during his tenure at the staunchly Catholic University of Toulouse, with the traditional prayer "Laus Deo virginique Mariae".[12] His piety was praised by his disciple Delassus, and the sincerity of his faith was never doubted by his contemporaries, even during the dark times of religious persecution in the Catholic stronghold of Toulouse.[13] It is perhaps indicative of the deep Catholic faith of Sanches that two of his sons became priests.[14]

The Collège de Guyenne in Bordeaux, which Sanches attended from 1562 to 1571, was one of the foremost schools in France at that time.[15] Founded as a college in 1533 by the municipality of Bordeaux, the Collège de Guyenne during the remarkable administration of André de Gouveia attracted distinguished teachers and scholars such as Mathurin Cordier, George Buchanan, Elie Vinet, and Marc-Antoine Muret. Gouveia, before coming to Bordeaux in 1534, had been the principal of the Collège de Sainte Barbe in Paris, which was a centre for Portuguese students and scholars under the official protection of King Manuel of Portugal.[16] As a

---

[11] See *Félix et Thomas Platter à Montpellier, 1552–1559, 1595–1599. Notes de voyage de deux étudiants bâlois* (Montpellier: C. Coulet, 1892), p. 196.

[12] It is interesting that this prayer does not figure at the end of the *Quod nihil scitur,* nor at the end of the *Carmen de cometa anni M.D.LXXVII,* both written and published before Sanches was appointed to the chair of philosophy in 1585 at the highly Catholic University of Toulouse.

[13] "Praeterea mirum eius in Deum devotionem, quem tanquam bonorum omnium fontem perpetuum certim restitutae sanitatis authorem indicavit, non possum quin recolam" (*Opera medica,* p. ẽ 4r.).

[14] See Senchet, *Essai sur la méthode de Francisco Sanchez,* p. XVI.

[15] Senchet, ibid., gives the date of Sanches's attendance at the Collège de Guyenne as 1562–69.

[16] See J. Quicherat, *Histoire de Sainte Barbe* (Paris: Hachette, 1860), I, p. 125. André de Gouveia persuaded Portuguese scholars such as his brother, António, and Jean de Costa to come to Bordeaux from the Collège de Sainte Barbe. Diogo de Teive came to the Collège de Guyenne from Toulouse. The Portu-

7

consequence of Gouveia's principalship of the Collège de Guyenne, close links were forged between Bordeaux and Portugal, especially after 1547, when Gouveia was asked by John III of Portugal to return to his native land in order to undertake a new reform of the University of Coimbra.[17] Gouveia was rightly called by one of his most famous pupils, Michel de Montaigne, who attended the college from 1539 to 1546, "le plus grand principal de France".[18] The Collège de Guyenne became renowned in Portugal for its programme of humanistic studies. Sanches's father would certainly have heard of the reputation of the Collège de Guyenne from his brother and would have a natural preference for settling in Bordeaux, rather than in other cities of south-west France.

The years that Sanches spent in study at the college were among the most prosperous and successful in its history. Many of the remarks Sanches makes in the *Quod nihil scitur* about his own education and that of his contemporaries can be better understood if one considers the programme of studies that he followed at the Collège de Guyenne. Fortunately an ample documentation exists, since Elie Vinet, who had followed Gouveia from the Collège de Sainte Barbe to Bordeaux in 1539, and had served both as principal and professor of Greek and mathematics during the years Sanches spent at the college, has described in his *Schola Aquitanica* the curriculum, timetable, and organisation of the Collège de Guyenne.[19] The primary aim of the college was to form students

guese scholars enjoyed a privileged status at the college. For a history of the college, see Ernest Gaullieur, *Histoire du Collège de Guyenne* (Paris: Sandoz & Fischbacher, 1874), and Roger Trinquet's *La Jeunesse de Montaigne* (Paris: Nizet, 1972), pp. 409–507, for many invaluable corrections of details in Gaullieur.

17 André de Gouveia invited several professors from the Collège de Guyenne to accompany him to Coimbra, such as George Buchanan, Nicolas de Grouchy, and Guillaume Guérente. Unfortunately, many were denounced to the Inquisition as Lutherans. George Buchanan was thrown into prison and others were banned from teaching in Portugal as a result of Jesuit intrigues. See Theophilo Braga, *Renascença*, pp. 583–7.

18 Michel de Montaigne, *Essais* (Paris: Gallimard, 1950), I, 26, p. 213.

19 Elie Vinet, *Schola Aquitanica,* trans. Louis Massebieau (Paris: Le Musée pédagogique, 1886).

well versed in Latin: "Latino sermoni cognoscendo haec schola imprimis destinata est".[20] Cicero's letters, orations, and oratorical treatises were the main Latin prose texts used in all classes, according to the level of ability, as models of style. Consequently it was natural for Sanches to write all his works in Latin, the language of the educated public and of all academics, even though, as he tells his reader in the preface to the *Quod nihil scitur*, he should not look for an elegant polished style, or verbal trickery, which was Cicero's manner. Indeed, the Latin of Sanches is deceptively simple: he parodies the rhetorical techniques used by the Scholastics, incorporates the strong vigorous concrete language of his contemporaries into the witty tirades, and constantly moves from elliptical philosophical statements to long discussions of the scientific evidence which negates a particular Aristotelian proof of knowledge, so that at times one has the impression of reading a scientific treatise.[21]

Students entered the Collège de Guyenne usually at the age of seven and finished the ten classes at the age of seventeen. Rhetoric was stressed increasingly during the last four years; students were also taught some elementary Greek through public lectures and, in their final two years, mathematics. As Woodward points out, "The existence of higher groups in philosophy and of public lectures in Greek and mathematics indicates the overlapping of school and university".[22] Indeed, the Collège de Guyenne also offered the first two years of university courses in the faculty of arts, since the University of Bordeaux had a very poor reputation in the arts. Readers in philosophy taught these courses, which consisted mainly of a study of Aristotelian logic in the first year, followed by courses in natural philosophy in the second year, when the principal texts studied were Aristotle's *Physica* and the

---

[20] Ibid., p. 6.

[21] See André Mandouze's preface to the elegant French translation of the *Quod nihil scitur* by Andrée Comparot, *Il n'est science de rien* (Paris: Klincksieck, 1984), where he analyses the problems of translating such a difficult Latin text.

[22] See William Harrison Woodward, *Studies in Education in the Age of the Renaissance* (Cambridge, 1906; rpt. New York: Russell & Russell, 1965), p. 143.

De caelo.[23] Vinet tells us that students were called *dialecti*, or *logici*, in the first year, and *physici* in the second year. It is more than likely that Sanches followed these courses before going on to the University of Bordeaux to begin his studies in medicine, if one accepts Cazac's statement that Sanches pursued his studies in Bordeaux to the level of the *maîtrise ès arts*, the equivalent of the modern French baccalaureate, before leaving for Italy in the early spring of 1571.[24] A further fact that supports Cazac's argument is that Sanches himself states in one of his medical works, the *Observationes in praxi,* that discharges from the chest and stomach were to be considered symptoms of serious illness, since he had observed the deaths of his own father and uncle from the flux in January 1571.[25] It was probably after these tragic family events that Sanches made his way to Italy, travelling through Languedoc and Provence, then visiting the northern Italian universities of Pisa, Bologna, Padua, Venice, Ferrara, and Florence before finally taking up residence in Rome, where his cousin from Lisbon, Duarte Paulo, lived.[26] Sanches's stay in Italy from 1571 to 1573 was to mark an intellectual turning-point in his life, for it was there that he first came into contact with the new interpretations of Galen's *Ars medica,* in which the question of method was a primary issue and the whole Aristotelian theory of demonstration was challenged.[27] It was also in Italy that he was introduced to the

[23] Woodward, ibid., pp. 139–54, gives a very useful account of the history of the Collège de Guyenne and of its programmes, based on Elie Vinet's *Schola Aquitanica,* which was first published in 1583. Vinet gives the following list of texts for philosophy: Porphyry, *Introduction;* Grouchy, *Préceptes;* Aristotle, *Categories, Peri Hermeneias, Prior Analytics* and *Posterior Analytics, De sophisticis elenchis, Physics, De caelo.* These texts were those normally prescribed for the university arts course.

[24] See Cazac papers, Boîte II.

[25] Sanches writes in his *Observationes in Praxi* in *Opera medica* (p. 368): "Secundum est, in morbis thoracis, alvi fluxum in malis habendum esse; quod nos etiam in Antonio Sanchez, parente nostro colendissimo, medicinae professore eximio, Patruoque Adamo Francisco observavimus".

[26] "Erat autem haec uxor Domini Duarte Paulo Viliponensis qui Romae habitabat nobis consangineus, ubi nos eam vidimus" (ibid. p. 366).

[27] For a discussion of Galen's method see Neal Ward Gilbert, *Renaissance Concepts of Method* (New York: Columbia University Press, 1960), pp. 100–5.

new medical advances in the realms of anatomy and physiology by the pupils of Vesalius, Colombo, and Fallopio.[28]

The union between medicine and philosophy, which Sanches often referred to in his works as being ultimately desirable, was, in the late mediaeval and Renaissance periods, a reality in the Italian universities, where the Galenic tradition was held in honour.[29] As Charles Schmitt has pointed out, arts and medical faculties were combined in the Italian universities, and "the statutes established a curriculum in which logic and philosophy were considered as a propaedeutic to medical studies proper".[30] It was not unusual to find famous scholars teaching courses in both philosophy and medicine.[31] The philosophical basis of medicine was to provide the theoretical approach, or scientific method, by which progress could be furthered in the practice of medicine. Thus it is likely that the initial reflections of Sanches on the problem of scientific method were directly inspired by his medical studies in Italy, where a much broader approach to medicine prevailed than in France.[32]

See also William F. Edwards, "Niccolò Leoniceno and the Origins of Humanist Discussion of Method", in *Philosophy and Humanism*, ed. Edward P. Mahoney (Leiden: Brill, 1976), pp. 283–305.

[28] See Salvatore Miccolis, *Francesco Sanchez* (Bari: Tipografia Levante, 1965), p. 13.

[29] Sanches writes in his philosophical treatise, *De longitudine et brevitate vitae liber* in *Opera medica* (p. 14): "Ultimo denique, ut Medicinam Philosophiae conjungamus, qua maxime ratione vita hominis produci possit, generalibus quibusdam praeceptis docebimus".

[30] Charles B. Schmitt, "Aristotle among the Physicians", in *The Medical Renaissance of the Sixteenth Century*, ed. Andrew Wear, R.K. French, and I.M. Lonie (Cambridge: Cambridge University Press, 1985), pp. 1–15.

[31] The archives of Padua University show that many famous humanists taught both philosophy and medicine. See Antonio Riccoboni, *De gymnasio patavino* (Patavii: apud Franciscum Bolzetam, 1598), pp. 11–51, who names the following professors of philosophy and medicine: Caietanus Thierens Vicetinus (author of many commentaries on Aristotle), Christophorus Ricinensis, Petrus Rocabonella Venetus, and Bernardinus Paternus, to mention but a few philosopher-physicians who taught at Padua.

[32] The best studies on the history of medicine at the University of Montpellier are Louis Dulieu, *La Médecine à Montpellier*, 2 vols. (Avignon: Les Presses

Sanches studied for two years at the famous college of La Sapienza in Rome. Renazzi writes in his history of Rome University that, after the first wave of enthusiasm for Plato and his doctrines, which Cardinal Bessarion had greatly encouraged, scholars were won over completely to Aristotelianism by the new translations from the Greek of Aristotle's works.[33] Henceforth Aristotelian philosophy was to dominate the teaching at Rome University until the end of the seventeenth century, and most of the professors spent their time emending or commenting Aristotle's works. Medical studies, which had fallen into disrepute during the fifteenth century, when medicine and astronomy were taught conjointly, flourished anew during the pontificate of Leo VI, and medicine became a discipline in its own right. Pope Paul III was bent on restoring the former glory of Rome University; during his pontificate the teaching of medicine was greatly enhanced by the founding of the chair of theoretical and practical medicine and the schools of anatomy and botany.[34] Scholars came from near and far to study medicine in Rome, which was known for its progressive medical curriculum. The study of natural history, botany, and anatomy was incorporated into medical studies. Rome became the first Italian city to have a botanical garden in which students could study rare and exotic plants. The works of Aristotle, Dioscorides, and other Greek writers on the nature of things were studied in depth and commented on in detail. Pliny's *Natural History* was diligently corrected, supplemented, and illustrated. This work of correction, which was stimulated by the publication of the original Greek texts of Aristotle, was entirely necessary, since many errors had crept into the Latin translations of Greek texts made by Arab physicians and philosophers, with sometimes dangerous uses of

Universelles, 1975), and Roland Antonioli, *Rabelais et la Médecine* (Geneva: Droz, 1976).

[33] Filippo Maria Renazzi, *Storia dell'Università degli Studi di Roma detta communemente La Sapienza* (Rome: Nella Stamperia Pagliarini, 1803), I, p. 164. Renazzi attributes the revival of Aristotelianism in Rome to the influence of Theodorus Gaza, who was invited to Rome by Pope Nicholas V in 1450, and was chiefly engaged in translating Aristotle and other Greek authors into Latin.

[34] Ibid., II, p. 107.

the wrong drugs being recommended. Niccolò Leoniceno, whose works are often referred to by Sanches, was one of the first medical humanists to criticise the fanciful botany of the Arabs in his *De Plinii et aliorum medicorum erroribus liber* (Ferrara, 1509).

In the field of anatomy spectacular developments had occurred which led to its being considered fundamental for the study of medicine and surgery. In 1572 Sanches, as a student at La Sapienza, listened to lectures from Bartolommeo Eustachio, remembered today for his description of the canal leading from the pharynx to the cavity of the middle ear, but who was a leading anatomist in his own day, renowned for his treatises on the movement of the heart and the arteries, the structure and function of the kidneys, and his many new discoveries of the function of valves in the veins. Yet Eustachio declared that he would never teach anything contrary to the principles of Galen, when much of Galen's teachings on anatomy had manifestly been demonstrated by Vesalius to be wrong.[35] Costanzo Varolio, a brilliant young scholar who succeeded Realdo Colombo in the chair of anatomy, did much to improve the teaching of surgery and published extensively. His *Epistolae medicinales* and treatise on the *De origine nervorum opticorum* made him one of the luminaries of medical science in Italy until his untimely death in 1575. The noted Andreas Bacci, who was appointed to the chair of botany in 1567, lectured on natural history. Arcangelo Piccolomini, who as a young man had studied philosophy in Bordeaux, was appointed to Rome University in 1569 and later held two chairs, one in practical medicine and the other in anatomy. Before coming to Rome the brilliant Piccolomini had already published a Greek-Latin edition of Galen's *De humoribus* in Paris (1556), accompanying it with his own weighty commentary. Girolamo Cardano, the famous mathematician, physician, and astrologer, whose *De rerum varietate* (1557) was attacked by Sanches in his commentary on the *De divinatione per somnum, ad Aristotelem,* came to Rome in 1571 after being deprived of his professorship at the University of Bologna; according to Renazzi, he was admitted to the Collegio de' Medici and given a papal

[35] Ibid., II, p. 189.

pension which enabled him to write his autobiography.[36] Sanches called Cardano "vero nostri saeculi et Philosophus et Medicus doctissimus" in his comments in the *De divinatione per somnum, ad Aristotelem*.[37] It was in Rome, too, that Sanches met and probably studied under the famous Jesuit mathematician Clavius, with whom he later corresponded from Toulouse concerning problems he had encountered in studying Euclid.[38]

Rome, then, constitutes in the biography of Sanches one of the most important and exciting intellectual periods of his life. Rome's superiority in the field of medical studies was due to the belief that the observation of nature, and of all natural phenomena, was of primary importance, and this was demonstrated by the new research carried out in the fields of anatomy and botany, and the related discipline of the pharmacological uses of plants.[39] The critical spirit, which animated much of the work of the medical humanists in the Italian universities in editing and commenting on the standard scientific texts of Aristotle and Galen, was continued by their disciples who taught at Rome University. The revolt against dogmatism in medical circles led to the discovery that progress in medicine was possible if one examined nature, free from the fetters of authority and prejudice. Sanches was to learn in Rome that a free enquiry into the nature of man and the physical world offered the promise of continuing progress in *scientia*, as opposed to *perfecta cognitio*. Medical empirical knowledge was to furnish a way out of the philosopher's sceptical dilemma. It is noteworthy that Sanches did not break with the past in medicine, as he did in philosophy: his commentaries on Galen in his *Opera medica* show his indebtedness to his precursors, and his final medical treatise bore the significant title *Summa Anatomica Libris quatuor*,

---

[36] Ibid., II, p. 219–20.

[37] See Sanches, *De divinatione per somnum, ad Aristotelem* in *Opera philosophica*, ed. Carvalho, p. 94. See also p. 99.

[38] Sanches, *Ad. C. Clavium Epistola* in *Opera philosophica*, ed. Carvalho, pp. 146–53.

[39] Sanches displays a wide knowledge of the medicinal uses of plants and was particularly interested in antidotes to poisons. See his *Pharmacopoeia* and *De theriaca ad pharmacopoeos liber* in *Opera medica*, pp. 417–514.

in qua breviter omnium corporis partium situs, numerus, substantia, usus, et figura continetur; ex GALENO, et ANDREA VESALIO, collecta. Additae sunt etiam Annotationes quibus COLUMBI et FALLOPII repugnantia cum GALENO et VESALIO continentur, et inter se.[40]

In 1573 Sanches returned to France and enrolled in the famous faculty of medicine at the University of Montpellier on October 21, completing the requirements for the doctorate on July 13, 1574. His rapid passage through the faculty of medicine at Montpellier has been commented on only briefly by scholars, and yet it illustrates the importance of his medical studies in Italy both in his professional formation as a doctor and later in his philosophical career. The length of studies at Montpellier depended on whether the prospective medical student possessed a *maîtrise ès arts* from a reputable university, since this was a prerequisite for entry into the faculty of medicine.[41] Presumably Sanches possessed a *maîtrise ès arts* from Bordeaux, as Cazac has stated, and so he was allowed to enrol in the faculty. Medical studies leading to the *licence* normally lasted three years and comprised two and a half years of formal studies in the faculty, followed by a six months' practicum in the surrounding area.[42] Some students, as was the case for Sanches, who had already taken courses in medicine at another recognised university, were allowed to proceed immediately to the *Baccalauréat* exams. Students were required to have a sponsor (*parrain*), who was a member of the teaching faculty of medicine at Montpellier. Sanches was sponsored by François Feynes, who held the chair of medicine.[43] The medical archives at Montpellier reveal that Sanches passed the *Baccalauréat* exams on November 23, 1573, just a month after his arrival in Montpellier. He was required to

---

[40] See *Opera medica,* p. 827. The translation of the title is: A compendium of anatomy in four books which contains succinctly the place, number, substance, function, and form of all parts of the body, drawn from the works of Galen and Andreas Vesalius. With additional notes also containing the criticisms made by Colombo and Fallopio of Galen and Vesalius, and of each other.

[41] The statutes of Montpellier University from 1240 onwards specified this requirement. See Dulieu, *La Médecine à Montpellier,* I, p. 37, and II, p. 56.

[42] Ibid., II, p. 63.

[43] François Feynes held the chair of medicine, *Régence* I, from 1563 to 1574.

comment on classical medical texts for four hours in front of his fellow-students. Then four exams followed (*per intentionem adipiscendi licentiam*) during which he was required to defend orally four theses whose topics were only known to him the night before the exam.[44] After the oral defence of the four theses came *les points rigoureux*, when the candidate was examined on the whole of medicine, defended two theses on pathology, and commented on one aphorism of Hippocrates. The *licence* was a mere formality, without exams, and was normally conferred immediately after the oral defence of the four theses. However, Sanches did not receive his *licence* until April 29, 1574, so that we can probably assume that the six-month period between November and April was spent in completing the requirements for the practicum.[45] Yet another set of exams, the *triduanes*, followed the *licence* after a further two years of study in the faculty, after which the doctorate was conferred on the successful candidate in a splendid ceremony which has been described by Félix and Thomas Platter in their accounts of their student days at Montpellier.[46] Sanches must have been granted a special dispensation from the normal two years' requirement of schooling, since he was awarded the doctorate from the University of Montpellier on July 13, 1574. His doctoral diploma is preserved in the library of the faculty of medicine at Montpellier.[47]

According to Dulieu, Sanches taught a course to the surgeon-apprentices in 1573 which his training in anatomy and surgery at Rome had qualified him to teach. These students were excluded from entering the faculty of medicine on the grounds that they were engaged in the practice of a manual profession. It was not until 1593 that chairs in anatomy and botany were founded at Montpellier and, in 1597, the chairs of surgery and pharmacy. Sanches also taught in the school of medicine in 1574 before presenting his candidature for the chair of medicine at Montpellier, which the death of François Feynes in June 1574 had left vacant.

[44] Dulieu, *La Médecine à Montpellier,* II, p. 59.

[45] Ibid., II, p. 63

[46] Ibid.

[47] There is a fine photographic reproduction of the original diploma in Dulieu, *La Médecine à Montpellier,* II, p. 70.

Unfortunately for Sanches there was a bitter ongoing dispute concerning a previous chair in medicine which had become vacant following the death of Antoine Saporta on November 7, 1573. Originally, the chairs of medicine, called *régences*, had been Crown appointments with a stipend of 100 livres per year, and the four *régents* did most of the official teaching of the medical programme in the university.[48] Only a *régent* could become the chancellor of the university. However, by a decision of the Parlement of Toulouse (which had legal jurisdiction over the university), it was required after 1574 that each *régence* be filled after an open competition for the chair was announced in every university in France, and each candidate was obliged to "dispute" for the chair, that is, to defend a number of theses on medical topics in front of the medical faculty. Nevertheless, certain families of doctors believed that the *régences* should continue in the family, and Jean Saporta was of the opinion that it was his right to inherit his father's chair. There were three candidates for Antoine Saporta's chair, all Protestants: Nicolas Dortoman, Jean Saporta, and Jean Blezin. Dortoman proved superior in the open competitive exam. But Jean Saporta appealed to the king, and, in an attempt to resolve the conflict between royal power and that of the Parlement of Toulouse, Charles IX decided to divide the chair between Dortoman and Saporta. However, upon the death of Feynes, Dortoman kept the chair of Antoine Saporta and Jean Saporta was appointed to Feyne's vacant chair on July 29, 1574. The chancellor of Montpellier University, Laurence Joubert, protested against this infringement of the normal procedures and insisted that an open competitive exam be held. Consequently four candidates presented themselves: Francisco Sanches, Jean Blezin, Jean Saporta, and Bermond Pagès. The twelve theses that were defended by the four candidates were found in the medical archives by Joseph Calmette and published by him in 1909.[49] Sanches opened the battle for the chair defending his three theses on August 2, 3, and 4, 1574, followed by Jean Blezin

[48] See ibid., II, pp. 17–23.
[49] Joseph Calmette, *Un Concours professionnel à la Faculté de Médecine de Montpellier au XVIe siècle*, (Toulouse: Imprimerie E. Privat, 1909).

on October 7, 8, 9, and, finally, by Jean Saporta on October 15, 16, 17. Pagès, according to Calmette, arrived too late for the oral defence of his theses and wrote his answers to the questions. The exams proved to be a pure formality: Saporta was again appointed (regularly this time) to the chair.

Dulieu believes that Sanches left Montpellier for Toulouse because he was disgusted with the proceedings over Feynes's chair.[50] Delassus, on the other hand, furnishes a more likely explanation in his preface to Sanches's *Opera medica* when he states that Sanches left Montpellier on account of the religious and civil strife in the city.[51] Many of Montpellier's citizens had embraced Huguenot beliefs and there were numerous skirmishes with loyal Catholics in the city. Montpellier became a Huguenot stronghold that did not surrender to royal power until 1622, when Louis XIII besieged the city. Veríssimo Serrão also offers what might have been an additional factor in Sanches's decision to go to Toulouse: the prospect of a vacant chair in medicine at Toulouse, where the regent Larroche was in poor health.[52]

It is evident that Sanches stayed too short a time at Montpellier to have been greatly influenced by the teaching of the medical faculty there. Moreover, although Montpellier had one of the most renowned schools of medicine in France, medical studies there were far more conservative and less practically oriented than those Sanches had undertaken in Rome. Hippocrates and Galen were the main authors studied, followed by Avicenna (the *Canon*), Rhazes (the *Almansor*), Paul D'Egine (*Traité*), Dioscorides (*De natura simplicium*), Gattinaria (*Practica*), and, in 1574 for the first time, Fernel's *Traité*.[53] Arabic medicine was still taught but to a far lesser degree than at the beginning of the sixteenth century.[54]

Sanches was to spend the rest of his life peacefully in Toulouse

---

[50] Dulieu, *La Médecine à Montpellier*, II, p. 41.

[51] "Sed eam cathedram frui diutius infanda pro Religione bella, et civilis Erynnis illum non passa sunt" (*Opera medica*, p. ē v.).

[52] Joaquim Veríssimo Serrão *Les Portugais à l'Université de Toulouse (xii–xvii siècles)* (Paris: Fundação Calouste Gulbenkian, 1970), p. 142.

[53] Dulieu, *La Médecine à Montpellier*, II, pp. 139–46.

[54] See Antonioli, *Rabelais et la Médecine*, pp. 44–8.

(1575–1623), where he found both fame and fortune. Toulouse was a devoutly Catholic city where heresy was severely repressed even to the extent of the death penalty being imposed. By order of Charles IX all professors and students at the university had to be Catholic.[55] Any newcomers to the city were closely watched for signs of Huguenot tendencies or adherence to the Jewish faith. It is thus not surprising that Sanches professed the most orthodox Catholicism in his philosophical and medical works.

From the foundation of the University of Toulouse medicine had always been taught in the faculty of arts. All courses in grammar, logic, and medicine continued to be taught in the faculty of arts, and it was not until the middle of the sixteenth century that medicine became a separate discipline with its own faculty.[56] The faculty of arts was the smallest and least renowned of all the faculties, law being the most prestigious faculty in the university. Yet the new faculty of medicine was to gain a certain prestige during the period 1572–1661 owing to the presence of several renowned Portuguese doctors: Manuel Álvares, Francisco Sanches, Pedro Vaz Castelo, and Baltazar Oróbio de Castro. Manuel Alvares occupied one of the two chairs in medicine from 1572 to 1612, and it may have been through his offices and friendship that Sanches decided to go to Toulouse.[57] Sanches was to be disappointed and frustrated for many long years in his efforts to obtain a chair of medicine, for it was only on the death of his friend Álvares in 1612 that he finally achieved his lifelong ambition.

During the years 1575–81, when Sanches did not hold a regular teaching position at the University of Toulouse, he devoted himself, so Delassus informs us, to intense philosophical reflection.[58] We know from Sanches's opening remarks in the dedicatory letter to his friend Diogo de Castro, the learned humanist, that the first

---

[55] Joaquim Veríssimo Serrão, in his well-documented study *Les Portugais à l'Université de Toulouse*, pp. 96–7, quotes from the laws passed by the Toulouse parlement in 1598 which were designed to stamp out heresy in the university.

[56] See Veríssimo Serraõ, ibid., p. 131.

[57] Ibid., pp. 132–3.

[58] "Hoc studendi seu meditandi genere suscepto nulli labori pepercit" (*Opera medica*, p. ẽ 3).

draft of the *Quod nihil scitur* had already been prepared in 1574.[59] Between 1574 and 1581, the date of the Lyons *editio princeps*, Sanches was busy revising and polishing the work. He also pursued his keen interest in mathematics. Delassus informs us that the first formal piece of research carried out by Sanches was the *Objectiones et erotemata super geometricas Euclidis demonstrationes*, which circulated in manuscript and was sent in a letter to his former teacher, the Jesuit geometrician Christopher Clavius, who had just published in 1574 a Latin translation and commentary on Euclid's *Elements*.[60] Although the entire correspondence is not extant, we do have a reply of Sanches to Clavius.[61]

The first published philosophical work of Sanches was the *Carmen de cometa anni M.D.LXXVII*, published in Lyons in 1578 by the printing house of Gryphius and dedicated to Diogo de Castro.[62] Sanches is described as a philosopher and doctor of medicine on the title page of the poem he wrote to protest against the ridiculous predictions of the astrologers after a comet had appeared in 1577. The fame of Sanches as a philosopher was to be

---

[59] The opening line of Sanches's dedicatory letter to Diogo de Castro, announcing the publication of the *Quod nihil scitur* in 1581, reads thus: "Cum nuper librorum scrinium evolverem, amicissime Jacobe, incidi forte in opusculum hoc, quod ante septennium edideram."

[60] Clavius's edition of *Euclidis elementorum lib XV. Accessit XVI de solidorum regularium comparatione* ran into four editions between 1574 and 1607.

[61] Sanches's letter to Clavius is published in Joaquim de Carvalho's edition of the *Opera philosophica*, pp. 146–53. The letter was originally published by Joaquim Iriarte in his article "Francisco Sánchez el Escéptico disfrazado de Carneadas en discussión epistolar con Cristóbal Clavio", *Gregorianum*, 21 (1940), pp. 413–51.

[62] According to Artur Moreira de Sá, Diogo de Castro was born in Vila Viçosa, the son of Dr. André de Castro, professor of medicine at the University of Coimbra and doctor to the dukes of Bragança. He was a knight of the Order of Christ and like his father was a member of the faculty of medicine at Coimbra. He was also known as a poet and novelist. See Moreira de Sá, *Francisco Sanches Prefácio e Selecção*, p. 55. Miccolis states that Sanches met him in Rome after de Castro, a high-ranking Spanish official, had fought in the battle of Lepanto (October 7, 1571). See Miccolis, *Francesco Sanchez*, p. 15. See also Henri Pierre Cazac, "Voyages du philosophe Francisco Sanchez en Italie et à Rome . . ." in *Journal officiel de la République Française*, 1903, p. 2476.

confirmed by the publication of the *Quod nihil scitur* in Lyons in 1581, and his reputation in Europe was to be established by the 1618 Frankfurt edition of the work in which the title was changed to *De multum nobili et prima universali scientia QUOD NIHIL SCITUR*. In all likelihood the change in title denotes a pirated edition. The importance of this edition will be discussed later with reference to Descartes and the seventeenth-century theological opponents to scepticism.

Sanches had hoped to obtain the chair of medicine at Toulouse made vacant by the death on April 30, 1581, of the regent Larroche. However, his rival, the Toulouse humanist Auger Ferrier, who was twenty years his senior and well known in his native city for his scholarly works, was appointed to the chair.[63] Sanches took over Ferrier's post at the Hôtel-Dieu on January 1, 1582, and remained as a doctor at the charitable institution for thirty years. From time to time he was called on to serve as *lecteur en chirurgie* on the faculty of medicine during the absence of a regent. This may account for the fragment of a treatise on bones found in the archives of the Hôtel-Dieu written by Sanches in 1584.[64]

Sanches seems to have found his duties at the Hôtel-Dieu rather onerous and ill paid. Veríssimo Serrão's study of the archives of the Hôtel-Dieu has revealed that Sanches made numerous requests to be allowed to resign from his position.[65] In spite of increases in salary, Sanches asked the board of governors of the Hôtel-Dieu to allow him to resign on account of ill-health in 1584, and they had to threaten him with prison and a fine, if he did not honour his three-year contract (1582–5). Further salary increases and the granting of a pension in 1589 must have persuaded Sanches to continue in the position of doctor at the Hôtel-Dieu until June 17, 1612, when he finally resigned his post and was replaced by

---

[63] Auger Ferrier was famous for his books on astronomy and Pythagorean doctrines, as well as his medical works on remedies for the plague and venereal diseases. Catherine de Médici, who was deeply interested in astronomy and the occult, was his patroness.

[64] See Senchet, *Essai sur la méthode de Francisco Sanchez*, p. XIV, and Veríssimo Serrão, *Les Portugais à l'Université de Toulouse*, p. 146.

[65] See *Les Portugais à l'Université de Toulouse*, p. 144.

Rodrigo Álvares, the son of Manuel Álvares, regius professor of medicine at the University of Toulouse.

In the early part of 1585 Sanches was appointed to a chair in philosophy at the university upon the death of the grammarian Bernard de Lapointe. It is a measure of his reputation and standing as a philosopher that the chair was offered to him without an open competition being announced.[66] Veríssimo Serrão believes that Sanches had already lectured on philosophy at the university before taking up the chair.[67] Sanches continued to fulfil the two functions of doctor at the Hôtel-Dieu and regius professor of philosophy until 1612. The burden of his medical duties and academic responsibilities in the faculty of arts undoubtedly accounts for the apparent absence of publications from 1581 onwards. Sanches does, however, refer in the *Quod nihil scitur* to many philosophical treatises that he was working on, and they may have never been completed or simply have been lost to posterity.[68]

Sanches remained as regius professor of philosophy for twenty-seven years (1585–1612) and ardently defended the rights of his faculty to propose candidates for the post of *recteur*, even though the faculty of arts was the least distinguished and the smallest compared to the other faculties.[69] The philosophical treatises published after his death in the 1636 Toulouse edition of all his works were probably written during his tenure as professor of philosophy. One can only surmise that the relatively small number of publications in philosophy, as compared to his massive output of publications in medicine, does not represent the work of twenty-seven years as professor of philosophy, and it is regrettable that Sanches's other philosophical works have not been found. On the other

---

[66] See ibid., p. 146. Veríssimo Serrão points out that there were two ways of obtaining a chair at Toulouse University: *la postulation,* in which the candidate was offered a chair by a decision of the teaching faculty on account of the candidate's outstanding merit; or *la prélation,* in which an open competition was held after all the universities in France had been informed that the chair was vacant.

[67] See Veríssimo Serrão, ibid., p. 146.

[68] Ibid., pp. 361–2.

[69] Ibid., p. 147 n. 95.

hand, Sanches himself may have preferred to devote himself to writing the many practical treatises on medicine, which were more relevant to his work as a doctor, and perhaps he considered that these publications would further his ambitions to obtain the chair of medicine.

During his tenure as regius professor of philosophy Sanches tried twice in vain to obtain a chair in the faculty of medicine. In 1588, following the death of Auger Ferrier, Sanches was a candidate for the chair of medicine, but Antoine Dumay, the queen of Navarre's doctor and a leading figure in Toulouse, was elected instead.[70] When Dumay died in 1611 Sanches was again a candidate for the chair of medicine. However, university politics once more conspired to frustrate his ambitions. Jean Queyrats, who had been appointed to the new chair of surgery and pharmacy created by royal decree of Henri IV in 1604, much against the wishes of the medical faculty at the University of Toulouse, decided that it would be prudent to abandon the new chair in favour of the chair left vacant by Dumay's death. Consequently Queyrats was elected to Dumay's chair in 1611 and Sanches, his arch-rival, was finally awarded the second chair in hygiene and therapy, after an open competition, when it became vacant upon the death of his fellow countryman, Manuel Álvarez, in 1612.[71]

[70] Underneath the portrait of Dumay in the faculty of medicine there is the following inscription: "Antonius Dumay in medicina regens electus 9 die mensis sept. 1588, vir capitolinus anno 1601. Obit mense martio anni 1611". See Veríssimo Serrão, *Les Portugais à l'Université de Toulouse*, p. 148. Although not one of Dumay's scholarly works has survived, he was nevertheless an important figure in Toulouse and had served as principal doctor and adviser to the queen of Navarre.

[71] There was a traditional antagonism between the faculty of medicine and the corporation of surgeons, since the faculty jealously guarded its privileges and despised the *chirurgiens barbiers* for practising a mechanical art. As Jean Queyrats was a famous man of science and enjoyed the royal patronage of Henri IV, the situation was rather delicate, for it became a struggle between royal power and local civic and academic autonomy. The medical faculty, and the town council of Toulouse, contested the royal appointment on the grounds that the statutes of the university required that an open competition be held. The corporation of surgeons supported Queyrats because the new chair of surgery

Sanches finally realised his lifelong ambition at the age of sixty-one and remained as regius professor of medicine for eleven years until his death in 1623. He was buried on November 16, 1623, in the Church of the Cordeliers in Toulouse. Both Guy Patin and Bayle give 1632 as the date of Sanches's death, but this is almost certainly a typographical error since the town register for 1623 states: "Du XVI novembre. François Chanche, docteur et régent en Médecine, âgé de soixante-treize ans, a esté ensevely aux Cordeliers, demeurant à la grand-rue".[72]

and pharmacy was the first official recognition of the status of their discipline. Barbot's researches into the medical archives of Toulouse University have revealed that an agreement was reached between Queyrats and the university whereby he consented to give up his chair in surgery and pharmacy, on condition that he be allowed to be a candidate for the first vacant chair in medicine. See Veríssimo Serrão, *Les Portugais à l'Université de Toulouse*, p. 149.

[72] Ibid., pp. 151–52. The initial wrong information given by Guy Patin in his *Naudaeana et Patiniana* led Bayle, and many subsequent biographers, into error concerning Sanches's date of birth and death.

III

Sanches's youthful rebellion against Aristotle in the *Quod nihil scitur* and in his other philosophical tracts was to result in a radical form of scepticism that makes him a unique figure in French Renaissance thought. For his scepticism was not, as many critics have conjectured, the fruit of his reflections on the works of Sextus Empiricus, recently made available in their Latin translations by Henri Estienne (*Hypotyposes*, 1562) and Gentian Hervet (*Adversus mathematicos*, 1569), but rather the consequence of his own refutation of Aristotelianism and the terminist logic of the Parisian Nominalists.[1] Popkin rightly observes that "Sanchez develops his

[1] Many critics, beginning with Bayle, have described Sanches as a "Pyrrhonian". In the sixteenth and seventeenth centuries, the terms "sceptic" and "Academic" were interchangeable, and no clear distinction was made between Academic scepticism and Pyrrhonism. For a discussion of the use of these terms, see

scepticism by means of an intellectual critique of Aristotelianism, rather than by an appeal to the history of human stupidity and the variety and contrariety of previous theories".[2] Indeed, unlike Montaigne (who saw in the contradictory doctrines of the different schools of philosophy an avowal of the fundamental incapacity of the human mind to reach truth and was deeply influenced by his reading of the *Hypotyposes* of Sextus Empiricus in the period 1575–80 and of Cicero's *Academica* in 1580–8), Sanches preferred to argue the case for radical scepticism by pointing out the errors and inconsistencies of the Aristotelian theory of science with its reliance upon the demonstrative syllogism.[3] Given the inadequacies of the Aristotelian system of knowledge and the failure of Scholastic dialectic to interpret anew and to develop Peripatetic doctrine in the light of recent scientific discoveries, Sanches was driven to seek the answer to the question of the right scientific method to be used in the quest for true knowledge by returning to a consideration of Galen's scientific methodology with its stress on empirical observation and experiment. Fundamental to understanding Sanches's rejection of Aristotelianism and adherence to an extreme form of scepticism is the importance of his training in medicine, which brought him into contact with Galenism and, in particular, with the many commentaries on the *Ars medica*. Thus it is the combination of two approaches to the theory of knowledge, the philosophical and the medical, which distinguishes Sanches's

Charles B. Schmitt, *Cicero Scepticus: A study of the Influence of the Academica in the Renaissance* (The Hague: Martinus Nijhoff, 1972), pp. 7–8. Senchet and Carvalho, in particular, stress Sanches's indebtedness to Sextus Empiricus.

It was at the Collège de Montaigu in the lectures and writings of Gaspar Lax, John Dullaert, and John Major that a renaissance of fourteenth-century nominalism arose at the beginning of the sixteenth century. Rita Guerlac, in her introduction to *Jean Luis Vives against the Pseudodialecticians: A Humanist Attack on Medieval Logic* (Dordrecht: Reidel, 1979), pp. 19–24, gives an excellent summary of the main figures in this revival of terminist dialectic and philosophy. See also Pierre M. M. Duhem, *Le Système du monde* (Paris: Hermann, 1959), X, pp. 72–131.

[2] Richard H. Popkin, *History of Scepticism from Erasmus to Spinoza*, p. 37.

[3] See Elaine Limbrick, "Was Montaigne Really a Pyrrhonian?" *Bibliothèque d'Humanisme et Renaissance*, 39 (1977), pp. 67–80.

contribution to the history of ideas in the sixteenth and seventeenth centuries.

Many scholars have commented on the close alliance between medicine and philosophy in the Renaissance medical curriculum where the study of Aristotle's works on logic (considered by many Renaissance university professors to be the true basis for scientific method), and on physics and natural history were held to be essential elements of the programme of studies to be followed by medical students.[4] One should not forget that medical students were required to spend their first two years in the faculty of arts prior to beginning their medical studies in the faculty of medicine. Sanches had the good fortune to have been trained both in France and Italy, where his keen and enquiring young mind benefited from the teaching of eminent scholars in both disciplines.

Sanches's first contact with the works of Aristotle had been made during the course of his studies at the Collège de Guyenne. As we have seen, the first year of the arts curriculum was spent in the study of Aristotelian logic and the second year in the study of Aristotle's natural philosophy, based on the *Physica* and the *De caelo*.[5] These texts were common to the curriculum of most faculties of arts whose teaching led normally to the conferment of the *maîtrise ès arts*, which was a prerequisite for entry into the higher faculties of theology, law, and medicine. Reulos has pointed out that even if the teaching of Aristotle was supposed to be based on the works of Aristotle, the actual study of Aristotelian logic was really founded on the summaries, or abridged versions, of Aristotle, which were themselves accompanied by weighty commentaries.[6] The most popular of these were the *Summulae logicales*

---

[4] The most valuable studies on the relationship between medicine and philosophy are the following: Gilbert, *Renaissance Concepts of Method;* John Herman Randall, *The School of Padua and the Emergence of Modern Science* (Padua: Antenore, 1956); Schmitt, "Aristotle Among the Physicians," in *The Medical Renaissance of the Sixteenth Century,* ed. Andrew Wear et al., pp. 1–15.

[5] See section II, note 23.

[6] Michel Reulos, "L'Enseignement d'Aristote dans les collèges au XVIe siècle", in *Platon et Aristote à la Renaissance,* ed. J.-C. Margolin (Paris: Vrin, 1976), pp. 147–54.

of Peter of Spain and the commentaries of George of Brussels, Lefèvre d'Etaples, and John Major, the Scottish theologian who was a regent of the Collège de Montaigu and leader of the Parisian school of nominalism.[7] Sanches would certainly have studied the introductory book on Aristotelian logic written by Nicolas de Grouchy, a former master at the Collège de Guyenne during the principalship of Gouveia. Grouchy's famous *Praeceptiones dialecticae* (1555) was a prescribed text in the curriculum of the college at the time Sanches was a student there and had been written by Grouchy in 1547 during his stay at the University of Coimbra when he accompanied André de Gouveia to Portugal.[8] Grouchy later taught at the University of Paris, and his *Aristotelis logica* (1549) had run into many editions by the year 1590. Jacques de Thou calls Grouchy an extremely learned man who was renowned for his dispute with Ramus during António de Gouveia's campaign to discredit Ramus and for his *Remarks on Aristotle*.[9] It must be remembered, as Walter Ong points out in his study of Ramism,

[7] Ibid., p. 149. Reulos quotes Robert Goulet's *Heptadogma* (1517), where, in chapter 6, "De artibus dialecticae ac eloquentiae", Goulet states: "In logica summe colatur et in eadem imitetur Aristoteles. Pro summulis Petrus Hispanus, commentarii ipsius Georgii Bruxellensis, Fabri Stapulensis aut domini Majoris, Scoti, nunc prae ceteris in pretio habentur". For additional information on George of Brussels, see Duhem, *Le Système du monde*, pp. 77–96.

[8] See Braga, *História da Litteratura Portugueza*, p. 583. Nicolas de Grouchy (1519–72) was an outstanding Hellenist, and the first edition of his *Aristotelis logica* was published in Coimbra in 1549. Grouchy was the author of several Latin translations of Aristotle among which the *Analytica posteriora* and the *De sophisticis elenchis* were included in Guillaume Guérente's edition of the *Aristotelis logica* (Parisiis: ex typographia T. Richardi, 1559). Charles Schmitt in *Aristotle and the Renaissance* (Cambridge, Mass.: Harvard University Press, 1983), pp. 166–7, note 35, points out that Grouchy revised nearly all of Périon's translations and that "Grouchy's translation of the *Organon* was included in the Casaubon edition of 1590". Guérente also taught at the Collège de Guyenne at the same time as Grouchy and wrote commentaries on Aristotle. For useful background information on the teaching of Aristotle at the Collège de Guyenne see Edilia Traverso, *Montaigne e Aristotele* (Florence: Felice Le Monnier, 1974).

[9] Jacques de Thou, *Historiarum sui temporis ab anno 1543 usque ad annum 1607, libri CXXXVIII* (Geneva: Pierre de la Rouiere, 1626), I, 708B.

that the teaching of Aristotelian logic in the university arts curriculum at Paris, and in other universities and colleges, was considerably affected (and limited also) by the need to simplify and systematise it for presentation to students who were only young adolescents.[10] Like Montaigne before him, Sanches reacted vigorously against the pedagogical versions of Aristotle's logic.[11]

Sanches's attacks on Aristotelian logic in the *Quod nihil scitur* should therefore be understood in the light of the teaching he had received at the hands of the Scholastic logicians who had rendered the obscure and difficult texts of Aristotle even more obscure with their commentaries.[12] Both in the arts curriculum and in the medical curriculum a disproportionate amount of time was spent on Aristotelian logic and the art of disputation. The obvious errors in the scientific works were challenged by some Galenists who, in their turn, were not anxious to see their source of authority discredited too readily by the discoveries of the anatomists and the pharmacologists.

There had already been serious objections made to Aristotelian doctrine by leading humanists at the beginning of the sixteenth century. The Spanish humanist Vives, whose works Sanches refers to in the *Quod nihil scitur*, was renowned for his constant attacks on the obscurity of Aristotle and of his commentators in his *De disciplinis* (Antwerp, 1531).[13] Even Aristotle himself, states Vives, would have laughed at the stupidity of his commentators and criticised them greatly.[14] Both as a critic of Aristotle and as an

---

10 Walter J. Ong, *Ramus: Method and the Decay of Dialogue* (Cambridge, Mass.: Harvard University Press, 1958), pp. 136–40.

11 See Trinquet, *La Jeunesse de Montaigne*, pp. 482–92.

12 Sanches writes: "What, then, does Aristotle say? 'Knowledge is a mental disposition, acquired by demonstration'. I do not understand; and, what is worst of all, it is *obscurum per obscurius*" (translation, p. 178).

13 Ioannes Lodovicus Vives, *De disciplinis libri XX* (Antwerpiae: excudebat M. Hillenius, 1531). The first part of the *De disciplinis* is often referred to as the *De causis corruptarum artium*.

14 "Profecto Aristoteles ipse, si nunc viveret, etiam si fuisset insolentissimus, cuiusmodi non fuit (nam multa modestiae eius signa impressa sunt in illius libris) sed si arrogantissimus fuisset, istorum tamen stultitiam irrideret, ac castigaret" (*De disciplinis*, liber quintus, "De philosophia naturae, medicina, et

adversary of the Scholastic dialecticians of his day, Vives exerted a wide and continuing influence on thinkers in the sixteenth century. In his *Adversus pseudodialecticos* (1520), which is a work of his youth attacking his former teachers of logic at the Collège de Montaigu in Paris, Vives criticises the formalism of the Scholastics, their abuse of sophismata, their corruption of language. In their hands language had become a jargon comprehensible only to themselves and their disciples, full of verbal quibbles, ugly barbarisms, and perverted meanings of words which had taken them ten, twenty years, nay sometimes a lifetime to understand.[15] In contrast, states Vives, "Aristotle does not entangle and detain his pupil in these stupid and dreary suppositions, ampliations, restrictions and verbal quibbles".[16] As a humanist with an excellent grounding in Greek, Vives claims that the Scholastic dialecticians did not have even a passing acquaintance with the original Aristotelian texts, which they knew only through the Latin translations and commentaries.[17]

Many passages in the *Quod nihil scitur* indicate a familiarity with the *De disciplinis*, an encyclopaedic work in which Vives discusses the causes of the corruption of three main branches of philosophy: language (grammar, dialectic, rhetoric); natural philosophy

artibus mathematicis corruptis", caput 2, p. 188, in *Opera omnia,* vol. VI [1785; London: Gregg Press, 1964]).

[15] "... ut gratulemur nostro seculo maxime queri illi solent Parisiis, unde lux totius eruditionis manare deberet, mordicus homines quosdam foedam amplecti barbariem, et cum ea monstra quaedam disciplinarum, velut sophismata, ut ipsi vocant, quibus nihil neque vanius est, neque stultius; quae cum exactius homines nonnulli ingeniosi consectantur, tum sua bona ingenia perditum eunt, tum tamquam fertiles agri, sed inculti, magnam inutiliam herbarum procreant copiam, somniant et confingunt sibi ineptias ac novam quandam linguam quam ipsi soli intelligant" (see Guerlac, *Jean Luis Vives against the Pseudodialecticians*, pp. 46–8).

[16] "... neque intricat et detinet Aristoteles suum discipulum frigidissimis et stultissimis suppositionibus, ampliationibus, restrictionibus, litterulis" (see Guerlac, ibid., pp. 78–9).

[17] "...nec ipsum certe Aristotelem, non dico in naturali vel morali philosophia, sed ne in dialectica quidem, vel de facie cognitum habent, quam se se tradere inverecunde profitentur, quum eam ipsi nunquam viderint" (see ibid., pp. 88–9).

(physics, medicine, mathematics); and moral philosophy (ethics, jurisprudence, theology). However much Vives may criticise Aristotle in the *De disciplinis* he still acknowledges him to be the outstanding author and philosopher of his age, remarkable for the keenness of his intellect and the manner in which he had illuminated all disciplines.[18] Sanches used similar words to praise Aristotle's contribution to knowledge.[19] Nevertheless, respect for the achievements of Aristotle in his time did not blind Vives, or later Sanches, to the tremendous constraints which the Aristotelian tradition had placed on the continuous search for knowledge. At the beginning of the *De dialectica*, the third book of the *De disciplinis*, Vives states that logic should be the means of access to and instrument of all studies and arts.[20] But logic had been corrupted at the hands of the Scholastic dialecticians and, in turn, the other arts of philosophy, medicine, and theology had been contaminated. It is interesting that Vives rejects the definitions of logic given by Cicero and Peter of Spain, preferring to follow the example of the Stoics, who had confined dialectic within the boundaries of judgment and made it the science of what is true, false, and neutral.[21]

In condemning speculative philosophy Vives advocated a theory of knowledge which, although pragmatic and undoubtedly deriving much of its theoretical formulation from the sceptical doctrines of the New Academy, rested on a firm belief in the divine origin and ordering of human knowledge. The sceptical

---

[18] "Fuit vir ille, mea quidem sententia, ingenii acumine, iudicio, dexteritate, prudentia, diligentia, atque studio, omnium cuiuscunque aetatis scriptorum facile praestantissimus, edoctus diutissime a magistro, non dicendi modo, sed etiam sapiendi, Graeciae totius Principe" (*De disciplinis*, liber primus, "Qui est de artibus in universum", caput 4, p. 31 in *Opera Omnia*, vol. VI).

[19] "To be sure, I think Aristotle stands supreme among the most gifted investigators of Nature; he is unrivalled among the wonderful intellects that the human race, in all its weakness, has produced" (translation, pp. 169–70).

[20] ". . . nempe aditum, atque instrumentum aliorum studiorum, et artium" (*De disciplinis*, liber tertius, "Qui est de dialectica corrupta", caput I, p. 110 in *Opera omnia*, vol. VI).

[21] ". . . credo Stoicos sequutus, qui intra judicandi fines Dialecticam concludunt, et eam finiunt *scientiam veri, et falsi, et neutrius*" (ibid. p. 112).

doctrine of probability which he propounds in the *De instrumento probabilitatis* and *De censura veri et falsi*, the two books in the *De disciplinis* which are likely sources for Sanches's own sceptical enquiry into the method of acquiring knowledge, serves merely to indicate to Vives the necessity for true humility on the part of the philosopher, who must accept the limitations of human reason when compared to the transcendental knowledge of God. Only God has perfect knowledge. Such was to be the conclusion of Sanches.[22] Vives constantly uses the terms *experimentum, experientia*, and *iudicium* when discussing how man may obtain limited knowledge of the natural world. Noreña carefully points out that Vives does not undertake a consistent and systematic investigation into philosophical method, nor does the use of the word *experimentum* mean anything more than "empirical observation".[23] Being firmly convinced that "philosophy is entirely founded on opinion, conjecture, and verisimilitude", Vives did not believe that it was possible for man to attain certain knowledge.[24] As he states at the beginning of the *De instrumento probabilitatis*, there are three sources of knowledge: the senses, authority, and reason based on experience. The common people trust the senses, particularly those of sight and hearing.[25] But these senses, Vives says, are affected by accidental causes, by circumstances such as the physical state of the body. Faith in authority, too, is misplaced since human authority may be wrong, of which Aristotle was a prime example. The only sure source of knowledge is reason, which relies on the facts presented by the senses and whose function it is to organise the

---

[22] See Carlos G. Noreña, *Juan Luis Vives* (The Hague: Martinus Nijhoff, 1970), pp. 247–53, 264–7, for an excellent survey of Vives's philosophical concepts. See *Quod nihil scitur*, p. 132.

[23] Noreña, *Juan Luis Vives,* p. 286.

[24] "Philosophia tota opinionibus et conjecturis verisimilitudinis est innixa" (*De tradendis disciplinis,* liber quintus, "De vita et moribus eruditi", caput 1, p. 417 in *Opera omnia,* vol. VI).

[25] "Ordo vero eorum, quae creduntur, hic est. Primam fidem arbitramur esse sensuum, hanc vulgus certissimam esse ducit, nec falli se ab illa posse, unde sunt illa, et vocem his auribus hausi. Ego hisce oculis vide" (*De instrumento probabilitatis,* liber unus, p. 84 in *Opera omnia,* vol. III).

31

evidence and make a judgment based on experience. Reason for Vives is a natural light (*lumen naturale*) which enables man to seize an approximation of truth.[26]

Although Vives had criticised the abuse of the syllogism by contemporary dialecticians in his *Adversus pseudodialecticos,* in the *De censura veri* he calls the syllogism "the true and perfect form of argumentation".[27] In his search for an instrument to examine the truth Vives examines the proposition in the first book of the *De censura veri,* and in the second book he discusses argumentation and, at great length, the different figures of the syllogism.[28] Since Vives was primarily more interested in the theory of language and in the art of discourse, he tended to view dialectic as the art of persuasion.[29] Consequently in the *De censura veri,* book II, Vives gives the Ciceronian term for syllogism, *ratiocinatio* (an exercise of

[26] Vives gives this definition of *lumen naturale:* "Dedit natura homini sensus in corpore, in animo vero acumen, quo cernat, speculetur, intelligat, appraehendat. Tum iudicium, quo sparsa et dissipata velut indagine quadam colligat, ad nanciscendum verum: quod cum se putat assecutum, acquiescit ei, quod verum iudicat, contrarium reiicit: quae sunt assensio, et dissensio. Hinc adjuvatur experimentis ac usu rerum, intentione animi, studio, sedulitate, memoria, exercitatione: quae quando sua cuique non sufficiunt, accedunt aliena per doctrinam homini ab homine traditam. Haec sunt cunctis mortalibus in commune proposita, quae quoniam nos naturae beneficio habemus, idcirco naturale lumen nuncupamus: et quae per haec assequimur, naturae lumine dicimur assequuti" (*De disciplinis,* liber quintus, "De philosophia naturae, medicina, et artibus mathematicis corruptis", caput 2, pp. 185–6 in *Opera omnia,* vol. VI. See also Noreña, *Juan Luis Vives,* pp. 249–50).

[27] "... germana et perfecta argumentatio" (*De censura veri,* liber secundus, "De syllogismo", p. 169 in *Opera omnia,* vol. III).

[28] Vives gives a useful summary of the eighteen figures of the syllogism: Barbara, Darii, Celarent, Ferio, Fapesmo, Darapti, Datisi, Fapello, Barboco, Felapton, Ferison, Disamis, Ferisco, Bocardo, Camestres, Baroco, Cesare, and Festino.

[29] See Noreña, *Juan Luis Vives,* p. 281, where he makes the following comparison between the two dominating perceptions of logic in the first half of the sixteenth century: "If Vives' books are the expression of a rhetorical conception of logic as a dialectic of persuasion, an art of discourse, and a theory of human communication, Ramus' popular writings symbolize the early shift toward logic conceived as an art of reason, a tool of scientific discovery and of the study of the thought-processes".

the reasoning powers), and refers mainly to Cicero's rhetorical and philosophical works; he also occasionally mentions Quintilian and Martianus Capella. The insistence on the rhetorical aspects of logic and the use of the formal syllogism set Vives's writings on the logic of probability apart from those of Sanches, who did not believe the Aristotelian syllogism could lead to truth.[30]

Vives's contribution to the search for a scientific method lies in his advocacy of practical learning for which his model was medicine. In spite of his criticisms of the education of young doctors, who, he says in the *De medicina,* are totally ignorant of the medical uses of herbs and lack knowledge of the psychological aspects of the art of healing, he does praise the art of medicine itself, since it was based on empirical observation (*experimenta*) and on judgment (*iudicium*).[31] The source for Vives's conception of *ars* was Galen's treatise *Methodus medendi,* which had been translated into Latin in 1519 by his friend Thomas Linacre and which became one of the best known and most widely quoted of Galen's works by philosophers and medical scholars alike.[32] Vives praises the works of the great medical authorities: Galen, Hippocrates, and Dioscorides, who had been rescued from oblivion, and from the bad translations and errors of their Arab commentators – Avicenna, Rhazes, and others – by the translations and commentaries of Niccolò Leoniceno, Ermolao Barbaro, Thomas Linacre, Wilhelm

[30] "For true knowledge is to understand, in the first place the nature of a thing, in the second place its accidents, where it has any. From which it follows that a 'demonstration' is not a 'syllogism resulting in knowledge'; rather, it is nothing, insofar as it merely demonstrates that the accident inheres in the thing, according to you (since for me, so far is it from demonstrating anything that it rather conceals something, and manages only to confuse the intellect), but takes for granted the definition of the thing itself" (translation, p. 203).

[31] "... medica ars; quae primum experimentorum audacia nata est, dum necessitas ad desperationem adigeret ut auderent tentare, quandoquidem nec quietis et cautis meliore loco res erant futurae; annota sunt experimenta vel in memoria eorum, qui essent adjuti, propinquorum, necessariorum, denique omnium qui cum admiratione ea animadvertissent" (*De disciplinis,* liber quintus, "De medicina", caput I, p. 198 in *Opera omnia,* vol. VI).

[32] *Galeni methodus medendi, vel de morbis curandis, T. Linacro interprete, libri quatuordecim* (Lutetiae, 1519).

33

Copp, Laurentius Laurentianus, Giovanni Manardi, and Johannes Ruellius.[33] By his emphasis on the study of nature itself, on the observation of facts, and on the final judicious choice (*iudicium*), Vives pointed the way to scientific method.

Another striking parallel between the thought of Vives and Sanches is to be found in their attitude towards the mathematical sciences: both disputed mathematical certainty. Vives admitted that the mathematical sciences do provide certain and indubitable proofs but only in the applied sciences such as perspective and music, architecture and optics, as well as dynamics, where precise measurement is required and can be demonstrated. Many eminent philosophers, too, says Vives, disagree among themselves as to the certainty of mathematics, since the very principles of the science are based on conjecture and are thereby open to challenge.[34] Vives himself considered mathematical speculation to be unproductive and sterile.[35] It is interesting to note that one of his admirers, the Spanish philosopher Fox Morcillo, elaborated on

[33] Niccolò Leoniceno (1428–1524), professor of medicine at the University of Ferrara, was famous for his translations and commentaries on Galen's *Ars medica*. His successor in the chair of medicine, Giovanni Manardi (1462–1536), continued in the same tradition of linguistic and textual commentary. See Gilbert, *Renaissance Concepts of Method,* pp. 102–5, for an analysis of Leoniceno's and Manardi's contribution to humanist exegesis on Galen. Ermolao Barbaro (1454–93), a distinguished Venetian humanist, translated and annotated Dioscorides' *De materia medica* and was renowned for his summaries and paraphrases of Aristotle. Wilhelm Copp translated and commented on many of the works of Galen and Hippocrates. Laurentius Laurentianus, too, was involved with Copp in the work of translating and commenting on Hippocrates and Galen. Joannes Ruellius was famous for his translation of Dioscorides. For Thomas Linacre, see Charles D. O'Malley's *English Medical Humanists: T. Linacre and J. Caius* (Lawrence: University of Kansas Press, 1965).

[34] In the *De disciplinis* (liber quintus, "De mathematicis"), Vives quotes Aristotle and Plato as believers in the certainty of the mathematical sciences, and Cicero and Seneca as philosophers who doubt the theoretical foundations of geometry.

[35] "Sed artes hae, quando ad usum pertinent, versae ad contemplationem usu remoto longissime, sunt ad ea evectae, quorum nullus esset fructus, sed tantum sterilis quaedam contemplatio, et inquisitione infinita, quoniam alia ex aliis sine modo ullo nascuntur" (ibid., p. 205 in *Opera omnia,* vol. VI).

Vives's ideas in his *De demonstratione, eiusque necessitate ac vi* (1556) and defended the necessity for mathematical demonstration.[36] Fox Morcillo disagrees with the followers of the New Academy who, influenced by Arcesilas and the Pyrrhonians, declared that there was no possibility of demonstration, or of science, that was irrefutable. On the contrary, he maintained that by experiment and daily observation the errors of the senses could be corrected, since nature has furnished us with the means not only of mechanical skills but also of knowledge.[37] It was possible to know something, declared Fox Morcillo, provided that an exact method of enquiry was established.[38] Fox Morcillo stated later in his *De naturae philosophia* (1560) that geometrical method was the most satisfying and that the definitions, axioms, and hypotheses of the mathematical sciences seemed true and certain to him, for at least they could establish probable opinion.[39]

In conclusion it should be noted that Vives's criticism of the Aristotelian system of knowledge opened the eyes of many later thinkers to the possibility that Aristotle's scientific vision was incorrect in many areas and that new advances in knowledge were continually being made. To argue that Aristotle was infallible in all of his writings was to deny the possibility of scientific progress and the evidence of history. This belief in progress and in the

---

[36] Sebastian Fox Morcillo, *De demonstratione, eiusque necessitate ac vi* (Basileae: per Ioannem Oporinum, 1556).

[37] "Nam nullam esse demonstrationem ac scientiam firmam et stabilem, quod recentiores Academici duce Arcesila cum Pyrrhoniis existimarunt, falsum est, et absurdum. Tollunt enim artes omnes, ac disciplinas praeclare fundatas et constitutas experimento, observationesque diuturna: tum sensibus errorem inducunt: principiaque non solum artium, sed cognoscendi, nobis etiam insita a natura, pervertunt" (ibid., pp. 7–8).

[38] "Quibus de ipsis priusquam differo, sicuti hactenus, in universum et sciri aliquid contra Academicos asservimus" (ibid., p. 17).

[39] Sebastian Fox Morcillo, *De naturae philosophia seu de Platonis et Aristotelis consensione libri V* (Parisiis: ex officina Iacobi Puteani, 1560). In the preface to his book dedicated to Philip I of Spain, who had asked him to tutor his son, Fox Morcillo writes: "atque in naturae Philosophiae petissimum, ut si qua in arte alia, probabilitas opinionum requiratur. Qua in re mihi ordo Geometrarum summopere placuit".

ceaseless quest for truth was characteristic of Vives's conception of philosophy, as it was to be of Sanches's own firmly held belief that the search for a true scientific method would enable man to lay a sure foundation for an all-embracing theory of knowledge.[40]

It is surprising that in none of his philosophical works does Sanches refer to Peter Ramus, the outstanding opponent of Aristotelianism in sixteenth-century France. Certainly Sanches would have heard of Ramus's reputation as the arch-enemy of Aristotle and as a *nouveau académicien,* if only for the reason that so many former masters of the Collège de Guyenne were involved in the defence of traditional Aristotelianism. For example, António de Gouveia, master at the Collège de Guyenne and brother of the famous principal, André de Gouveia, had published a defence of Aristotle against Ramus in 1543.[41] Moreover, Nicolas de Grouchy, who had taught at the Collège de Guyenne and subsequently at the universities of Coimbra and Paris, campaigned with António de Gouveia against Ramus. Undoubtedly there existed strong ties between the defenders of Aristotelianism in Bordeaux and Paris. Ramus's fame as an anti-Aristotelian was established by his *Aristotelicae animadversiones* (1543), an attack on Aristotle along the lines already drawn by Valla, Agricola, and Vives, as Gouveia and Pierre Galland did not fail to point out.[42] Like his predecessors, Ramus criticises the obscurity of Aristotle, the abuse of the demonstrative syllogism (which leads to a dialectical circle), and the failure of Aristotelian method.[43] Since Ramus was to propose the

[40] Noreña argues that it is the identification of the *lumen naturale* with a firm Christian moral sense that enables Vives to propound a philosophy in which "the search for truth is not an individual effort but a cooperative undertaking, subject to the law of constant historical progress" (Noreña, *Juan Luis Vives*, p. 249). Sanches, too, at the beginning of the *Quod nihil scitur,* maintains that Aristotle, like other humans, was fallible and that each generation brings a set of different opinions concerning the truth. However, what really matters is that man should continue his quest for knowledge.

[41] See Gilbert, *Renaissance Concepts of Method*, p. 133, and Ong, *Ramus*, pp. 22–4, 214–20.

[42] See Ong, *Ramus*, p. 22.

[43] In his commentary on the *Posterior Analytics* Ramus writes: "Primo itaque capite praecipit ut intelligenter et perspicue loquamur: in quo nugatoriam

fusion of dialectic and rhetoric, and to dismiss Galenic method as argument, Scholastic foolishness, and a synthesis of many methods, it is possible that Sanches deliberately chose to ignore Ramist method because of its close association with rhetoric, which Sanches despised.[44]

In his other philosophical treatises Sanches continues his critique of Aristotle's scientific works and displays a profound knowledge of even the minor tracts. As a Christian and believer in a divinely ordered universe, Sanches naturally opposed the dogmatism of Aristotle and his followers, particularly with regard to the teleological view of nature and the conception of the soul. As an adherent of Galenism, Sanches is highly critical of the scientific errors of Aristotle and uses his medical experience to reveal the false assumptions and inconsistencies in Aristotelian doctrine. In his first published work, the *Carmen de cometa anni M.D.LXXVII* (1578), Sanches was concerned with refuting in the name of reason and experience the absurd predictions of the astrologers after a fiery comet had appeared in the skies of Europe in 1577.[45] A wave

obscuritatem suam valde arguit et se iudicio suo damnat, quod de industria (ut Aristotelei testantur) et verbis, et sententiis perobscuris utatur ... Definit rursum scire, per demonstrativum syllogismum intelligere: quod falsum, et reprehendum est: potest enim omnis scientia, omnisque disciplina solis definitionibus, divisionibus, exemplis, sine ullo perfecto syllogismo haberi: et valde ridicula ea disciplina esset, quae perfectis syllogismis tota contexeretur, qualis videlicet nulla est" (*Petri Rami Veromandi, Animadversionum Aristotelicarum libri XX* [Lutetiae Parisiorum: apud Ioañem Roigny, 1548], pp. 185–6). Ramus gives several examples of the absurdities the syllogism can engender when the reasoning becomes circular in book 18, p. 406:

Omnis homo est rationalis
Omne risibile homo est:
Omne risibile est rationale
Circulo concluditur propositio

[44] Sanches states that "elegant language is seemly for rhetoricians, poets, courtiers, lovers, harlots, pimps, flatterers, parasites, and people of that sort, for whom elegant speech is an end in itself; but, for science, accurate language suffices" (translation, p. 171). Later on he observes: "As for rhetoric and poetry, they distort everything, and abuse every device. The practitioners of all of these arts merely employ useless loquacity" (p. 176).

[45] Artur Moreira de Sá has published a facsimile reproduction of the 1578 edition

of fear had swept over Europe, creating a resurgence of superstitious belief in judiciary astrology, and many prophets of misfor-
tune had seized the opportunity to make alarming predictions of
terrible wars, famines, plagues, floods, fires, droughts, rebellions,
and the downfall and death of great princes.[46] Moreira de Sá
observes that about 139 works, including translations and re-
editions, were written about the comet of 1577.[47] Among such
prophets was Franciscus Junctinus (Francisco Guintini), whose
*Discours sur ce que menace devoir advenir la comete apparüe à Lyon le 12
de ce mois de Novembre de 1577. laquelle se voit encores à present* had
greatly aroused the ire of Sanches.[48] Composed in the manner of
Lucretius, the *Carmen de cometa anni M.D.LXXVII* attacks in the
name of reason and scientific fact the false prophecies of Junctinus,
Leopoldus, Albumasar, Auger Ferrier (a rival of Sanches at Toulouse), Cardano, and others mentioned in historical accounts of
astrology.[49] His contemporaries who still believed in the supersti-

  entitled *O Cometa do ano de 1577 (Carmen de cometa anni M.D. LXXVII)* (Lisbon:
  1950), which is accompanied by an excellent introduction, notes, and Portuguese translation by G. Manuppella. C. Doris Hellman discusses the major
  impact the comet of 1577 made upon astronomical thought in her study *The
  Comet of 1577: Its Place in the History of Astronomy* (1944; rpt. New York: AMS
  Press, 1971). Sanches writes in the preface addressed to his friend Diogo de
  Castro: "Cum tamen postea etiam ex doctioribus quosdam animadverterem
  his praedictionibus animum adhibere fidereque plus quam ratione dignum sit,
  antiqua nimirum superstitione Arabum Aegyptiorumque non solum in hoc,
  verum et in aliis pluribus rebus ad nostra usque tempora per manus deducta,
  cum tamen nulla alia fundetur ratione quam male capto experimento, tunc
  exarsit animus aliquantulum, vel eo maxime quia Iunctini cuiusdam de hoc
  comete opusculum ad nos pervenit, quo doctus vir pluribus experimentis
  probare nititur semper crinita astra aliquid portendere mali" (Carvalho, *Opera
  philosophica*, p. 123).

  [46] See Hellman, *The Comet of 1577*, pp. 296–306.
  [47] Moreira de Sá, *O Cometa*, p. 13. Hellman, *The Comet of 1577*, gives an extensive bibliography of all known published tracts.
  [48] Franciscus Iunctinus (Junctinus or Guintini) was an Italian astrologer and
  mathematician whose work was published in Lyons and Paris in 1577.
  [49] Leopold of Austria discussed comets in his *Compilatio de astrorum scientia*
  (Augsburg, 1489). Sanches was familiar with Albumasar's *De magnis conjunc-
  tionibus,* translated by John of Seville and published in 1515 in Venice. Auger
  Ferrier had published his *Liber de diebus decretoriis secundum pythagoricam doc-*

tions of the Babylonians and the Egyptians are mocked unmercifully by Sanches for their ignorance and credulity, since common sense and historical and scientific facts have clearly proved that no value can be attributed to predictions based on the appearances of comets. The forty-page poem, written in hexameters, sets out in a series of twelve arguments and counter-arguments the rational explanations of natural phenomena and ends, like the *Quod nihil scitur,* with the lines: "What is taught has no more strength than it derives from him who is taught". This poem continues the sceptical dialectic of the *Quod nihil scitur* and is dedicated, as was the *Quod nihil scitur,* to his dear friend Diogo de Castro, who delighted in contemplating Nature and her laws.

Aristotle's views on comets are expounded in the *Meteorologica* in which he adopts the method of first stating, then refuting, the views of his predecessors, a method Sanches was to employ also in his *Carmen de cometa anni M.D.LXXVII.* As Doris Hellman has shown in *The Comet of 1577: Its Place in the History of Astronomy,* Aristotle's explanation of comets held an important place in the history of cometary theory.[50] Even though comets could not be observed accurately as physical phenomena, Aristotle believed it was possible to furnish a rational explanation of their origin, constitution, and motion. His conception of a comet as being a fiery exhalation, rather like a shooting star, often fringed or bearded, led him to accept as a natural consequence that comets are harbingers of wind and drought owing to their fiery constitution. Sanches did not believe in Aristotle's theory of the generation of comets, nor that their attendant consequences were drought, famine, and pestilence. However, his main objective in the *Carmen de cometa anni M.D.LXXVII* was to combat the false predictions of contemporary astrologers in the name of reason, as he states in the preface, and his critique of Aristotle is moderate.

Sanches's remaining philosophical tracts, the *De divinatione per somnum, ad Aristotelem,* the *De longitudine et brevitate vitae liber,* and

trinam et astronomicam observationem (Lugduni: J. Tornaesius, 1549). For an interesting study of the role of astrology in the Renaissance, see Eugenio Garin's *Astrology in the Renaissance* (London: Routledge & Kegan Paul, 1983).
[50] See Hellman, *The Comet of 1577,* pp. 19–23.

the *In lib. Aristotelis physiognomicon commentarius,* were all published posthumously and form part of the 1636 edition of the *Opera medica* to which the philosophical works were added.[51] Most probably during his tenure of the chair of philosophy Sanches was called on to lecture on these minor works of Aristotle and felt obliged to clarify and comment on the Aristotelian corpus in the light of his own medical knowledge.

The opening remarks of the *De divinatione per somnum, ad Aristotelem* refer to his long, self-imposed silence and period of contemplation (1575–81), and in the same spirit as the *Quod nihil scitur,* Sanches asks, "What else is our science other than rash confidence combined with absolute ignorance?"[52] Given the infinite variety, inconstancy, and contradictions of all philosophical opinions on nature, who would dare to claim, asks Sanches, that he knows anything at all? Thus he himself had resolved to spend the rest of his life in leisurely contemplation rather than wear himself out in fruitless quarrels and disputations. But a sense of duty and the responsibilities of his position had led him to renounce this project. So, says Sanches, "We must be mad along with all the others, or, if we alone are mad, we must measure our madness against that of the others".[53] Sanches proposes to discuss this minor and obscure work of Aristotle in order to show what is believable and what should be avoided, according to perfect reason.

Presumably the *De divinatione per somnum, ad Aristotelem,* as Cazac has conjectured, formed part of Sanches's introductory lectures at the University of Toulouse when he was first appointed to the chair of philosophy in 1585.[54] It appears as the second of his philosophical treatises in the 1649 Rotterdam edition of Sanches's

[51] The title of the 1636 Toulouse edition is *Opera medica. His iuncti sunt tractatus quidam philosophici non insubtiles.*

[52] "Quid enim aliud est scire nostrum, quam temeraria fiducia cum omnimoda ignorantia coniuncta?" (Carvalho, *Opera philosophica,* p. 91).

[53] "Decreveramus iamdiu potius silere, et mutam agere nobiscum Philosophiam, quam cum tot fatuis publice insanire, insaniamque nostram publicis tum concertationibus, cum praelectionibus, tum denique operibus manifestam omnibus facere, et quod peius fortasse sit, in eandem alios, si ita contingant, trahere" (ibid., p. 91).

[54] Fonds Cazac, Boîte III.

Tractatus philosophici following immediately after the *Quod nihil scitur*. The treatise examines the history of the belief in divination, drawing heavily on Cicero's *De divinatione* throughout, and attacks vigorously the *De rerum varietate* and the *De subtilitate* of Girolamo Cardano, the famous Italian mathematician, physician, and astrologer.[55] Although Sanches calls Cardano the most erudite philosopher and doctor of his age, he berates him for being irrational, even demented, for saying that divination was a true conjecture of future events and governed by reason.[56] Perhaps the 1556 French translation of Cardano's works by Richard le Blanc inspired Sanches's hostile and lengthy criticism of Cardano.[57] Certainly he quotes extensively, sometimes several pages at a time, from Cardano's writings on oracles, whose prophecies Cardano held to be of divine origin, and which Sanches affirms is not only an absurd belief but also one which is contrary to the Christian religion. In fact, Sanches carries on a long dialogue with Cardano throughout the *De divinatione per somnum, ad Aristotelem,* insulting him in the most virulent language for his belief in demons, so that at times the treatise appears to be a pretext for a powerful indictment of one of the most famous contemporary scholars, rather than a commentary on Aristotle's work.[58]

[55] In 1554 Cardano published his celebrated treatise on astrology *In C. Ptolemaei Pelusiensis IIII de astrorum iudiciis* in Basel.

[56] "Cardanus vero nostri saeculi et Philosophus et Medicus doctissimus, simul etiam saepe omnino irrationalis, et deliro potius ... *Divinatio, inquit, est coniectura vera de futuris, non certa ratione habita*" (Carvalho, *Opera philosophica,* p. 94).

[57] Jerome Cardan, *Les Livres de Hierome Cardanus ... intitulez de la subtilité, et subtiles inventions, ensemble les causes occultes, et raisons d'icelles. traduis de latin en françoys, par Richard le Blanc.* Nouvellement reveuz, corrigez, et augmentez sur le dernier exemplaire latin de l'auteur, et enrichy de plusieurs figures necessaires (Paris: G. Le Noir, 1556).

[58] "Quomodo ergo refers? inani coniectura, vano experimento, inartificiosa consequentia; denique totis paginis confirmas dictum tuum, te de daemonibus nihil effatu dignum scribere, sed solas meras nugas: ita ut pudeat me tantum Philosophum talia litteris mandasse, et qui aliorum fallacias, et nugas videret, et detegeret, in peiores incidisse. Trahit te gloriae cupiditas in absurda, ne aliquid ignorasse videaris, et non naturam ingenio superasse" (Carvalho, *Opera philosophica,* pp. 115–16).

41

Sanches inclines to the view that Aristotle did not condemn divination by means of dreams, and observes that Aristotle seemed to favour Cicero's belief that it was possible to have a presentiment of the future.[59] He himself prefers to call presentiment an "internal vision of things hidden" (*interna visio occultorum*) which is dependent on the senses and the mind.[60] However, since knowledge, too, is internal vision, Sanches makes a distinction between the two forms of internal vision by stating that knowledge is the result of rational discourse.[61]

For most Renaissance men the physical presence of demons was a matter of belief, as the studies of Lucien Febvre and Jean Céard have amply demonstrated.[62] Sanches, like Montaigne, was unusual in refusing to subscribe to current beliefs which he considered to be irrational and superstitious. Aristotle, on the

---

[59] "Praesentire enim possumus et divinare certo, quamvis nihil praedicamus, non autem praedicere certo, nisi praesenserimus. Huic etiam sententiae videtur favere Aristoteles, dum divinationem quae per somnum fit, non omnino contemnendam esse dicit, et saepe evenire ea quae in somniis praedicuntur, et saepe etiam aliter quam praedictum est" (ibid., pp. 94–5).

[60] "Ita ut iam hactenus habeamus divinationem esse, internam visionem occultorum. At vero, quia scientia videtur esse etiam interna visio occultorum (quae enim per scientiam habentur, occulta sunt omnino sensui, quamvis non intellectui)" (ibid., p. 95).

[61] ". . . ut differentiam inter scientiam et divinationem constituamus, oportet addere definitioni, non habita rationis discursu. Scientia enim habetur ratiocinatione, divinatio vero omnino sine discursu, si divinatio futura sit" (ibid., p. 95).

[62] Lucien Febvre points out in his study *Le Problème de l'incroyance au 16e siècle* (1942; rpt. Paris: Albin Michel, 1968) that, for the many humanists who believed in demonology, the world was "peuplé d'esprits, de démons, de créatures semi-divines, qui sont les agents, les instruments de la causalité" (p. 414). Jean Céard's study *La Nature et les Prodiges* (Geneva: Droz, 1977) traces the development of the belief in monsters, as signs and portents of disorder in nature, and rightly stresses the climate of anxiety created by the civil and religious wars in France which led to people accepting the existence of *mirabilia* in nature. A recrudescence of belief in demonology in the latter part of the sixteenth century is indicated by the fact that the *Malleus maleficarum* was reprinted sixteen times between 1574 and 1621, whereas in the previous fifty years there was no known edition (see Céard, *La Nature et les Prodiges*, p. 357).

other hand, was extremely circumspect about the problem, neither openly supporting nor denying that there were demons, and calling all that was below the divine regions a demon. Cardano, however, in his usual mad manner, states Sanches, had argued that demons were visible, tangible entities, going so far as to assert that his own father had a "familiar" (demon).[63] Sanches's scepticism would not allow him to believe the popular theories about demons. Nevertheless, as a devout Christian, it was incumbent on him to accept what the Bible said about demons and other miracles, since that was a matter of faith and not of reason.[64] Sanches vehemently disagrees with Cardano's view that demons had been entrusted with the task of taking care of men, for that was surely the task of angels.

In the final pages of the *De divinatione per somnum, ad Aristotelem* Sanches prefers to give a medical explanation of dreams, which are, he says, purely a continuation of all the sensory and intellectual impressions that assailed the body and mind when awake.[65] Quoting Hippocrates's *Liber de insomniis*, Sanches justifies his own observations of the many sensory perceptions that are stimulated when one is dreaming, many of which are dependent on the good health or poor health of the body. In conclusion

[63] "Non videtur Arist. daemones aperte asserere, neque negare, sed solum daemonium vocare quod infra divinum est. Academici quidam, et Philosophi nonnuli alii multa de daemonibus commenti sunt; et Cardanus, de quo antea, eo dementiae pervenit, ut tractabiles, visibilesque daemones dixerit, et patrem suum familiarem unum habuisse, et quasi asseclam, imo subditum" (Carvalho, *Opera philosophica,* p. 107).

[64] "At nos quibus illuxit veritas per Evangelium Domini nostri Jesu Christi, et fatemur bonos et malos daemones esse, ut tales agnoscimus quales sacra scriptura depingit, idque nullo rationis lumine ... sed sola fide victi, captivantes intellectum ad illius obsequium, ut ait Divus Paulus" (ibid, p. 107).

[65] "Mira est animi nostri natura, ut et videatur nihil esse, neque posse sine corpore; et tamen sine eo videatur et esse, et agere posse; ut in somno. Quamvis enim per vigilias non videat, neque audiat, neque cogitet absque corpore, nihilominus per somnum quiescente omnino corpore, ipse per se ipsum quasi solutus externa cura, non distractus adventitiis obiectis, et totus ad domicilium suum conversus, in idque contractus, eius partes omnes perreptare videtur ... in summa, quaecumque corporis, aut animae munia, ea omnia anima ipsa in somno obit" (ibid., p. 120).

Sanches reiterates that we cannot predict the future with certainty and that the art of divination is a total fiction, falsehood, and deceit. He believes Aristotle was wrong to say that men of low intellect have the ability to predict by means of dreams, since their minds are empty and easily filled with imaginary forms; far less the intelligent, for the opposite reason. Yet many intelligent men predict the future, as do idiots! Aristotle stated more judiciously at the end of his treatise that men of a melancholy disposition were more apt to foretell future events. Sanches's closing words to his readers are a restatement of his faith in scientific method: one must state only that which agrees with reason and experience.[66]

The *De longitudine et brevitate vitae liber* is unique among Sanches's philosophical tracts in that he comments on this minor work of Aristotle, using his knowledge of both philosophy and medicine to refute Aristotelian doctrine.[67] Sanches comments scornfully on Aristotle's works, claiming that Aristotle was not a physician used to confronting theory with daily experience. Sanches felt able to criticise much of what Aristotle had written on the problem of longevity, as opposed to brevity, of human, animal, and plant life; he preferred to trust his own practical observations and medical knowledge.[68] Sanches's commentary on Aristotle's scientific writings on the structure of animals' bodies, the theories of generation, of perpetual motion, and of the psychology of the soul, reveals an intimate acquaintance with the entire Aristotelian corpus. The treatise is a dazzling display of

---

[66] "Diximus solum quod tum ratione, cum experimento hactenus assequi potuimus: tu vero si quid certius habes, id sequere, et nos bona fide mone" (ibid., p. 122).

[67] "Hactenus vitae essentiam, eiusque causas, longae itidem brevisque praecipuam unam, scilicet animam, demonstravimus, adversus Aristotelem, aliosque eius sequaces. Nunc protensae, curtaeque, ex instituto, methodoque nostra, rationes investigemus ... Ultimo denique, ut Medicinam Philosophiae coniungamus, qua maxime ratione vita hominis produci possit, generalibus quibusdam praeceptis docebimus" (ibid., pp. 64–5).

[68] "Nec enim Medicus erat. Ob id etiam fere omnia quae et de corporis humani structura, et de his quae ad Medicinam spectant, memoriae prodidit, absurda, aut saltem mutila, obscura, et ut sibi incognita, sic etiam nobis reliquit" (ibid., p. 68).

erudition, probably designed to show Sanches's students that the scientific teachings of Aristotle were invalid where medical science was concerned, and that it would be better to follow the recommendations of doctors, if one wished to lead a healthy and long life. Indeed, the final two chapters are full of practical medical advice on personal hygiene, diet, and rest.

Sanches again pointed out, as in his other philosophical works, the absurdities, inconsistencies, and confused arguments that Aristotle presented in the *De longitudine et brevitate vitae liber*. The first part of his treatise deals with some of the historical philosophical problems that Aristotle, according to Sanches, did not coherently reconcile with his scientific thought. The second part approaches Aristotle's works from a medical viewpoint.[69] As a Christian philosopher, Sanches consistently disputes Aristotle's view of the soul, or life force, throughout the treatise. He maintains that it is the soul which gives life to the body and that one cannot attribute agency and intentionality to natural phenomena.[70]

The *In lib. Aristotelis physiognomicon commentarius* is Sanches's shortest work. The text, now considered apocryphal, was still attributed to Aristotle in the sixteenth century. It was translated and commented on by the Segovian physician Andres de Laguna, and published in Paris in 1535.[71] Sanches was the first to express doubts concerning Aristotle's authorship of this text.[72] There was

---

[69] See Carvalho, *Opera philosophica*, pp. 202–4, for a detailed analysis of the arguments advanced by Sanches.

[70] "Videtur Aristoteli. Causas enim longitudinis et brevitatis vitae, ad corpus omnes refert. Sed non sic res habet. Imo contra, maximum praecipuumque momentum habet anima tum in diversis, tum in eadem specie, ad producendam, aut coarctandam vitam" (ibid., p. 62). "Cur autem vegetabilia diutius vivunt quam animalia? Multae sunt rationes. Prima et praecipua est Dei voluntas, et Naturae eius ancillae, ordo" (ibid., p. 65).

[71] *Aristotelis Stagiritae de physiognomicis liber unus*, per Andream a Lacuna Secobiesem nunc primum ab infelici superioris versionis (a verbo absit iactantia) editione in feliciorem latinitatem restitutus (Parisiis: apud Ludovicum Cyaneum, 1535). Presumably Laguna was referring to Bartolommeo della Rocca's translation of 1515.

[72] "De authore major est ambiguitas. Nam prima quidem pars operis sane omnino redolet Aristotelis stylum, docendi methodum, et gravitatem. At

a certain contemporary interest in the art of judging character from facial features, and Sanches himself thinks that it would be a useful skill in such an age of hypocrisy. Both Cardano in his *Metoposcopia* (1550), and Giambattista Porta in his *De humana physiognomia* (Naples, 1586), had defended the art of physiognomy. Sanches thinks that it would be of interest to his students before they began their study of Aristotle's *Meteorologica* after the feast of Saint Luke, for him to comment on this useful little book. He proposes to interpret the work according to the principles of the natural sciences and medicine.[73] Although Sanches does not condemn the art of physiognomy, he does point out the difficulty of judging character from facial features, which are constantly modified by transitory passions, by the changing state of the body, and by the ability of men to dissimulate their true character. Consequently he judges the art of physiognomy to be far from certain and totally dependent on the skill of the observer.[74]

All of Sanches's philosophical works reveal a deep and intimate knowledge of Aristotle's logical and scientific works. His vituperative attacks against Aristotle and his commentators, the Scholastic dialecticians whose way of teaching logic and natural philosophy had dominated French and Italian universities into the late Renaissance, were motivated by a profound conviction that the only path to true knowledge was to go back to first

vero secunda, quae incipit a capite septimo, multoque magis a capite octavo usque ad finem, non adeo secure eius authoris dici debere videtur" (Carvalho, *Opera philosophica,* p. 84). Förster notes in volume I of his *Scriptores Physiognomonici* (Leipzig: Teubner, 1893), p. xix, that Sanches was the first to doubt the authenticity of this text. Sanches believed that no other scholar had commented on the *Physiognomicon:* "Extant quidem in plurima Aristotelis opera commentarii doctissimorum quorundam virorum. In hoc autem, nullius" (Carvalho, *Opera philosophica,* p. 83).

[73] "Conabimur ergo quantum vires ferre possint nostrae, tum Physicis, tum Medicis axiomatis adiuti, authoris sensa et concipere et vobis manifestare" (ibid., p. 84).

[74] "Dicimus ergo primum, quamvis Aristot. probaverit, aliquam esse Physiognomizandi artem, eam tamen non esse usque adeo certam, ut non falli unquam possit qui ea utitur, maxime vero si non sit valde expertus: et id commune est omnibus artibus" (ibid., p. 87).

principles, which could be demonstrated by experience and observation of the facts. Aristotle and his successors had constructed a maze of words, a system of knowledge based on chimeras and fictions, unconnected with factual truth, which only resulted in ignorance of the true nature of things.[75] Proudly Sanches announces in the *Quod nihil scitur* and his other philosophical tracts that he intends to write a book on the method of knowing.[76]

[75] Typical of Sanches's invective against Aristotle is this opening remark made to his students in his *In lib. Aristotelis physiognomicon commentarius:* "At scitis qualis hic author sit, quam scaber, inaccessus, obscurus, concisus, incomprehensibilis saepissime, nisi artificiosa coniectura, subtilique mentis acumine" (ibid., p. 83).

[76] The *Quod nihil scitur* concludes with these words: "Interim nos ad res examinandas accingentes, an aliquid sciatur, & quomodo, libello alio praeponemus: quo methodum sciendi, quantum fragilitas humana patitur, exponemus. VALE."

IV

In his quest for knowledge Sanches was led to contemplate first of all the mathematical sciences. Although the manuscript of Sanches's *Objectiones et erotemata super geometricas Euclidis demonstrationes* no longer exists, a letter sent by Sanches to Christopher Clavius gives important indications of his philosophical adherence during the period 1574–81.[1] Clearly Sanches was going through a sceptical crisis, since he calls himself "Carneades Philosophus" in

[1] The Jesuit Christopher Clavius, professor of mathematics at the Collegio Romano, corresponded with most of the eminent mathematicians of the day. Much useful information on Clavius can be gleaned *passim* from Paul L. Rose's study *The Italian Renaissance of Mathematics* (Geneva: Droz, 1975). Clavius rejected Copernican cosmology but did recognise the importance of Copernicus's restoration of astronomy. He was responsible for ensuring the publication of Maurolico's important optical treatises, the *Photismi* and *Diaphana* (Naples, 1611; Lyon, 1613). It is noteworthy that Galileo submitted his *Theoremata circa centrum gravitatis* to Clavius in 1587 at Rome.

both his opening salutation and closing words to Clavius.[2] The philosopher Carneades of the New Academy had developed a theory of probability which would enable the sceptic to function in society and thereby avoid the criticism that the suspension of judgment led to inaction and ignorance.[3] Although there is no absolute criterion of truth, for no perceptual statement is free from error, Carneades believed that one could give qualified assent to a concurrence of credible impressions.[4]

Sanches begins his reply to Clavius by speaking of his own despair of finding true knowledge, for which he had searched so long: "I had long searched through the realms of physics and mathematics but I had not found truth there. As I continued my investigations into this matter some men said that truth had established itself in an intermediate zone between the natural and

[2] The letter begins with a greeting to "Sapientissimo, piissimoque viro D. Christophoro Clavio, Carneades philosophus S [alutem]", and ends with the phrase: "Sum enim alter Carneades, non gloriae inanis, sed veritatis, et tui amantissimus. Vale. Carneades Philosophus" (Carvalho, Opera philosophica, pp. 146 and 153).

[3] The best exposition of Greek scepticism is still Victor Brochard's Les Sceptiques Grecs (Paris: Imprimerie Nationale, 1887). For his assessment of the doctrine of Carneades, consult pp. 127–85. Charlotte Stough explores systematically the epistemology of the Greek sceptics in her Greek Skepticism: A Study in Epistemology (Berkeley: University of California Press, 1969) and points out that "Carneades' criteria introduce the notion of evidence as reasonable ground for a perceptual assertion" (p. 62).

[4] Sextus Empiricus outlines the doctrine of Carneades in the Adversus mathematicos and uses a medical analogy, which would have pleased Sanches, to define the criterion of truth for the Academic: "And just as some doctors do not deduce that it is a true case of fever from one symptom only – such as too quick a pulse or a very high temperature – but from a concurrence, such as that of a high temperature with a rapid pulse and soreness to the touch and flushing and thirst and analogous symptoms – so also the Academic forms his judgment of truth by the concurrence of presentations, and when none of the presentations in the concurrence provokes in him a suspicion of its falsity he asserts that the impression is true" (Sextus Empiricus, Against the Logicians, trans. R. G. Bury [London, 1933–49; rpt., Cambridge, Mass.: Harvard University Press, 1961], II, pp. 179–80).

the supernatural worlds, that is to say, in the realm of mathematics".[5] However, mathematics, states Sanches, presented more formidable pitfalls than physics and metaphysics, and hardly deserved the name of science.[6] "True science", declares Sanches, "is to know God first of all, then Nature, which is subject to him; to know both internally and externally, as they say, or as Aristotle says, to know a thing by its causes".[7] Sanches states that mathematics may require much ingenuity and cleverness, but it is not a true science. Furthermore, in the related field of astronomy many fundamental suppositions had been proved wrong, as Copernicus had demonstrated most clearly. Even geometry, whose axioms should furnish certainties, seemed to have many chinks in its theoretical formulations. Since the evidence furnished by the senses is untrustworthy, reason must remedy any deficiencies. Sanches confesses to Clavius that, although he does not despair entirely of geometric certainty, he does not have great confidence in geometry.[8]

According to Sanches, the mathematical sciences cannot furnish a model of scientific knowledge, for their very principles are doubtful, as is their theoretical development.[9] For example, one supposes that there are points, but their existence and manner of being may be doubted. And the same applies to lines and

---

[5] "Olim ergo post peragratam Physicam Metaphysicamque, neque in eis inventam veritatem, de ea percontanti responsum est a quibusdam, in medio eam loco inter naturalia, transnaturaliaque sedem posuisse, hoc est in Mathematicis" (Carvalho, *Opera philosophica,* p. 146).

[6] "Omitto quod vix Mathematicas disciplinas scientias vocare audeam, ut quae magis sensu quam mente egeant, et proinde certiores sint, si quid hic certum sit" (ibid., pp. 146-7).

[7] "Vera enim scientia est Deum primo, deinde Naturam eius ancillam intus et extra, ut aiunt, aut ut Aristoteles rem per causas cognoscere" (ibid., p. 147).

[8] ". . . et si demonstratio illa esset Euclidis, iam aperte de Geometriae certitudine desperassem; quamvis non adeo multum ei fidam, ut alibi fortasse ostendam" (ibid., p. 149).

[9] "Multa ergo sunt in Mathematicis dubia, non solum in principiis, sed etiam in progressu" (ibid., p. 147).

surfaces.[10] For Sanches, mathematical definitions depend on "hypotheses" (postulates of existence) that have yet to be fully proved. Many ambiguities and errors had crept into mathematical reasoning. This was particularly true of the related science of astrology. Indeed, Clavius himself was well aware of the fallacious suppositions of astronomers and astrologers, since he had laboured long over the calculations necessary for the reform of the calendar.[11]

Sanches's scepticism concerning the mathematical sciences is understandable. Carneades had attacked geometry and mathematics because their theories depended on conjecture.[12] Sanches, too, was unwilling to accept that inductive reasoning could lead to certainty. Consequently, like Carneades, he was prepared to accept an approximation of the truth.[13]

[10] "Nam primo puncta supponunt, quae dubitatur, an sint et quomodo? et lineas, et superficies" (ibid., p. 147).

[11] Pope Gregory XIII abolished the ancient calendar in March 1582. Presumably Clavius had been working already on his calculations for the *New Style* (Gregorian calendar) when Sanches studied under him in Rome. Although Lilio Ghiraldi was the author of the new system, he died before the introduction of the new calendar and Clavius had the major responsibility of verifying the calculations.

[12] Sanches was thoroughly familiar with the philosophical works of Cicero and knew the arguments advanced by Carneades in the *Academica,* II, 116–18.

[13] "Sed satis promovet homo, si proxime ad veritatem accedat. Ad quam ego, ut quantum humano ingenio fieri potest, quam prope collimem, minimeque aberrem, omnia nimis anxie et scrupulose examino" (Carvalho, *Opera philosophica,* p. 148).

V

From the beginning of the *Quod nihil scitur* Sanches stresses that "the goal of my proposed journey is the art of medicine, which I profess, and the first principles of which lie entirely within the realm of philosophical contemplation".[1] Like Galen, whose

[1] Translation, p. 171.

treatise *Quod optimus Medicus sit quoque Philosophus* was often invoked to justify the importance of philosophy in the medical curriculum of the universities, Sanches himself firmly believed in the philosophical foundations of medicine and pursued throughout his life his dream of finding a method which could be universally applied, and which would enable him to establish "a kind of scientific knowledge that is both sound and as easy as possible to attain".[2] It was widely accepted in the sixteenth century, both in the Aristotelian tradition and in the Galenic medical tradition, that the alliance between philosophy and medicine was desirable and, indeed, beneficial.[3] As a consequence the question of method in the interrelated disciplines of philosophy, medicine, and the natural sciences became a dominant issue in intellectual debate during the Renaissance: it was still considered possible that a philosophical method could be successfully applied to the sciences.

Sanches's quest for "the proper method of acquiring knowledge"[4] should not be considered as an isolated, personal investigation: it was part of a growing dissatisfaction within the community of scholars with a traditional conceptual framework that was badly in need of total revision and restructuring. The violence of Sanches's feelings of revolt against the domination of the Aristotelians in the teaching methods used in the arts–medical curriculum of the universities is shown by his use of militaristic language and metaphors in the opening and concluding sections of the *Quod nihil scitur*. Proudly he calls the proposition "Nothing is known" his battle colour.[5] In his letter to Diogo de Castro he speaks of his work marching off to the field "like a soldier bent on storming the citadel of falsehood", which, of course, is the syllogistic stronghold of the Aristotelians.[6] Dialecticians draw up

---

[2] Ibid., p. 290.

[3] See Schmitt, "Aristotle among the Physicians", in *Medical Renaissance of the Sixteenth Century,* ed. Wear et al., pp. 2–5.

[4] Translation, p. 167.

[5] "Let this proposition be my battle colour – it commands my allegiance – 'Nothing is known'" (translation, p. 173).

[6] Ibid., p. 166.

words "in line of battle, bidding them to fight not as individuals but in combination", whereas rhetoricians parade words for a pretty effect, "like those who simulate troops of cavalry and military camps at public shows and spectacles".[7] Words are "troops" fighting the battles of the philosophers.[8] What then becomes of the poor student, whose only desire is knowledge, when faced with the verbal disputes of his professors, who bear the name of "men of science", yet "turn into brutes" and "fight to the death about what X or Y *meant* to say," resorting to the arms of "insults, invectives, defamatory libels, and abuse"?[9] The mind of the unfortunate "tyro" is torn apart and mauled to pieces by the everlasting arguments of his teachers! Like Galen, Sanches underlines the importance of method in teaching: "For in teaching, *nothing* possesses such importance as method".[10] However, once more disappointment and sorrow await the student: "Whom is he to follow, whom to believe? This one; that other; or no one".[11] The student may choose to be free and independent, which is Sanches's own advice to his reader. If not, he must defend the teachings of his master and turn "into a soldier, who follows his commander wherever he may drag him, in order to fight for *him,* no longer mindful of himself; and with *him* he perishes".[12]

The eclectic method (which was followed by Galen), of selecting from all the philosophers whatever the student approves of, is a freer course that requires great powers of judgment.[13] But new dialectical weapons are constantly being forged so that even if a person has truth and justice on his side, just as in war, "he may yet perish outwitted by skill and trickery".[14] Sanches considers

[7] Ibid., p. 176.
[8] Ibid., p. 176.
[9] Ibid., p. 267.
[10] Ibid., p. 269.
[11] Ibid., p. 272.
[12] Ibid., p. 272.
[13] "But if he puts equal trust in all or in none, so that he may select from all of them whatever he approves of, this is indeed a freer course, but it is also more difficult; for enormous powers of judgment are needed by the person who attempts to resolve their differences" (ibid., p. 272).
[14] Translation, p. 273.

that this tendency to verbal trickery was furthered by Aristotle's "science" of syllogisms and remembers the torments he suffered as a student looking for the defect in a syllogism when he might have better spent his time gaining understanding of a natural cause.[15] Syllogisms are cleverly constructed snares designed to entrap the adversary. Sanches declares that nothing is more harmful to the sciences than this dialectical method of teaching, which has become the very basis of scientific method, or as Sanches calls it, "scientific instruction in syllogisms".[16] Although Aristotle himself had written another work entitled *Sophistical Quibbles,* says Sanches, so that he might rescue men from the deceptions of syllogisms, this work proved to be a poisonous antidote, less powerful than the poison of the demonstrative syllogism.[17] Sanches therefore proposes to show the reader how he "can employ another and a better method than this one of syllogisms".[18] It is evident that Sanches was fully aware of the conflict in purposes which had arisen following the adoption of a method of teaching that perpetrated fallacious reasoning and led to error in the scientific method derived from this system of teaching. Sanches was to propose in embryonic form a scientific method based on experimentation and a weighing of the facts by the faculty of judgment in which experience, too, was to play a decisive role.[19]

The *Quod nihil scitur* has as its main objective the destruction of the Aristotelian system of knowledge, which had proved sterile and restrictive of the free pursuit of truth, and concludes with the promise of a new method of philosophical and scientific enquiry.

[15] Ibid., p. 273.
[16] Ibid., p. 274.
[17] Ibid., p. 274.
[18] Ibid., p. 276.
[19] Gilbert, in *Renaissance Concepts of Method,* states: "With regard to experimentation as a confirming stage in the application of scientific method, we have no evidence of an explicit formulation of such a doctrine in our period" (p. 223). Much work remains to be done on the medical-philosophical approach to science in the sixteenth century before one can make such a dogmatic statement.

Unfortunately, the destructive elements of Sanches's attacks against Aristotle and his followers were to be remembered the most by his contemporaries. Sanches was considered a complete sceptic because he proclaimed time and time again that "nothing is known", thus seemingly rejecting the accumulated knowledge of the past and the weighty authority of the Aristotelian tradition. Yet Sanches's ultimate aim was to build a system of knowledge on true and sound foundations.[20] His concern, as a physician and a scientist, was to have a true "understanding of natural phenomena".[21] His goal, as a philosopher, was to find the "proper method of acquiring knowledge". His rejection of past philosophical systems was an attempt to "assess the facts for themselves, under the guidance of sense-perception and reason".[22] As Sanches states towards the end of his enquiry, the two necessary and complementary methods of obtaining knowledge are judgment and experience.[23] This double procedure, long used by the school of medical empiricists and incorporated into Galen's epistemology, was to provide the basis for scientific investigation, not only in the field of medicine, but also in all the sciences. The remarkable scientific vision of Sanches, expressed simply and briefly in the final pages of the *Quod nihil scitur,* was limited by his philosophical scepticism, which led him to doubt the validity of experimentation on the grounds that only the "external aspects of events" are revealed, and to question the accuracy of judgment.[24] Nevertheless, *experience,* a vital key concept in Sanches's philosophical and medical treatises, and the final step in the Galenic

---

[20] In the translation, p. 275. Sanches compares Aristotelianism to an ancient building on the point of collapse which has to be constantly shored up and reinforced, and whose foundations are built on sand or are of fragile materials.

[21] Ibid., p. 168.

[22] Ibid., p. 168.

[23] "Those methods consist of experience and judgment. Neither of these two can properly retain validity without the other" (translation, p. 278). Sanches uses the term *experimentum* (see *Quod nihil scitur,* p. 157), which may be interpreted as referring to experiments which provide a body of experience.

[24] Translation, p. 278. Sanches goes on to ask: "How *many* experiences can a mere youth command? Few enough. How, then, is he to judge aright on the basis of only a few?"

method, can be handed down from one generation to the next by means of books.[25] Yet this experience transmitted by books is open to contestation: books propagate many errors and false opinions, and their meaning cannot always be comprehended. The young student must be prepared, states Sanches, "if he wished to learn anything, to study continually, to read what has been written by everyone, and to compare this information experimentally with *facts*".[26] Ill-health, mental affliction leading to melancholy, even premature death – all await the young scholar! There is no consensus among the authorities, for they have "totally divergent experimental findings".[27] Consequently, perfect scientific knowledge would appear to be beyond the reach of man.[28] Sanches, therefore, seeks "a kind of scientific knowledge", and to obtain this he proposes to examine *Things* and to discuss in another book whether anything is known, and how it may be known. Thus, with the promise of expounding in his next book the *method of knowing*, Sanches ends the *Quod nihil scitur*.[29]

Sanches undoubtedly considered the *Quod nihil scitur* to be the preliminary discourse in a series of philosophical treatises dealing with method, the nature of things, and the nature of the soul.[30] As we have previously stated, these treatises were either not written or were lost to posterity. But even without the other treatises the *Quod nihil scitur* stands in its own right as an important philosophical enquiry into the problem of knowledge and the method of acquiring knowledge. Like Descartes's *Discours de la méthode*, it is

---

[25] See Owsei Temkin, *Galenism: Rise and Decline of a Medical Philosophy* (Ithaca: Cornell University Press, 1973), pp. 15–16, for a discussion of Galen's concept of experience.

[26] Translation, p. 282.

[27] Ibid., p. 287.

[28] "You have, then, observed the difficulties that place scientific knowledge beyond our reach" (ibid., p. 289).

[29] Sanches refers twice in the *Quod nihil scitur* to the book on method on which he was currently working. See the translation, pp. 276 and 290.

[30] There are several references throughout the *Quod nihil scitur* to these three treatises. For the *Enquiry into Things*, see the translation, pp. 212, 230, 247, 250, 254, 261, and 290. For the *Treatise on the Soul*, see pp. 193, 229, 239, and 264 of the translation.

the account of Sanches's feelings of immense deception with previous philosophical systems and his decision "to examine the facts themselves as though no one had ever said anything about them, which is the proper method of acquiring knowledge".[31]

The impact of Galenist medical philosophy on Sanches's thought in the *Quod nihil scitur* remains to be considered. There is no doubt that Sanches greatly admired Galen, even though he was aware of the errors and contradictions in the Galenic teachings, for he refers constantly to the many works of Galen in his medical and philosophical treatises.[32] As Richard Durling has shown, there was an extraordinary renewal of interest in the works of Galen during the Renaissance.[33] The great European presses of Paris, Lyons, Basel, and Venice published no less than 630 editions, commentaries, and translations of Galen between 1525 (the date of the Aldine *editio princeps*) and 1560, when publication of Galen's voluminous works began to decline.[34] Paris, where the faculty of medicine was known for being a stronghold of Galenism during the years famous scholars such as Guinter, Copp, and Sylvius taught there, heads the list of major centres for the publication of Galen's works with 191 items, followed by Lyons with 158 items.[35] Lyons was an important publishing centre during the

---

[31] Translation, p. 167.

[32] In his commentary on Galen's *De crisibus* Sanches writes: "Non possum non valde admirari Gal. divinum ingenium in omnibus artis partibus, sed maxime in morborum naturae cognitione, praecognitione, et in pulsuum materia. Eique tantum tribuo propter multam, quae in eius operibus elucet, eruditionem doctrinamque, ut facile et in omnibus assentiar, credamque" (*Opera medica*, pp. 651–2). Many of Sanches's medical works are commentaries on Galen. In his anatomical treatises Sanches refers to the criticisms of Galenic anatomy made by famous contemporary scholars such as Vesalius, Colombo, and Fallopio. Likewise, in his commentaries on the causes and symptoms of diseases, Sanches mentions Joubert, Fernel, and Argenterius (see *Opera medica*, pp. 722, 725, and 741 ff.).

[33] Richard J. Durling, "A Chronological Census of Renaissance Editions and Translations of Galen", *Journal of the Warburg and Courtauld Institutes*, 24 (1961), 230–305.

[34] See ibid., pp. 242–3.

[35] Ibid., p. 243.

Renaissance and specialised in providing scholarly editions of medical and philosophical works for the universities of Montpellier and Toulouse. It was normal for an ambitious young scholar like Sanches to seek to have his first works, the *Carmen de cometa anni M.D.LXXVII* and the *Quod nihil scitur*, published in such a prestigious city where they would be assured of wide distribution.

Naturally the *Ars medica* and other well-known medical works of Galen were published the most frequently, accompanied by learned commentaries by the most illustrious humanist scholars of the day. Medical practitioners certainly possessed many of Galen's practical treatises. Françoise Lehoux in her fascinating study of the archives of sixty-six medical families living in Paris in the sixteenth and seventeenth centuries reveals that their libraries contained mainly medical works, both classical and modern, and that Galen headed the list with 145 volumes indicated in the library inventories, followed closely by Hippocrates with 121 volumes.[36] These figures do not include the enormous number of commentaries on the works of Galen and Hippocrates also found in the inventories. Two of the doctors studied, Lemaignan and Baudesson, possessed fifteen and fourteen works of Galen, respectively.[37] Although not every doctor or university professor of medicine could afford the sumptuous folio editions of Galen's *Opera omnia,* smaller and less expensive editions of individual works were available, and pocket editions in octavo for the university student were brought out by the Parisian publishers Simon de Colines and Gerhard Morrhius, followed closely in 1546 by the Lyonnese publisher Rouille, who flooded the market with his 16mo editions.[38]

The importance of the work of the translators and commentators on the Galenic corpus in the sixteenth century must be taken into account when assessing Sanches's own contribution to the great on-going debate on method. The revival of Galenism was due in

---

[36] Françoise Lehoux, *Le Cadre de vie des médecins parisiens au XVIe et XVIIe siècles* (Paris: Picard, 1976), p. 471.

[37] Ibid., p. 472.

[38] See Durling, "Chronological Census", p. 242.

large measure to the efforts of scholars such as Leoniceno, Linacre, Manardi, Guinter, Copp, Sylvius, Fuchs, Thomas à Veiga, and many others who had laboured over the years to translate the original Greek text into a Latin free from the errors of the Arabic translators. Their copious commentaries provided a comprehensive review of previous translation errors, medical theory, and philosophical issues raised by the confrontation of the Galenic texts with traditional (Aristotelian) scientific thinking. Whether their work was motivated by a humanistic quest for textual purity and a desire to establish Galenic orthodoxy, as Bylebyl has suggested, or represented the efforts of leading physicians to "stamp out the corruption of the true medicine by the Arabs and the utterly futile (*ineptissimum*) crowd of medical barbarians", as Wightman has stated, it is evident that medical thought was constantly being challenged and reassessed during the sixteenth century.[39]

As a physician, Sanches was familiar with the Latin translations of Galen made by Leoniceno and Guinter, the commentaries of Thomas à Veiga, and the manuals of Leonhart Fuchs on the art of medicine.[40] Sanches frequently quotes the names of these famous

[39] See Jerome J. Bylebyl, "The School of Padua: Humanistic Medicine in the Sixteenth Century", in *Health, Medicine and Mortality in the Sixteenth Century*, ed. Charles Webster (Cambridge: Cambridge University Press, 1979), pp. 340–1. See William P. D. Wightman, *Science and the Renaissance* (Edinburgh: Oliver & Boyd, 1962), I, pp. 212–13. R. K. French gives an interesting definition of the term "barbarian" as applied by the Hellenists to the Arab translators, mediaeval surgeons such as Guy de Chauliac, and contemporary surgeons lacking university training, in his article "Berengario da Carpi and the Use of Commentary in Anatomical Teaching", in *The Medical Renaissance of the Sixteenth Century*, ed. Wear et al., pp. 71–4.

[40] For information on Leoniceno see Edwards's excellent article, "Niccolò Leoniceno and the Origins of Humanist Discussion of Method", in *Philosophy and Humanism*, ed. Mahoney, pp. 283–305. Charles Singer in his *A Short History of Anatomy and Physiology from the Greeks to Harvey* (New York: Dover, 1957), pp. 105–6, emphasises the influence Guinter (Johannes Günther von Andernach or Winther, 1487–1574) exerted through his students (Vesalius, Servetus, Rondelet, Dryander), as well as through his translations of Galen, Oribasius, Paulus Aegineta, Alexander of Tralles, and Caelius Aurelianus. For information on Fuchs, see W. P. D. Wightman, *Science and the*

scholars as authorities for certain points he wished to emphasise for his medical students in his practical treatises. As his theoretical treatises on method and the nature of things are not extant, it is difficult to judge how much he was influenced by the current debate on method. Certainly Leoniceno's explanation of the prologue on method in Galen's *Ars medica* was known to generations of students in the sixteenth century.[41] Leoniceno, by his insistence on the Greek sources of Galen, rescued the prologue of the *Ars medica* from the Aristotelians, for he argued that it was not possible to apply the Aristotelian forms of demonstration to the interpretation of Galen's theory of scientific method. Leoniceno considered Averroës and the other Arab commentators to be barbarians, guilty of having contaminated the purity of the original Greek text with their faulty translations. Henceforth, after the publication of Leoniceno's translation and commentary on the *Ars medica* in 1508, the methodological connection between Galen, Aristotle, and Averroës was severed: two distinct camps were formed within the scholarly community, that of the *medici,* who followed Leoniceno, and that of the *philosophi,* who still adhered to the Aristotelian tradition.[42] Leoniceno was also responsible for focussing attention on the idea that method was "a logical instrument for the *organizing or restructuring of a science as a whole*", as Edwards has pointed out in his seminal article "Niccolò Leoniceno and the Origins of Humanist Discussion of Method".[43] It would seem, therefore, that Sanches belonged more to the school of medical humanists who preferred to go back to the original

Renaissance, 1, pp. 213–17, and also Andrew Wear's "Explorations in Renaissance Writings on the Practice of Medicine", in *The Medical Renaissance of the Sixteenth Century*, pp. 121–3, 133–5. Thomas à Veiga's commentaries on Galen have received no attention from scholars and yet there were two editions of his *Commentariorum in C. Galeni opera* brought out by Plantin in 1564 and 1566, and a third in Lyons in 1593.

41 See Durling, "Chronological Census", p. 282. The numerous reprints attest to the popularity of Leoniceno's work on the prologue to the *Ars medica*, his *De tribus doctrinis ordinatis.*

42 See Edwards, "Niccolò Leoniceno and the Origins of Humanist Discussion of Method", in *Philosophy and Humanism,* ed. Mahoney, p. 301.

43 Ibid., p. 284.

Galenic teachings, free from the Scholastic tradition with its underpinning of Aristotelian logic and natural philosophy. Certainly Sanches shared with Leoniceno the concept of method as "rational argument" leading to scientific knowledge. However, he does not debate method according to the *doctrina ordinata* of definition, demonstration, division, and resolution established by Leoniceno in the *De tribus doctrinis ordinatis*.[44] One can only presume that in the planned sequel to the *Quod nihil scitur* Sanches would have dealt fully with the question of the proper method to follow, drawing on his experience in the field of medicine.

The many translations of Galen's works and numerous manuals on the art of medicine written by the internationally renowned German humanist physician Leonhart Fuchs (1501–66) testify to the popularity and wide diffusion of Galenist medical theory and practice in the sixteenth and seventeenth centuries.[45] All aspiring medical students and doctors were familiar with Fuchs's *Compendiaria ac succinta admodum in medendi artem introductio* (1531), a short practical guide in which Galen's indications of the cause of an illness were reflected in the logically prescribed treatment for the patient.[46] For the third edition of 1548 the work was revised and expanded, then reissued under a new title, *Methodus seu ratio compendiaria cognoscendi veram solidamque medicinam ad Hippocratis et Galeni scripta recte intelligenda mire utilis*. Fuchs, like Leoniceno, argued for a return to the *prisca medicina* of Galen and his followers (Aëtius and Paul of Aegina, both of whom are referred to in Sanches's medical treatises) and for the use of "a method or *ratio* for treatment which would reflect Galen's views, especially as they related to the indications for cure".[47] Finally, under a new title,

---

[44] Ibid., p. 293. An excellent overview of the problem of method in Renaissance medical writings is given by William P. D. Wightman, "Quid sit methodus? 'Method' in Sixteenth Century Medical Teaching and 'Discovery'", in *Journal of the History of Medicine*, 19 (1964), pp. 360–76.

[45] See Durling, "Chronological Census", p. 297, for a list of Fuch's translations.

[46] See Wear, "Explorations in Renaissance Writings on the Practice of Medicine", p. 123.

[47] Ibid., p. 121.

Institutionum medicinae, Fuchs's original short manual became a huge authoritative work of 809 pages in which he presented in great detail the theory of medicine in Galenist terms, stressing in particular Galen's physiology.[48]

Thomas à Veiga's commentaries on the medical works of Galen were first published in 1564 by Plantin at Antwerp.[49] Sanches cites Veiga more than any other commentators on Galen in his medical works. Veiga, who had studied at the University of Coimbra, dedicated his commentaries to King Sebastian I of Portugal. In his preface Veiga refers to the fact that Galen, although he was greatly admired, was the object of many criticisms made by famous contemporaries such as Vesalius, Fernel, Montanus, Argenterius, and Triverius. These criticisms Veiga compares to those made by Galen when commenting on Aristotle's works, and he views them as a rejuvenation of the Galenic text.[50] Veiga follows Leoniceno in his discussion on method and makes the same major point: that method applies to the entire system of knowledge, not just to the solution of one particular proposition.[51] Reason and experiment, according to Veiga, are the instruments for making medical discoveries.[52] In his commentary on the *Ars medica,* Veiga reviews the question as to whether medicine is an art or a science: Hippocrates and Plato both consider that medicine is an art, Plato judging it to be the art of conjecture; Galen affirms that medicine is a science but, according to Veiga, confuses the two notions of "art" and "science"; Aristotle calls medicine at one moment an art and at another, a science. In an attempt to reconcile these conflicting viewpoints presented by the greatest medical and philosophical authorities of the past, Veiga concludes that med-

---

[48] See Wightman, *Science and Renaissance,* I, pp. 214–17.

[49] Thomas à Veiga, *Tomus primus commentariorum in C. Galeni opera* (Antwerpiae: C. Plantin, 1564).

[50] "... id quod idem Galenus in Aristotelis scriptis antea fecerat: in quibus locis. jejuna est Galeni lectio" (ibid., p. 6).

[51] "Nam et hic de ordine tradendi totam artem agit, non de demonstranda una aliqua propositione" (ibid., p. 12).

[52] "... instrumentum inveniendae medicinae est ratio et experimentum" (ibid., p. 15).

icine can be defined both as an art and as a science, since it may be divided into two branches: theory and practice.[53]

Sanches's familiarity with the works of Leoniceno, Fuchs, and Veiga indicates his interest, both as a philosopher and as a physician, in the current debates on method and the art of medicine. Apart from the *Ars medica* another work of Galen, the *Methodus medendi,* figured prominently in sixteenth-century discussions. It is noteworthy that in Durling's census of editions of Galen the *Methodus medendi* ranks eighth in popularity. Significantly, the *Methodus medendi* was the first work of Galen to be printed in Greek and received a wide diffusion in Europe following the publication of Thomas Linacre's excellent Latin translation in 1519, which ran into fourteen separate editions between 1519 and 1598.[54] Guinter's Latin translation of the *Methodus medendi,* published in Paris by Simon de Colines in 1528, enjoyed great popularity, too, since its smaller format made it more accessible for medical students.[55] Much of what Sanches writes about method clearly echoes the Galenic teachings and though he does not quote directly from the *Methodus medendi* in the *Quod nihil scitur,* he does refer to this treatise in his *De longitudine et brevitate vitae,* as well as in his medical works.[56] It should perhaps be remembered that in the *Quod nihil scitur* Sanches was discussing theories well known to any medical student who had taken

---

[53] "Et has duas partes vocat saepe Galenus duo medici crura: quorum altero deficiente necesse est medicum claudicare: possuntque ea comparatione vocari pars theorica et practica" (ibid., p. 19).

[54] According to George Sarton, *Galen of Pergamon* (Lawrence: University of Kansas Press, 1954), p. 25, the *Ad Glauconem de medendi methodo* was published in Greek by Zacharias Callierges in Venice in 1500. See Durling's "Chronological Census", p. 293, for a list of all the editions and translations, and his article "Linacre and Medical Humanism", in *Linacre Studies: Essays on the Life and Work of Thomas Linacre c. 1460–1524,* ed. Francis Maddison, Margaret Pelling, and Charles Webster (Oxford: Clarendon Press, 1977), pp. 76–106, for an assessment of Linacre's contribution to the translation of Galen's works.

[55] See Vivian Nutton, "Humanist Surgery", in *The Medical Renaissance of the Sixteenth Century,* ed. Wear et al., p. 79.

[56] For the references in the *De longitudine et brevitate vitae* see Carvalho's edition of Sanches's *Opera philosophica,* pp. 75, 78, 79.

courses in the faculty of arts, and there was no need to indicate sources. It is highly likely that Sanches used Guinter's edition of the *Methodus medendi*. However, since one of Sanches's major criticisms in the *Quod nihil scitur* was levelled against the disproportionate importance accorded authority in the teaching carried on in the universities, it is not surprising that Sanches did not burden his own text with the customary copious references to classical sources.[57]

Finally, in evaluating the impact of Galenic thought on Sanches, his own academic training as a physician must be remembered. Galen reigned supreme in the university medical curriculum, followed, at a distance, by Hippocrates. For example, at the University of Montpellier, where Sanches completed his formal medical degrees, during the period 1501–1600, thirty-eight works of Galen were prescribed texts as compared to sixteen works of Hippocrates.[58] Many of Galen's works were taught repeatedly, the *Techne* or *Ars parva* being taught thirty-eight times over a period of thirty-four years, and the *De arte curativa ad Glauconem* twenty-six times.[59] Two hundred and forty-two university medical lectures were devoted to examining Galen's medical works, compared to ninety-seven given to the teachings of Hippocrates.[60]

The philosophical writings of Galen were of equal importance in the academic training of physicians, even though many of them had been lost. However, Galen's voluminous medical works furnished many valuable insights into his own epistemology and much information on the history of philosophy, for as a youth in Pergamum Galen had attended lectures given by the disciples of the four major schools of thought: Platonism, Aristotelianism, Stoicism and Epicureanism. One of Galen's works, in particular,

---

[57] Sanches himself warns the reader: "And you should not ask me to quote many authorities, or to treat my authorities with deference; deference is rather the mark of a servile, untrained mind than of one that is freely investigating the Truth" (translation, pp. 171–2).

[58] See Dulieu, *La Médecine à Montpellier*, II, pp. 142–3.

[59] Ibid., p. 143.

[60] Ibid., p. 145.

the *De Hippocratis et Platonis placitis,* was an excellent source of information on Plato, Hippocrates, Aristotle, and the Stoics: its rediscovery and translation during the early Renaissance was hailed with delight by classical scholars.[61] Another Galenic work, his short commentary on the Hippocratic maxim *Quod optimus Medicus sit quoque Philosophus* was widely known during the Renaissance after Erasmus in 1526 had translated it from the Greek, together with the *De optimo docendi genere,* under the title *Exhortatio ad bonas arteis . . . de optimo docendi genere, et qualem oporteat esse medicum.* Erasmus's translation of the *De optimo docendi genere* was included in both the 1562 edition of Sextus Empiricus's *Hypotyposes Pyrrhonianae* and the 1569 joint edition with the *Adversus mathematicos.*[62] Galen's criticisms of the Academic sceptics and the Pyrrhonians supplied precious information on sceptical doctrines. It is interesting that Sanches mentions Galen's *De optimo docendi genere* in a marginal note to the *Quod nihil scitur,* and this is the only possible indication that he may have read Sextus Empiricus.[63]

As we have said, much of Galen's philosophical thought is disseminated throughout his medical writings. Galen considered philosophy to be an instrument, a useful way or method of attaining truth and knowledge, particularly as it applied to medicine. After surveying the major philosophical systems he concluded that there were basic principles common to all branches of knowledge that transcended the differences among the philosophical sects. In his *De libris propriis* Galen confessed that the conflicting views held by philosophers had both dismayed and discouraged him, and

---

[61] See Charles Daremberg, *La Médecine: histoire et doctrines* (Paris, 1865; rpt. New York: Arno Press, 1976), pp. 90–4, for an analysis of the *De Hippocratis et Platonis placitis.* I have been unable to consult Philip De Lacy's translation of this work. Gilbert discusses the impact of this treatise on Ramus in his *Renaissance Concepts of Method,* pp. 21–2, 138–41.

[62] The five-page translation of the *De optimo docendi genere* is described on the title page of Sextus Empiricus's works as *Claudii Pergameni contra Academicos et Pyrrhonios* and appears after Diogenes Laertius's life of Pyrrho.

[63] See p. 184, n. 44. Galen's work appeared in the 1562 and 1569 editions of Sextus Empiricus.

were it not for the fact that all sects agreed on the reliability of mathematical proof, he might have become a Pyrrhonian sceptic.[64] Sanches, of course, was to dispute in his letter to Clavius the reliability of geometrical proof.[65] Above all it is Galen's quest for a true scientific method that informs the *Quod nihil scitur*.[66] The fundamental Galenic criteria, expounded in the *De methodo medendi*, of *reasoning* and *experience* become the two criteria that Sanches accepts as means of discovering truth.[67]

Indubitably Galen exercised a powerful and continuous influence on Sanches in all aspects of his philosophical and medical writings. Like Galen, Sanches campaigned against blind acceptance of received opinions, for "Authority bids us *believe*, whereas Reason *demonstrates*; the former is more suited to faith, the latter to the sciences. Accordingly I shall establish, by rational argument, those propositions that seem to me correctly stated by others; those that seem incorrectly stated I shall disprove".[68] In one sense the *Quod nihil scitur* could be understood as a logical demonstration of the main proposition "Nothing is known", without recourse to the Aristotelian definition of demonstration as "a syllogism that gives birth to knowledge".[69] Demonstration involved careful evaluation of scientific evidence, according to Galen, and for Sanches, too, it was necessary to observe the facts with the intention of seeking in them the basis of judgment.[70] Galen adhered to the Aristotelian doctrine that perception and intelligence are the sources of knowledge.[71] Sanches, too, in his

---

[64] Gilbert, *Renaissance Concepts of Method*, p. 14, gives this quote from *Melanchthoniana paedagogica*: "Galenus fatetur se pene in amentiam Pyrrhoniorum delapsum esse, nisi Geometria vidisset tantam vim esse demonstrationum".

[65] "Multa ergo sunt in Mathematicis dubia, non solum in principiis, sed etiam in progressu" (Carvalho, *Opera philosophica*, p. 147).

[66] See Gilbert, *Renaissance Concepts of Method*, p. 14.

[67] Ibid., p. 19.

[68] Translation, p. 172.

[69] Ibid., p. 181.

[70] "Therefore anyone who wishes to *know* something ... must study *facts*" (ibid., p. 277).

[71] See Temkin, *Galenism*, p. 11.

address to the reader states quite clearly: "I would address myself to those who, 'not bound by an oath of fidelity to any master's words', assess the facts for themselves, under the guidance of sense-perception and reason".[72]

Nevertheless, Sanches does cast doubt on the absolute validity of sense-perception and the internal processes of the mind which lead to cognition and, finally, knowledge (*scientia*). For the senses perceive only the "outward appearances of things", the "accidents", and the mind cannot achieve perfect understanding, grasp the internal principles of all objects, but merely gropes, doubts, supposes, and conjectures.[73] It is at this point in the *Quod nihil scitur* that Sanches advances a series of well-known sceptical arguments that demonstrate the unreliability of the senses. And it is at this point, too, that Sanches attacks in eight pages of argument Galen's influential treatise *De usu partium corporis humani* for his praise of the marvellous perfection of the human body in which each organ and part is perfectly adapted to its function.[74] Sanches denies that a perfect body can exist, capable of performing the most perfect operations, the highest of which is intellectual understanding, the foundation of science.[75] Likewise he challenges the argument from design, in which Galen praises the Creator in Aristotelian terms that are contrary to Christian belief.[76]

In the final analysis, even Galenism with its stress on the constant search for truth, the need for objective assessment of the facts using the two criteria of reason and experience, failed to satisfy Sanches's rigorous requirements for absolute certitude. But it is

[72] Translation, p. 168.
[72] See ibid., pp. 236, 237, 244.
[74] Ibid., pp. 256–8. See Temkin, *Galenism*, pp. 24–7.
[75] "To whom has a perfect body been given? To no one (even if a physician loudly denies this)" (translation, p. 256).
[76] Galen ascribed to Asclepius and to Nature herself the wonderful design of the cosmos and rejected the Judaeo-Christian belief in an omnipotent God. Sanches states the idea of perfection in Christian terms: "Now, what is more perfect than the work of Creation? It is performed by the only perfect being, God, who is perfection itself. By what means? By means of His wholly perfect power; which alone is utterly perfect, because it is the only *infinite* power, and because it is God Himself" (translation, p. 258).

important to note that the dogmatism of Sanches's proposition "Nothing is known" is modified at the end of the *Quod nihil scitur* by the admission that his purpose was "to establish, as far as I am able, a kind of scientific knowledge that is both sound, and as easy as possible to attain". As a philosopher Sanches may doubt the possibility of attaining true knowledge, but as a physician he realised that the natural philosopher had to proceed by observation of the facts and judgment based on experience.

VI

In the eyes of his contemporaries and those of posterity Sanches epitomised the sceptic whose doubt as to the possibility of knowledge was summed up by the interrogative *Quid?*[1] The different interpretations of his sceptical attitude reflect an understandable confusion in the use of the two terms *Sceptique* and *Pyrrhonien*. These terms were often used interchangeably in the philosophical debates of the sixteenth and seventeenth centuries. They denote a philosophical and methodological view or approach, distinguished by a refusal to make dogmatic statements of any kind, and by the withholding of assent. Thus free enquiry may continue, or the desirable state of *ataraxia* be attained. This confusion was prompted by the fact that even in classical antiquity the distinction between the Pyrrhonian and Academic schools of scepticism was a very subtle one, and Sextus Empiricus himself felt obliged to devote a chapter in his *Outlines of Pyrrhonism* to a discussion of the essential differences between the sceptics and Academics.[2] A further complication ensued in the late Renaissance when the terms *Académique* and *Pyrrhonien* also came to be used interchangeably. For example, Montaigne in the "Apologie de Raimond Sebond" makes no clear distinction between Academic scepticism and Pyrrhonian scepticism, except when he is directly

---

[1] An interesting discussion of the meaning of Sanches's *Quid?* takes place in John Owen's *The Skeptics of the French Renaissance*, pp. 619–20.
[2] See *Sextus Empiricus*, trans. Bury, I, pp. 133–45.

quoting the words of Sextus Empiricus.[3] Even as late as 1665 we find Pascal, in his "Entretien avec M. de Sacy," speaking of Pyrrhonian doubt and Academic doubt without distinguishing the two sceptical attitudes.[4]

Montaigne's undoubted influence on the evolution of sceptical thought in the seventeenth century, due to his exposition of Pyrrhonian doctrine in the "Apologie", led to great discussions in the middle of the century among the Jansenists at Port Royal, and in circles connected with Descartes, as to whether Pyrrhonian scepticism led to atheism.[5] Pyrrhonism was equated with all forms of scepticism and was a highly fashionable doctrine. It is thus not surprising that Delassus, in his biography of Sanches which prefaces the 1636 Toulouse edition of the *Opera medica*, affirms, quite wrongly, that Sanches followed the Pyrrhonian suspension of judgment.[6] As a consequence Bayle, who relied heavily on Delassus for his article on Sanches, declared of Sanches: "C'etoit un grand Pyrrhonien".[7] So the myth of Sanches's Pyrrhonism persisted into the twentieth century, to be perpetuated by some historians of philosophy who classify Sanches as a Pyrrhonian.[8]

---

[3] See Limbrick, "Was Montaigne really a Pyrrhonian?" p. 67.

[4] See Elaine Limbrick "Le Pyrrhonisme est le vrai", in *Mélanges sur la littérature de la Renaissance à la mémoire de V.-L. Saulnier* (Geneva: Droz, 1984), pp. 439–48.

[5] As an indication of the popularity of Montaigne's *Essais,* thirty-seven editions were published between 1580 and 1669, but, in 1676, the *Essais* were placed on the Index. For an assessment of the polemics surrounding Descartes's use of hyperbolical doubt, see Popkin, *The History of Scepticism from Erasmus to Spinoza,* pp. 172–213. Jansenist attitudes towards Pyrrhonism are best reflected in Arnauld and Nicole's *La Logique ou l'Art de penser* (1662; rpt. Paris: Flammarion, 1970).

[6] "Non eo tamen Pyrrhoniorum more dubitandi vel potius cavillandi aestu abreptum Professorem nostrum credendum est, praesertim in rebus divinis et sensuum fide, sed haesisse solum in rebus incertis et ad ἐποχήν Pyrrhoniam recurrisse, vel suspendisse iudicium in his quae in fugacibus coniecturis ebulliunt" (ē 2v. – ē 3r.).

[7] See *Dictionnaire historique et critique par Mr. Pierre Bayle,* article on Sanchez.

[8] See Frederick Copleston, *A History of Philosophy* (1946–75; rpt. New York: Doubleday [Image Books], 1963), III, part 2, pp. 35–6. Copleston, doubtlessly influenced by Bayle, calls Sanches "another Pyrrhonian".

Yet nowhere in Sanches's philosophical and medical works is there any mention of his adhering to Pyrrhonian scepticism, and a close examination of the references and sceptical arguments used in the *Quod nihil scitur* has not revealed any clear evidence that Sanches had even read the works of Sextus Empiricus.

The *Quod nihil scitur* is an enquiry into the possibility of knowledge, inspired by a belief that the alliance between philosophy and medicine was a necessary and vital part of the discovery of a new method for ascertaining the nature of things and the principles of knowledge (*scientia*). Whereas other sceptical writers of the Renaissance, such as Agrippa von Nettesheim, Omer Talon (Audomarus Talaeus), Guy de Brués, and Montaigne, were concerned with the fundamental problem of the criterion of truth and its epistemological and theological implications, Sanches himself was primarily intent on destroying the Aristotelian system of knowledge and, notably, the demonstrative syllogism which was supposed to produce *scientia*. If knowledge is an "accumulation of many syllogistic inferences", then nothing is known.[9] Aristotelian science results only in nescience. Hence the title of Sanches's treatise. Only free independent enquiry, using a new methodological approach, can possibly hope to establish "a kind of scientific knowledge that is both sound and as easy as possible to attain".[10] The *Quod nihil scitur* begins with the dogmatic assertion that nothing is known, demonstrates this proposition by an attack on every article of Peripatetic epistemology, and ends, paradoxically, with the promise of attaining probable scientific knowledge, once the method of knowing has been determined. Complete doubt thus leads to a kind of scientific knowledge, provided that the due methodological steps have been respected: observation of the facts, daily experimentation resulting in a body of scientific experience, all subjected to the final assessment of sound judgment based on rational discourse.[11]

[9] Translation, p. 189.
[10] Ibid., p. 290.
[11] Brochard's fine study *Les Sceptiques Grecs* stresses the importance of the doctrine of probability, favoured by Carneades and the New Academy, for the progess of the sciences (see p. 175).

Sanches's treatise differs greatly from other sceptical works of the Renaissance by its independence of spirit, non-reliance on authority, and limited use of ancient sceptical arguments. At the beginning of the *Quod nihil scitur* Sanches tells his reader: "And you should not ask me to quote many authorities, or to treat my authorities with deference; deference is rather the mark of a servile, untrained mind than of one that is freely investigating the Truth. In my reasoning, I shall follow Nature alone. Authority bids us *believe,* whereas Reason *demonstrates;* the former is more suited to faith, the latter to the sciences".[12]

Sanches's refusal to recognise the authority of ancient philosophers sets him apart from his contemporaries who still respected humanist values, underlines the daring originality and independence of his thought, and explains the attractions that the New Academy under Carneades held for him. It was the only school of sceptical thought that proposed a constructive form of scepticism by allowing assent to a concurrence of credible impresions that are consistent and have been tested, and thus laid down the criteria for a doctrine of empirical evidence.[13]

Sanches's predecessors and contemporaries, on the other hand, had been deeply influenced by the rediscovery and revival of the classical sources of ancient scepticism, and drew principally on the arsenal of sceptical arguments to be found in the works of Cicero (chiefly the *Academica*), Diogenes Laertius's *Lives of Eminent Philosophers,* Saint Augustine's *De civitate Dei* and the *Contra Academicos,* and the sceptical writings of Sextus Empiricus after

---

[12] Translation, pp. 171–2.

[13] Nicholas Rescher in his stimulating critical reappraisal, *Scepticism* (Oxford: Blackwell, 1980), argues persuasively that "a nonfoundationalist approach to cognitive validation via the mechanisms of plausibility and presumption affords the means for dispensing with the idea of self-evidencing bedrock, and so averts the impact of the 'No Foundation' Argument" (p. 153). Plausibility and presumption are, according to Rescher, "the probative tools of inquiry" (p. 172) and are at the heart of scientific method. Thus, when Carneades states that the wise man can assent to a complex of credible impressions that hang together like the links of a chain, he is laying the foundations for a scientific method that depends on a series of tests to determine the reliability of experience.

the publication of Henri Estienne's Latin translation of the *Hypotyposes* in 1562, followed in 1569 by Gentian Hervet's Latin edition of all of Sextus Empiricus's works, including his own translation of the *Adversus mathematicos*. Both Popkin and Schmitt have thoroughly explored the importance of the two main schools of sceptical thought, the Academic and the Pyrrhonian, in the intellectual crisis brought on by the Reformation with its culmination in what has been called the *crise pyrrhonienne*.[14]

The sceptical writers of the Renaissance used many of the arguments advanced by the Academic and Pyrrhonian sceptics to attack all forms of dogmatism: Aristotelian, Stoic, and Epicurean. They wished to demonstrate the futility of philosophical systems that claimed to provide a reliable method of acquiring knowledge. An important part of their intellectual critique of the dogmatists was to expose the various and contradictory doctrines of the major schools of thought so that the reader would arrive at the inevitable conclusion that all knowledge is simply opinion. Their main artillery in the battle waged against the dogmatists was supplied at first from the series of sceptical arguments put forward by Arcesilas and Carneades of the New Academy, and later by the Pyrrhonian sceptics whose more radical expression of doubt was systematised in the tropes of Aenesidemus.[15] The most frequently used sceptical arguments were those that cast doubt on the reliability of the senses and the validity of the reasoning processes of the mind, which depended on a subjective apprehension of reality that was, in turn, influenced by conditions in which false impressions could be just as convincing as true impressions. Favourite sceptical arguments concerned with the sense of vision cited the examples of the stick that appears bent in water, the iridescent plumage of the dove (or pigeon), and the apparent size of the sun relative to the position of the viewer. The states of

---

[14] See Popkin, *The History of Scepticism from Erasmus to Spinoza*, pp. 18–41, and Schmitt, *Cicero Scepticus*, pp. 9–77.

[15] Sanches relied on the summaries of the ten tropes of Aenesidemus and the five tropes of Agrippa given by Diogenes Laertius in his life of Pyrrho. Diogenes Laertius gives a lengthy account of the sceptical doctrines of Pyrrho and his followers in book 9 of his *Lives of Eminent Philosophers*.

dreaming (as opposed to waking), madness, and bodily health were all invoked in arguments concerning true and false impressions that affected the mind's judgment. Finally, the relativity of all customs, institutions, laws, and religious beliefs, as revealed in both historical and contemporary accounts of different civilisations, was a major argument used in inducing doubt. Whereas the sceptics of the New Academy were prepared to give qualified assent to an assertion that appears credible or probable, the Pyrrhonian sceptics maintained that it was impossible to acquire knowledge about reality and advocated that the wise man should suspend judgment in order to enjoy *ataraxia* (tranquillity).[16]

For the predecessors of Sanches scepticism seemed to offer a solution to the problem of the criterion of truth which would resist the challenges presented by the changing spiritual, moral, and scientific horizons of man in an age racked by civil and religious wars, where confusion, chaos, and destruction seemed to prevail. There was a natural recourse to authority in an effort to stem the rising tide of dissatisfaction with established ideologies. There was also a counter-reaction: a desire to tear down the old edifices of the church, state, and the sciences in order to rebuild on sure and solid foundations. The very language of sceptical writers is revealing: architectural metaphors abound even in the epistemological treatises of Sanches and Descartes.[17]

---

[16] "The end to be realized they hold to be suspension of judgment, which brings with it tranquillity like its shadow: so Timon and Aenesidemus declare" (Diogenes Laertius, *Lives of Eminent Philosophers* [London: William Heinemann, 1950], II, 9, pp. 517–19).

[17] Sanches refers to the collapse of Aristotelianism in the following terms: "like some ancient building that keeps threatening to fall down, or else one built on sand and on an unstable site, with foundations made of fragile materials; a building that must be continually shored up with wooden props, or reinforced with stone, mortar, and so forth, since cracks keep continually opening in its structure on this side or that. Just so, as the syllogistic discipline continually crumbles...its inhabitants and craftsmen continually struggle to prevent it from collapsing" (translation, p. 275). See the interesting opening remarks of Jean-Joseph Goux on the use of architectural metaphors in Descartes's *Discours de la méthode* in his article "Descartes et la perspective", *L'Esprit Créateur*, 25, no. 1 (1985), pp. 10–20.

Sanches is not a typical representative of mainstream scepticism in the Renaissance. Only to a minimal degree do we find reflected in the *Quod nihil scitur* and the other philosophical and medical works of Sanches the religious and ethical concerns that stirred deeply the minds and hearts of other sceptical writers of the sixteenth century. Sanches's declaration that nothing is known is a dialectical strategy: his main critique is of the Aristotelian doctrine of knowledge and its methodological implications for medicine and the sciences. Unlike other sceptical writers he does not attack the Stoic or Epicurean philosophies that had attracted many adherents during the Renaissance, nor does he share their conviction that all value judgments are mainly determined by law, custom, and tradition. Finally, at no point does Sanches advocate the complete suspension of belief in order to enjoy *ataraxia,* nor does he adhere to the Pyrrhonic belief that we live in a world of phenomena and that, therefore, investigation into the real nature of things is, of necessity, speculative and cannot be based on experience.

Certainly there are interesting parallels to be drawn and affinities to be observed between the *Quod nihil scitur* and other sceptical treatises of the sixteenth century. Agrippa von Nettesheim, for example, in his *De incertitudine et vanitate scientiarum et artium* (1530), one of the earliest works that can be said to express a sceptical viewpoint, rejects all human knowledge on the grounds that it consists of unreliable opinions and has led to the sin of intellectual pride.[18] Faith in God and in the Holy Scriptures is the only path to truth. His condemnation of the arts and sciences is based on invective rather than on a series of reasoned arguments.[19]

[18] "Moreover, al Sciences are nothinge els, but the ordinaunces and opinions of men, so noysome as profitable, so pestilent as holsome, so ill as good, in no parte perfecte, but doubtful and full of errour and contention" (Henry Cornelius Agrippa, *Of the Vanitie and Uncertaintie of Artes and Sciences,* trans. James Sanford, ed. Catherine M. Dunn [Northridge: California State University, 1974], pp. 17–18). Chapter 1 "Of Sciences in general" clearly states Agrippa's opposition to the arts and sciences, since science has ruined faith.

[19] See Charles Nauert, *Agrippa and the Crisis of Renaissance Thought* (Urbana: University of Illinois Press, 1965), pp. 299–300. Nauert argues against

The fideistic viewpoint that Agrippa expresses was to become a significant factor in the development of a Christian scepticism in the sixteenth and seventeenth centuries.[20] Sanches, too, stresses the ignorance of man compared to the perfect knowledge of God and comments on the disproportion between man and God, between the finite and the infinite, since God is measureless, limitless, and cannot be comprehended by the intellect.[21] Certain critics have insisted on Sanches's debt to Nicholas of Cusa, Saint Augustine, and Raimond Sebond in the formulation of his religious thought, but Sanches rarely indulges in metaphysical discussion and, whenever he does, it is with the object of refuting Aristotle or Galen.[22]

Two sceptical treatises and two translations that were published at Paris in the mid-sixteenth century, all dedicated to the powerful cardinal Charles de Lorraine, reveal the growing importance of sceptical doctrine in the ongoing philosophical and theological debates.[23] Omer Talon's *Academia*, which accompanied his edition of Cicero's *Academica posteriora* (1547), was primarily a defence of the philosophical freedom which Academic scepticism offered and an attack on the Aristotelian dogmatists who still dominated the

Popkins's refusal to consider the *De vanitate* as a valid piece of sceptical argumentation.

[20] "And so large is the libertee of the Trueth, and the largenesse thereof so free, that it cannot be perceived, with the speculations of any Science, nor with any straite iudgement of the Sences, nor with any argumentes of the Arte of Logike, nor with any evident proofe, with no *Sillogismes* of *Demonstration*, nor with any discourse of mans reason, but with Faithe Onely (Agrippa, *Of the Vanitie*, p. 16).

[21] "Such is the philosophers' 'infinite', if there *is* such a thing, and – in our own realm – God, of whom there can be no measure or limit, and hence no comprehension by the intellect" (translation, p. 224).

[22] See Marcel Sendrail, *Le Serpent et le miroir* (Paris: Plon, 1954), p. 81. Andrée Comparot's study of Sebond, Vivès, and Montaigne in *Amour et Vérité* (Paris: Klincksieck, 1983) indicates many affinities between the thought of Sanches and the aforementioned authors without, however, substantive evidence.

[23] Both the *Academia* by Talon and the *Dialogues* by Brués were dedicated to the Cardinal of Lorraine, as was also the 1569 edition of Sextus Empiricus by Hervet.

teaching of philosophy in the University of Paris.[24] Although the main motivation behind Talon's valuable exposition of Academic philosophy was, doubtlessly, his desire to aid his friend Ramus in his battle with the Aristotelians, as Charles Schmitt has convincingly demonstrated, his advocacy of the Academic sceptical method, as a means of counteracting the infinite errors engendered by human credulity, shows certain common features with the final arguments of the *Quod nihil scitur* in which Sanches comments on the desirability of teaching the student to think critically without recourse to authority.[25] Talon, like Sanches, understood the importance of Academic probabilism for the natural sciences and arrived at the same conclusion: God alone has true knowledge, for man can know only the accidents and not the causes of things.[26] As for religious matters, Talon declares that faith carries more weight than any demonstrations dreamed up by the philosophers: one must believe before one can attain religious truth.[27]

The second sceptical treatise that gives an interesting account of the doctrines of the New Academy is Guy de Brués's *Les Dialogues contre les nouveaux académiciens* (Paris, 1557).[28] One of the first philosophical works written in the vernacular in support of the nationalistic aims of the Pléiade group of poets, the *Dialogues* has

---

[24] Talon writes at the end of his treatise: "Haec est Academicorum, id est verorum hominum (utrunque enim tantundem valere existimo) propria et germana libertas, nullius hominis legibus et institutis in philosophia necessario parere" (*Academia*, I, p. 20).

[25] See Schmitt, *Cicero Scepticus*, p. 87.

[26] "Itaque licet Academicus sapiens in physicorum disciplinis interdum probabile aliquid inveniat, quod sequatur; procul tamen aberit a scientia et accurata cognitione causarum quae latent in tenebris, et, ut ante diximus, soli Deo certa scientia notae sunt; satisque habebit, si de elementis, de animalibus, de stirpibus, de caeteris naturae generibus non per causas, quae rem quaeque constituant, sed per accidentia et adiunctas qualitates physicorum more philosophetur" (*Academia* [1550], II, p. 97).

[27] See Elaine Limbrick, "Ce dernier tour d'escrime", *Cahiers de l'Association Internationale des Etudes Françaises*, no. 33 (May 1981), p. 56.

[28] See the excellent modern edition of *The Dialogues of Guy de Brués. A Critical Edition with a Study in Renaissance Scepticism and Relativism*, ed. Panos Paul Morphos (Baltimore: Johns Hopkins University Press, 1953).

as its main objective the prevention of the corruption of young people by perfidious sceptical arguments that seek, by maintaining that everything consists in opinion, to destroy all belief in God, the state, and its various institutions, as well as in the sciences and other disciplines.[29] Although ostensibly an attack against the pernicious *nouveaux académiciens,* using the form of the Ciceronian dialogue to present different philosophical positions assumed by Ronsard and other members of the Pléiade, the *Dialogues* has led some modern scholars to misinterpret the author's professed intent because of the undue importance accorded to the defence of the Academic position. Yet Brués, like other sceptical writers, affirmed clearly his orthodox Catholic beliefs and his sincere desire to place religion beyond the reach of Academic doubt.[30]

The 1562 and 1569 translations of the works of Sextus Empiricus renewed and stimulated great interest in scepticism as a philosophical doctrine that was of the greatest use in destroying all forms of dogmatism and seemed to offer a solution to the many problems confronting the theologian, philosopher, and scientist who were very conscious of living in a time of tremendous change and instability. Henri Estienne, the great Renaissance printer and translator of the *Hypotyposes,* states in his preface to his friend Henri Memmius that his purpose is to make madmen of all the dogmatic philosophers of the day who were infected with atheism and, at the same time, to spare other lovers of philosophy great labour by furnishing them with a treasure house of erudition.[31] Gentian Hervet, in his dedicatory epistle to the cardinal Charles de

---

[29] "Or voyant que les opinions que nous avons conceües, nous rendent amys ou bien ennemys de la verité, qui est le vray but de toutes sçiences, j'ay mis peine en ces miens dialogues de prevenir la jeunesse, et la destourner de croire ceux qui disent que toutes les choses consistent en la seule opinion, s'efforçans par mesme moien d'abolir et mettre à mespris la religion, l'honneur de Dieu, la puissance de nos superieurs, l'autorité de la justice, ensemble toutes les sciences et disciplines" (ibid., p. 88).

[30] See Schmitt, *Cicero Scepticus,* pp. 103–8.

[31] See Jean Grenier's excellent introduction to *Oeuvres choisies de Sextus Empiricus,* trans. Jean Grenier and Geneviève Goron (Paris: Aubier, 1948), pp. 21–4 in which the influence of Sextus Empiricus on Renaissance thinkers is studied and Estienne's preface is quoted.

Lorraine of the *Adversus mathematicos,* stresses that Pyrrhonism demonstrates that no system of human knowledge can resist the assaults of arguments that can be opposed to it, and that the only certainty is divine revelation. Sextus provides many arguments against present-day heretics who measure the supernatural world with rational arguments drawn from the nature of things and who do not understand because they have no belief. In particular, Hervet dislikes intensely the Calvinists and New Academicians, whom Gianfrancesco Pico della Mirandola had already attacked.[32] Finally, scepticism, because it contests all human theories of knowledge, teaches humility, counterbalances the excesses of the dogmatists, and prepares young people to trust only the doctrine of Christ.

The prefaces to the two translations are indicative of the major developments in the use of Pyrrhonism by theologians and philosophers in the late Renaissance and early seventeenth century in France. Pyrrhonian doubt emerged as a powerful weapon, used by the Counter-Reformers, in meeting the challenge of Calvinist theologians, and resulted in a new form of Christian fideism in which faith in the Catholic tradition and respect for the authority of the church were placed in a logically unassailable position.[33] For the philosopher the works of Sextus Empiricus provided many new sceptical arguments with which to assault the citadel of the Aristotelians and all other dogmatisms. The Pyrrhonian suspension of judgment enabled him to lead a life in accordance with his natural inclinations while obeying the laws, customs, and beliefs of his society. For the scientist the destruction of the Aristotelian scientific tradition was certainly hastened by the methodological approaches of the Academic and Pyrrhonian schools of scepticism.[34] The role of doubt, with its contrasting of the pros and cons for any hypothesis, was clearly critical in the testing of new scientific theories.

---

[32] Ibid., p. 24. See also Popkin, *The History of Scepticism from Erasmus to Spinoza,* p. 20, for an assessment of Pico's Pyrrhonism.

[33] See Popkin, ibid., pp. 67–82.

[34] See Schmitt, *Cicero Scepticus,* p. 11.

"Sanchez le sceptique", as he was called by his contemporaries, acquired his reputation simply because he demonstrated convincingly that true knowledge in the Aristotelian sense of knowing a thing in terms of its causes was a logical impossibility.[35] Compared to his predecessors his knowledge of ancient sceptical sources was very limited. The only direct references are supplied by the annotations in the margin of the *Quod nihil scitur,* and these references are to three sources in which he found useful summaries of the main tenets of Academic and Pyrrhonian doctrine: Galen (*De optimo docendi genere liber*), Diogenes Laertius (*Lives of Eminent Philosophers,* Book 9), and Plutarch (*Adversus Colotem*). From the few direct references he makes to sceptical doctrine in his other works we can only conclude that he considered himself to be a follower of the New Academy. In his letter to Christopher Clavius he introduces himself as *Carneades Philosophus* and ends with this definition of himself: "Sum enim alter Carneades, non gloriae inanis, sed veritatis, et tui amantissimus. Vale. Carneades Philosophus".[36] As we have already noted, the letter to Clavius was written during the period when Sanches was actively engaged in rewriting and polishing up the manuscript of the *Quod nihil scitur* and, therefore, can be assumed to reflect his sceptical attitude at that time.[37] Two other references in Sanches's medical works

---

[35] Rescher points out that scepticism is irrefutable if one uses the standard kinds of refutatory argumentation (see *Scepticism,* p. 7). Sanches cleverly uses the wheel argument to enmesh the Aristotelians over the definition of knowledge as "understanding something by means of its causes", then goes on to quote Aristotle's own objection: "If the only knowledge is, in fact, that which is acquired by demonstration, while its first principles are incapable of being demonstrated, then there will be no knowledge of the first principles, and hence there will be no knowledge" (translation, p. 198). Thus Sanches uses the confused thought of Aristotle himself to refute one of the basic tenets of Aristotelianism.

[36] See Carvalho, *Opera philosophica,* pp. 146 and 153.

[37] Schoock indicates in his history of scepticism that Carneades was responsible for the transition from the negative dogmatism of NIL SCIRE to the more constructive and open-ended scepticism of DUBITARE (*De scepticismo pars prior,* p. 20). Like Sanches, Schoock drew on Diogenes Laertius for this interpretation of the doctrines of the New Academy.

indicate that in the practice of medicine he preferred the method of the Academic sceptics who affirmed nothing and enjoyed freedom of choice.[38] In his role as a physician, when called on to make a diagnosis of a disease, he examined the evidence and then followed what seemed more probable.[39]

The sceptical arguments that Sanches uses for his critique of perceptual statements were all well known and their exact attribution is difficult to ascertain. His own annotations reveal that some were definitely taken from Galen, Diogenes Laertius, and Plutarch; others were based on Sanches's medical observations. Certain arguments may have their origin in Cicero's *Academica*, possibly even Sextus Empiricus, and could have been transmitted second-hand through the works of Sanches's contemporaries, but one can only conjecture as to the original sources when faced with a text so bare of positive indications.

Among the sceptics of the sixteenth century only one other writer besides Sanches made a major contribution to the diffusion of sceptical ideas: Michel de Montaigne. The fame and influence of the *Essais de Michel de Montaigne* have tended to eclipse the modest success of the *Quod nihil scitur* and yet Sanches argues the case for philosophical scepticism far more cogently than did Montaigne in the "Apologie de Raimond Sebond". The structure of Sanches's argumentation is far better organised, philosophically more satisfying, and ends on a positive constructive note. However, the *Quod nihil scitur* was intended as the first of a series of treatises on the problem of knowledge, and its range and potential audience were limited. Sanches wrote his treatise in Latin for the philosophical and medical community with the intention of destroying present-day Aristotelian dogmatists. Montaigne, on the other hand, wrote in the vernacular and addressed a far wider public of *honnêtes hommes* who were well educated but not interested in

---

[38] "Quae tamen iudicanda aliis relinquimus, et Academicorum more nihil affirmantes, cuique liberam eligendi potestatem concedimus" (*De pulsibus*, p. 606).

[39] "Nos tamen quod probabilius videtur sectantes, dicemus, solutiones continui a diversis rebus diversa esse sortitas nomina" (*In librum Galeni de differentiis morborum commentarii*, p. 711).

reading a formal philosophical discourse. Sanches dealt with two particular issues: the criterion of truth and the search for philosophical method. Montaigne ranged over every field of human endeavour applying ancient sceptical theories to contemporary issues in theology, philosophy, the sciences, ethics, and the judicial and political systems. Above all Montaigne made his contemporaries aware of Pyrrhonian scepticism with its doctrine of total doubt, which had tremendous repercussions on intellectual debates in the seventeenth century.[40]

It is a strange fact of intellectual history that both Montaigne and Sanches were to be labelled Pyrrhonians because of their use of doubt as a philosophical method, in the manner of the Academic sceptics, as a way of arriving at the criterion of truth which would allow qualified assent to the objects of experience. Both use an interrogative form of scepticism: the elliptical *Quid?* of Sanches and the *Que sais-je?* of Montaigne imply that the search for knowledge is a continuous process and that cognition is ultimately possible. Both begin their philosophical enquiry with a quotation from the first line of Aristotle's *Metaphysics*: "All men by nature desire to know", and reach the same conclusion that experience can provide probable grounds for belief.[41] As Christian sceptics, Sanches and Montaigne subscribe to the view that perfect knowledge exists only in God and that there is beyond the world of phenomena a transcendent reality: God.[42] It is astonishing that

[40] Still the best study by far on the question of Montaigne's influence is Alan M. Boase, *The Fortunes of Montaigne: A History of the Essays in France*, 1580–1669 (1935; rpt. New York: Octagon Books, 1970).

[41] Sanches greets his reader with the first line of the *Metaphysics*: "Mankind has an inborn desire to know." Montaigne begins his most famous essay "De l'experience" (*Essais*, book 3, chapter 13): "Il n'est desir plus naturel que le desir de connaissance," and in the third line of the essay states: "Quand la raison nous faut, nous y employons l'experience". It should be noted that the title *Essais* has the connotation of trial, test, and experiment.

[42] In the *Quod nihil scitur* Sanches writes: "Only He, being Himself perfect wisdom and understanding, and perfect intelligence, enters into all things, is wise in relation to all things, comprehends everything and understands everything...But how shall little Man, imperfect and wretched as he is, comprehend other things, he who is incapable of comprehending the self that

there is no evidence of reciprocal influence when one considers that the *Essais* of Montaigne were first published in 1580, preceding the *Quod nihil scitur* by one year, and that even in the 1588 edition of the *Essais* there is no mention of Sanches.[43] Their common Portuguese-Jewish heritage and upbringing in Bordeaux, where they both attended the Collège de Guyenne, admittedly with an interval of twenty-three years separating their studies at the famous institution, do not reveal even the slightest piece of evidence that they knew one another. Yet, as advocates of a mitigated scepticism, Montaigne and Sanches were responsible for a re-examination of all claims to knowledge by thinkers in the seventeenth century, some of whom mistakenly claimed that all sceptics were Pyrrhonians and therefore to be considered the enemies of science and of religion.[44]

is *in* him and *with* him?" (translation, p. 239). In the *De longitudine et brevitate vitae* he states, "Esse Dei non tempore mensuratur, sed totum praesens, totum simul est" (Carvalho, *Opera philosophica*, p. 57). At the beginning of the "Apologie de Raimond Sebond", Montaigne is careful to refute Sebond's critics (who had accused him of advancing weak rational proofs of the existence of God), by proclaiming in Augustinian terms: "C'est la foy seule qui embrasse vivement et certainement les hauts mysteres de nostre Religion" (p. 484). Then a few pages later Montaigne attacks the presumption and pride of the atheists and proposes to "leur faire baisser la teste et mordre la terre soubs l'authorité et reverance de la majesté divine. C'est à elle seule qu'appartient la science et la sapience" (p. 493). All the quotations from the *Essais de Montaigne* are taken from the Pléiade edition (Paris: Gallimard, 1950).

[43] Pierre Villey in his *Les Sources et l'évolution des Essais de Montaigne* (1908; rpt. New York: Burt Franklin, 1968), pp. 209–10, considers it likely that Montaigne possessed a copy of the *Quod nihil scitur* and that some of the ideas of Sanchez may have influenced the beginning of the chapter "De l'experience". Montaigne was distantly related to Sanches through his mother, Antoinette de Louppes (Lopez), who was descended from Portuguese Jews. However, there is no factual evidence, by way of textual references, of reciprocal influence.

[44] The Jesuit François Garasse spearheaded the attacks against the Pyrrhonists of the day in a series of three works: *Apologie du Père François Garasse, de la Compagnie de Jesus, pour son livre contre les athéistes et libertins de nostre siècle* (1623) *La Doctrine curieuse des beaux esprits de ce temps, ou prétendus tels* ... (1624), and *La Somme théologique des véritez capitales de la Religion chrestienne* (1625). The Franciscan Jean Boucher denounced the two most dangerous

81

It was in the seventeenth century that Sanches acquired his reputation for being a sceptic of the most dangerous kind and his treatise became well known in theological and philosophical circles. Most important, it was in association with the debates concerning Descartes's use of methodological doubt as a means of testing the evidence for knowledge that the name of Sanches was invoked. Many scholars have pointed out the close affinities between Sanches's prologue to the *Quod nihil scitur* and the beginning of Descartes's *Discours de la méthode*.[45] The significant factor linking the name of Sanches to that of Descartes was the role doubt played in their quests for philosophical certitude and which led the enemies of Descartes, particularly those in the Dutch universities of Utrecht, Groningen, and Leiden, to place them both in the camp of the Pyrrhonian sceptics.[46]

The first reference to Sanches of which Descartes himself was

nouveaux Pyrrhoniens, Montaigne and Charron, in his monumental work, *Les Triomphes de la Religion Chrestienne* (1628). Marin Mersenne's *La Vérité des sciences contre les septiques ou pyrrhoniens* (1625) is an important analysis of the implications of scepticism for the sciences and a defence of scientific knowledge. See Popkin, *The History of Scepticism from Erasmus to Spinoza*, pp. 110–50, for a critical survey of the philosophical and theological battles waged in France against the Pyrrhonians.

[45] See Joseph Moreau, "Doute et savoir chez Francisco Sanches", *Portugiesische Forschungen des Görresgesellschaft*, 1st series, *Aufsätze zur Portugiesischen Kulturgeschichte*, vol. I (1960), pp. 26–30.

[46] Apart from a few pages in Francisque Bouillier's *Histoire de la Philosophie Cartésienne*, 3rd ed. (Paris: Ch. Delagrave, 1868) and Paul Dibon's *La Philosophie Néerlandaise au siècle d'or* (Paris: Elsevier, 1954), little has been written on the role of the Dutch philosophers and theologians, Voetius and Schoock, both traditional Aristotelians, in the anti-Cartesian battles in Holland. Voetius did succeed in 1642 in having the *philosophia nova et praesumpta* condemned by the faculty of the University of Utrecht on the grounds that it was contrary to the true and ancient philosophy, turned the young away from the study and understanding of Scholastic terms, and led to scepticism and irreligion (see Bouillier, *Histoire*, p. 264). Having attacked Descartes's disciple, Regius, Voetius then attacked Descartes quite openly and contrived to have the magistrates of the city of Utrecht summon Descartes to appear before them on charges of atheism and calumny. Fortunately Descartes had powerful protectors in the persons of the Prince of Orange and the French ambassador to Holland and the summons was quashed.

probably apprised was made by Heubnerus in a letter to Mersenne, dated August 19/29, 1641, in which he mentions that Sanches's *Quod nihil scitur* brilliantly and wittily exaggerates the difficulties of acquiring true knowledge yet does not advance to the state of hyperbolical doubt in the manner of Descartes.[47] Mersenne was a close friend and regular correspondent of Descartes and kept him up-to-date with all the intellectual happenings in Europe through his vast network of correspondents. As Gouhier points out, Descartes probably knew the *Quod nihil scitur* and may have read it during his studies at the Jesuit college in La Flèche.[48] It has been advanced by some scholars that Sanches had a direct influence on the *Discours de la méthode* on the grounds that Descartes read the 1618 Frankfurt edition of the *Quod nihil scitur* when he was in Frankfurt for the coronation of the Emperor Ferdinand II in 1619, and that afterwards he began to reflect on the method "pour bien conduire sa raison et chercher la vérité dans les sciences" which he describes in the second part of the *Discours de la méthode*.[49] However, after analysing Cazac's conjectures and those of Iriarte, Carvalho has rightly concluded that, although there are significant parallels between certain passages of the *Quod nihil scitur* and the *Discours de la méthode*, there

[47] "Haud dubie iamdudum legisti libellum FRANCISCI SANCHEZ, titulo, *quod nihil scitur*. Difficultates scientiaer verae acquirendae egregie e ingeniose exaggerat; sed tamen ad hyperbolicas eiusmodi dubitationes, quales Cartesianae sunt, non progreditur" (quoted in *Oeuvres de Descartes*, ed. Charles Adam and Paul Tannery [Paris: Vrin, 1971], III, p. 439).

[48] See Henri Gouhier, *Les Premières Pensées de Descartes* (Paris: Vrin, 1958), p. 116. Etienne Gilson, in his historical commentary on the *Discours de la méthode*, remarks that Descartes was referring to a sceptical tradition which had inspired many authors (Montaigne, Charron, Sanchez, La Mothe Le Vayer, etc.) when he mentions the difficulty of distinguishing between true and false impressions when awake or dreaming, and in his second *Réponses* he mentions: "... encore que j'eusse vu il y a longtemps plusieurs livres écrits par les Sceptiques et Académiciens touchant cette matière, et que ce ne fût pas sans quelque dégoût que je remâchais une viande si commune" (Descartes, *Discours de la méthode*, ed. Etienne Gilson [Paris: Vrin, 1967], pp. 291–2).

[49] Descartes employs terms and architectural metaphors similar to those of Sanches when he describes how in Germany he meditated on his new method. See *Discours de la méthode*, ed. Gilson, pp. 11–14.

are radical differences in their approach to the problem of knowledge.[50] Etienne Gilson's magnificent commentary on the *Discours de la méthode* does demonstrate the extent of Descartes's indebtedness to Montaigne, Charron, and Sanches. Gilson suggests that Descartes may have been thinking of Sanches when he stated: "Non que j'imitasse pour cela les sceptiques, qui ne doutent que pour douter, et affectent d'être toujours irrésolus".[51]

The bitter attacks on Descartes by Gisbert Voetius, rector of the University of Utrecht, and by his disciple, Martin Schoock, in the *Admiranda methodus novae philosophiae Renati Des Cartes* (1643), were part of a campaign by traditional Aristotelian scholars to discredit Descartes by calling him a Pyrrhonian sceptic, because his method of hyperbolical doubt undermined the very foundations of the Aristotelian system of knowledge.[52] Schoock, however, in a later work, the *De scepticismo pars prior* (1652), does not include Descartes in the list of modern sceptics but singles out Sanches above all others for having revived the delirious arguments of ancient sceptics.[53] It is interesting that Schoock cites a

[50] "A diferença implica divergências profundas e radicais. Assim, Sanches, não foi, nem podia ir, além da apreensão do que lhe era dado como real, pelo que o seu ideal de Ciência se apresenta como essencialmente mostrativo. Descartes, pelo contrário, foi do concreto à superestrutura, isto é, à construção de um mundo *real*, coerente lògicamente com dados tidos por consistentes, recusando-se a aceitar, como Sanches, que o *imediato* da experiência fosse a expressão da realidade autêntica" (Carvalho, *Opera philosophica*, p. 188).

[51] "Le pyrrhonisme de Montaigne, grossièrement interprété, pouvait à la rigueur passer pour le scepticisme d'un homme qui ne doute que pour douter; mais la formule s'appliquerait mieux au scepticisme de Sanchez ... dont le *Quod nihil scitur* (Lyon, 1581) était très répandu. On notera, dans la préface de cet opuscule, un texte qui devait inviter Descartes à marquer la différence entre son doute méthodique et le Scepticisme, à cause du parallélisme frappant entre leurs deux expériences ainsi qu'entre les conclusions que tous deux en avaient tirées" (Descartes, *Discours de la méthode*, ed. Gilson, p. 267).

[52] Dibon points out that Schoock, in the *Admiranda methodus*, was merely serving as Voetius's straw man, and later completely disavowed the offensive accusations made against Descartes in the book (see *La Philosophie Néerlandaise au siècle d'or*, p. 182).

[53] "... ac prae aliis Franciscus Sanchez in opusculo, quod inscripsit *de multum nobili et prima universali scientia, quod nihil scitur*, in quo antiquorum

passage from the *Quod nihil scitur* when he demonstrates that Descartes's *cogito* was an irrefutable truth that not even the most convinced sceptic could overturn.[54] Schoock also quotes extensively from Sanches's sceptical arguments against the validity of sensory perception when he seeks to prove that experience and reason have shown that sensory data are reliable.[55] In the eyes of the Dutch theologians, Sanches was the patron (*patronus*) of modern scepticism, and his attacks against Aristotle were viewed, as the subtitle of Schoock's work suggests, as undermining not only the certainty of all disciplines but also the theoretical basis of philosophy.[56] The publication of the 1618 Frankfurt edition and of the 1649 Rotterdam edition of the *Quod nihil scitur* seems to have had a major impact on the European philosophical scene and contributed to Sanches's reputation as the leading sceptical thinker among modern Pyrrhonians.

Gabriel Wedderkopff continued Schook's attacks against Pyrrhonism in his *Dissertationes duae quarum prior de Scepticismo profano et sacro praecipue remonstrantium* (1665), which stressed that scepticism was extremely dangerous for the Christian religion as it easily lapsed into atheism. According to Wedderkopff, Sanches was the principal restorer of Pyrrhonian scepticism. In addition, Wedderkopff states that he shares Voetius's opinion that Descartes's scepticism was a leading cause of contemporary atheism.[57] Daniel

Scepticorum deliria non solum ab ovo revocavit, sed etiam classes, ex quibus argumenta sua petere solent" (Schoock, *De scepticismo pars prior*, p. 69).

[54] See Schoock, *De scepticismo pars prior*, 88–91. The passage relevant to the *cogito* is quoted as follows: "Certus quidem sum, me nunc haec, quae scribo, cogitare velle scribere, et optare ut vera sint, et ut a te approbentur: nec tamen nimis curare: sed cum considerare nitor, quid sit haec cogitatio, hoc velle, hoc optare, hoc non curare, sane deficit cogitatio, frustratur voluntas, incessit desiderium, augetur cura. Nil video quod captare aut comprehendere possim" (*Quod nihil scitur*, [1618], p. 83).

[55] *De scepticismo pars prior*, pp. 228–34.

[56] *De scepticismo pars prior* sive Libri quatuor: quibus, qua antiquorum, qua recentiorum SCEPTICORUM deliria, ex suis principiis solide discutiuntur, atque certitudo non minus disciplinarum universalium, quam Philosophiae Theoreticae asseritur.

[57] "Cum primis illa a Renato Descartes libertas ac Scepticismus introductus, quo in dubium vocare vult ipsa naturalis luminis principia atque axiomata, quod

Hartnack's long and erudite treatise *Sanchez aliquid sciens* (1665) is a line-by-line refutation of the *Quod nihil scitur* in the tradition of the Scholastic commentary, which, in spite of its boring prolixity, does illustrate the importance the Dutch and German theologians attached to Sanches's treatise. Consequently Hartnack goes to great pains to quote every ancient authority who has ever written on the subject of scepticism, including the Nominalists, and opposes the sceptical arguments with quotations from Aristotle, Averroës, Saint Augustine, Zabarella, and Francis Bacon. A similar work by Johann Ulrich Wild, *Dissertationes quinque quod aliquid scitur,* was published in Leipzig in 1664.[58]

The judgment pronounced by seventeenth-century commentators on Sanches, that he was a Pyrrhonian sceptic of the kind most dangerous to religion and to the sciences, was to be enshrined for ever in Bayle's *Dictionnaire historique et critique*. Only the Abbé Joly, in his critical remarks on Bayle's dictionary, fully appreciated Sanches's true intentions in writing the *Quod nihil scitur* and carefully pointed out that Bayle's words "C'etoit un grand Pyrrhonien" were in need of some modification:

Sanchez ne portait pas le Pyrrhonisme aussi loin qu'on le pourroit croire par la seule inspection du titre de son traité. Cet Ecrit, à proprement parler, est une espèce de méthode, à peu près semblable à celle que Descartes a suivie dans la suite, dont le fondement est un doute, sur tout

> sane neque pium nequo periculo caret, vix etiam aliquis a se impetrabit ut impressam menti de Deo cognitionem eripi creda oblivione ac deletione quum saepius quidem ea notitia obscura reddatur per naturam tamen penitus obliterari nequeat ... Neque extra periculum est, quod facilis inde prolapsus ad Atheismum nefandum sit, ut demonstratum legere licet apud Voetium in disput. de Atheismo" (*De scepticismo profano et sacro*, pp. 60–1).

[58] The article on Sanchez in Bayle's *Dictionnaire historique et critique* states in a footnote: "Jean Ulric Wildius le réfuta dans des thèses intitulées *Quod aliquid scitur*, soutenues à Leipsic l'an 1664". The book is seemingly unobtainable in European and North American libraries. Professor Schrenck of Strasbourg University informs me that Wild, a native of Strasbourg, studied in Leipzig and presented the *Dissertationes quinque quod aliquid scitur* for his M.A. degree in 1664.

ce que l'on veut examiner; doute par lequel on veut se mettre en état de chercher la vérité sans aucun préjugé.[59]

Joly goes on to state that Sanches does not attack any article of faith and does distinguish between certainty and uncertainty and that a Pyrrhonian would have spoken in different terms.[60] All the doubts that Sanches discusses are those any reasonable man might consider.[61] Moreover, Sanches's promise to write a book on the "method of knowing" was a positive proof of his anti-Pyrrhonism.[62] Later in the eighteenth century, Formey, a French historian of philosophy, was equally convinced that not all sceptics were atheists and, in reviewing Sanches, comments: "Sentant bien que la Philosophie qu'il étoit obligé d'enseigner, formilloit d'absurdités et de contradictions, il ne put s'empêcher de l'attaquer par un petit Ouvrage sur la Science, où il se proposa de faire voir que nous ne savons rien".[63] Thus an attempt was made by certain eighteenth-century thinkers to reassess critically the different strands of sceptical thought, and to situate Sanches among those sceptics who had made a positive contribution to the history of philosophy by his advocacy of a new method of enquiry based on systematic doubt.

[59] L'Abbé Joly, *Remarques critiques sur le dictionnaire de Bayle,* 2 vols. (Paris: Hyppolite Louis Guérin, 1748), p. 710.

[60] "Par exemple, examinant ce que c'est que la pensée, il dit à la page 57 "Certus quidem sum, me nunc haec, quae scribo, cogitare, vel scribere, et optare ut vera sint, et ut a te approbentur . . . Sanchez distingue donc la certitude d'avec l'incertitude. . . . Un Pyrrhonien auroit parlé bien autrement" (ibid., p. 710).

[61] "Sanchez ajoute à la page suivante: "Dixi, de his quae in nobis sunt, aut fiunt, nos esse CERTOS QUOD IN RE SINT. Jamais Pyrrhonien fit-il un pareil aveu? . . . Presque tous les points, où il entasse doutes sur doutes, sont effectivement des points sur lesquels un homme sensé peut être quelquefois indécis" (ibid., p. 710).

[62] "J'ajoute seulement qu'il finit son Traité par une promesse qui est un témoignage positif de son Anti-Pyrrhonisme: Interim, nos ad res examinandas accingentes, an aliquid sciatur, et quomodo, libello alio proponemus: quo METHODUM SCIENDI, quantum fragilitas humana patitur, exponemus. Vale" (ibid., p. 711).

[63] See Jean-Henri Samuel Formey, *Histoire abrégée de la philosophie* (Amsterdam: H. Schneider, 1760), p. 246.

On the whole, however, posterity has tended to misjudge Sanches's real intentions in writing the *Quod nihil scitur* and has been too ready to place him among the ranks of the Pyrrhonians. The importance attached to the translations of Sextus Empiricus and their impact on sixteenth and seventeenth-century philosophical debates has tended to obscure the genuine contribution made by Academic scepticism to the constant attacks against the Aristotelian concept of scientific method. The Academic sceptics advocated a system of methodological doubt which would free the human mind from the fetters of the past and enable the sceptical enquirer to re-establish knowledge on a firmer empirical basis. Sanches's scepticism is philosophically anchored in the Academic scepticism of the school of Carneades and confirmed by his own experiences as a physician who adhered to the Galenic method with its insistence on judgment and empirical observation.

QVOD NIHIL SCITVR

TEXT AND TRANSLATION

The basis of the text is the second edition of 1581 (referred to here and in the notes following the text as *1581²*), incorporating the *Errata* printed at the end of that edition. At the few places where *1581²* clearly fails to yield the reading intended by Sanches, a correction (whether from the 1581¹, the 1618 or the 1636 edition, or from a later emendation) has been inserted in the text, and the origin of the correction, together with the *1581²* reading, has been added in a footnote.

There are no paragraph-divisions in the *1581²* text; in the translation I have added these at my own discretion, bearing in mind the guiding and ever-present principle of giving a clear account of Sanches's meaning. In matters of spelling and punctuation, I have adhered as closely as was reasonably possible to Sanches's practice, retaining his abbreviations but ignoring all accents, except those on Greek words. In roman capitals, Sanches uses *V* for consonant and vowel alike (only once employing capital *U*); this has been followed here. Where lower case is employed, Sanches has one form for *u* and *v* at the initial position, and another for letters within the word, making no distinction between instances where a vowel follows and those where it does not. I decided to print *v* in the initial position wherever it precedes a vowel, but *u* elsewhere; later I found that the most widely used modern edition, that of 1955, does the same. Again, Sanches (or his printer) chooses either capital *S* or long ſ at the opening of a sentence, apparently at random; for the sake of clarity it was necessary uniformly to employ capital *S* in this position. For the same reason, although I have adhered to Sanches's punctuation as faithfully as possible, I have been obliged at least once to substitute a semicolon (not, apparently, a feature of the printer's italic fount) for a full stop.[1]

The translator of such a work as this cannot avoid the problem posed by the words "knowledge" and "science." Plainly the second of these nowadays has overtones that were absent in the sixteenth century; on the other hand, one frequently has occasion to speak of particular "sciences", rather than "branches of knowledge", not only because it is less cumbersome as an expression, but also, and more importantly, because to imply the present existence of a corpus of knowledge appears to beg the entire question raised by Sanches. Equally troublesome is the failure of English to distinguish unequivocally between the two "kinds" of knowing for which French uses *savoir* and *connaître*, while German uses *wissen* and *kennen*. Here the English translator must be empirical – and, it will seem to some, inconsistent – having regard solely to the precise meaning intended in the context. In dealing with Sanches, I am inclined to suspect that a translator who made a fetish of "consistency" would quite often end up misleading the reader. This, at least, I have striven not to do; but one can never be certain that one has succeeded, and for this reason I have placed in the margin of both the text and the translation the page numbers of the *1581*[2] edition, adding (in the Latin text only) the symbol // at the place where the new page begins. It will thus be possible easily to compare the English text with the original, and to verify whether the new Latin text accurately reproduces the substance of the old.

D.F.S.T.

---

[1] In editing the text I have discarded the marginalia; only the indications of sources deserve attention, and these are amplified in the commentary.

Franciscus Sanchez Philosophus et Medicus Doctor

QVOD NIHIL SCITVR

INTEGERRIMO, DISERTISSIMOQVE VIRO IACOBO A CASTRO, FRANCISCVS SANCHEZ S. P.

Cum nuper librorum scrinium euoluerem, amicissime Iacobe, incidi forte in opusculum hoc, quod ante septennium edideram, cōdideramque usque in nonū annum illius consilio: reperique id adeo tineis & blattis laceratum, ut si biennium adhuc distulissem in lucem proferre, timendum erat, ne tunc potius in ignem, quam in lucem mittere necesse fuisset. Id me coëgit illud praepropere abortare. Sed quemadmodum humani partus non solum qui nonum attigere mensem, verum & septimestres etiā vitales sunt, sic septenne hoc infectum superstes esse poterit. Est & alia ratio. Parturimus propediem nonnulla alia, quibus hoc praevium esse oportet. Quod si tandiu expectandum foret donec nil corrigi, nil mutari posset, Sisyphi saxum volueremus, nunquam finis lambendi ursi, nil daremus in vulgum unquam. Adde quod usu saepe venire videmus, ut qui multoties opus idem repetunt ut forment, tandem deforment.[1] Exeat igitur bonis auibus in campum, falsitatem expugnaturus miles. Quod si ab hostibus premi contingat, moneo in castra, a Castro amantissime, se recipiat tua: nullibi enim tutior esse possit. Sed ne forsan fores illi praecludas, non antea cognito, eum tibi mitto cum mandatis, ut quamprimum te ex nobis salutet, amicitiam nostram confirmet, insignique tuo instructus in militiam prodeat. Excipe ergo cum laeta fronte, & in numerum tuorum ascribe, nosque cum illo. Vale, Tolosae.

[1] deformant *1581²*, deforment *1618 Errata*.

Innatum homini velle scire: paucis concessum scire velle: paucioribus scire. Nec mihi ab aliis diuersa fortuna successit. A prima vita, Naturae contemplationi addictus minutim omnia inquirebam. Et quāuis initio auidus animus sciendi quocumque oblato cibo contentus esset utcumque: post modicum tamen tempus indigestione praehensus reuomere coepit omnia. Quaerebamque iam tunc quid illi darem quod & perfecte amplecteretur, & frueretur absolute: nec erat qui desiderium expleret meum. Euoluebam praeteritorum dicta, tentabam praesentiū corda: idem respondebant: quod tamen mihi satisfaceret, omnino nihil. Vmbras quasdā fateor veritatis referebant aliqui: nullū tamen inueni, qui quid de rebus iudicandum sincere, absoluteque proferret. Ad me proinde memetipsum retuli; omniaque in dubium reuocans, ac si a quopiam nil unquam dictum, res ipsas examinare coepi: qui verus est sciendi modus. Resoluebam usque ad extrema principia. Inde initium contemplationis faciēs, quo magis cogito magis dubito: nil perfecte complecti possum. Despero. Persisto tamen. Magis. Accedo ad Doctores auide ab eis veritatem expetiturus. Quid ipsi? Quisque sibi scientiam construit ex imaginationibus tū alterius, tum propriis: ex his alias inferunt: & ex his iterū alias; nil in rebus perpendentes, quousque labyrinthum verborum absque aliquo fundamento veritatis produxere: ex quo tandem non res intelligas naturales; sed nouarum rerum, fictionumque texturam discas: quibus intelligendis nulla sufficiat mens. Quis enim quae non // sunt intelligat? Hinc Democriti Atomi, Platonis Ideae, Numeri Pythagorae, Aristotelis Vniuersalia, agens intellectus, & intelligentiae. His ignaros expiscantur, se incognita, Naturaeque recondita inuenisse prodentes. Credunt hi, facileque ad Aristotelem conuolant, voluunt, euoluunt, memoriae mandant: isque doctior est, qui plura ex Aristotele nouit recitare. Quibus si vel minimum neges, muti fiunt: te tamen blasphemum clamant. Si contra arguas, sophistam. Quid his facias? Miserum. Decipiantur qui decipi volunt. Non his scribo: nec proinde scripta legant mea. Non deerit tamen inter eos aliquis, qui lectis, nec intellectis, (quid

92

enim asino cum lyra?) dente ferire tentet. Ast rumpitur impactus adamanto malleus: Aesopicaque serpens, limam dum rodere putat, dentes frangit proprios. Cum iis igitur mihi res sit, qui nullius addicti iurare in verba magistri, proprio marte res expendunt, sensu, rationeque ducti. Tu igitur quisquis es eiusdem mecū conditionis, temperamentique: quique de rerum naturis saepissime tecum dubitasti, dubita modo mecum: ingenia nostra, naturamque simul exerceamus. Sit mihi liberum iudicium, non irrationabile tamen. Tibi tale & concedo, & precor. At dices forsan, quid post tot, tantosque viros tu nobis adferre potes noui? Tene expectabat Veritas? Minime quidem. Sed nec illos expectauerat antea. Nil igitur noui. Si sic, cur scripsit Aristoteles? Aut cur tacebimus nos? An ille Naturae potestatem determinauit totam, ambitumque uniuersum complexus est? Non crediderim, licet doctissimi quidam ex recentioribus ei nimis addicti sic praedicent: eum insuper vocantes Veritatis Dictatorem, Veritatis tribunal, Veritatis rempub. dignis sane tanto laudato, & tanto laudante epithetis: sed quae magis laudem ex alterius laudatione, & verborum ornatu affectare videantur, & mereantur; quam Veritatis rempub. In hac enim, ut & in eiusdē tribunali, nil nisi Veritas. In illo autem quot ab hac aliena? Sane plurima, ut suo quoque loco videbimus. Et acutissimi isti eius alumni & laudatores, in pluribus ei repu- / / gnarunt; ab eodem, credo, Veritatis tribunali compulsi: nisi malint ab ambitione, & liuore. Hercule Aristotelem inter acutissimos Naturae scrutatores plurimum valere iudico; unumque esse praecipuum ex mirabilibus humanae infirmitatis ingeniis. Nullibi tamen errasse, non assererem: plurima ignorasse affirmo; in multis haesitasse; non pauca confuse tradidisse; alia succincte perstrinxisse; quaẹdam tacite praeteriisse, aut fugisse, video. Homo erat, ut & nos: quique coactus saepe humanae mentis torporem, infirmitatemque detegit. Nos eandem dolentes hic & manifestamus, & exercemus, & exhaurimus; dum plurima cogitando elicimus, quae ut a veterum decretis abscedunt, sic ad Veritatis accedere videntur. Tale est iudicium nostrum. Succedunt temporibus tempora, sic hominum diuersae opiniones: quorum quisque se verum inuenisse credit: cum ex mille varia opinantibus solus unus inuenisse potest. Liceat igitur & mihi cum reliquis, aut

93

etiam absque illis, idem inquirere: forsan attingam. Plures enim
canes facilius praedam venantur uno. Nil itaque mirum tibi
videatur, si post tot, ut arguis, tantosque viros tantillus ego
lapidem hunc moueam: soluit enim quandoque a vinculis mus
leonem. Nec proinde tamen Veritatem tibi omnino polliceor, ut
qui eam, ut alia omnia, ignorem: inquiram tamen in quantum
potero: tuque utcumque apertam, & e latebris excussam
persequeris. Nec tamen eam arripere speres unquam, aut sciens
tenere: sufficiat tibi quod & mihi, eandem agitare. Hic mihi
scopus, his finis est: hunc tu quaerere etiam debes. Quo posito, a
principiis rerum exordium sumentes, grauiora Philosophiae capita
examinabimus, ex quibus facilius reliqua colligi possint. Nec enim
in his inmorari in votis est omnino: ad Medicam quippe artem
viam affectamus, cuius professores sumus: cuiusque principia
omnia Philosophicae contemplationis sunt: ut eadem manu duos
simul moueamus lapides: nec enim aliter vita sufficeret. Excus-
andus subinde venio, si dum Veritati inquirendae studeo, minu-
tiora quaedam con- / / tempsero. Non igitur a me comptam &
politam expectes orationem. Darem quidem si vellem: sed labitur
interea veritas, dum verbum pro verbo supponimus, ambagi-
busque utimur: hoc namque est verba dare. Si id vis, pete a
Cicerone, cuius hoc munus est: sat enim pulchre dixero, si sat
vere. Decent bella verba Rhetores, Poëtas, aulicos, amatores,
meretrices, lenones, adulatores, parasitos, & his similes, quibus
belle loqui finis est. Scientiae sufficit proprie, imo necessarium est:
quod tamen cum illo stare non potest. Nec a me postules
multorum autoritates, aut in autores reuerentiam, quae potius
seruilis & indocti animi est, quam liberi, & veritatem inquirentis.
Solam sequar ratione Naturam. Autoritas credere iubet; ratio
demonstrat: Illa fidei; haec scientiis aptior. Proinde quae ab aliis
recte dicta videbuntur, ratione confirmabo: quae falso, eadem
infirmabo. Faxitque Deus, ut quo ego animo haec tibi vigilans
elaboro, eodem tu elaborata excipias vigilans, sanaque mente
iudices: & quae falsa videbuntur, firmis rationibus, (quod ut
Philosophi est, sic mihi valde gratum) non infirmis iniuriis, (quod
ut foeminarum, sic Philosopho indignum, & mihi omnino
ingratum) quod cum liuidi, tum ignari quidam faciunt, lacessas:

quae vero sana, approbes & confirmes. Quod ut fiet spero, sic tu maiora prope diem expecta. Vale. Ex Tolosa, Kal. Ianu. Anno redemptionis. M.D. LXXVI.

QVID? //

Franciscus Sanchez Philosophus et Medicus Doctor

1

QVOD NIHIL SCITVR

Nec unum hoc scio, me nihil scire: Coniecto tamen nec me, nec alios. Haec mihi vexillum propositio sit, haec sequenda venit, Nihil scitur. Hanc si probare sciuero, merito concludam, nil sciri: si nesciuero, hoc ipso melius: id enim asserebam. At dices: si probare scias, contrariū sequetur, aliquid enim scis iam. At ego cōtra prius conclusi, quam tu argueres. Iam incipio turbare rem: Ex hoc ipso iam sequitur, nil sciri. Forsan non intellexisti, meque ignarum aut cauillatorem vocas. Verum dixisti. Melius ego te, quia non intellexisti. Ignari igitur ambo. Iam ergo nesciens conclusisti quod quaerebam. Si intellexisti ambiguitatem consequentiae, aperte vidisti, nil sciri: sin minus, cogita, distingue, & mihi solue nodum. Acue ingenium. Persequor. A nomine rem ducamus. Mihi enim omnis nominalis definitio est, & fere omnis quaestio. Explico. Rerum naturas cognoscere non possumus, ego saltem: si dicas, te bene, non contendam. Falsum tamen est: Cur enim tu potius? Et hinc nil scimus. Quod si non cognoscamus, // 2 quo pacto demonstrabimus? Nullo. Tu tamen diffinitionem dicis esse quae rei naturam demonstrat. Da mihi unam. Non habes. Concludo ergo. Amplius, rei quam non cognoscimus quomodo nomina imponemus? Non video. Sunt tamen. Hinc circa nomina dubitatio perpetua, & multa in verbis confusio & fallacia: quin & in his omnibus quae modo protuli forsan. Conclude tu. Dices definire te rem quae est homo hac definitione, Animal rationale mortale, non verbum. Nego. Dubito enim rursus de verbo

95

animal, & de rationale, & alio. Definies adhuc haec per superiora
genera & differentias, ut vocas, usque ad Ens. Idem de singulis
nominibus quaeram. Tandem de ultimo Ente: nec enim scis quid
significet. Non definies, quia non habet superius genus, dices.
Non intelligo hoc. Nec tu. Nescis quid sit Ens. Minus ego. Dices
tamen in quaestionibus tandem quiescendum. Hoc non soluit
dubium, nec explet mentem. Prodis coactus ignorantiam.
Gaudeo. Et ego. Procedo. Una res homo est, eam tamen pluribus
insignis nominibus, Ente, substātia, corpore, viuenti, animali,
homine, & tandem Socrate. An non haec verba sunt? Sane. Si
idem significant, superflua: Si diuersa, non eadem res & una
homo. Plura dicis in eodem considero homine, quibus singulis
propria attribuo nomina. Rem magis dubiam facis. Nec hominem
intelligis totum, qui magnum quid est, crassum, & sensu per-
ceptibile: & in tam minima diuidis, quae sensum effugiunt cer-
tissimum omnium iudicem, ratione indaganda fallaci & obscura!
Male agis, & decipis me, & magis te. Quaero, quid in homine
vocas animal, viuens, corpus, substantia, Ens? Nescis ut antea.
3 Nec ego. Et id // volebam. Dicam tamen inferius. Dein peto, quid
hoc nomen qualitas, significat? quid Natura? anima? vita? Dices,
hoc. Negabo facile: aliud enim. Proba. Recurris ad Aristotelem.
Ego ad Ciceronem, cuius munus est verborum significationes
ostendere. Dices non tam proprie loquutum Ciceronem, nec tam
exquisite. Ego contra contendam: hanc enim Cicero exercebat
artem, non Aristot. Si amplius quaeras, alios adferam Latinae
linguae excultores, vel Graecae: idem enim est. Nulla inter eos
concordia, nulla certitudo, nulla stabilitas, nulli limites. Quisque
ad libitum verba dilacerat, hinc inde distorquet, & proposito suo
accommodat. Hinc tot tropi, tot figurae, tot regulae, tot mix-
tiones, quibus omnibus Grammatica constat. Quid autem Rhe-
torica & Poetica non peruertunt? Quibus non abutuntur modis?
Atque hi omnes loquacitatem tantum exercent inutilem, sed ad
libitum, soluteque, ut dicunt. At Dialectica seu Logica eandem
etiam, sed non eodem modo: verba enim in ordinem disponit, in
aciem parat, prohibetque disparata pugnare, sed coniunctim: dat
leges: coërcet, permittit, cogit. Denique illae similes sunt eis qui
turmas & castra effingunt in publicis ludis & spectaculis, in quibus

plus decoris quam roboris desideratur: Hae contra eis qui ad
Martem serio se comparant, quibus plus virium quam pulchritu-
dinis inesse conuenit. Omnibus autem verba milites sunt &
obiectum. Cui horum credes magis? Dubium est. Quisque sibi
credi vult. Nec hoc sufficit. Verborum significationes magis aut
omnino a vulgo pendere videntur, ab eoque proinde petendas esse:
Quis enim nos loqui docuit nisi vulgus? Nam & hac ratione fere
omnes qui hactenus scri- / / pserunt, ea quae frequentius in 4
hominum ore sunt pro fundamēto disputationis sumpsere: ut ille,
Tunc nos aliquid scire dicimur, cum eius causas principiaque
cognoscimus: Et alter, Sumendum vero & hic omnium consensu
approbatum principium, quod omnes homines tunc se sanos
existimant, cum &c. In vulgo autem an aliqua certitudo &
stabilitas? Nequicquam. Quomodo ergo in verbis quies unquam
erit? Iam non est quo fugias. Dices forsan quaerendum esse, qua
significatione qui primum imposuit usus fuerit. Quaere igitur: non
inuenies. Sed iam satis. An non plane de nomine omnis quaestio?
Mihi sane probasse videor. Si neges, praecipuae quaestionis
probationem confirmabis. Sed mox probabitur melius. Ergo quid
scientiae nomine intelligendum sit videamus. Nam si haec nulla
sit, nullus subinde ab ea denominabitur sciens. Quid Aristoteles?
Hūc enim (ut qui acutissimus fuit Naturae scrutator, quemque ut
plurimum sequitur Philosophorū maior turba) pro omnibus aliis
examinasse sufficiat: ne, si cōtra omnes pugnandum esset, in
infinitum abiret opus, Naturamque item aliorum more dimittere-
mus. Quid igitur ille? Scientia habitus per demonstrationem
acquisitus. Non intelligo. Et hoc pessimum. Obscurum per
obscurius. Sic homines decipiunt. Quid habitus? Minus scio quam
quid scientia. Minus tu. Dic, firma qualitas. Adhuc minus. Quo
plus procedis minus promoues, quo plura verba maior confusio.
Detrudis me in lineam praedicamētalem, & inde semper ad Ens,
quod nescis quid sit. At nonne ad praedicamenta reducenda
omnia? Sane. Quid inde? In labyrinthum omnia ducenda. Quid
Praedicamenta? Series verborum lōga. Mirum, quid dixi? Dico. // 5
Verborum alia communissima, Ens, verum, bonum, si velis: Alia
minus communia, substantia, corpus: Alia propria, Socrates,
Plato. Illa significāt omnia: Ista plura: Haec unum. Sequitur,

quum dicunt, Socrates est homo, & hinc animal, &c. significari, hoc quod ostendo (Socratem intellige) sic vocari particulari nomine: Cum aliis autem figura similibus, communi nomine, hominem: Cum equo & reliquis quae mouentur, dissimilis tamen sunt figurae, animal: Communissimo cū rebus omnibus, Ens. De reliquis Praedicamentis idem. Non sufficit id. Simplicibis verbis non contenti, ut rem difficiliorem efficiant, communibus utuntur apposita differentia aliqua: ut pro homine, Animal rationale mortale: quorum quodlibet primo difficilius est. Vbi enim multitudo ibi confusio, & quo ampliora verba eo confusa & obscura magis. Hoc minimum. Super haec mira construunt. De verborum hac serie (Praedicamenta vocant) plura disputant, de ordine, de numero, de capite, de differentia, de proprietatibus, de reductione omnium rerum ad illa, haec reducunt ad rectam lineam, illa ad latus: Haec per se, illa ratione sui contrarij: Haec communia sunt duobus, illa male reducuntur ad illud: Haec non habent ad quod reducantur. Ergo vel si sit coelum, si non obtinuit locum in praedicamento, iam nihil est. Quid dicam? In infinitas hinc trahuntur nugas. Amplius adhuc verborum verba confingentes, omnino se, miserosque audientes in profundum ineptumque Chaos prouoluunt. His tota plena Aristotel. Logica, multoque magis quas post eum conscripsere recentiores, Dialecticae. Communiora enim nomina vocant genera, alia

6 species, Differentias, Propria, Indiuidua. / / Si quaeras, quid hoc. Commune quid abstractum per intellectum. Aristotelis fictio Ideis non dissimilis. De abstractione statim. De intellectu agente (noua res) abstrahente aut illuminante, (potius obscurante) & de intelligente, unde consurgit uniuersale quod est animal. Eo rem ducunt, ut asinus significet[2] mentem istorum Logicorum, quae non nisi communem asinum comprehendere potest, imo eum formare: quum tamen quilibet eorū particularis asinus sit. Quid dices? An non haec verba & stultitiae? Verum quidem. Atque hoc de simplicibus tantum terminis, Praedicabilia vocant. De quibus adhuc quot, quae, quid? Nihil, nugae. Iterum vocant haec aequiuoca, illa uniuoca, analoga, deuominatiua, terminos, voces,

---

[2] significem *1581*[2], significet *1618 Errata.*

verba, dictiones, simplices, compositas: complexas, incomplexas: mentales, vocales, scriptas: a placito, a Natura: primae intentionis, secundae intentionis: categorematicas, syncategorematicas: vagas, confusas: innumerasque alias nominum denominationes, rursusque harum alias: & circa harum quamlibet subtiles admodum disputationes formant, adeo sane subtiles, ut vel minimo ictu in nihilum impellas. An tu hoc scire vocas? Ego nescire. At nunc incipimus. Si verbum verbo iungas, hoc opus hic labor est: subiectum, praedicatum, copulam, propositionem, definitionem, diuisionē, argumentationemque constituunt. Horum rursus infinitas alias species, differentias, conditiones. Quid dicā? Dum mentem scientia perfici aiunt, amentes omnino fiunt: qui rerum Naturas & causas inuestigare deberent & praedicant, nouas fingunt: quique plura & obscuriora fingit, doctior ille: unde & de sophismatis etiā / / scientiam scripsit ille. 7 Sic fictio fictionem soluit, & clauus clauum pellit: similesque mihi videntur iis qui Necromantiae, incantationibusque operam dant, quorum qui versutior est, ut aiunt, alterius actiones conatusque eludit, irritos facit, soluit, impeditque. Quod impij quidam olim Diuino Mosi obiecerunt de serpente, qui magorum alios deuorauit. Sic nostri hi incantatores verbis confisi, nil scientes, plura tamen se scire produnt, ne inscitiae arguantur. Ego contra inscitiam libenter confiteor meam, libentiusque tuam[3] detego. Nil scio. Minus illi. Quid igitur obscuris verbis mentes nobis obliniūt? Haec de habitu. Iā quid illud est: Demonstratio? Diffinies iterū, Syllogismus scientiā pariens. Circulum comisisti, meque proinde & te decepisti. Sed quid Syllogismus? Mirum, arrige aures, extende phantasiam: nec enim tot verba capiet forsan. Quam subtilis, quam longa, quam difficilis Syllogismorum scientia. Sane futilis, longa, difficilis, nulla Syllogismorum scientia. Ah blasphemaui. Verum, quia verum dixi. Iam lapidibus dignus sum. Tu contra fustibus, quia decipis. Ignorantia enim meretur utcumque veniam, fallacia supplicium. Audi, proba hominem esse ens. Sic dicis, Homo substantia est: haec ens: ergo homo ens. De primo dubito & secundo. Probas, homo corpus est: hoc substan-

---

[3] suam *1581*[2], tuam *1618 Errata.*

tia: ergo homo substantia. Iterum de ambobus. Dicis, homo
viuens: hoc corpus: ergo homo corpus. Et de istis. Sic, homo
animal: hoc viuens: ergo homo viuens. Summe Deus quae series,
quae farrago, ut probes hominem esse ens! Obscurior probatio
quaesito. Adhuc nego hominem animal esse. Quid dices? Nō sunt
8 plura genera. Quo fugies? / / Ad definitionem animalis, quae est,
viuens mobile & sensile: Talis homo. Vtrumque nego: sequere.
Viuens est corpus quod nutritur: tale animal: ergo. Haec proba.
Corpus est substantia tribus dimensionibus constans: Viuens tale
est: ergo. Vtrumque falsum. Substantia est ens per se: quale corpus
est: ergo. Et haec quoque probari velim. Non potes amplius. Quid
ens tandem est? Nescis ut antea. Quid his Syllogismis perfecisti?
Non probasti hominem esse ens, quod petiueram primum: imo
per lineā tuam tum descendens, tum ascendens, ut altum illud Ens
mihi appropinquaret, tibi maximum periculum, mihi metum
peperisti, ne cadens totus comminuereris, meque si subtus
comprehendisses, idem: remque tandem ita dubiam ut ante erat,
aut forte magis dereliquisti. Atqui primas solum propositiones
probare tibi semper videbaris, secundas ne attigisti quidem. Quod
si primas probasses, & ad secundas deuenissemus: in his magis
turbareris. Quid igitur decipis me tuis istis verborum concatena-
tionibus? Facilius ego. Ens significat omnia, hominem, equum, &
asinum &c. ergo homo est ens: equus & asinus. Si primum neges,
non probabo: nam nescirem. Proba tu mihi, si scis. Neque tu
quoque. Nil igitur scimus. Redeo ad syllogismos, quorum
subtilissima scientia tota corruit. Dixi iam supra: nomina alia
communissima, ut Ens, verum: Alia minus, substantia, qualitas:
Alia particularia, Plato, Mithridates. Intermedia plurima, quae nec
tot ut illa, nec tam pauca ut haec significant: corpus, viuens,
animal. Hinc facile est quaerenti, an homo substantia sit? sic
ostendere uno verbo. Substantia significat omnia quae per se sunt,
9 / / unde & hominem, & lapidem, & lignum: ergo homo substantia
est. At ipsi ambages quaerentes, ne in contemptum veniat eorum
scientia, si facilis sit, difficilem & laboriosam verborum inuolucro
efficiunt: demonstrasse se, & scientifice probasse iactantes, hominem esse substantiam, sic in Barbara, inexpugnabili castello:
Omne animal est substantia. Omnis homo est animal. Ergo omnis

homo est substantia. Verum dixisti, sed inscienter, & obscurius quam poterat sciens. Idem enim est ac si diceres, substant: \m significare tam viuentia, quam non viuentia: & viuentia significare hominem & cerasum: ergo a primo ad ultimum, significare substantiam hominem. At per tot intermedios gradus confunditur mens, imo subinde magis dubitat de singulis intermediis. Nonne hoc illud est quod dixerat alibi idem, Quod de praedicato dicitur, idem de subiecto dici? haec autem nominum passiones sunt. Sicut & illud, Quod est multis modis dicitur: si nomen hominis unum significat: principium aliud dicitur: causa autem uno modo dicitur: natura dicitur uno modo: necessarium dicitur. Denique quidquid est in illius Methaph. reliquisque operibus, nominum definitio est. Vnde de nomine omnis quaestio fere est: an substantia de homine dicatur, & sic de aliis. Quod cum scire nullus certo possit, nec rerum nec verborum scientia aliqua est. Dic, denuo verba imponamus. Permitto. Sciemus ergo iam verbum hoc, hoc significare. Falsum: nescis quid sit verbum, nescis quid sit hoc, nescis quid sit significare: ergo nescis verbum hoc hoc significare. Probo sequi: nam ignoratis partibus ignoratur totum. At tu mecum par-
/ / tes, & totum: ergo nihil scimus. Quare ergo ignarum me & te, 10
tu idem ignarus, verborum ignorantia maxima, subtilem tamen scientiam vocas, obscuraque farragine, maiori ignorantia cumulas? Vt gnarus appaream, dices. At contrarium euenit: dum enim falsa ridiculaque canis, scire te tamen multa praedicas, ego ignarum omnino coniicio, qui nescias te nihil scire. Quod si scias, deceptorem mendacemque, qui prodas te multa scire. Hoc enim unum semper maxime ab aliquo expetiui, quod modo facio, ut vere diceret an aliquid perfecte sciret: nusquam tamen inueni, praeterquam in sapienti illo, proboque viro Socrate, (licet & Pyrrhonij, Academici, & Sceptici vocati, cum Fauorino id etiam assererent) qui Hoc unum sciebat, quod nihil sciebat. Quo solo dicto mihi doctissimus iudicatur: quāquam nec adhuc omnino mihi explerit mentem: cum & illud unum, sicut alia, ignoraret. Sed ut magis assereret se nil scire, illud unum se scire dixit: qui proinde quum nihil sciret, nihil nobis scribere voluit. Idipsum saepe in mentem venit mihi. Quid enim dicam quod falsitatis suspectum non sit? Mihi enim humana omnia suspecta sunt, & haec ipsa quae scribo

modo. Non tacebo tamen: saltem hoc libere proferam, me nihil scire: ne tu in vanum labores veritatem inquirendo, sperans eam aliquando aperte tenere posse. Quod si deinceps aliquid cum reliquis exagitabo eorum quae in Natura sunt, hoc supposito, crede si velis, non tamen curo: vanitas enim omnia, dicebat sapientissimus ille Salomon, omnium doctissimus quos nobis superius memoriae dedit saeculum: quod aperte demonstrant eius

11 // opera, inter quae primas tenet aureus ille libellus, Ecclesiastes, aut Concionator dictus. Sed redeamus ad scientiam. Quid mouerit Aristotelem tot tantaque de verborum contextura disserere: quid Vniuersalia illa fingere: & an sine his omnibus scire aliquid possimus, ostēdam inferius ubi de modo sciendi. Interim ex eodem nulla scientia est. Vide: scientia per demonstrationem habetur. Quid haec? Somnium Aristotelis, non dissimile Platonis reipub. Ciceronis oratori, Horatij poetae. Nulla, nullibi. Depinxit quidem ille sat prolixo sermone: at nullam unquam dedit, nec post eum aliquis. Sin minus, da tu; mitte mihi. Non habes, scio. Sed nec syllogismum alium formauit usquam, nisi cum eas struere docuit: tuncque non ex significantibus terminis, sed ex elementis A, B, C, idque difficulter adhuc. Quod si significantibus usus fuisset, nunquam peregisset opus. Ad quid ergo deseruiunt hi? Quid in his docēdis tantum laborauit? Quid post eum tantum laborant adhuc reliqui? In scribendo non utimur his, nec ipse. Nulla his unquam parta scientia, imo deperditae multae, turbataeque sunt horum causa. In arguendo, & inter disputandum, simplici contenti consequentia, minus adhuc illis utimur: alias enim nunquam disputatio finem haberet, semperque de reducendo syllogismo in modum, in figuram, conuertendo, infinitisque aliis tricis certandum esset: imo & stulti quidam hodie id agunt, negantque, quidquid in modo & figura situm non est: tanta horum est stupiditas, scientiaeque huius syllogisticae arguties utilitasque, ut rebus in totum oblitis, ad umbras se conuertant. Vnde subit

12 mirari acutum alias Auerroum, // postque eum plurimos, quae Aristot. laxo dixit sermone, inutili, tantoque labore in syllogismos reducere conatum, eosque infallibiles, certissimos & demonstratiuos esse ubique ostendere voluisse, cum nihil minus sit, ut postea ostendemus. Contra vero non mirum est Augustinum Christianae

Ecclesiae splendidissimam[4] facem omnes alias scientias suo marte sine praeceptore didicisse, praeter hanc syllogisticam. Aliae enim in rebus fundantur, haec vero figmentum subtile est, nulliusque usus, imo plurimi nocumenti: ut quae homines a rerum contemplatione reuocet, in seque detineat, quod melius in discursu operum nostrorum videbis. Hoc vero multum differt ab eo quod isti dicunt, modum scilicet sciendi esse, principiumque sine quo scientia non sit. Qui verum quidem, sed inscienter dicunt. Eorum enim scientia haec est, nil aliud sciunt quam syllogismū ex nihilo struere, scilicet ex A, B, C: si autem ex aliquo instruēdus esset, obmutescerent, ut qui nec minimam intelligant propositionem. Sed iterum ad nos. Quid ergo? qui docet domum struere, ipse nec struxit unquam, nec scit, nec eius discipuli? cur credam sic struendam? Quod si nulla demonstratio, nulla ergo scientia. Quin & illud falsum, Demonstratio habitum scientificum parit. Nam ab ignaro, apto tamen scire, scientia prodit, solum ostēdente demonstratione rem sciendam: hoc enim vel verbum ipsum demonstrationis ostendit. Quinimo nec minimam unquam rem, aut propositionem intellexi ego ab Aristot. aliisque: sed illorum dictis commotus ad quamlibet rem contemplandam me accinxi, illorumque contradictionibus & difficultatibus perspectis, / / ne ego 13 iisdem inuoluerer, iis dimissis ad res confugi, inde iudicium petiturus: idque mihi fuit Aristot. quod Timotheum reliquis cantoribus fuisse idem Aristot. ait: quod scilicet nisi talis extitisset Aristot. Plato, & alij, forsan non ego talis extitissem. Vnde quam stulti sint qui ab authoribus totam, solamque scientiam quaerunt nil in rebus considerantes, facile est videre. Non ergo qui mihi rem aliquam videndam digito indicarit, visionem in me parit, sed potentiam visiuam excitat, ut in actum reducatur. Vnde & illud mihi stultum admodum videtur quod quidam astruunt, Demonstratiōe ex aeternis & inuiolabilibus necessario concludere & cogere: cum forsan talia nulla sint, aut si quae sint, nobis omnino incognita ut talia sunt, qui tum maxime corruptibiles, paruoque admodum tempore violabiles multum simus. Quare contra vera scientia, si quae esset, libera esset, & a libera mente: quae si ex se

---

[4] splendissimam *1581*[2], splendidissimam *Comparot.*

non percipiat rem ipsam, nullis coacta Demonstrationibus percipiet. Cogunt hae proinde ignaros, quibus sola fides sufficit. Cur
igitur ex Aristot. plures hinc inde ignare colligis propositiones, ex
quibus tandem syllogismum Barbarum construis, qui nec earum
unam intelligas? Consulerem tibi melius, mitte Philosophiam, ad
eam enim omnino ineptus es: at optimus fores architectus, aut
sutor, aut si velis cerdo, qui ligna, lapides, pannos, & coria in
figuram, non Barbaram ut tu, sed politam componunt, non quaerentes quid lignum, lapis, pannus, aut corium sit, sed quomodo ex
his domum, vestem, aut calceos Caesari effingant, quemadmodum tu Caesarea utens potestate labirynthum struis, quo & te
14 & miseros / / tibi similes illaquees, quibus deest rationis filum. Sed
nec tu aliquid scis: alios tamen docere praedicas: Nec ego, tibi
tamen illud persuadere conor. Vnde cum tu illa nescias, nec hoc
poteris percipere: Nec ego, cum omnia nesciam, tibi hoc demō-
strare. Igitur nil scimus. Id adhuc ostendo. Insequor definitionem
scientiae. Habitum explicant multarum conclusionum congeriem.
Mirum quomodo res omnino dimittentes semper ad figmenta sua
reuertantur, similes catae Aesopicae in virginem mutatae, quae
tamen post mutatam formam etiamnum mures insectabatur.
Verum quidem his scientia talis est: nil enim aliud sciunt praeter
multas conclusiones, res nullas. Quis unquam visionem per
specierū congeriem definiuit? scientia autem nil aliud est, quam
interna visio. Quod si scientia conclusionum congeries est, liber
hic scientiam multam habet. Proteruus es: dices fortasse habere
scientiam scriptam, iuxta illud, quod alius est terminus vocalis,
alius scriptus, alius mentalis. Non intelligo. Concedo tamen. Quid
sequitur? Nec te, nec me aliquid scire. Probat id Aesopus, qui inter
Grammaticum & Rhetorem conseruos venalis positus, ultimus
interrogatus quid sciret, respondit, Nihil. Quomodo hoc? Quia
inquit, Grammaticus & Rhetor nil mihi sciendum reliquerunt: (hi
enim antea interrogati quid scirent, responderant, omnia) sic nunc
liber hic multa scit per te, alius item plura, & omnes alij similiter:
ergo nil nobis relinquitur sciendum. Pergo. Si dixissent, plurium
rerum congeriem in mente, fortasse melius: non tamen omnino
verum. Vnius enim rei solum scientia esse potest. Imo unius
15 cuiusque rei per se solum est scientia, / / nec plurium simul:

quemadmodum & unius solum cuiusque obiecti visio una: nec enim duo simul licet perfecte respicere, sic nec duo simul perfecte intelligere, sed aliud post aliud. Vnde & illud, Pluribus intentus minor est ad singula sensus. Quemadmodum autem omnes homines specie, aut melius, nomine sunt unus homo, sic visio una dicitur, etiamsi plurium rerum sit, & plures numero visiones: sic Philosophia una scientia dicitur, etiamsi plurium rerum contemplatio, quarum cuilibet propria contemplatio, & scientia cuiuslibet post contemplationem una est. Nec id etiam verum est, multarum rerum cumulum in mente scientiam esse: quod quidam inepte cogitant, eos doctos proferentes qui plura viderint, audierint, recitareque subinde possint, tum in eadem scientia, tum in diuersis. Quum potius qui omnia amplecti vult, omnia perdit. Sufficit enim una scientia toti orbi, nec tamen totus hic ei sufficit. Mihi vel minima mundi res totius vitae contemplationi sat superque est, nec tamen tandem eam spero me nosse posse. Quomodo igitur tot scire unus homo valeat? Imo, crede mihi, multi sunt vocati, pauci vero electi. In te ipso experire, rem aliquam contemplare, vermem si velis, eius animam: Nil captare possis. Fateor quidem haec in mente necessario esse debere, ut quis ea sciat: non tamen id scientia est, sed memoria: quemadmodum nec congeries specierum in oculo visio est, (si ita visio fiat) quamuis haec sine illis fieri non possit. Videmus namque eos qui aliquid fixe imaginantur, quicquid se sensibus offerat, nil tamen sentire, quamuis tunc & oculis & auribus spectra imprimantur. Haec eadem ratione // illi omnia in omnibus esse asserebant. 16 Quomodo enim, dicunt, cognoscemus ea quae extra nos sunt? ergo in nobis omnia erant, euoluendo tamen inuenimus, & hoc scire. At falluntur nimium. Primo quod asserant in nobis asinum esse, (forsan in illis est) leonem, & reliqua. Qui enim id fieri potest, ut ego sim in leone, & leo in me? Chymeram fingis. Atque o utinam probarent nos aliquid scire: tunc enim concederemus illis consequentiam: scilicet, Nil sciri potest quin sit in nobis. Omnia sciuntur. Ergo omnia sunt in nobis. Nunc autem maior dubia est: falsa minor. Quomodo ergo concludes? Deinde male arguunt, si sufficere putant, ut sciamus, ea quae sciuntur in nobis esse. Quamuis enim id forsan conduceret, si fieri posset, non tamen inde colligitur in nobis omnia esse, imo contrarium: cum sane in nobis corpus, anima, intellectus, facultates, imagines, pluraque alia sint, quae tamen neutiquam perfecte cognoscimus. Sed hanc quaestionem, an scilicet omnia in nobis sint, in libris Naturae ex professo tractabimus: nunc sufficiat tetigisse quae ad propositam tractationem conducunt. Non igitur in nobis existentes vel res, vel rerum imagines scientiam efficiunt, aut scientia sunt: sed memoria ab his impletur, quas inde mens contemplatur. Hinc etiam iam illud efficio, pessime scientiam habitum vocari. Hic enim qualitas est difficulter mobilis: scientia qualitas non est: nisi visionem qualitatem dicere velis: potius mentis actio simplex, quae vel primo intuitu perfecta esse potest, nec amplius manet quam a mente fit: quemadmodum nec visio. Cuius contemplationis

17 cognitionisque, quae a mente fit, imago memoriae mandata / / in ea retinetur: quae si bene fixa sit, habitus dicetur: sin minus, dispositio. Haec vero memoriae tunc propria erunt, non scientiae. Si retulerit postea, memorare dicetur scita, non scire: nisi cum illa contemplatur: quemadmodum qui visa recitat, non videt. Multa tamen scire dicitur, qui sic scita memoria tenet, quod ea omnia & sciuerit antea, & scire possit cum volet: nā vel minimo ictu ea respiciendo intelligit: quia iam antea intellexit. Vnde liquet habitum plurium rerum in memoria non dici scientiam, nisi eaedem antea ab intellectu fuerint cognitae. Sed & alius scire nostrum (mirum) nil aliud esse quam recordari dicebat: Animam scilicet nostram ante nos omnia scire, in nobis omnia obliuisci, dum in corpus mergitur, pauloque post quasi ab occasu expergefactam reminisci. Sed parcat alias doctissimus vir, leue admodum figmentum, hoc[5] est, nec experientia, nec ratione confirmatum: sicuti & plurima alia quae de anima somniauit, ut in tractatu de Anima ostendemus. Hunc autem errorem Aristot. saepe confutauit. Cuius rationibus relictis, ut quae a quolibet legi in eo possunt, nos quod ad rem nostram attinet eundem examinemus. Si dixisset ille se, vidisse animam suam antequam immergeretur in corpus suum omnia scientem, forsan credidissem: tuncque non homo, sed larua, aut phantasma esset.

[5] hos *1581²*, hoc *1581¹*.

Sane quae ante me fuerint nescio: quod video vix credo: quomodo ergo somnia tua credam? Dic, Aut antequam anima ingrederetur corpus, sciebat, aut non. Non dices hoc. Tunc, Aut scientia illa animae recordatio solum erat, aut non. Si erat: ergo ab alia anima quae in ea erat, quaeque antequam in ea esset sciebat / / omnia. Et 18 de hac iterum, scire suum recordarine est? In infinitum te duco. Si non per aliam recordatur animam, sed per seipsam, ergo oblita fuerat antea. Quare? Et si oblita fuerat, antequam hoc accideret, an scire suū recordari adhuc erat? Iterum in infinitum. Si scire animae non erat recordari, eadem immersa in corpus an amittit scire illud? Si non amittit, ergo scit ut antea. At antea per te scire suum non erat recordari. Quod si per immersionem in corpus, ut dicis, quasi noui domicilij commercio attonita per tempus maneat sui immemor, recordabitur quidem postea eorum quae oblita fuerat, non tamen sciet denuo: quemadmodum & nos eorum quae antea sciebamus obliti, tandem recordamur: non tamen haec recordatio scire est. Si vero amittit, non postea recordabitur. Eorum enim recordamur quae in memoria quidem aut imaginatione adhuc sunt, non tamē cogitationi sese offerunt. Vnde occasione aliqua excitata aut similis rei, aut alterius per consequentias in phantasiam exeunt, cum recordatione tamen, quod antea ibidem essent. Quod si omnino erasa fuissent, non recordatio esset, sed noua impressio: quemadmodum iis accidit, qui ob morbum' vel nominis proprij obliuionem incurrunt perfectam: quos postea si discere contingat, non dices recordari: omnimoda enim contra obliuione teneri vel ipsum vulgus dicit, subindeque denuo ac si pueri essent instruendos: ipsique negant se unquam antea illa quae docentur sciuisse. Non igitur scire recordari est. Praeterea quoties recordamur, dicimus, hoc sane antea oblitus fueram, memini enim nunc sic, aut sic actum fuisse. Quod si id animae contingeret ut recordaretur / / solum, diceret etiam puer cum doceretur, & ego 19 haec sciebam antea, nunc memini. Quis autem hoc dicit? Item si anima antequam in corpus demersa esset sciebat, postea eadem sciet, non homo. Dicere autem animam scire an non ineptum? Denique rem dilucidiorem efficiamus, de nomine enim quaestio est. Aut scire & recordari idem significant, aut non. Idem non. Cur enim uno pro alio indifferenter non utimur? Quin & canes

etiam recordari non dubito: unum enim non dudum percussi de industria, qui quoties postea me videt adlatrat mihi, ictuum sane memor. At canes scire quis dicet? Forsan non vis recordari canes propter Aristot. At de hoc postea. Recordantur saltem foeminae & pueri, nihil tamen sciunt. Imo recordamur quidem omnes, nil tamen scimus. Quod si idem non significant, cur pro eodem sumpsit? Si aliquod eorum superius est ad aliud, cur non aliquam adiecit differentiam, quae illud restringeret? Homo enim animal est, sed non solum, quia etiam equus:· quare huic quadrupes addimus, illi bipes. Non igitur significant idem: ergo diuersae res sunt scire & memorare. De hoc nil nunc. Ad aliud. Quid adhuc scire est? Rem per causas cognoscere, aiunt. Nec adhuc omnino bene: obscura definitio. Sequitur enim statim quaestio de Causis difficilior prima. An omnes causas oportet cognoscere ad cognoscendam rem? Efficientem minime: quid enim ad mei cognitionem confert pater meus? Quid etiam finis? Deinde, si causatum perfecte cognoscere velis, & causas etiam perfecte cognoscas oportet. Quid sequitur? nil sciri, si efficientis, & finalis causae perfectam cognitionem habere velis. Ostendo. Ad cog-
20 nitionem mei perfectam // patrem meum perfecte cognoscere oportet: ad hunc cognoscendum, patrem eius antea cognoscas necesse est: post hunc alium, & in infinitum. De aliis rebus item. De finali idem. Dices te non considerare particularia, quae sub scientiam non cadunt, sed uniuersalia, hominem, equum &c. Verum quidem, & id antea dicebam. Sciētia tua non est de vero homine, sed de eo, quem tu tibi fingis: proinde nil scis. Esto, considera tuum illum fictum hominem: non illum scies, nisi eius causas cognoueris. An non efficientem habet? Non negabis. Hanc iterum si scire velis, eius efficientem cogita. Non finem facies, nec proinde scies quid tuus ille homo sit: nec quid verus esset sciebas: ergo nil scis. Forsan recurres ad Deum opt. max. primam omnium causam, omniumque finem ultimum: ibique standum dices, nec in infinitum eundum. De hoc postea. Sed nunc volo. Quid inde? Nil scis. Fugis infinitum, & incidis in infinitum, immensum, incomprehensibile, indicibile, inintelligibile. An hic sciri potest? Minime. At omnium causa est per te. Ergo ad effectuum cognitionem eius cognitio necessaria est ex definitione tua. Ergo

nil scis. Si efficientem, & finalem ad rei cognitionem non arbitraris necessarias, cur non distinxisti in definitione tua? ego enim omnes intelligebam cum absolute protulisti, Rem per causas cognoscere. Sed & alibi ille omnes comprehēdit & numerat, efficientem, materialem, formalem, & finalem, cum dixerit, tunc rem nos cognoscere putare, cum eius primam causam tenemus. At do tibi (quamuis dari nec debeat, nec licite possit) efficientem & finalem non necessarias esse. Supersunt duae, materialis, & formalis, quas credo intelligis / / cognoscendas esse. Sed istud minus. Si formam 21 scire velis, per causas ipsius scias oportet, ex definitione tua. Non per efficientem & finalem, ut antea. Ergo per materialem & formalem. At non habet. Non igitur scies. Quod si hanc non scias, nec id cuius forma est scies: ignoratis enim partibus, ignoratur totum. De materia idem dicam, quae adhuc simplicior est, minusque Ens, & cuius forsan nulla est causa, saltem efficiens, materialis, & formalis secundum Aristot. De finali enim dubitari possit. Quid dicis? Sufficit quaecumque causarum cognitio ad rei scientiam habendam, licet non sit perfecta. Fabulae sunt. Impossibile est totum perfecte cognoscere, quin partes perfecte cognoscas. Quod si id etiā dederim: quaero an formae & materiae scientia haberi possit? Concedes, ut qui omnia scire te profitearis. Iterum, an per causas? Si non: ergo definitio tua nulla. Si sic: de illis causis repeto an sciri possint? Non minus quam illa, imo magis: simpliciora enim per te notiora natura sunt, proindeque ex se scibilia magis. An per causas? In infinitum. Nulla ergo definitio. Imo & nil scis ex iisdem rationibus. Atque obiecit ille quidem alias hoc ipsum sibi, Si scientia vere solum illa est, quae per demonstrationem habetur, principia autem prima demonstrari non possunt, non horum erit scientia, nullaque proinde scientia erit. Sed non satisfecit, dicens, non omnem scientiam esse demonstratiuam, sed eorum quae mediis vacant indemonstrabilem esse. Nam inde sequitur non simpliciter prolatum illud, Scire est rem per causas cognoscere, verum esse: & illud, Scientia est habitus acquisitus per demonstrationem: si aliqua est quae per demonstrationem non habe- / / tur. Melius autem dixerat alibi, excusarique poterat, si 22 semper eodem modo loquutus fuisset, perfecteque aliquando scientiam explicuisset. Nunc autem cum ubique vagus, confusus,

& inconstans sit, excusationi locum praecludit. Dixerat porro, Rerum quarum sunt principia, causae, & elementa, scientiam ab horum cognitione pendere. Quod ridiculum est quomodo exponant eius sequaces. Ad verba enim & syllogismos res deflectentes (antiquo obsopiti errore in eoque putrescentes) principia interpretantur, scientiae cuiusque primas, notasque, & suppositas propositiones: quas ipsi etiam principia & dignitates vocant: causas explicant medias propositiones, quae inter illa fiunt & rem probandam: elementa vero, subiectum, praedicatum, copulam, medium, maiorem extremitatem, minoremque. An non subtile commentum hoc est? an potius delirium? sic eorum princeps fallitur modicum. Illi non eum percipientes nec sequentes, adhuc magis: quousque tandem in tot vanitates prolabuntur, sensim a veritate deficiendo. Sed ad illum redeamus. Non excusari potest. Superius dicebat primorum principiorum scientiam esse, sed indemonstrabilem. Alibi primorum principiorum cognitionem intellectum, non scientiam vocat: male tamen. Horum enim, sicut & aliorum, si haberetur, perfecta scientia esset. Nunc autem cum horum non habeatur, nec eorum etiam habetur quorum haec principia sunt. Vnde sequitur nihil sciri. Deinde quid scientia aliud est, quam intellectus rei? tunc enim scire aliquid dicimus, cum id intelligimus. Sed nec verum est duplicem esse scientiam. Vna
23 enim & simplex esset, si quae esset, sicut & una / / visio, duplex tamen habendi modus: unus simplex, cum simplicem rem cognosceremus, ut materiam, formam, & spiritum, si velis: alius compositus, ut ita dicam, cum compositam rem, quam prius explicare oporteret, & singulas partes cognoscere, tum demum totum. Vltimum autem hunc modum semper praecedit primus: non tamen hunc semper sequitur ille. In his autem omnibus Demonstratio nil deseruit aliud, quam forsan ostendere rem sciendam. Sed iam satis: plura enim diximus, quam nihil scienti conuenire videbatur. At non praeter rationem dicta haec sunt. Hucusque enim aliorum ignorantiam, circa scientiae definitionem, cognitionemque subinde ostendi: nunc meam proferam, ne solus ego scire aliquid videar. Ex quo videre poteris quam inscientes simus.[6] Quae enim hucusque a pluribus recepta fuere, mihi falsa

[6] scimus *1581*[2], simus *Thomson*.

videntur, ut iam ostendi: quae deinceps dicam, vera. Forsan contrarium iudicabis tu, & fortassis verum erit hoc: unde sequitur
confirmatio propositi, Nil sciri. Iam igitur quid scire sit videamus,
ut inde an aliquid sciatur magis manifestum euadat. SCIENTIA
EST REI PERFECTA COGNITIO. Ecce facilem, veram tamen
nominis explicationem. Si quaeras genus & differentiam, non
dabo: verba enim haec sunt definito magis obscura. Quid cognitio? Sane nescirem explicare aliter: & si aliter hanc definirem, de
hac iterum definitione idem quaerere posses, & eius partibus. Sic
nunquam finis, perpetua nominum dubitatio. Qua ratione scientiae nostrae tum infinitae, tum omnino dubiae sunt: conantibus
nobis rerum Naturas demonstrare verbis, rursus hae // aliis: quod 24
tum difficile, tum impossibile est. Nil scimus. Alicubi standum
dicis in quaestionibus. Verum, quia aliud non possumus. Sed
nescio quid sit cognitio, defini mihi. Dicerem rei comprehen-
sionem, perspectionem, intellectionem, & si quid aliud est, quod
idem significet. Si de hoc adhuc dubites, tacebo: sed petam a te
aliud. Si dederis, de tuo dubitabo: sicque perpetua laboramus
ignorantia. Quid superest? Extremum remedium: tu tibi ipse
cogita. Cogitasti, menteque forsan cognitionem apprehendisti: sed
nil minus. Ego etiam mihi comprehendisse videor. Quid inde?
Dum de cognitione postea tecum loquor, qualem comprehēdi,
talem suppono: tu contra qualem tu. Hoc ego assero eam esse: tu
contra illud. Quis componet litem? qui nouit quid ipsa vere sit.
Quis ille est? Nullus. Quisque sibi doctissimus videtur: mihi
omnes ignari. Forsan solus ego ignarus sum: sed id saltem scire
vellem. Non possum. Quid igitur dicam deinceps quod ignorantiae suspicione vacet? Nihil. Cur ergo scribo? Quid ego scio. Cum
stultis stultus eris: homo sum: quid faciam? perinde est. Reuertor.
Nihil scimus. Suppone nominis (scientiae) explicationem a me
traditam, ut oratio procedat: hincque colligamus nihil sciri:
supponere enim non est scire, sed fingere: quare ex suppositis
fictiones prodibunt, non scientia. Vide quo nos duxerit oratio iam,
Omnis scientia fictio est. Patet. Scientia per demonstrationem
habetur. Haec definitionem supponit: non possunt enim probari
definitiones, sed debent credi: ergo demonstratio ex suppositis
scientiam supposititiam producet, non firmam & certam. Haec

111

omnia ex te concludunt. Deinde, in omni scientia per te sup-
25 ponenda / / principia sunt, nec de his disputare illi conuenit. Ergo
quae sequuntur ex his supposita erunt, non scita. Quid miserius?
ut sciamus, ignorare oportet. Quid enim supponere aliud est,
quam quae nescimus admittere? Nonne melius esset principia
prius scire? Nego tibi artis tuae principia: proba. Non est
arguendum contra negantes principia, inquis. Nescis probare.
Ignarus es, non sciens. At spectat ad superiorem seu communem
scientiam aliarum probare principia. Ille igitur forsan omnia sciet
qui comunem hanc scientiam habet: tu nihil. Qui enim ignorat
principia, ignorat & rem. Sed quid communis illa scientia est?
Mirum quomodo sibi officia partiantur artifices isti, limitibus se
separant, quemadmodum stultum vulgus sibi tellurem adaptat
partiturque. Quin potius imperium scientiarum struxere: quarum
regina supremusque iudex scientia communis est: ad quam su-
premae deferuntur lites. Haec leges caeteris dat, quas ratas accipere
oportet: nec aliarum alicui in huius messem manum immittere
licet impune, nec inter se sibi. Sic tota vita litigant de subiecto
scientiae cuiusque, nec est qui hanc litem (potius ignorantiam)
dirimat. Hinc si quis de astris in Physica agat, aut in quantum
Physicus, aut in quantum Astrologus, inquiunt, hoc facit: & alius,
hoc ab Arithmetico mutuatur: sed & alius a Mathematico furatur
illud. Quid hoc? An non puerorum fabulae? hi enim in communi
loco, platea, foro, vel campo, hortos struunt, tegulis cancellant, &
quisque alteri sui hortuli aditum interdicit. Video quid hoc. Cum
omnia quisque amplecti non posset: hic sibi partem hanc elegit, ille
26 aliam discerpit. Hinc nihil scitur. Cum enim / / omnia quae hoc in
orbe sunt, in unius compositionem conspirent: nec haec sine illis
stare possunt, nec haec cum illis conseruari: quodque priuatum
gerit munus, diuersumque ab alio: omnia tamē ad unum conferunt: haec causant illa, haec ab illis fiunt. Indicibilis omnium
concatenatio. Nil ergo mirum si ignorato uno, ignorantur &
reliqua. Cuius causa fit, ut qui de astris agit, eorum motus &
causas motuum considerans, quid astrum sit, quid motus a Phy-
sico accipiat quasi probatum: deinde motus solum contempletur
varietatem multitudinemque. De reliquis eodem modo. At hoc
scire non est. Verum enim scire est, rei naturam primum cognosse,

secundo loco accidentia, ubi accidentia res habet. Ex quo sequitur demonstrationem syllogismum scientificum non esse, imo nihil esse, ut quae solum accidens inesse demonstrat secundum te, (mihi enim tantum abest ut aliquid demonstret, ut potius abscondat, nihilque aliud agat quam turbare ingenium) rei vero definitionem supponat. Nihil ergo sciunt quicumque demonstrationibus fidunt, ab eisque scientiam expectant: qui etiam has damnant, nihil per te: & ut modo probabo. Ergo nil scimus omnes. In scientia igitur, si definitionem admittas meam, tria sunt, res scienda, cognitio, & perfectum: quorum quodlibet singillatim[7] nobis expēdendum erit, ut inde colligamus nihil sciri. Res primum quọt sunt? Forsan infinitae, non solum in indiuiduis, sed in speciebus. Negabis infinitas. At non probabis finitas: nec enim vel minimam earum partem numerare potuisti: ego vix hominem, & equum, & canem noui. Ergo de hoc iam nil scimus. Nam nec tu finem omnium rerum vidisti, / / finitas tamen asseris: nec ego earum infinitatem 27 vidi: infinitas tamen esse coniecto. Quid certius? videris tu: mihi nihil. Sed quid infinitas ad rei unius cognitionem, dices, impedire potest? Multum per te: principia enim cognoscere oportet ad cognoscendam rem: forsan materiam & formam: at in infinito infinitae materiae forsan sunt distinctae specie: (quanquam tu materiem specie ab aliquo distingui nolis, ut qui eam omni forma priues: de quo postea). De formis nullum dubium: at de infinito nulla scientia. Sed dices, infinitarum etiam rerum eadem materia esse potest. Verum quidem: sed etiam potest non eadem esse, proindeque multiplex. Aliae enim res forsan sunt a nostris omnino diuersae, quas nullus nostrum nouit. Quod vero potest & esse & non esse, dubium est quod eorum sit. Scientia autem de eo quod est, quodque aliter esse non potest, per te est. Nec necesse est infinitas esse res ut diuersa sit materia: nam & tibi qui finitas credis nondum constat, nec constabit unquam (possum tamen falli) an materia coeli eadem sit quae horum inferiorum. Quin & an non spiritibus propria est materia quamuis simplices dicantur? Sane. Asseris tu plura esse eorum genera, pluresque subinde differentias. Ergo conueniunt in aliquo communi: id per te materia est: differuntque alio: id forma. Accidentia vero nonne & illa habent mate-

[7] sigillatim *1581*[2], singillatim *Thomson*.

riam propriam? Tu vocas genus eorum materiam: differentiam
vero formam. An astrorum eadem quae coeli materia? Non scis:
videtur quod non. Ergo & principia quae, quotque sint ignoratur,
quamuis finitae sint res. Nec stabitur unquam in principiis: sed ho-
28 minis principia sunt elementa: / / horū, materia haec & forma haec:
huius materiae & huius formae alia simpliciora: leonis, asini, ursi
itidem: sic in infinitum. Atque de formis nil dubium, quod in
infinito erunt infinitae. At principia praecognoscere oportet. Dices
elementa non esse principia, de quo postea. Imo nulla erunt principia. Infiniti enim principium nullum est. Sed sint finitae res: nil
scies magis. Nec enim primum nosti principium omnium neces-
sarissimum: quare nec & reliqua, quae ab eo deriuantur. Nil ergo
scimus. Deinde in rebus aliae a se, ex se, in se, per se, & propter se
tantum sunt, (liceat nobis ita loqui) qualem dicunt primam causam
Philosophi, nostri Deum: aliae omnes ab hoc, non a se, non ex se,
non in se, non per se, non sibi solis, nec propter se: sed aliae ab
aliis, ex aliis aliae, aliae in aliis, aliae propter alias. At utrasque res
cognoscere oportet. Deum autem quis perfecte nouit? Non videbit
me homo & viuet. Proinde solum licuit Moysi videre eum per
posteriora, id est, per opera sua. Vnde ille, inuisibilia Dei per ea
quae facta sunt intellecta conspiciuntur. Tum & illud nosse oportet, scilicet quae res quas causent, & quomodo, ut sciamus quid
perfecte. Talis autem concatenatio in rebus omnibus est ut nulla
ociosa sit, quin alteri obsit aut prosit: quinimo & eadem pluribus &
nocere, & iuuare plures nata est. Ergo omnia cognoscere oportet
ad unius perfectam cognitionem: illud autem quis potest? Nusquam
vidi. Et ob hanc eandem rationem scientiae aliae aliis fauent, & una
ad alterius cognitionem confert. Imo, quod magis est, una sine
aliis sciri perfecte nō potest: proindeque coguntur aliae ab aliis
mutuari. Earum namque subiecta sic etiam se habent, ut unum ab
29 alio mutuo de- / / pendeat, & aliud etiam mutuo aliud efficiat.
Vnde sequitur rursus nil sciri. Quis enim omnes nouit scientias?
Subiiciam breue aliquod exemplum, ne haec improbata maneant.
De homine sufficiet. Hic basiliscum odit: fertur enim eum hominis
saliua ieiuni interfici: basiliscus hominem & mustellam, quae eum
sola dicitur perimere: mustella basiliscum & murem: mus mustellam & catum: catus murem & canem: canis catum & leporem:

lepus canem & viuerram. Atque satis haec sint de antipathia. Homo item non quocunque vescitur cibo, delectaturque: sed boue, ariete &c. Haec non quocunque oblato, sed feno, auena, palea: haec iterum non quacumque terra, sed hac vel illa: haec rursus terra non omnia producit, sed haec vel illa: ad quod plurimum confert hoc vel illud coelum. Haec de sympathia. Quomodo haec omnia fiunt? Cuiuslibet horum naturam oportet nosse prius quam hominem probe noscas. Homo item quia nutritur, crescit, viuit, generat, corrumpitur, ratiocinatur, statim quaerendum est de anima, & eius facultatibus. Huius ratione, de plantis, qua anima viuant: de animalibus: de inanimatis, Contrariorum enim eadem est scientia. Generatio autem et[8] corruptio a quo fiunt? a qualitatibus contrariis. Statim de his, de elementis, de superioribus corporibus: nam Sol & homo generant hominem: de introductione animae, de introductione formarum, de actione & passione, de qualitate, de quantitate, de situ, de relatione: quia sedet, quia generat, quia calescit. Illud rursus quia in quiete fit: istud in instanti: hoc in tempore: vidēdum quid tempus. Statim de coelis & eorum motibus: tempus enim est, / / ait ille, (licet male,ut suo loco videbimus) numerus motus 30 secundum prius & posterius. Quia mouetur motu recto & deorsum: illico quid sursum, deorsum: de centro mūdi, de polis, partibus eius. Quia videt, & hoc media luce: statim de coloribus, de spiritibus, & speciebus, de luce, & luminoso:,[9] de Sole, astrisque. Quia corpus est, & est in loco: de corpore, de substantia, de loco, de vacuo. Quia locus finitus dicitur: de finito & infinito. Quia generat & generatur: statim de causis omnibus usque ad primam. Quia ratiocinatur, de anima intellectiua & eius facultatibus, de scientia & de scibili, de prudentia & reliquis habitibus, ut vocant. Quia interficit: quia nunquam contentus viuit: quia pro patria vitam morti exponit: quia subleuat aegros & egentes: de bono, & malo: de ultimo & summo bono: de virtute, & vitio: de animi immortalitate. Quodcunque autem horum secum ducit omnes alias res, quas prosequi fastidiosum esset. Idem dicas de quacumque minima re. Id exemplo familiarissimo communis horologij cognosces. Si

---

[8] est *1581*[2], et *1581*[1].
[9] luminoso:, (double punctuation in *1581*[2]).

enim quomodo horas pulset scire velis, oportet ut a prima ad ultimam omnes circunspicias rotas: quidque primam moueat, & quomodo haec aliā, & haec alias duas, sicque usque ad ultimam per-
uenire. Quod si praeter id quod horas pulset horologium, easdem
etiam exterius in gnomone digito ostendat: monstret praeterea Lu-
nae motus, auctionem, defectionemque: Solis item per Zodiacum
discursum perfectum eodem quo in coelo fit tenore, (quae omnia
& plura alia nos in portatili horologio secundum verum astrorum
cursum ostendi vidimus) sane rem difficiliorem efficies, nec vel
31 mini- / / mā earum rerū quomodo fiat percipere poteris, quin totā
fabricam ex integro soluas, examines, singulasque partes & earum
munus teneas. Idipsum tibi repraesentabit vitreus orbis admirabili
artificio ab eximio Archimede Syracusano constructus: in quo omnes sphaerae, Planetaeque eodem modo quo in vera hac machina,
& mouebantur & conspiciebantur: flatu per canaliculos & ductus
quosdam omnia symmetrice agente. An non oportebat, si quomodo id fieret nosse vellet aliquis, totam perfecte machinam,
eiusque partes usque ad minutissimam cum muniis callere suis?
Idem in nostro hoc orbe existimandum est. Quid enim in eo
inuenias quod non moueat & moueatur, mutet & mutetur, aut
unum aut utrumque patiatur? sed quanto plura in vero orbe & sunt
& fiunt quam in Syracusano vitreo, tanto difficilius est illum, quam
hunc totum complecti: non tamen minus necessarium ei qui scire
vult. Vide quo peruentum sit. Vna solum scientia est, aut esset si
haberi posset, in natura rerum: non plures, qua omnes res perfecte
cognoscerentur: quando una sine aliis omnibus perfecte cognosci
non potest. Eae quas habemus vanitates sunt, rapsodiae, fragmenta
obseruationum,[10] paucarum & male habitarum: reliqua imagina-
tiones, inuenta, fictiones, opiniones. Vnde non inepte omnino
dicebat ille, hominum sapientiam stultitam esse apud Deum. Sed
reuertamur unde digressi eramus, hincque collige unā esse omnium
rerum scientiam. Quotiescumque enim de re aliqua incidit sermo,
huius occasione de alia agendum, de alia iterum propter hanc, &
tertio propter istam de alia. Sic in infinitum iremus, nisi in medio
32 cursu pedē / / retraheremus, & id non sine scientiae detrimento.

---

[10] observationem *1581²*, observationum *1618 Errata*.

Vnde lex illa in scientiis consurgit, Non omnia in omnibus. Videbant enim omnia ex omnibus sequi, ne tamen eorum scientia finem non haberet, limites statuere conati sunt, quos tamen seruare nequeunt: (quomodo enim limites seruabunt, quos natura non patitur?) unde eadem necesse est millies in eodem opere, & in diuersis repetere: quod facile ostenderemus in quolibet authore, sed longum esset. Nonne omnia quae in praedicamentis, dixit ille eadem in Physicis, & Metaphysicis repetit? & quae in his, in aliis passim? Galen. autem noster quam prolixus est? Vix caput unum inuenias in quo non legas: Et de his quamuis alibi fusius dixerimus, non nocebit si iterum breuiter quod ad propositum spectat repetamus: Vel, Hoc sufficit quod ad praesens institutum attinet, reliqua enim tali in lib. reperies: aut denique similem aliam dictionem. Quod manifeste ostendit, ad unius rei cognitionem aliarum etiam cognitionem necessariam esse, quando & ad unius productionem, conseruationem, aut destructionem, omnium aliarum concursus necessarius est, ut in rerum examine fusius probabimus. Idem confirmant etiam qui disputationem de re aliqua suscipiunt: tantum enim abest ut, si hominem animal esse probare instituant, id efficiant, ut contra per medios syllogismos discurrentes ab uno in aliud, tandem deueniant vel ad coelum, vel ad inferos, secundum media quibus utitur probans, & secundum negata ab alio. Quod enim demonstrationis inuentor de eis tradit, per medias veniendum ad prima usque principia, ibique standum, fictio est: sicut & alia circa / / eandem rem dicta. Nec enim talia sunt certa, numerata, 33 atque ordinata media, per quae libere possimus procedere: neque principia in quibus animus quietus contentusque sistere possit. Quod si tu talia aliqua habes, gratum facies, si mihi mittas. Expectasne adhuc ampliorem inscitiae nostrae probationem? Dabo. Vidisti iam difficultatem in speciebus. De indiuiduis autem fateris nullam esse scientiam, quia infinita sunt. At species nil sunt, aut saltem imaginatio quaedam: sola indiuidua sunt, sola haec percipiuntur, de his solum habenda scientia est, ex his captanda. Sin minus, ostende mihi in natura illa tua uniuersalia. Dabis in particularibus ipsis. Nil tamen in illis uniuersale video: omnia particularia. In his autem quanta varietas conspicitur? Mirum. Hic omnino fur: ille homicida: ille non natus nisi ad Grammaticam: alius scientiis

omnino ineptus: ab incunabulis hic crudelis & truculentus: nulla
arte ille a vino arceri potest: a venere iste: a ludo hic: alter aut
viso, aut etiam olfacto fele animo linquitur: ille pomum nunquam
gustauit, nec alium gustantem videre potest: alter carnem: alter
caseum: alius pisces: ex quibus omnibus nos quosdam nouimus.
Alius numismata, vitrum, pennas, lateres, lanam, omnia denique
vorat & coquit indifferenter: ille rosae odore aut aspectu labitur in
syncopen: iste foeminas odit: haec cicuta nutritur: hic diu noctu-
que stertit: ego saepius libros iratus proieci, aufugi musaeolum:
at in foro, in campo, nunquam nihil cogito, nec unquam minus
solus, quam cum solus: nec minus otiosus, quam cum otiosus:
34 mecum hostem habeo, non possum euadere: & ut / / ille ait, meip-
sum vito fugitiuus ut erro, Iam sociis quaerens, iam somno fallere
curam. Frustra: nam comes atra premit, sequiturque fugacem.
Denique sunt homines quidā, quos maxime dubites an rationales,
an potius irrationales vocare debeas. At contra bruta videre est,
quae maiore cum ratione rationalia dicere possis quam ex hominibus aliquos. Respondebis unam hyrundinem non facere ver, nec
unum particulare destruere uniuersale. Ego contra contendo uniuersale falsum omnino esse, nisi omnia quae sub eo continentur ita
ut sunt & amplectatur, & affirmet. Quomodo enim verum esset,
dicere omnē hominem rationalem, si plures aut solus unus irrationalis sit? Si dicas, in hoc homine defectum esse non in animo,
sed in corpore eius instrumento, forsan verum dices, sed pro me.
Nec enim homo solus animus est, nec solum corpus, sed utrumque
simul: ergo altero defectuoso, defectuosus homo erit: quare nec
simpliciter homo: corpus enim de essentia eius est, quemadmodum & animus, & non corpus simpliciter, sed tale corpus. Ex
quo sequitur ridiculum esse quorundam dictum, Animam scilicet
hominis sub figura rotunda vel qualibet alia, quam ea qua omnes
sumus, esse posse: illudque hominem fore. Qualem nescio an ipsi
quandoque viderint. Si viderunt, mihi fauent. Nam illum eiusdem
rationis cum nostris esse non crediderim: hominem tamen dicunt,
& verum. Quis scit? Nullus. Si non viderunt, cur talem fingunt,
qualem forsan natura producere non potest? Quod si potest, quomodo aeterna erit propositio illa, Anima actus corporis physici
35 organici &c? Haec / / illorum sciētia est. Quin & illud absurdius

multo est, Nullis scilicet existentibus hominibus verum esse dicere, Homo est animal. Impossibile enim supponunt ut falsum inferant. Nam si in philosophia loquaris, nunquam homines deerunt: quia mundus est aeternus: si in fide, an deerit esse Christus dominus? Vides quomodo utrinque impossibile est suppositum tuum. At nonne scis ex praeceptore tuo, possibili posito in esse, nullum sequi inconueniens, impossibili autem admisso, plurima? Sed esto, sit possibile: si homo non est, quomodo homo animal erit? Pro essentia dicunt supponere verbum (Est) ibi, non pro existentia, solumque copulam esse. Proindeque propositionem illam aeternam esse, & in scientiis semper ita sumi: quin & ante creationem hominis veram fuisse propositionem illam: & in mente diuina omnes fuisse rerum essentias. Hinc de Ente & Essentia mira scribunt. Quid magis vanum? Sic verba a propria significatione detorquent & corrumpunt, ut alius ipsorum sermo sit a paterno omnino diuersus, idem tamen. Cumque ad eos accedas ut aliquid discas, verborum, quibus antea usus fueras, significationes sic immutant, ut iam non res easdem & naturales designent, sed illas quas ipsi finxere, quo tu sciendi auidus, harumque nouarum rerum omnino ignarus eos de his subtiliter disputantes & disserentes, qualesque sibi in insomniis apparuere, miro tamen artificio referentes, audias, mireris, colas, reuerearisque ac acutissimos naturae scrutatores. Mirum quanta barbaries. Quid simplicius, quid clarius, quid magis usitatum verbo hoc (Est)? De eo tamen quanta disputatio? Pueri Philosophis do- // ctiores sunt, a quibus si quaeras, an domi 36 pater sit, respondent esse, si sit: si quaeras an nequam sit, negant. Philosophus de nullo homine asserit esse animal. Nec illud absurdum minus est quod quidam astruere conātur, Philosophiam non alio idiomate doceri posse, quam vel Graeco, vel Latino: quia, inquiunt, non sunt verba quibus vertere possis plurima quae in illis linguis sunt, ut Aristotelis ἐντελέχεια, de quo hucusque frustra disputatur quomodo Latine verti debeat: apud Latinos Essentia, Quiditas, Corporeitas, & similia quae Philosophi machinantur: quaeque cum nihil significent, a nullo etiam nec intelliguntur, nec explicari possunt, nedum vulgari sermone verti, qui res solum veras, non fictas nominibus propriis omnes designare solet. Huic adde friuolam aliorum sententiam verbis nescio quam vim propriam assignantium, ut inde dicant nomina rebus imposita fuisse secundum earum naturam. Quo ducti non minus stulte etiam quidam verborum omnium significationes ab aliquo trahere conantur: ut lapis, quia laedat pedem: humus ab humiditate, inquiunt. Et asinus unde? a te, quia sine sensu es: a enim Graece, & Latine saepe priuat: sinus, quasi sensus: ergo asinus, idem est quod sine sensu: & hoc idem quod tu. An non bona est etymologia? De aliis omnibus curiose magis, quam vere aut utiliter idem inquirunt: sicque omnia deriuatiua aut composita faciunt, nullum simplex nec primum: quod quam vanum ignarumque sit quis non videt? Si lapis dictio pro natura rei imposita est, ut dicis: an haec est lapidis natura ut laedat pedem? Non, puto. Sed esto. Quomodo (laedo) 37 naturam damni quod significat / / repraesentat? Quomodo (pes) pedis naturam significat? In infinitum imus. Humus etiam ab humiditate non dicitur: nam contra terra siccissimum est omnium elementorum per te. Sed sit humidissima, & inde dicatur humus, unde dicetur humiditas? Si aliud des unde haec dicatur, idem de illo quaeram. Iterum in infinitum. Si tandem cesses in aliquo, illud quidem non habebit quomodo naturam rei, quam significat, ostendat. Ex eo enim omnia ante illud media naturam rei repraesentare videbantur: quia ab aliis deriuabantur, quae aliquid significabant, usque ad ultimum, quod a nullo alio deriuatur per te: alias enim iterum de illo quaererem. Quot autem simplicia sunt? fere omnia. Praeterea si (panis) pro rei natura impositus est, quid Graece ἄρτος aut Britanice Bara, aut Vasconice Ouguia: quorum diuersitas in sonitu, in literis, in accentu tanta est, ut nullo communicare dicas? Si unam solum dicas linguam pro rerum natura impositam esse, cur non item aliae? aut quae illa? Si dicas Adami primam, verum quidem est: poterat enim, quia rerum naturas nouerat, ut testatur author Pentateuchi: & tunc sane desiderandum esset ut Philosophia sua, aut quam habemus, suo etiam idiomate conscripta esset. Nec, si tu dixisses tunc eam alio sermone doceri vel explicari non posse, quam illo Adami, ego id negarem: sed dicis non nisi Graeco, aut Latino, quae pro rei natura imposita non sunt. Quid quod perpetuo voces corrumpuntur: extantque Galli libri, Hispanique, in quibus verba plurima inuenias, quorum significata 38 omnino ignorātur? Et apud Latinos nonne verba sunt obsoleta / /

plurima, quotidieque de nouo alia finguntur? Idemque in sermone
contingit, atque in aliis rebus ut usu continuo inmutetur, tandem-
que tanta mutatio cōtingit, ut omnino degeneret & diuersus fiat:
unde est quod periit iam omnino antiquus sermo Latinus in Italum
nunc vulgarem transformatus: Graecus eodem modo. Si qui autem
libri superstitē utramque linguam seruant, adeo ab antiquo illo
splendore differunt, ut si nobis sua lingua loquētibus adessent
Demosthenes, aut Cicero, forsan deriderent. Nec hoc solum, sed
hic ab illo mutuatur dictiones plurimas, ille ab alio: sicque puto
nullam legitimam synceramque nobis superesse linguam. Nulla
ergo vocibus rerum naturas explicandi facultas, praeter eam, quam
ab arbitrio imponentis habent: eademque vis [cani] ad significan-
dum panem est ac canem, si ita placeat. Sunt quidem verba quaedam ab effectu, vel accidente aliquo rebus imposita, non tamen a
natura. Quis enim rerum naturas nouit, ut secundum eas nomina
illis imponat? Aut quae nominibus cum rebus est communitas?
Illa vero sunt quae vocamus propria, ut si hominem risibilem
voces, vel flebilem: in quibus tamen primitiua, scilicet risus &[11]
fletus, nullam vim habent, nisi quam ab arbitrio nostro accepere.
Sic alipes Mercurius, armiger, & similia composita. Sunt & alia
quae similitudine sonitus, voces imitantur eorum quae significant,
proinde Onomatopeicae dicta, ut cucurire gallinarum, crocitare
coruorum, rugire leonum, balare ouium, latrare canum, hinnire
equorum, mugire boum, frendere porcorum, stertere dormiētium,
susurrus aquarum, sibilus, tinnitus, timpanū, / / clangor, & ille, 39
Baubantem est timidi pertimuisse canem: & alter, Et tuba terribili
sonitu taratantara dixit: & alius, Quadrupedante putrem sonitu
quatit ungula campum. Neque in his quoque aliqua naturae demonstratio eorum quae significant, sed similitudo sonorum. Minus etiam in verbis omnibus deriuationem quaerere oportet: aliter namque iretur in infinitum. Sed longius processimus, quam
putaueram. Reuertor. Hominum ipsorum quanta varietas etiam
in specie? alicubi omnes breuissimi sunt, pygmaei dicti: alibi prae-
grandes, Gigantes: alij omnino nudi incedunt: villosi[12] alij, totoque

---

[11] & & *1581*[2], & *1636*.
[12] vilosi *1581*[2], villosi *1618 Errata.*

121

corpore capillati: quin alij omnino sermonis expertes ferarum modo in syluis degunt, cauernis conduntur, aut etiam auium ritu in
arboribus stabulantur, sed & nostros homines si quando contingat
rapere, maxima cum voluptate deuorant: alij de Deo & religione
nil solliciti omnia communia habent, filios quoque & uxores:
vagantur, nec sedem fixam habent. Contra alij Deo & religioni
astricti pro his sanguinem intrepide fundunt. Quisque sibi propriam ciuitatem, domum, foeminam, familiamque habere vult,
habitamque usque ad mortem tuetur: illi post mortem cum amicis
viuis, uxoribus, & supellectile terrae aut igni mandantur: hi nil
horum curantes inhumati manent: alter viuum se laniari, dissecari-
que in partes patitur & conatur: ille fugiēdam mortem omnino
censet. Non finem faceremus si omnes omnium mores recensere
vellemus. An tu his eandem rationem, quā nobis, omnino putes?
Mihi non verisimile videtur. Nihil tamē ambo scimus. Negabis
40 forsan tales aliquos esse homines. Non contendam: sic ab / / aliis
accepi: his sunt pleni antiquorum recentiorumque libri, nec impossibile videtur: quin & aliqui forsan sunt alij magis his a nobis
diuersi in aliqua orbis parte, nobis nondum aperta, aut fuere, aut
erunt. Quis enim de omni quod fuit, quod est, aut quod erit
certum quid proferre potest? Dicebas heri perfecta scientia tua,
imo & a plurimis saeculis, totam terram Oceano circumflecti,
eamque in tres diuidebas partes uniuersales, Asiam, Aphricam,
Europam. Nunc quid dices? nouus est inuentus mundus, nouae
res, in noua Hispania, aut Indiis Occidentalibus, Orientalibusque.
Dicebas etiam Meridionalem & sub Aequatore positam plagam
inhabitalem aestu esse, sub Polis vero & extremis Zonis propter
frigus. Iam utrumque falsum esse ostendit experientia. Strue aliam
scientiam, falsa enim iam prima est. Quomodo ergo aeternas,
incorruptibiles, infallibiles, quaeque aliter habere non possint propositiones tuas asseris miserrime vermis, qui vix quid sis, unde sis,
quo eas, ac ne vix quidem scias? De aliis tum animalium, tum
plantarum speciebus pro diuerso orbis situ idem dicere licet: tanta
quippe in diuersis plagis eiusdem, ut vocas, speciei dissimilitudo
est, ut diuersas dicas species, & sunt. Nil tamen ambo scimus:
quippe qui formas utriusque non cognoscamus, per quas ipsae
distinguuntur. Addit etiam ad ignorantiam nostram rerum ali-

quarum prohibitus accessus nobis, vel propter locum, vel propter
tempus, quarum maxima pars est. Hinc eorum quae in mari, quae
in intima terra, quae in supremo aëre, quae denique in supremis
corporibus fiunt & sunt, maxima dubitatio. Nec sine ratione: omnis enim a sensu / / cognitio est: a quo cum illa percipi non possint, 41
nec sciri subinde possunt: imo multo minus quam quae nobiscum
sunt. De his enim quod sint non dubitamus, de illis autem plurima dicuntur, quae esse nec certum est, nec ratio id cogit: quin
quandoque contrarium, ut suo loco dicemus. Huc etiam spectat
de pluralitate mundi quaestio, de eo quod extra coelum est, &
similes. Nec hoc solum, sed & in diuersis terrae partibus (quas
unus & idem omnes perlustrare non potest, necessarium tamen
est) propter nuper dictam rerum varietatem variae sunt hominum
opiniones, nullaque scientia. De his vero quae longo tempore ante
nos facta sunt, de his quae postea fient, quis certi quid asserere
potest? Huius occasione tanta hucusque de mundi principio, aut
aeternitate inter Philosophos disceptatio, de eiusdem duratione &
fine controuersia: cui finem nullus imposuit, quod sciamus, nec
forsan imponet ex scientia. Quomodo namque corruptibilis de
incorruptibili, finitus de infinito: denique qui per instans solum
viuit ac si non viueret, est quasi non esset, de sempiterno certo
quid ostendere valeat? Cuius (an sit) quaestio, quemadmodum &
reliquorum, fundamentum est aliarum quaestionum, de qua penitus nil ipse nouit, nec nosse potest. At de his omnibus nobiliores
sunt, maximeque necessariae ad aliarum omnium rerum cognitionem in Philosophia dubitationes, quarum ignorantia aliarum
subinde inscitiam inducit. Quod vero nil perfecte sciri possit, humano modo, apparet ex eo quod Peripateticus cum reliqua schola
conantur innumeris rationibus ostendere mundum esse aeternum,
nec habuisse initium, nec habiturum finem: idque persua- / / sum 42
est Philosophis. Vnde Romanus ille Naturalem hystoriam suam
inde auspicatus est. Et certe si humana ducaris ratione potius id
iudicabis. Nam venisti in mundum iam factum, & pater tuus, &
aui tui: discesseruntque illi, & discedes tu: videsque alios & nas-
centes & morientes, ipso manente. Nec est aliquis qui asserat aut
voce, aut scripto, se aut vidisse mundi principium, aut vidisse
alium qui viderit, aut qui audierit ab alio se vidisse. Et, ut dicit

Sapiens, Generatio praeterit, & generatio aduenit, terra autem in aeternum stat. Oritur Sol & occidit, & ad locum suum reuertitur, ibique renascens gyrat per medium, & flectitur ad Aquilonem. Lustrans uniuersa in circuitu pergit spiritus, & in circulos suos reuertitur. Omnia flumina intrant in mare, & mare non redundat. Ad locum unde exeunt flumina reuertuntur, ut iterum fluant. Cunctae res difficiles, non potest eas homo explicare sermone. Audisti sententiam Philosophorum: tamen vides contrarium omnino esse verum, secundum fidem, mundumque & creatum esse, & finem habiturum, saltem secundum qualitates quas modo habet. Non enim anihilabitur, iuxta illud regij prophetae, Et sicut opertorium mutabis eos, & mutabuntur &c. Quae quidem omnia sciuntur ex reuelatione diuina, non ex humano discursu. Nec enim id fieri potest. Vnde diuinus legislator Moses, diuinam hystoriam suam diuino efflatus spiritu diuine a mundi creatione orditur, contra omnino ac fecit Plinius. Proinde excusationem aliquam habet Philosophorum opinio: sed nullam pertinacia in non credendo, &
43 contumacia in fidem. Sed regrediamur. / / Est & alia ignorantiae nostrae causa, rerum quarundam tam magna substantia, ut a nobis omnino percipi non possit: quo in genere Philosophorum Infinitum est, si quod illud est: nostrorum Deus, cuius nulla mensura, nulla finitio, nec subinde a mente comprehensio aliqua esse potest. Nec immerito: comprehēdentis enim ad comprehensum proportio certa esse debet, ut aut comprehendens comprehenso maius sit, aut saltem aequale (quamuis hoc vix fieri posse videatur, ut aequale aliud aequale comprehendat, ut videbimus in tractatu de loco: sed nunc demus): nobis autem cum Deo nulla proportio, quemadmodum nec finito cum infinito, nec corruptibili cum aeterno: denique eius collatione nihil potius sumus quam aliquid. Hac eadem ratione ille omnia nouit, ut qui omnibus maior, superior, praestantior, aut melius, ne collationem cum creaturis facere videar, maximus, supremus, praestantissimus sit. Quaecumque summo huic opifici propinquiora sunt, ea ratione nobis incognita etiam sunt. Est aliud rerum genus his omnino aduersum, quarum tam minutum esse est, ut vix a mente comprehendi possit. Et harum maxima copia, cognitio maxime necessaria ad scientiam, fere tamen nullam habemus. Talia forsan sunt accidentia omnia, quae pene nihil sunt:

124

adeo ut hucusque nullus fuerit qui eorum naturam perfecte explicare potuerit, quemadmodum nec reliquarum rerum. Nil scimus;
quomodo ergo explicabimus? Neque mirum est, si aliqui accidentia
nihil in se esse iudicarint, sed solum quaedam nobis apparentia,
quae pro varia nostri conditione dispositioneque varia apparent: ut
qui febrit, omnia calida iudicat: cui lingua / / flaua bile aspersa est, 44
omnia amara. Alia adhuc in rebus superest inscitiae causa nostrae,
aliquarum scilicet perpetua duratio, rursus aliarum perpetua generatio, perpetua corruptio, perpetua mutatio. Ita ut nec illarum
rationem reddere possis, cum non semper viuas: nec harum, cum
& nunquam eadem sint omnino, & modo sint, modo non sint.
Hinc fit ut de generatione & corruptione disputatio sub iudice
adhuc sit, de qua alibi quid sentiamus proferemus. Quot generationis? quot corruptionis modi? Illa ex semine, ex ouis, ex fimo,
ex putredine, ex rore, ex puluere, ex limo, ex halitu, ex carie,
ex pluribus aliis. Haec a calore, frigore, ruptione, dissolutione,
oppressione, nec certus forsan numerus est. Si de phoenice verum
dicunt, ex cinere combusti parentis oritur vermis, ex quo alius fit
phoenix. Vermiculi qui nobis sericum faciunt omnino exsiccantur,
post longum tempus renascuntur, tanquam ex semine, ex granulis
quibusdam alij. Struthium oua fixe inspiciendo animare ferunt:
ursum lambendo efformare catulum. Ficus, nuces, ligna in vermes
abeunt, & lapidescunt. Arborum folia quarundam Iuuernae fluuio
imminentium, si in eum cadant, piscium naturam subeunt. Aliarum plurium frondes in terram cadentes volitantia animalia efficiūtur. Gallae, triticum, folliculi lentisci, & populi, medulla cardui
fullonum, caseus, caro, terebinthus in vermes mutantur & volucellos. Et, quod magis mirandum, in Britanico Ocoeano, si verum
narrat ille, auis anatis figura, rostro de putridis naufragiorum reliquiis pendet, donec inde soluta pisces ad sui alimoniam quaeritet:
quam Vascones Ocoeani incolas, Craban, / / Britones, Bernach- 45
iam, vocare ait. Addit & regi Frācisco Galliarum allatam concham,
cui intus anicula fere perfecta erat, quae alarum fastigiis, rostro,
pedibus, haerebat extremis oris ostraci. Oua in Aegyptiis ad Cairum in fornacibus animantur, temperato ignis calore: & alicubi
etiam in fimo. Inter pisces plures non dubito esse, & inter aues
producendi modos. In his autem quae vita carent non pauciores.

125

Destruendi totidem. Inter ortum & interitum quot mutationes fiunt? Innumerae. In viuentibus nutritio perpetua, auctio ad tempus, status, declinatio, generatio, variatio partuum, mutatio, defectus, additio, perfectio morum, actiones, opera diuersa, contraria saepissime in eodem indiuiduo: denique nulla quies. Nec mirum si aliquorum sententia fuerit, de homine uno post horam non asseri posse eundem esse, qui ante horam, non omnino explodenda, imo forsan vera. Tanta quippe est identitatis indiuisibilitas, ut si punctum solum vel addas, vel detraxeris a re quapiam, iam non omnino eadem sit: accidentia vero de indiuidui ratione sunt, quae cum perpetuo varientur, subinde & indiuiduum variari contingit. Scio, dicis, dum eadem forma maneat, idem semper esse indiuiduum: ab illa enim unum quid dicitur: nec accidentium horum minutias identitatem mutare. Dixi identitati nihil mutandum, alias non idem omnino esse. Vna forma unum facit. Eadem forsan informat semper, sed non idem: in hoc enim perpetua mutatio, ut in corpore meo. At ex utroque componor, ex anima praecipue, ex corpore paulo minus, quorū aliquo variato, & ego varior. Sed id
46 alibi latius & oportunius. Atque hucusque de / / totis animalibus. Quod si partes respicias, multo maior dubitatio. Cur sic hae? cur illae? an aliter melius? an peius? cur non plures? cur tot? cur tantae? cur tam paruae? Nunquam finis. In inanimatis idem. Quid igitur fixum de rebus tam mutabilibus, quid determinatum de rebus tam variis, quid certum de rebus tam incertis? Nil sane. Orta hinc proinde est de introductione formarum, earundemque principio tanta disceptatio, quantam nunquam finiet aliquis. Quod si addere velis monstra quae indies fiunt, tot, tamque diuersa, maxime in homine, promiscuos sexus in aliquibus speciebus, & aliarum specierum indiuiduis: mixtas species, ut ex asino & equa mulus, aut ex equo & asina hinnus, ex lupo & cane lycisca, ex tauro & equa hinnulus, quae vulgata sunt apud nos: quanquam & ex canis & vulpis, tigridis, hyaenae, lupique, cum quibus misceri aiunt, coitu tertia species fieri debeat, ut & ex cameli cum equa, galli cum perdice, & si verum est quod de ossifraga dicunt, ex vulture & aquila gignitur. In arboribus eadem mixtio cernitur & plantis aliis, ut in caulorapo, malopersicis, amigdalopersicis, & pluribus aliis, quibus insitione media acquiritur natura inter insitum, & id cui

inseritur. Si denique addas mutationes specierum, ut ex tritico saepe lolium, & ex lolio triticum quandoque, & ex secali auena fit: si mutationes sexus in quibusdam hominibus, a virgine in virum, ut illi dixere, rem omnino difficilem efficies, nec scies quid hoc, quomodo, a quo, quare. Minus ego. Atque in his quae anima carent maior mutatio, maior diuersitas in generatione, in corruptione. Amplius nobis sciendi ansam / / adimunt eiusdem rei varij, 47 multi, sed & contrarij effectus: eiusdem contra effectus variae, multae, sed & contrariae causae. Exemplum unum (ne nimis prolixus sim, cum in rerum examine haec latius discutienda sint) tibi sit calor, qui idem generat, corrumpit: dealbat, denigrat: calefacit, frigefacit: attenuat, incrassat: segregat, congregat: liquat, cogit: exsiccat, humectat: rarefacit, densat: extendit, contrahit: ampliat, coarctat: dulcorat, amaricat: grauat, allevat: mollit, durat: trahit, pellit: mouet, cohibet: laetificat, tristat. Quid denique non agit calor? Hic numen sublunare est, dextera naturae, agens agentium, mouens mouentium, principium principiorum, causa causarum sublunarium, instrumentum instrumentorum, anima mundi. Nec immerito in prima Philosophia antiqui plurimi ignem primum credidere principium. Merito Trimegistus ignem Deum vocauit. Optima cum ratione Aristot. Deum, ardorem coeli potuit appellare, licet coeli ardorem Deum esse non crediderit: proindeque in hoc a Cicerone male taxatur. Quid enim Dei Opt. Max. melius potentiam, virtutem, speciemque aliquam eius ineffabilis diuinitatis nobis suggerat igne? Ipsemet hoc insinuauit, in ardenti rubo fideli seruo se primum ostendens: & in columna ignis dilectum populum per desertum ducens: & in igneis linguis super electorum conuentum descendens. Vides quanta calor agat: simplex tamen accidens est, cuius ratio, sicut & aliarum rerum, incognita est. Quomodo tot obit munia solus? Difficile intellectu, difficilius dictu, difficillimum, vel impossibile forsan, utrumque. Distinguunt tamen id quod per se, ab eo quod ex acci- / / denti fit: varietatem 48 subiecti obiiciunt, quorum quodlibet difficilius est primo. Quis hanc varietatem exacte nouit? Nullus. Solum probabilia quaedam dicunt: quod certo sciunt, nihil. Sed de his postea. Sufficiat nunc nosse, nos nil plane nosse. Eadem ratione a contrariis causis idem productus effectus ambiguitatem nobis parit maximam. Frigiditas

& a motu fit, ut in cordis, thoracis, arteriarum, calidaeque aquae agitatione, & a quiete, ut si homo a motu calens quiescat. Caliditas itidem a motu, in cursu: a quiete, si quiescat cor, aut bullientem aquam non moueas. Nigrities a calore, in Aetiopibus: a frigore, in demortuo, aut diu suspenso membro: praecipue si compressione spiritus per arterias transitus impediatur. Putredo, ab omnibus qualitatibus, dempta siccitate. Nec hoc solum, sed unum contrarium ab alio contrario producitur: calor a frigore, in calce frigida macerata, in nobis, fontibus, terra, hyberno tempore: unde sententia, Ventres hyeme & vere calidissimi. Frigus a calore, in cōbustis corporibus calidis, in Aetiopibus, qui frigidi sunt interne, & nos etiam aestate. Quomodo haec fiant penitus non intelligo. Ergo nec alij? Non necessario concludo. Videtur tamen. Quid ipsi de his[13] dicāt audio: non tamen propterea rem magis cognosco. Idipsum ego cogitabam antea: sed non satiabat animum. Nam si quid perfecte cognouissem, non negassem, imo vehementer clamassem prae laetitia: nil enim foelicius mihi euenire potuerit. Nunc autem perpetuo angor moerore, desperans me quid perfecte scire posse. Aut ergo solus ego omnium ignarissimus: aut mecum omnes alij. Vtrumque credo verum. Sed scirem tamen aliquid, si alij etiam aliquid / / sciunt: nec enim verisimile est mihi soli omnino aduersam fuisse naturam. At nil omnino scio. Neque tu. Plures aliae sunt in rebus nobis occasiones ignorandi, quae & longum, & inutile esset omnes huc transferre, cum in singulis earum tractatibus eas tibi videre liceat, & ipse ubique ostendam ubi de eis sermo fuerit. Solum unam aut alteram adhuc addam praecipuas. Rerum varietas, multiplex forma, figura, quantitas, actiones, usus tot tamque diuersi mentem sic nobis circumueniunt, aut melius, distrahunt, ut secure non possit quid vel proferre, vel sentire, quin ex alia parte obsideatur, & cogatur opinioni[14] cedere: sicque hinc inde varia nunquam sistitur. Si asserat albedinem (ut de coloribus sufficiat exemplum adduxisse) a calore fieri, arguit eam nix, glacies, Germani: si a frigore, cinis, calx, gypsum & os, usta. Si ab humiditate, haec: si a siccitate, illa. De nigredine totidem contingunt dubita-

---

[13] de de his *1581*[2], de his *1636*.

[14] opinioni *1581*[2] *Errata* (opinione *1581*[2] *text*); the alteration may be regretted in the absence of *e.g. alterius*; cf. *sentire*, above.

tiones. Quid vero dicas de mediis? Quam temperiem illis assignabis? Atque extrema adhuc videntur manifestam habere causam, ut
nix frigus, cinis calorem: quia utrumque sensu deprehenditur.
Quid vero dicas de maculatis animalibus panthera, pardo, cane, &
similibus? Quid de herbis, dracunculo, carduo argentato, trifolio
maculato? Quid de floribus vetonicae altilis, violaeque variegatis?
Quid de turcico phaseolo? Quid de auibus, pauone, psittaco? An
pauoni, maculatis floribus, pardo, in eadem pinna, flore eodem,
eodem capillo, diuersa assignabis temperamenta? Atque hi permanentes colores sunt. Quid de Iride dices, de columba variegata,
de vitro aqua pleno, & alio sine aqua: quae varie soli exposita, / / 50
aut ex vario videntis situ tam varios proferunt colores? Merito
mutus eris, ut & ego. In omnibus aliis, quae supra enarrauimus,
multo magis. Nec unquam finis: quo plus scrutamur, plures sese
offerunt tricae, magis confundimur, difficilius expedimur. Vbi
enim multitudo, ibi confusio. Sic non immerito Philosophiam
nostram liceat conferre Minois labyrintho: in quem ingressi regredi
non possumus, nec explicare nos: si pergamus, in Minotaurum
incidimus, qui nobis vitam adimit. Hic finis studiorum nostrorum,
hoc praemium irriti & vani laboris, perpetuae vigiliae, labor, cu-
rae, solicitudo, solitudo, priuatio omnium deliciarum, vita morti
similis, cum mortuis degendo, pugnando, loquendo, cogitando, a
viuis abstinere, propriarum rerum curam ponere, animum exer-
cendo corpus destruere. Hinc morbi: saepe delirium: semper mors.
Nec labor improbus aliter omnia vincit, nisi quia vitam adimit,
mortem accelerat, quae ab omnibus liberat. Sic qui moritur omnia
vicit: tantumque abest ut verum sit quod ille dicit, ut contra omnino eueniat. Ait autem

> Ad summam sapiens uno minor est Ioue, diues,
> Liber, honoratus, pulcher, rex denique regum.
> Praecipue sanus: nisi cum pituita molesta est.

Vide quomodo pituitam coactus aperuit tandem. Sed alibi contrarium dicitur, & verius.

> Ipse licet venias Musis comitatus Homere,
> Si nihil attuleris, ibis Homere foras.

129

Et idem Horat. melius inferius

> 51

> *Scilicet uxorem cum dote, fidemque, & amicos,*
> *Et genus, & formam regina pecunia donat. / /*
> *At bene nummatum decorāt Suadela, Venusque.*

Verum quidem id est nunc quod & ille alibi.

> *Curia pauperibus clausa est, dat census honores,*
> *Inde grauis iude, inde seuerus eques.*
> *In pretio pretium nunc est, dat census honores,*
> *Census amicitias, pauper ubique iacet.*

Nihili fit doctrina, & cedunt armis togae, concedunt laureae linguae. Nauci fiunt literati. Quid igitur nos consumimus? Nescio. Sic fata ferunt. Dedit Deus filiis hominum occupationem hanc pessimam, ut in ea occuparentur. Cuncta fecit bona in tempore suo: & mundum tradidit disputationi eorum, ut non inueniat homo opus quod operatus est Deus ab initio usque ad finem. Non absimilis etiam videtur eadem Philosophia (ut unde digressi eramus regrediamur) Hydrae Lerneae, quam Hercules expugnauit. Nostram autem non est qui vincat. Abscisso capite uno, emergunt centum ferociora semper. Deest enim mentis ignis, qui perfecte rem unam cognoscens, reliquis difficultatibus pullulandi occasionem auferat. Concludamus. Cognitio omnis a sensu trahitur. Vltra hāc, omnia confusio, dubitatio, perplexitas, diuinatio: nil certum. Sensus solum exteriora videt: nec cognoscit. Oculum nunc sensum voco. Mens a sensu accepta considerat. Si hic deceptus fuit, illa quoque: sin minus, quid assequitur? Imagines rerum tantum respicit, quas oculus admisit: has hinc inde spectat, versat, inquirendo, quid hoc? a quo tale? cur? Et hoc tantum. Nec enim videt aliquid certi. Nonne hoc vult illius fabula? in qua grus vulpem ad prandium 52 inuitans, ei scyphum angusti oris vitreum pulte plenum / / obiecit: ad quam vulpes linguam, osque admouens, aliquid prehendere eius, quod videbat, ferculi cogitans, irrito conatu, vindictam grui, similem ab eadem vulpe antea passae iocum, dedit. Simili ratione pictis uuis aues ille delusit: dum hae rostro impetentes, ut comederent, rostrum tabulae illidunt. Alter vero istum, velo sic affabre delineato, ut verum videretur, decepit: dum hic, quasi iam vicisset tumidus, accurrens videndae picturae cupidus, velo coopertam credens, manum tabulae admouet ut velum amoueat, tabulamque offendit solam. Sic nobis natura res obiicit cognoscendas. Et hoc dicebat ille alibi: intellectum nostrum ad rerum naturas, sicut nicticoracis oculum ad Solis lumen, se habere. Per simulacra de rebus indicat. An ergo rectum potest esse iudicium? Tolerabile id esset, si omnium rerum, quas scire cupimus, simulacra a sensu haberemus. Nunc autem contra, praecipuarum rerum nulla habemus. Solum accidentium, quae ad rei essentiam, ut dicunt, nihil conferunt: a qua vera scientia est: vilissimaque sunt omnium entium. Ab his de aliis omnibus coniectare oportet. Quae ergo sensibilia sunt, crassa, abiecta, (ea sunt accidentia, compositaque) nobis utcumque nota sunt. Quae contra spiritalia, tenuia, sublimia, (ea sunt principia compositorum, coelestiaque) nullo modo. Haec tamen natura sua cognoscibilia magis sunt: quia perfectiora, magis entia, simpliciora, quae tria perfectam cognitionem producunt. Nobis minus: quia a sensibus magis remota. Quae autem his magis propinqua, nobis magis cognita: non alia ratione, quam quia a sensu melior dependet cognitio nostra. Natura autem sua mini- / / me cognoscibilia: quia imperfectissima, fere nihil. Ens vero 53 cognitionis omnis: imo actuum omnium & motuum obiectum, subiectum & principiū est. Vides quāta in rebus nobis ignorādi occasio praebetur. Videbis melius ubi ad earū explicationem venerimus. Haec enim uniuersaliter solum dicta sint. At haec non demōstrant, sciri nihil: Nec demonstrare id proposui: (ut, demonstrare, tua significatione utar) nec possem. Nam nihil scitur. Sat est obiecisse tibi difficultates. Si has vincere possis, aliquid scies. Sed non poteris: nisi tibi clanculum demissus alius de nouo sit spiritus. Potest forsan id fieri: sed nondum vidi. Nunc vero de eo quod est, non[15] de eo quod potest esse, agimus. Atque haec quae in rebus sunt, minima sunt, si eis, quae in cognoscente sunt, obstaculis conferantur. Qui namque perfecta, acutissimaque mente praeditus esset, inculpatoque sensu, forsan posset omnia vincere (ut tibi hoc gratis concedam: licet non possit, etiam si perfectissima

---

[15] non non *1581*[2], non *1618 Errata*.

omnia nactus sit). Sed nunc contrarium apparet. Secundum igitur
in definitione scientiae erat, cognitio, in qua tria spectantur. Res
cognita, de qua supra: cognoscens, de quo infra, & cognitio ipsa,
quae actus est huius in illam. De hac nunc. Sed breuiter quātum
poterimus. Proprium enim locum obtinet in tractatu de Anima. Et
sane difficilima est, perplexitatisque plena animae, eius facultatū,
actionumque contemplatio: si quae alia. Praecipue vero in hac,
quam nunc quaerimus, cognitione. Cum nil dignius sit anima,
nil excellentius hac unica cognitione. Quam si perfectam haberet,
Deo similis esset: imo Deus ipse. Nec enim perfecte cognoscere
54 potest // quis, quae non creauit. Nec Deus creare potuisset: nec
creata regere, quae non perfecte praecognouisset. Ipse ergo solus
sapientia, cognitio, intellectus perfectus, omnis penetrat, omnia
sapit, omnia cognoscit, omnia intelligit: quia ipse omnia est, &
in omnibus: omniaque ipse sunt, & in ipso. Imperfectus autem,
& miser homunculus quomodo cognoscet alia, qui seipsum non
nosse potest, qui in se est & secum? Quomodo abstrusissima
naturae, inter quae spiritualia sunt, & inter haec anima nostra, qui
clarissima, apertissima, quae comedit, quae bibit, quae tangit,
quae videt, quae audit, penitus non intelligit? Profecto quae nunc
cogito, quae hic scribo, nec ego intelligo, nec tu lecta intellecta
habebis. Iudicabis tamen forsan pulchre & vere dicta. Et ego talia
existimo. Nil tamen uterque scimus. Immerito proinde ille, licet
doctissimus vir, Viuem absurdum vocat: quod mentis naturae per-
scrutationem obscuritatis plenam dicat. Imo ego, si illius opinio
absurda est, absurdissimus esse volo: qui non solum obscuritatis
plenam censeo, sed caliginosam, scabrosam, abstrusam, inuiam,
pluribus tentatam, nulli superatam, nec superandam. Forsan ille,
ut erat acutissimo ingenio, facilem habuit. Et sane perpulchre, &
scite, ut plaeraque omnia de quibus egit, animam persequutus est.
Sed non omnino absolute, non ex ordine, non totam. Plaeraque
protulit, quae verborum ambitu exteriori mentē decipiunt famem-
que affatim ingesta retundere videntur. Quae tamen, si penitius
scruteris, tandem fucum produnt, remque, ut antea, difficilem
relinquunt: ut suo loco ostendemus. Nunc autem quod ad praesens
55 spectat negotium, subiiciamus. Quid cogni- // tio? Rei apprehēsio.
Quid apprehēsio? Apprehende tu ex te. Nec enim ego in mentem

omnia tibi possum ingerere. Si adhuc quaeris, dicam, intellectionem, perspectionem, intuitionem. Si adhuc de his quaeris, tacebo.
Non possum. Non scio. Distingue tamen apprehēsionem, a recep-
tione. Recipit enim canis hominis speciem, lapidis, quanti: non
tamē cognoscit. Imo recipit oculus noster, nec cognoscit. Recipit
anima saepe, & nō cognoscit. Vt cum falsa admittit: cum tardo
ingenio obscura offeruntur. Distingue etiā cognitionem proprie
dictā, quam nunc descripsimus, quam tamen nō cognoscimus ab
alia improprie dicta: qua quis cognoscere dicitur ea, quae alias
vidit, & memoria tenet propriis signis ornata. Nam hac cognitione
dicitur puer cognoscere patrem & fratrem: & canis dominum, &
viam per quam iuit. Diuide denique omnem cognitionem in duas.
Alia est perfecta, qua res undique, intus & extra perspicitur, in-
telligitur. Et haec est scientia, quam nunc hominibus conciliare
vellemus: ipsa tamen non vult. Alia est imperfecta, qua res quo-
modolibet, qualitercumque apprehenditur. Haec nobis familiaris.
Maior tamen, minor, clarior, obscurior, variis denique partita
gradibus, pro variis hominum ingeniis. Hanc duplicem faciunt.
Aliam externam, quae per sensus fit: sensualem subinde vocant.
Aliam internam, quae a mente sola, sed nihil minus. Aliter haec
pensanda sunt. Vnum cognoscens homo est. Vna cognitio in om
nibus his. Eadem enim mens est quae externa, & quae interna
cognoscit. Sensus nil cognoscit: nil iudicat: solum excipit quae
cogniturae menti offerat. Quemadmodum aër non colores, non
lucem videt: quamuis hos excipiat visui // offerendos. Tria tamen 56
sunt quae a mente diuersimode cognoscuntur. Alia omnino externa
sunt, absque omni mentis actione. Alia omnino interna, quorum
quaedam sine mentis opera sunt. Alia non omnino sine hac. Alia
partim externa, partim interna. Deinde, illa se per sensus produnt:
ista nullo modo per hos, sed immediate per se. Haec denique
partim per hos, partim per se. Explicemus haec. Color, sonus,
calor non possunt menti per se offerri, ut ea cognoscat, nisi sui
speciem (per receptionem specierum nunc sensationem fieri recipi-
amus) organo ei recipiendae apto imprimant, quae eadem, vel sibi
similis alia menti offertur, ut eam cognoscat, aut rem, cuius illa est
species, per illam. Quae autem ab intellectu ipso omnino fiunt,
quorumque ille pater est, & quae intus in nobis sunt, nō per alias

133

species, sed per seipsa se produnt & ostendunt intellectui. Talia sunt plurima quae sibi ipse fingit: ut etiam cum pluribus discursibus aliquid noui excogitat, concluditque: & cum intelligit ipse intellectionem suam: & cum coniunctiones, diuisiones, comparationes, praedicationes, notionesque in se facit, ad eaque animum aduertens cognoscit per seipsa. Secundi autem generis sunt omnia interna cum intellectu eadem, quae tamen sine eius opera fiunt, aut sunt: ut voluntas, memoria, appetitus, ira, metus, & reliqua pathemata, & quidquid aliud internum est, quod ab ipso intellectu cognoscitur immediate per se. Sunt denique plurima quae partim per sensus ad eum deueniunt: partim ad eo fiunt. Canis, magnetis natura nullo modo sensu capi potest. Vestita ergo colore, magnitudine, figura, per sensus ad animum defertur. Hic eam illis spoliat 57 // accidentibus. Quod reliquum est considerat, versat, confert: denique naturam quandam sibi fingit communem, ut potest. Intelligentias in coelis mihi inculcant isti Philosophi. Ego audio quid dicant: sed non intelligo. Quamuis aliquid fingo, quod intelligentiam mihi referat. Aërem tactu utcumque percipio: sed sane nullam habet imaginem in mente mea: nisi quandam, quam ego mihi finxi, corporis cuiusdam quasi incorporei: nescio quid. Vacuum eodem modo cogito. Infinitum comprehendo, nunquam finem comprehendendo: sed in media eius cogitatione quiesco coactus, cogitans, infinitum esse, quod in infinitum addendo, in infinitum imaginando, nunquā apprehensione terminabo. Sic speciem fingo terminatā quidē, sed cuius neutra extremitas terminata & perfecta est, sed quasi defectuosa, cum hac notione, quod non terminata sit, nec terminabilis: quia ei in aeternum addi possunt partes infinitae ex utroque extremo. Quid facias? Misera est conditio nostra. In media luce coecutimus, saepe lucem cogitaui, semper incogitatā, incognitā, incomprehensam reliqui. Idem est, si voluntatem, intellectum, aliaque, quae sensibus non percipiuntur, contempleris. Certus quidem sum, me nunc haec, quae scribo, cogitare, velle scribere, & optare ut vera sint, & ut a te approbentur: non tamen hoc nimis curare: sed cum considerare nitor, quid sit haec cogitatio, hoc velle, hoc optare, hoc non curare, sane deficit cogitatio, frustratur volūtas, increscit desiderium, augetur cura. Nil video, quod captare, aut apprehendere possim. Et quidem in hoc superatur cognitio, quae sine sensu de internis sit, ab ea, quae de externis per sensus habetur: in hac enim habet intel- / / lectus quid captet, 58 hominis scilicet, lapidis, arborisque figuram, quam a sensu hausit: videturque sibi hominem comprehendere per eius imaginem. In illa vero, quae de internis fit, nil inuenit quod comprehendere possit: discurritque hinc, inde, more coeci palpans, si quid tenere queat. Et id tantum. Contra autem certitudine vincitur cognitio, quae de externis per sensus habetur, ab ea, quae de internis, quae aut in nobis sunt, aut a nobis fiunt, trahitur. Certior enim sum, me & appetitum habere, & voluntatem: & nunc hoc cogitare, modo illud fugere, detestari, quam templum, aut Socratem videre. Dixi, de his quae in nobis aut sunt, aut fiunt, nos esse certos quod in re sint. Nam de his, quae discursu, & ratiocinatione de rebus iudicando opinamur, &[16] colligimus quod ita in re sint, ut nos iudicamus, incertissimum est. Certiusque multo mihi est, chartam hanc, cui inscribo, & esse, & albam esse, quam eandem ex quatuor elementis compositam: & haec in ea actu esse: & formam aliam ab illis eam habere. Denique, si ea quae in nobis sunt, aut a nobis fiunt, demas: certissima omnium cognitio est, quae per sensus fit: incertissima omnium, quae per discursus. Nam haec non vere cognitio est: sed palpatio, dubitatio, opinatio, coniectura. Ex quo illud rursus emergit, scientiam non esse, quae per syllogismos, diuisiones, praedicationes, & similes alias mentis actiones habetur. Sed si fieri posset ut, quemadmodum externas rerum qualitates quomodocumque sensu percipimus, sic internam rationem cuius-cumque rei amplecteremur, tunc vere scire diceremur. At hoc nullus unquam potuit, quod sciamus. Vnde nihil scimus. De cogni-tione porro, quae de internis: / / & de alia, quam non cognitionem, 59 sed opinionem voco : quae per coniunctiones, negationes, com-parationes, diuisiones, & alias mentis actiones fit, suo loco amplius agetur, ubi utriusque inscitia manifestabitur. Nunc autem de ea solum, quae de externis per sensus habetur, nonnihil dixisse suffi-ciat. In hac duo sunt media: quandoque tria, aut quatuor: sed duo semper, per quae sensatio fit: siue illa intro, siue ex tramissione

---

[16] colligimus *1581²* *Errata* (& colligimus *1581²* *text*); the correction seems mistaken, and I have not followed it.

135

fiat. Nec enim nunc id nos morabitur. Alterum internum, oculus. Alterum externum, aër. An per haec aliquid perfecte cognoscitur? Nequaquam. Nam non per aliud cognosci debet, quod perfecte cognosci debet: sed per seipsum ab ipsomet cognoscente immediate. Nunc autem rerum substantia per accidentia, quae sensibus percipiuntur, se prodit: aut contra his se abscondit. Mens, de rerum substantia per fallaces sensus informatur, aut alias decipitur. Quomodo ergo perfecte aliquid scire possimus? Atque de substantiis rerum scientia esse debet, ex te. De accidentibus vero an perfecta cognitio? Hoc minus. Iuuabat unum, quod scilicet percipiuntur sensu. Nocent plura, quod nil pene sunt: quod ad mentem nec ipsa perueniunt, sed eorum imagines solum: quod denique sensum saepissime fallunt. Hoc propter medij, tam externi, quam interni, varietatem in substantia, situ, & dispositione. Sufficiat de uno, aut altero sensu dixisse. De visu. Qui etiamsi perfectissimo organo fiat, & sensuum certissimus, nobilissimusque sit, saepissime tamen fallitur. Externum medium varium esse solet: varie proinde sensum afficit. Aër, commune, res videtur melius referre:
60 omnis enim coloris expers apparet. Aqua / / aliter representat. Haec naturalia. Artificialia plurima, vitrum, cornu derasum, cristallus, & similia. Cui horū credes? Visu non solum colores discernuntur, sed magnitudo, numerus, figura, motus, distantia, asperitas, luciditas: & quae ad haec referuntur: ut aequalitas, similitudo, velocitas: & horum contraria. Aqua, obscura reddit corpora, bina, maiora, alias minora, alterius figurae, crassiora, mobilia, laeuia. Nec semper hoc, sed alias aliter. Aër quandoque crassa, in Austro, obscura, magna, duplicia in Echo, in Sole, in Luna: quandoque contra. Quin & picta quandoque sculpta, viuaque apparent: sculpta quoque saepissime viua. Vitrum, cornu, & cristallus ut lubet, maiora, minora: crassa, tenuia: eiusdem coloris, varij coloris: pro artificis denique voluntate. Hinc tot speculorum, specillorumque diuersitates. Quod horū melius refert, & verius? Nescias certo. Si aërem dicas, & negauero, non probabis. Sed volo. At quandoque maiora, aliquando minora refert. De colore multo maior dubitatio. Quando illi credendū? Quādo naturae suae magis propinquus, minusque ab extraneo affectus. At quis illius naturam nouit? Quis simplicem vidit? Perpetua mutatio a Sole, Luna, & aliis superne:

inferne, terra, aqua, & mixtis. De vitro & aqua idem censendum:
imo difficilior solutio. Duo enim sunt externa media in visu, qui
per vitrum aut aquā fit, aër, & illa. Monetam vasculo lato impone:
humi residere fac vas: a quo eo te semoueris, donec monetam
non videas amplius. Tunc iube aqua impleri vas: videbis statim
monetā, & maiorē quam antea. Cur nō poteras antea per aërem
videre, cum per te optimū sit medium? Cur nunc / / maior apparet 61
moneta? Nescimus. Opinari licet aliquid tantum: & nos id dicemus
cum ad rerū examen ventum erit. Atque haec de substantia externi
medij: ad quā etiā referuntur crassities, vel tenuitas, magnitudo,
vel paruitas, figura haec, vel illa medij, per quod videtur aliquid.
Haec enim quamuis in aëre non omnia reperiātur: tamen in factitiis
mediis multum variare faciunt rem visam. Crassum enim vitrū
aliter ostendit, quam tenue: quadratum aut rotundum aliter, quam
triangulare: magnum aliter quam paruum. Ostendunt id variae
fabricatae cristalli, vitrique normae, per quas res erectas, vel
inuersas, huius, vel alterius coloris, figuraeque videas: denique
diuersas ab eo quod sunt. Multum mare & ipsum coeruleum
conspicitur, & quae sub eo sunt, eodem colore notat. Paucum
contra album. Quomodo fit id? Nescis. Nec ego. Situs rei varius
variare solet etiam sensum. Medij itidem. In specillis id manifestum est: si oculo admoueas aliter referunt, quam si paululum
remoueas. In aëre non minus. Lucerna cominus aequalis apparet,
oblonga, quieta, parua, fulua: eminus rotunda, radians undique, &
inequalis, scintillans, & mobilis (unde Aristot. demonstrationem
suā assumpsit, ut probet Planetas esse prope nos: quia nō scin-
tillant) magna, clara, & sine colore. Quae longe sunt, obscura
apparent, parua: quae prope nimis, aut non videntur,·aut aliter
quam sunt. Quid facies? Medium tenendum. Vbi est medium
illud? An ad duos passus, aut quolibet alio certo numero? Qui
longe a nobis est, etiamsi celerrime currat, tamen lente admodum moueri videtur: praecipue si deorsum ex / / alto, aut contra 62
inspicias. Quae sensim fiunt sensum effugiunt: ut radij motus in
horologio. Quomodo certo indicabis? Ignoras. Magis ego. Nec
vero hoc parum scire refert. Hinc enim emergit perpetua dubitatio
de magnitudine stellarum: ut de distantia, de celeritate, de loco
taceam: quae omnia inde videntur pendere. Quae enim ad manus

habemus, licet utcumque identidem, & diuersis sensoriis, si communia sint, explorare, & certius proxime cognosse. At illa quis potest? Nec illa solum. Si e longe baculum aquae semiimmersum videas, contortus, aut refractus apparebit. Dices integrum tamen esse: quia alias expertus es. At fractus sit, apparebit nihilominus fractus. Non enim hic valet contrariorum ratio. Asseres integrum esse, superiori ratione: & tamen falsum est. Quid facies, nisi ab aqua extrahere possis? Dubius manebis. In coloribus vero quantum intersit situs, ostendit Iris, vitrū aqua plenū, columba variegata, sericae telae ex diuersis contextae coloribus, vicinitas corporis splendentis alterius coloris (ut etiam, si plano perpendiculariter imponas auream, argenteamue laminam: multoque magis si deorsum inclines): quae omnia huc atque illuc mota varium admodum referunt colorem. In quo situ verum ostendere colorem dices? In eadem parte modo ruber, nunc fuluus, dein caeruleus. Quis horum proprius? Dubitare tantum licet. Numerum autem, figuram, motum, magnitudinemque a vario variari situ, (quoad sensum intelligimus, nō in se) non est quod prolixius ostēdamus: cum id quotidiano usu experiri possis. Atque sufficiant haec de situ. Externi medij variam dispositionem 63 ea, quae per id referuntur, variare est ne- // cesse. Iam partim diximus. In crasso aëre obscura apparent omnia, parua. In tenui contra. In prato omnia viridia fiunt. Circa rubra, aut crocea, his notantur corpora. In multa luce videre nō licet: praecipue alba, aut maxime lucida corpora. In tenebris minus. Circa has, vel illam, dubie, & fallaciter. Quod medium? Designa tu. Sed & in aëre, artificioso igne illustrato, alij ac alij videntur colores, aliaeque figurae, pro materiae ignis varietate. Si medium vitrum sit, aut cristallus, pro horum coloribus, variisque figuris, & consistentia, aliter, atque aliter res significantur. Haec media sunt, per quorum medium res videntur. Alia vero per superficiem ostendunt. In his nulla constantia. Quot figurae monstrosae, ridiculae, multiplicatae, inuersae, truncatae? Quid nō fingunt specula? Quid de his iudicabis? An figuram vides illam? Non est: quomodo videas? Vides tamen: quomodo id? Non sine ratione ignoras. Transeamus iam ad internum medium, in quo tot contingunt difficultates. Elato oculo uno, aut in transuersum deducto, (quanquam aliter

Arist. senserit) binae res apparent. Vnde mirum, quod qui stra-
bismo laborant binas res omnes non videant. Sed rationem in
rerum Examine reddemus. Idipsum illud contingit, si in latus
recumbens, corpus aliquod coram te habeas, quod inferiorem
oculum cooperiat. Tunc enim superior oculus omnia, quae infra
corpus illud sunt, percipiet: alter vero solum corpus illud: nec
distincte, sed nubis modo. Sic altero, quae post corpus sunt,
inspiciente, altero ipsum corpus, simul videmur videre corpora
duo, quorum unum supra aliud est. Facilius autem id experieris, si
oculum unum ad externum angulum / / mouens, quae a latere 64
sunt respicias. Tunc enim altero oculo illuc vergente, nasus se
obiicit videndus, apparetque umbrae modo ea, quae ab altero
oculo videntur, superinducere. Eodem modo si digitum oculis
praesentes, non tamen eum inspicias: sed ad ea, quae aut post eum,
aut ad latera sunt, animum vertas, duplex nihilominus apparebit.
Idē continget, si ambos oculos ad nasum vertas: duplicia omnia
videbūtur. Moto oculo uno, quae videntur, moueri videntur. Imo
ex duabus apparentibus rebus, altera mouetur, quiescente alia. Sed
& altera ad dextram, ad laeuam altera mouetur, si librum in-
spiciens, oculos per seipsos sine digiti adminiculo iugiter moueas,
lineas solum respiciens non legendo. Accedit etiam ad haec oculi
situs profundus, vel eminens, natura, aut casu. Quorum maxima
in videndo diuersitas. Multoque magis, si altero profundo, alter
eminens sit. Si quoque elatior alter, alius depressus: sed hic mani-
festus error. Illic autem, ubi uterque aut profundus, aut eminens,
nullus. Ad situm etiam refertur maior, aut minor palpebrae com-
missio, aut apertio. Si lucernam inspicias conniuentibus oculis,
apparebunt plurimi radij ad oculos protendi: mouenturque ad motū
palpebrae: si omnino aperias, quiescunt, nec tam longi sunt. Sufficiant haec exempli causa: ex quibus tu alia complurima cōiectare,
experirique poteris. Colores a vario oculi situ non minus, quam a
vario rei videndae, mediique situ mutantur. Sed iam dictum est.
Haec tu forsan minimi facis: nec scientiam impedire posse cogitas.
At longe aliter res habet. Mouerunt enim haec illas, ut & de omni
quod sensibus apparet, dubitarent: & crederent, / / colores non in 65
rebus permanentes esse: sed a luce fieri, variarique. De quo alibi
dictum a nobis est, ut videbis. Sed iam pergamus ad substantiam.

139

Interna media quinque numerantur a Philosophis, visus, tactus, gustus, auditus, olfactus. Diuersae horum omnium substantiae. Proinde & diuersae etiam res ab eis percipiuntur: sunt tamen quaedam communes. Tetigimus supra: magnitudo, numerus, figura &c. Percussionem unam videt oculus: binum audit ictum auris: si non vidisset oculus, sine dubio duos iudicasses fuisse ictus. Esto coecus: percutiam bis: aut ego semel: alius autem procul a me, statim post me, quasi altera Echo. Dices ab aliquo monitus, si nunquam vidisti, Echo esse: & falsum. Imo vide. Iubeo alium clam post me percutere. Dices Echo, non est. Currente equo iudicat saepissime auris duos esse. Aut si duo sint, aequali tamen gradiantur passu, unum: imo oculus, si e longe sit: si plura sint quae moueantur, magis utrumque fallitur. In magnitudine non minus. Quod oculus paruum, auris magnum: & contra. In figura multo magis decipitur oculus, quam tactus: quemadmodū & hic minus, quam ille in magnitudine. Quae prope sunt, distantissima quandoque videntur visui, & auditui: magis tamen huic: alias contra. Non minus fallitur tactus in distantia: cui si magnum calidum adsit, etiamsi longe: tamē prope iudicat esse, propter magnam impressionem. Naribus quoque saepissime imponitur. Quid multa profero? Nil certius sensu: nil eodem fallacius. Cui credes? an auri? an oculo? Lupum auribus tenes. Sequere. Accedit maximum: horum omnium instrumentorum variae dispositiones, quae ut plurimum // nos aberrare cogunt. Varij oculorum colores, varia temperamenta, consistentia, substantia, quantitas, situs, perspicuitasque spirituum, & humorum, qui in eis habentur, an non maximam diuersitatem pariunt in videndo? Quod si medice magis agatur, tunicarum substantia, optici nerui eadem, & quantitas spirituum, humorumque haec omnia, & perspicuitas, quantum visum variare solent? Saepe ab externa causa muscas, floccos, aranearum telas, & similia videre videmur: cum tamen non sint. Oculo inflammato, omnia rubra apparent: bile perfuso, citrina: si humor pupillae incumbat, perforata, aut velo obducta, aut magna, aut parua, aut dupla, aut obscura. Vitia haec sunt morbosa: sed sanorum alij longe, alij prope: alius clarius, obscurius alius: hic magna, ille parua: hic rubra, ille crocea videt. Nullus denique aut perfecte, aut eodem modo ut alij. Quid ergo prohibet per oculum

66

140

tot obnoxium mutationibus, imo & in se tam varium, per aërem
non minus, imo magis mobilem, & incertum, res varias, incertas,
instabiles, aliter atque ipsae sunt, nos percipere? perpetuo falli?
nunquam certi aliquid deprehendere, nec proinde asserere posse?
Oculus vero omnium sensorium praestantissimum, certissimum-
que est. Quod si ad alia te cōuertas, multo maius dubium. Quomodo quod calidum semper est, de calido aut frigido recte iudicabit?
Sumus autem semper calidi. Qua ratione fit, ut, qui in termis, aut
balneis arte factis sunt, frigidam iudicent urinā, & aquam tepidam:
falso per te. An non quaecunque tangimus, aëri exposita sunt, &
ab eo afficiuntur? an non ab eodem nos perpetuo afficimur? an
non & hic / / ab aqua, terra, & astris? Quid igitur cogit, aquam 67
frigidam dicere? Quid aërem calidum? Multum calidis, minus calida frigida apparent. Tales forsan sumus nos. Ergo aqua calida.
Hyeme, quia a frigido maxime afficimur externo, nuper hausta a
fonte aut puteo aqua calida apparet, quia minus frigida: aestate
quantumcunque calida, aër, si curras, vel flabello moueas, frigidus
videtur: cum tamen per te calidus sit: & tunc temporis multo
magis. Quid ergo caliditas? Quid frigiditas? Vt videamus quae
calida sint, aut quae frigida, ratio nil hic potest. Quis eorū rationem nouit? Nullus. Sensibus committendum iudicium. At etsi
sensus optime perciperet, discerneretque qualitates illas: non tamen
proinde sciret: sed solum cognosceret, quemadmodum rusticus
asinum suum a vicini boue, aut suo distinguens. Nunc autem nec
hoc praestare potest tantum. Quid ergo scimus? Nihil. Discurre
per alios sensus. Minus. At haec est potior cognitio nostra. Quid
faciet mens sensu decepta? Decipi magis. Falso uno supposito,
plurima infert: hinc alia (paruus enim error in principio, magnus
est in fine). Tandem ubi falsitatem videt, (veritas namque unica
est, & sibi constans) regreditur: quaerit locum defectus causam.
Non inuenit: suspicatur hoc, vel illud medium. De hoc iterum
quaerit, an verum, an falsum. Nosse non potest, quia supra sensum
est. Probabiliter agitat. Sic in infinitum. Nulla conclusio. Perpetua
dubitatio. Age, in te experire. Non impono. Si tecum essem: facile
verbis ostenderem omnia dubia esse: at charta non tot patitur: &
properamus ad rerum examen: in quo experientia hoc indigitabo.
Ex / / superioribus potuisti utcumque videre. Melius deinceps 68

141

videbis. Insequor definitionem meam. Iam dictum est de re: & de mediis ad cognitionem: nunc de cognoscente. Quot in hoc ignorandi occasiones? Innumerae. Vita breuis: ars vero longa, imo infinita: aut potius ea quae arti subiacent, aut quibus ars subiacet. Occasio autem praeceps: experimentum periculosum: iudicium difficile. Nec vero solum seipsum praestare oportet opportuna facientem: sed & assidentes, & exteriora. Mirum, diceres Aphorismum in nostri gratiam factum fuisse, in quo difficultates eius, qui aliquid scire debet, proponuntur: quas tu partim iam vidisti, partim videbis nunc. Sic incipiamus ab incipiente homine: hunc enim in Aphorismo, per eum, qui oportuna facit, intelligimus. Semel natus hic cerea moles est, fere omnis capax figurae, tam in corpore, quam in anima: sed magis in hac. Ita ut non male tabulae rasae, in qua nihil pictum est, conferatur: nec tamen omnino bene, in ea omnia depingi posse, asseratur. Nec enim omnes ad literas apti sunt, etsi omnia necessaria illis subministrentur. Atque an in anima depingi possent rerum naturae? infiniti? vacui? Non videtur. Nunc autem non est. Duo ergo in nuper nato sunt: nil actu impressum: potentia plura, vel pauca: haec, vel illa. Omnia, nulli. Est haec passiua potentia tantum: cui opponitur passiua alia impotentia: qua quis pluribus, vel paucis, his, vel illis omnino ineptus est. His duabus communicant nobiscum etiam bestiae aliae. Quippe psyttacus prima illa potentia sermones imitari potest humanos: quos simia secunda impotentia non potest. Haec contra, prima potentia

69 plurima // ad hominis imitatiōe exequitur, quae psyttacus ob secundam impotentiam nequit. Sic inter homines hic ad Grammaticam ineptus omnino: ad nauigationem maxime aptus. Ille contrario modo. Est autem nobis potentia actiua, qua carent bruta, quaque scientiae inueniuntur, & artes. Sed de hoc, ubi de Anima, latius agetur. Nunc sufficiat adduxisse haec, ad ea quae sequuntur, intelligenda. Quam pauci ergo ex tot hominum millibus scientiis apti sunt, etiam his quales habemus? Vix unus, aut alter: perfectae autem nullus. Ostendo. Perfectus homo sit oportet, qui perfecte aliquid scire debet. An aliquis talis est? Quod vero talis esse debeat, vide. Animam tu quidem dicis in omnibus aeque perfectam (eius naturā ignorans, ut alibi monstrabimus): corpus vero in causa esse cur hic doctior, ille minus, ille nullo modo. Volo. An anima nostra

142

satis perfecta est, ut aliquid perfecte sciat homo? Non. Sed sit. Cui ergo minus perfectū corpus est, minus perfecte sciet: cui magis, magis: cui maxime, perfectissime. Hoc enim rationabilius videtur colligi ex te, quam contrariū. Cui datū est perfectū corpus? Nulli: vel clamāte medico: aut si daretur, nō nisi per instans duraturū. Quod si neges, nō probabo nūc: alias probaturus. Petā tamen aliquod a te: & scio quod nō dabis. Ignoras enim, ut & ego. Perfectissimū autem cum Gal. voco corpus, quod temperatissimum, quod pulcherrimum. Atque ille temperatissimum tantum (licet & compositiónis meminisse debuisset, propter instrumentarias actiones) perfectissimas edere operationes omnes vult. Inter quas intellectio, a qua sciētia pendet, primas tenet. Sed & id ratione fulcitur. / / Fuere medicorum quidam, qui asseruere, medicum, ut 70 perfectus esset, omnes morbos prius pati debere, quam perfecte de his iudicare posset. Et non videtur omnino inepta opinio: licet satius esset tunc non esse medicum. Nam quomodo de dolore sententiam feret rectam, qui nunquam doluit? Quos autem & dolores, & morbos in nobis ipsis experti sumus, melius in aliis & dignoscimus, & curamus. Sic quomodo coecus, aut luscus, de coloribus? surdaster, de sonis? paraliticus, de tactilibus qualitatibus iustum ferat iudicium? Perfecte ergo videat oportet, qui de coloribus: audiat, qui de sonis: palpet, qui de tactilibus: gustet, qui de gustabilibus: moueatur, qui de motu: digerat, qui de digestione: doleat, qui de dolore: imaginetur, qui de imaginatione: memoret, qui de memoria: intelligat, qui de intellectione perfecte iudicare velit. Alias, ut inquit Gal. erit nauta ex volumine: qui securus in scamno sedens, optime portus, scopulos, promontoria, Scyllas, & Charybdes depingit: denique nauem per culinam, aut super mensam optime ducit. Si vero mare conscendat, eique clauum triremis committas, in scopulos, in Scyllas, in Charybdes, quas tam bene norat antea, infliget. Aut ut ille, qui in foro deperditum asinum, aut canem, proprius describens signis, proclamat: quem tamen si coram habeat, non cognoscat. Et hac ratione dicitur Christus Dominus miserias humanas subire voluisse: ut expertus calamitates nostras, magis misereretur. Melius enim qui pauper aliquando fuit, pauperi, qui captiuus, captiuo, qui denique miser, misero: quam qui nunquam pauper, captiuus, miser, illi, isti, huic,

143

71 compatitur. Perfectissimum ergo // corpus requirit perfectissima cognitio. Sit haec ultima ratio. Perfecta omnia perfectis gaudent, a perfectis fiūt, & per perfecta. Quid perfectius creatione? A solo perfecto, perfectione ipsa, Deo fit. Quo medio? Perfectissima eius potentia, quae sola perfectissima, quia infinita sola, quia ipse Deus. Reliqua omnia perfectiora a perfectioribus fiunt. Quae a corporibus coelestibus fiunt, ab imperfectiori fieri non possent. Ratio horum omnium. Agens, in passum utcunque abit, transit. Quodlibet enim cupit in se aliud transformare. Quod non potest, nisi se illi communicet. Dumque hoc agit, ab alio repatitur: dum hoc conseruare se in suo esse conans (quod etiam inditum est omni enti: unde & illud sequitur, velle scilicet in se aliud conuertere: ne sui unquam finis eueniat) partim resistit: partim, aliud in se conuertere etiam volens, quantum potest suam in agens extendit, & exercet potentiam, imprimitque vim: sed quia inferius illi viribus est, vincitur in pugna, cogiturque alterius vexillum sequi, & se in illud inserere, primo exuto habitu. Si ergo agēs perfectum est: & actio perfecta esse debet: & media ad actionem exequendam: & patiens quod actionem recipit, in quantum hanc recipit: licet aliter imperfectum sit. Quod si actionem non sequatur patientis conuersio in agens, saltim opus, quod a tali actione fit, perfectum a perfecto agente est, imperfectum ab imperfecto. Orta enim, ut dicunt medici, attestantur suis principiis. Quod quid est, id agit: & quale quid, tale agit, mediis ubique idoneis. Talia sunt quae agenti similia. Sic enim melius ambo in patiens conspirant. Perfectum ergo agens
72 melius perfectis // adiutum instrumentis, & mediis, in patiens aget, opusque intentum peraget, quam imperfectis. Vide id in omnibus, tam naturalibus, quam voluntariis actionibus. Sol perfectissimum omnium corporum (unde plurimi Deum illum existimarunt) quam edit actionem? Perfectissimam: similem Dei actioni. Hic enim creat: ille generat omnia: qui secundus est a creatione gradus. Sed differunt. Nam Deus a se, solus, ex nihilo, & sine medio, aut instrumento creat. Sol a Deo potentiam habens, cum homine, ex semine, & medio calore hominem generat. Licet quandoque etiam sine congenerante plurima solus generet, ut murem ex stercore, ranam ex puluere cum pluuia, locustam, pulicem, culicem, lacertam, scarabeum, pediculum, & plurima alia animal-

ia: & inter plantas philitidem, ceterach, politrichum, adianthum, lichenem, pulmonariam, viscum, fungum: & inanimata omnia, aurum, argentum, lapides, gemmas omnis generis: & elementa ipsa ex seipsis inuicem. Sed obiicies forsan Solem corrumpere etiam: quae est pessima actio, & imperfecta, si generatio perfecta est. At non ita habet. Nec enim corrumpit, sed dum generat, necessario corruptio sequitur. Quod autem generet primo, patet. Prius enim est ens non ente: actus priuatione, dignitate, praestantia, & natura. Corruptio autem non ens est, priuatio, destructio huius entis, nihil. Ergo prior generatio corruptione. Ergo ad illam sequitur haec: non contra. Ergo generat Sol primo: corrumpit ab euentu, & ex consecutione. Quod inde etiam manifestum fit. Nullum enim ens propter nihilum agit, aut nihilum / / intendit. (Vnde & 73 neque malum per se: malum enim priuatio boni est, quasi nihil) omnia namque propter finem. Nihil autem finis enti esse non potest. Finis enim perfectio est: quae inter entia primas occupat. Nihil priuatio, destructio, defectus, mera entis negatio. Quo alio quam infestissimo nihili nomine nil ipsum vocabo? omnino perfectioni, entique oppositum, inimicum. Nil denique. Quis illud intendet? quis quaeret? Omnia naturaliter id fugiunt. Nil me, praeter hoc nihil, perterret, tristat, animum prosternit: dum cogito, me aliquando illius aulam inuisurum: nisi fides spe, & charitate comitata, metum hunc, nihilque, simul eius causam, destrueret, meque confirmaret, post compositi huius dissolutionem, indissolubilem cum Deo Opt. Max. nexum promittendo. Sol ergo perfectissimum omnium corpus, corruptionem intendat, efficiat? Generat ergo. Quo medio? Calore, omnium qualitatum perfectissima, praestantissima, actuosissima. Videbis hoc in rerū Examine. Lucem tu etiam addis: sed ego non consentio. Tamen pro me stat. Illustrissima res est lux, amicissima, charissima. Vitam huic conferunt: ut mortem tenebris. Exhilarat nos. Ea media pulcherrimas omnium res cognoscimus, plurimas.[17] Deus se lucem vocat. Sine luce coecutiamus, obdormiamus, obmutescamus, tanquam mortui vagemur, nec solum nos discernentes, nedum rerum naturas cognoscentes. Vides quantum in tenebrosa, nubilosaque nocte

---

[17] pluririmas *1581²*, plurimas *1636*.

silentium? Pene alterum chaos videtur, mors. Sane sine luce viuere nollem. Vtriusque parens Sol, utroque, calore scilicet & luce, ad
74 genera- / / tionem utitur, ut tu vis. Quod vero non ad corruptionem, ostendunt haec eadem. Accedente ad nos Sole omnia reuiuunt, renascuntur, pullulant, germinant, frondescunt, florent, fructificant. Animalia frigore torpentia, & semicorrupta, omninoque corrumpenda, si diutius abfuisset astrum, e latebris exeunt, ad motum promptiora fiunt, laetantur, currunt, saltant, gestiunt, canunt, ad generantis astri aduentum apta generationi fiunt, in hanc laeta feruntur. Denique ver & aestas generatio sunt, & vita. Ego tunc solum viuo. Abeunte autem a nobis dextro Dei oculo, (sic enim Solem libet vocare) omnia languent, torpent, labuntur, pereunt. Quid autumnus & hyems nisi perpetua mors? mortem frigidam, gelidam, rigidam, horridam, pallentem vocant poëtae, & merito. Vitam contra floridam, virentem, vegetam. Mors a frigore est: vita a calore: calor a Sole. Hic ergo perfectissimus omnium corporum, perfectissima omnium qualitate, calore, perfectissimam omnium actionum naturalium, generationem scilicet, edit. Haec de naturalibus. In voluntariis autem, nonne pictor, sculptor, cytharedus, melius pinget, sculpet, pulsabit, si perfectioribus, quam si imperfectioribus utantur mediis & instrumentis? An bene canet raucus, saltabit claudus, scribet qui inconcinnam habet manum? Qua quidem manu quod perfectius a natura excogitari potuit instrumentum? Nullum sane, ut optime Gal. noster prosequitur. 1. de Vsu p. Perfectissimum autem omnium animalium homo ad perfectissima inter coetera animalia opera edenda, perfectissimo
75 etiam omnium / / eguit instrumento. An si imperfectius fuisset istud, potuisset ille tam perfecta exequi munia, totque, quam exequitur. Non, cogito. Sed quorsum tot? Huc: ut probemus: omne perfectum producere perfectum , & uti perfecto ad eius productionem. Quid inde? Hoc. Humana anima perfectissima omnium Dei creaturarum, ad perfectissimam omnium, quas edere potest, actionum, perfectam scilicet cognitionem, perfectissimo eget corpore. Quid? dices: a corpore non pendet intellectio, nec ab eo ullo modo iuuatur, sed solummodo ab animo perficitur. Hoc falsum est, ut alibi probauimus. Vanum est dicere, animum intelligere, ut & audire. Homo utrumque agit: utrobique corpore,

& animo utens: & quodcumque aliud cum utroque simul exequens: nihilque, non utroque fauente, conferente, agente. Sed, si in dictis tuis consistas, idipsum probatur. Cur hic doctior, ille minus? Animus aeque perfectus in utroque. Ergo in corpore defectus, ut tu dicebas. Ergo doctior perfectiori potitur corpore, quomodocumque illo utatur, siue ad imaginandum, siue ad intelligendum. Ergo doctissimus perfectissimo. Ille autem est vere sciens. Quale autem sit perfectum corpus, diximus iam. Cumque illud nusquam inueniatur, nusquam etiam perfecta cognitio, neque proinde scientia, quae idem est. Sed dices forsan: ad intelligendum non agere nos brachiis & cruribus: proinde etsi illa defectuosa sint, modo cerebrum bene habeat, sufficere. At deciperis: si membra a primordiis generationis praue conformata sunt, defectus fuit aut in materia ex qua // facta sunt, aut in virtute formatrice. Vtroque 76 modo aliquod ex principibus membris, aut plura imperfecta sint necesse est. De materia non est dubium: ex eodem enim semine fiunt membra omnia. Virtus autem non debilis primo per se est: sed quia deficiunt spiritus, aut temperies, eius praecipua instrumenta. Quocumque autem horum deficiente, etiam in internis defectus est. Sed etsi solum in externis esset, ab his internis communicaretur. Debilia enim extrema non perfecte attrahunt, retinent, coquunt, expellunt: unde sanguis inficitur excrementis. Ab hoc spiritus, & membra interna: si post formatum perfectum corpus & natum, deformitas accidat: vel ab interna: vel ab externa causa accidit. Quomodocumque contingat, interna etiam eodem modo, quo si a primordiis eueniret, alterat, & a perfectione disturbat. Denique perfectum corpus aut nusquam est: aut per momentum tantum durabit. Nullus ergo sciens. Nil scitur. Sed dices forsan: etiam imperfectum corpus scientiis aptum esse. Videtur enim difficile creditu, nullum ex hominibus scientiis idoneum. Ego vero hoc, ut & plura alia, libens concedo. Non tamen quodcumque. Nam neque tu id vis:? neque probaueris unquam. Certo ergo quodam temperamento praeditum esse illud necesse est. Quale est illud? Forsan non dabis. Sed esto, dederis. Hic nuper natus quot subit mutationes ab aëre, loco, motu, cibo, doctrina? Cogita tutemet. Si diues, delicate tractatur, pinguescit, totus corporeus fit, ineptus ad studium. Anima enim & corpus utcumque

147

contraria expetunt, per te, ut in Anima dicemus. Quin neque
77 parentes eum studio & laboribus // consumi permittunt: sed in
corporis [curam],[18] & ad corporis cultum componunt omnia: de
moribus solum (& o utinam) modicum soliciti. Et (ut hominum
maior pars facit, & quidem prudenter, natura ad hoc impellente)
sanitati, & diuitiis, reliquisque, quae vitam beatam efficere possunt, studere docent: unde euenit ut tam pauci studio literarum
incumbant. Sed esto, permittant, & velint parentes: puer detrectat.
Corpus enim otium semper expetit: labor nobis inimicus omnibus.
Diuitiae reuocant animum, delitiae disturbant, pellicit mundus.
Illeque sane summus mihi est Apollo, qui, cum huius seculi bonis
frui queat, his neglectis, rerum contemplationi se dedit, miserrima
omnium status permutatione. Sed rara auis in terris. Omnes aut ad
laudem, aut dignitates, aut diuitias: vix unus scientiam amplectitur
propter seipsam: sicque tantum quisque laborat solum, quantum
sufficiat ad acquirendum finem, non scientiae, sed ambitionis suae.
Egeni autem ad studia plurimi aduolant, tristi principio, aduerso
medio, turpi fine. Tristis enim egestas est, quae impellit, eadem
impedit: eadem satiata finit scientiam pauperis. Non enim amplius
student, quam ut eam fugere valeant. Hinc illud: ingenium volitat,
paupertas deprimit illud. Et illud: Diuinū ingenium plena cru-
mena facit. Et ille: Quaerenda pecunia primum est: Virtus post
nummos. Vtque sine Cerere & Bacho friget Venus, sic Pallas.
Psittaci proinde vino poto melius garriunt, discuntque: & quidam
etiam homines. Vnde: Foecundi calices quem non fecere disertum?
Quid non tentare cogit fames? Quid plura refero? Nunquam finem
78 facerem. Sit haec // conclusio. Studenti nullus finis esse debet
alius, quam scire. Egeno vero hic aut non est, aut eo solum est, ut
egestatem vitet. Quare qui propter ventrem studebat solum, hoc
repleto obdormit, scientiasque post tergum mittit, quibus non
delectatur, quia ineptus est illis: si vero aptus delectetur, impedit
egestas: & hoc miserandum. Quod si adhuc & diuitem, & pauper-
em omnia necessaria habere ad scientiam contendas, & voluntatem
non deesse, supponamus sic esse, vide quae sequātur difficultates.
Incipiens uterque instruendus est. Quis enim tam foelix, ut ex se

---

[18] *1581*[2] seems to have omitted a word; I have supplied *curam*.

doctus euadat? Atque quot miseriae in instructione! quam pauci
bonos nanciscuntur doctores! Hi vel propter praemij paruitatē, vel
ob desidiam, vel ob inualetudinem, vel ob egestatem, (cui dum
prouident, studio vacare nequeunt) vel ob inuidiam, vel ob metum,
vel ob superbiam, vel ob amorem, vel ob inimicitiam, vel ob dis-
cipulorum ineptitudinem, (si talem de eis conceperint opinionem)
vel (quod omnium pessimum, magisque crebrum) ob inscitiam: hi
inquam ob haec omnia, vel plura, aut veritatem, si nouerint utcunque, celant, aut falsa docent. Quo quid calamitosius tyroni euenire
possit? Hic enim credit, ut & conuenit, & necesse est incipienti:
semelque ebibitum errorem, vix unquam in posterum, quacunque
ratione id coneris, deponere potest. Tanta est recipiendi, retinen-
dique vis puerilibus annis: praecipue si praeceptoris authoritas
maxima fuerit. Vnde illud: Quo semel est imbuta recens seruabit
odorem Testa diu. Hinc illorum Αὐτὸς ἔφα tam illiberum, indig-
numque Philosopho. Hac ratione & ille cum incipiente simplex
paciscebatur prae- / / mium: cum eo autem qui sub alio didicerat 79
praeceptore, duplum: cum duplo etiam labore opus esset, altero
ad eradicandum errorem, quē iam ebiberat,[19] ad seminandam veritatem altero. Hinc Philosophorum sectae natae sunt: illudque,
Iurare in verba magistri. Vnde tot tantaque effundunt: hic pro
defensione huius: ille contra, ut expugnet: volumina implent de in-
telligendo praeceptore: nouas fingunt, infinitasque explicationes,
intelligentias, distinctionesque, quas nunquam ne somniauit quidem ille. Quinimo & tam stulti aliqui sunt, ut omnia, quae ab
hoc, vel illo authore tradita sunt, defendere se posse iactent:
ad idque se parent nugis, tricisque adeo circunsepti, & armati,
ut venatorem dicas, qui retibus turdos, fictoque sibilo aucupari
tentet. Quibus ipsimet irretiti, seipsos explicare nequeunt: sicque
incidunt in foueam, quam aliis parabant: moreque Aesopici aucu-
pis, dum columbo insidiantur, a colubro capiuntur. Et quemadmodum ij qui tormentis utūtur bellicis, (hacquebutas, aut sclopetos
vocant) dum, ut alium occidant, oculo admouentes uni, ut recta
feratur glans, ignem pulueri immittunt, si obstructa nimis fuerit

---

[19] ebiberat *1581*[2], biberat *1618 Errata* (an unnecessary correction; cf. a few lines
above, *semel ebibitum errorem*).

machina, contrarium experiuntur, quam volebant: recalcitrante scilicet illa, caputque illis confringēte. Sic hi dum aliis machinantur falsa, ipsi falsis inuoluuntur. Alij colligunt praecipua, Epitomasque faciunt. Alij in tabulas digerunt, in capita, in libros, quae ab aliis confuse scripta sunt. Alij contra ampliant, addunt, extendūt, commentantur, & commentiuntur plurima. Alij superstitiosa, fatuaque pietate, dissidētes conciliare, in pacemque omnino bellantes
80 redigere conantur. Alij contra eadē sen- / / tientes inimicos faciūt, dum diuersa scribere, & intelligere affirmant. Alij opus hoc illius esse asserunt. Alij contra, sed alterius. In his autem omnibus probandis, quibus non utuntur argumentis? quid non fingūt? quid non tentant? quid non excruciantur? Si non sufficiāt falsa probabilia, utuntur veris improbandis, contumeliis scilicet, inuectiuis, famosis libellis, iurgiis. Denique his non contenti, ad arma veniunt, ut quae ratio non potuit, vis cogat, militum modo. Sic qui scientifici dicūtur, bruta fiunt. An nō haec furor, & insania? Qui naturam inuestigare dicuntur, nil minus quam id agunt: dum quid hic, illeue voluerit, non quid hoc, illudue in natura sit, digladiantur: totamque in illis absumunt vitam, similes cani, qui visam umbram in aqua carnis, quam ore ferebat, hac dimissa, sectatur irrito, inanique conatu: tauroque, qui hominem sectans, inuento huius pallio, in id saeuit, hominis amplius non solicitus, immemorque. Sic illi naturam quaerentes, ad homines se conuertunt, illam omnino relinquentes. Proinde nil ipsi sciunt aliud, quam psittacorum more referre ea, quae in aliis scripta inuenere, prorsus ignari earum quae proferunt. Et horum quidem maxima in scientiis multitudo: qui autem naturam ipsam in se scrutetur, vix ullus, aut saltem admodum pauci, quique apud illos, & vulgum indocti iudicantur. Nec mirum. Iudicat enim quisque pro natura sua reliquos. Sic doctus doctum iudicat, & laudat, quia percipit quae dicit: indoctus negligit, quia non capit: contra extollit inertem, quia idem cum eo sentit. Simile enim simili gaudet, dissimile
81 respuit. Sub quocumque autem / / horum infoelix iuuenis literas ebibat, ut frequentius ebibit, (foelicissimus enim ille est, qui sub experto magistro, vereque docto initiatus est, ut & rarissimus) actum est de eius scientia: nisi aliquo actus sydere resipiscat. Atque si semper sub eodem studeat doctore, (quod vix unquam fieri

potest) semper errabit, si semel errauerit. Imo continuo magis errabit. Paruus enim error in principio, magnus est in fine: & dato uno absurdo, plurima sequuntur. Quis autem est qui semel non erret? Aut quis qui semel erret? Dubito an semper non erremus. Quod si a pluribus doceatur, hoc opus, hic labor est. Pauci quos aequus amauit Iupiter, aut ardens euexit ad aethera iudicium, diis geniti, potuere ab erroribus se expedire: tenent media omnia syluae difficilimae. Dum diuersi hi perpetua contentione se agitant, miserum incipientis ingenium misere distrahunt, dilacerantque. Hic illi hoc inculcat: ille contrarium persuadere conatur. Quis enim duos in omnibus conuenire vidit? Atqui maximum veritatis, proindeque & scientiae alicuius, certitudinis indicium est doctorum concordantia. Veritas enim semper sibi constat. Contra vero nil magis arguit incertitudinem scientiae, quam diuersitas opinionum artificum. Quod commune est omnibus sciētiae cuiuslibet doctoribus: ut inde colligas etiam quam parum certitudinis scientiis insit nostris. Sic debilem tyrunculum aduersi doctores trahunt in confusionem, ambiguitatemque. Qui subinde nescit quo se vertat: sed prout illi videtur vel huic, vel illi adhaeret: saepius decipienti. Hic enim plurimum garrit, ut mos est illis qui falsa astruunt: sicque pauperē iuuenculū ad se trahit, / / qui 82 victorem iudicat eum, qui magis clamauit. En tibi scientem. Sic multo tempore in his versatur procellis: saepius tota vita. Quod si ad methodum docendi accedamus, non hic erit minor difficultas, quinimo maior: siue eos, qui viua voce docent, spectes, siue qui scriptis. Eadem enim utriusque ratio. Porro maxima hinc discenti accedit vel utilitas, si bona methodo utatur doctor: vel difficultas, & damnum, si peruersa. Nihil enim tantum in docendo momentum habet, quantum methodus: quae subinde tam varia hominibus est: quaque uti scire non minus laboriosum, ingenioque plenum est, quam utile: nec minus rarū, quam necessarium. Nullus proinde est qui huic plurimum non studeat, insudetque: paucique admodum, aut fere nullus, qui vel scopum attigerit, vel attigisse credatur. Cum enim ars infinita forsan sit, ut iam diximus, vita vero omnium breuissima rerum, cui illam commensurare oportet vel docere, vel discere volenti, maximam nobis imponit curam, conantibus scilicet infinitum finito metiri, & quod magis est,

comprehendere: unde tanta scriptorum varietas. Quorum hic artem contrahere (cui vitam producere non licet, quod potius esset, & necessarium) dum nititur, longiorem efficit viam, difficilioremque breuitate, subindeque obscuritate sua (Nam obscurus, fio dū breuis esse laboro) tempus nobis absumens, quod rebus intelligendis, non eius scriptis impendi deberet: capitaque rerum solum nobis deuoranda dat. Alter dum artē fuse, ut est, prodit, in primis consenescit principiis, nosque cum illo. Hos, qui impatientes laboris sunt, quique acutiore ingenio, damnant: quod
83 pluribus verbis, quae hi / / breuibus perciperent, inculcent. Laudāt vero morosi & rudes, quibus nihil unquam satis explanatum. Illos cōtra. Si quis medio scribat modo, (si quis forsan sit) ab his omnibus improbatur: & quod nō sat breuis, & quod iusto breuior. Medium enim utrique extremo utcūque contrarium est. Ab iis solum commendatur, qui medio etiam gaudent, & ipsi mediocres. Hi rari admodum, sicut & pulchra omnia, incognitique. Iam docti alij ab his iudicantur: ab illis contra. Hic loquitur compte, pulchreque: ille aspere, & rude. Aliorum hic labores surripit, pro suisque venditat, repetit alius integras suas paginas, sui immemor: hic omnia ubique miscet, & cōfundit, ille nuda omnia & indiscussa relinquit: garrulus hic, & sophista, ille seuerus, & grauis: hic nouorum inuentor acutus, ille veterum assertor ineptus. Quid denique dicam? Quis omnibus placuit unquam? Nec natura ipsa, ut quam quidam damnare, increpareque ausi sunt. Tanta est in rebus varietas, ut natura in his lusisse cernatur, confusioneque nostra sibi placuisse videatur: ut nos eam hinc inde quaerentes, coram nobis existens deluderet, irrideretque. Nec in variis solum rebus varietas conspicitur. Idem homo modo vult, modo recusat: modo id asserit, tandem idem damnat: iam hoc profitetur, de quo si eum mane quaeras, non meminit amplius, nec meminisse vult. Sed & in hac coeli parte nunc vigent literae, tandem omnimoda brutalitas. Illic olim omnia ensis & arma, nunc nihil habes praeter libros. Et, quod magis, haec opinio nunc placet omnibus, hic Doctor in pretio est, mane omnino aliter. Horum omnium exempla
84 videbis si hystorias legas: adducam / / tamen unum, alterumue. Quid olim Aegypto, Graeciaque luculentius in literis? Quid in idolis colendis fertilius? Vbi illustriores viri, tum in scientiis qui-

buslibet, tum etiam armis? Nunc vero nec ibi musaeum inuenias, nec idolum, nec insignem virum. In Italia, Gallia, Hispania nec per somnium doctor erat: omnia Mercurius, & Iupiter. Nunc hic sedent Musae, hic habitat Christus. Iam in Indis quanta hucusque regnauit ignorantia? Iam nunc astutiores, religiosiores, doctioresque sensim nobis fiunt. Sit hoc satis. Quid ergo faciet in tanta rerum varietate calamitosus iuuenis? Quem sequetur? Cui credet? Huic, illi, nulli. Sic ipse elegit, si liber sit. Sin minus, vel totus huic, vel totus illi, vel totus nulli. Quod horum melius? In omnibus fallacia & miseria. Si totus se dedat alicui, seruus fit, non doctus: illiusque dogmata quo iure, quaque iniuria tuetur quantum potest. Sic fit miles, qui ducem sequitur quocumque trahat, ut pro eo pugnet: non memor amplius sui, cum eoque perit. Sic iuuenis noster, eiusque scientia perit, quoties se alicui pertinaciter adnectit. Nec enim sine dispendio veritatis quis potest iurare in verba magistri. Quod si omnibus aeque credat, aequeque nulli: ut ab omnibus excerpat, quae sibi videantur, magis liberum hoc est: sed & difficile magis. Quanto enim iudicio eget qui horum lites dirimere conatur? Quisque pro se suas habet rationes, argumentaque, ut sibi videtur, inexpugnabilia. Neque tamen inter hos iudicium ferre sine iudicis periculo est: qui pro quocumque tulerit sententiam, pro eo sibi standum etiam proponat. Quod si male iudicauerit, sententiae suae // poenam feret. Ignorabit enim 85 veritatem, sicut & alter pro quo male sententiam tulit, quod pessimum est. Sed & pro quocumque sententiam ferat cum eo contra alium semper illi pugnandum est: alio semper negocium facescente ambobus, nouaque fingente arma, quae repellere necesse est. Saepeque contingit, ut, quemadmodum in bello quis, quanquam aequitate, armis, & viribus maior hoste sit, arte tamen & astu circunuentus pereat: sic qui veritatem tenet, tueturque, argumentis contrariis obruatur: quibus cum resistere nequeat, animum despondet, veritatemque deserit, ut hosti se dedat. Hoc ut saepe contingit, sic veritatem obfuscat, dum qui falsa adstruit acutus est, subtilisque. Et id promouit ille syllogistica sua scientia, in qua optima consequentia ex falso quandoque verum sequitur. Sic verum nunc cum vero, nunc cum falso mixtum non discernitur: sed nunc verum falsum apparet, nunc falsum verum. Sicque qui

153

melius retes syllogisticos extendere nouit, hic quod vult adstruit.
Cumque ignari docendi essent veritatem, cauendumque omni
modo ne deciperentur, praecipue quibus eam inueniendi non est
potestas: ille contra eis insidias struere docuit, quibus veritatem, si
eam utcumque tenent, deserant: quam alias, nisi telis his circum-
uenirentur, tenerent. Sic vidi ego quandoque garrulum sophistam
conantem persuadere ignaro cuipiam, album esse nigrum: cui hic:
Ego non intelligo rationes tuas, quia non studui ut tu: bene tamen
sentio, aliud esse album a nigro: argue tu modo quantumcumque
86 volueris. Et sane memini, dum / / Dialecticae initiarer fere puer,
a prouectioribus aetate, & studio in certamen saepe prouocatum,
ut ingenij mei periculum facerēt: qui subinde fallaces syllogismos mihi obiiciebant: quorum ego fallaciam non vidēs, aliquando
onere premebar, falsaque concedebam, non tamen manifeste falsa:
cum tamen manifeste falsa sequebantur: tunc cruciabar admodum,
si statim defectum non ostendissem: nec quiescebam donec inuenis-
sem. An nō satius fuisset, tempus, quod in quaerendo defectu
syllogismi absumebam, in cognoscenda causa aliqua naturali dis-
pendere? Denique apud hos syllogizantes ille doctior est, qui melius
garrit: ille verum protulit, qui decipulam optime construendo,
socium, aut aduersarium vicit, eoque redegit, ut aut concederet
infallibiles quas vocant consequentias: (quas negare esset ridiculum, & impium: plenae tamen sunt rimis, laqueisque, quos qui
non videt, ab eis captus cogitur dare manus, concedereque quod
alter volebat, falsum licet) vel cum captum se videat, nec tamē
dolum percipiat, fere obmutescat. Hāc vocant scientificam syllogismorum doctrinam: qua nil ad scientias perniciosius. Quod
ille ipse videns, cauillatorim aliam scripsit, ut ab illorum decep-
tionibus eriperemur. Sic venenum bibendum didit: postea alexi-
pharmaco curare tentat, & ipse venenoso. Sed fortius est primum:
proindeque vincit plurimum, interimitque veritatem. Cui ut resis-
tant posteri, quot commenti sunt conditiones? quot alias fallacias?
quot volumina suppositionum, indissolubilium, exponibiliū, ob-
ligationum, reflexionū, modalium? Vide quanta subtilitas, &
87 scientia, quanta eius vis. Iam altera Circe Dialectica est: in / /
asinos eos conuertit. Nil certius. Pontem struxere in medio scientiae suae, quem asinorum pontem vocant. An non digni sunt

auena, propter praeclarum inuētum? Prope pontem iacent asini depicti, Circeas bibentes aquas: quibus inebriati, circa pontem perpetuo rudunt. Mihique fere idem accidisset, ni Vlissis carminibus adiutus, incantantes vitassem pontis dominas Circeas syllogismorum figuras. Quid non cruciantur miseri asini illi pro fulcienda antiqua habitatione? Quibus modis Dialecticam suam Circem honorant, defendunt, laudant, depingunt: similes Aeneae, qui sui oblitus, Italiaeque quam petebat, omnino immemor, effoeminatus, & vecors, lasciuua indutus clamyde, Didoni factus in mancipium, huic totus studebat, hanc colebat unam: quousque a Mercurio monitus erubuit, cognouitque apertis oculis se misere illaqueatum esse: depositaque statim foemina, virū assumpsit, deincepsque magnae orbis partis factus est dominus, Virtute duce, comite Fortuna. Atque o utinam Mercurius ego essem nostris Aeneis, ut relicta infirma, incantatriceque Dialectica, ad naturam se conuerterent: fierent forsan multi orbis domini. At ipsi nunc adhuc coeci perpetuo magis se illaqueant, ipsimet sibi laqueos parantes tot, ut nunquā legendi finem facias: quemadmodum nec ipsi unquam scribendi finem faciunt, noua quotidie adaperta ruina: simili veteris alicuius aedificij, lapsumque minantis ratione, aut in arena, instabilique loco, & ex fragili materia conditi, cui perpetuo supponendi postes, admouendi lapides, calx, similiaque, perpetuo eo hinc inde dehiscente. Sic continuo labante syllogistica doctrina, (quae nullo modo consistere potest, friuola, & / / inanis) continuo 88 etiam laborant eius incolae, & artifices, ut ruinam impediant. Atque haec docent ad se venientes iuuenes: his confundunt eorum ingenia primum: his eos exercent. Res autem quaerat quicunque velit. Sicque per manus currit haec pernities ab uno ad alium, ita ut tota vita nil scias. Sed dices forsan: quid ergo, visne imperatoris modo quaecunque dixeris rata esse sine ratione, & probatione, quod alienum iudicant omnes? Nec id volo: sed ostendam postea quomodo ratione, probationeque alia meliori, quam hac syllogistica uti possis. Iuuenis ergo noster, quem ad scientiam promouebamus, in his difficultatibus quid faciat? Iisdem se inuoluere, ut & ante eum praeceptores eius fecere, idipsumque eum docent: & ipse credit. Quid enim, non credat artificem qui ad discendam artem ad eum venit? Ergo qualis ille, talis hic: inscius ille, &

hic quoque. Iam difficile admodum est semel ebibitum errorem vomere. Suppone tamen hūc iudicio fretum suo: & postquam sub his longo tempore eorū didicerit scientiam, videritque dissensiones in opinionibus, sententiam ferre velle: quod ut rarum admodum inuentu, sic & scire cupienti utilissimum, & omnino necessarium. Quantum id periculi habeat, antea ostendimus. Nunc vero quantum difficultatis. Si recte ipse iudicaturus sit, res de quibus inter eos lis est optime consideret oportet: quod pauci faciūt. Pauci proinde sunt, qui quae proferunt intelligent: qui tamen volumina implent aliorum laboribus: componunt authores, quos ipsi non intelligūt, proinde & saepe male: iudicant de eorum controuersiis, & id quoque male. Intēti enim solum authoribus dissidentibus, ab
89 aliisque mu- / / tuato hinc inde auxilio, ut utētes Arist. testimonio, & aliorum, ex horum dogmatibus alia inferētes, & ex his alia: sic contra hūc vel illū sententiā proferūt: nō ostēdentes, sic rē se habere; sed sic videri Aristot. Sic illi, sic huic, sic colligi ex hoc theoremate, illoque. Quae omnia forsan magis dubia sunt eo, de quo quaestio est. Sic ipsi dū iudicium ferre stulte conantur de aliis, iudicādi ipsimet veniūt, imo & cōdemnādi. Quid enim ad rē, quod hoc ille, vel hic dixerit? An propterea verum est? Non fieri potest. Omnium enim rerum principia essent athomi, aër, aqua, ignis, terra, materia, forma, priuatio, chaos, lis, amicitia, magnum, paruū, aether, unum, numerus: quae omnia a diuersis rerum principia iudicantur. Ergo verum dixit, non qui quod alter dixerit, sed qui quod res est dixit. Cur ergo nobis tam obstinate hunc, illumue obiiciunt, quem negasse impium, haereticumque, ut ipsi dicunt, sit? Atque & ille ipse dixit, (quod fatui isti authoriductores non aduertunt, aut saltem fingunt se non aduertisse) Non propterea quod quis affirmarit, vel negarit, sed quia in re sic, vel sic sit, propositio vera vel falsa est. Idem enim ipse olim expertus est in similibus fatuis, cum Platoni aduersaretur, quod nos in his, cum illi, & aliis. Quibus tamen responsum satis duxit hoc, quod amicus erat Plato, sed magis amica veritas. Et alibi, Authoritas, inquit, ab extra est, parum habēs momenti. Sed video quid ignaros hos tam obseruantes in praeceptorem suum faciat. Nil sciunt extra ipsum, omnia in isto, omnia ab isto: in re nihil vident. Proinde nō mirum, si, cum non habeant aliud, quo vel asserant quod volunt,

vel destruant quod tu vis, non mirū inquam, / / si stomachentur 90
simplici negatione[20] victi. Docti autem cum res in promptu habeant, quas negare non possunt ignari: nisi velint experiri an
calidus sit ignis, si negent: non egent authoritatibus. Res ergo
contemplari oportet ei, qui aliquid scire velit, iuuenique proinde
nostro. Sed an hoc facile? Heu! Nullibi tantus labor: nullibi tanta
ambiguitas: nullibi tam pauca scientia. Vidisti iam antea quanta in
rebus diuersitas, quanta mutatio, quantam denique scire cupienti
pariant difficultatem, inaccessumque. Videbisque clarius ubi res
ipsas examinare aggressi fuerimus. Nunc vero prosequamur impedimenta ex parte discentis: sicque huius libelli finem faciemus.
Duo sunt inueniendae veritatis media miseris humanis: quādoqui-
dem res per se scire non possunt, quas si intelligere, ut deberent,
possent, nullo alio indigerent medio: sed cum hoc nequeant, adiu-
menta ignorantiae suae adinuenere: quibus propterea nil magis
sciunt, perfecte saltem sed aliquid percipiunt, discuntque. Ea vero
sunt experimentum, iudiciumque. Quorum neutrum sine alio stare
recte potest: quorumque utrumque quomodo habendum, adhi-
bendumque sit, in libello huic proximo, quem indies parturimus,
latius declarabimus. Interim vide ex hoc Nihil sciri. Experimentum fallax ubique, difficileque est: quod etsi perfecte habeatur,
solum quid extrinsece fiat, ostendit: naturas autem rerum nullo
modo. Iudicium autem super ea, quae experimento comperta sunt,
fit: quod proinde & de externis solum utcumque fieri potest, & id
adhuc male: naturas autem rerum ex coniectura tantum: quas quia
ab experimento non habuit, nec ipsum quoque adipiscitur, sed
quandoque contra- / / rium aestimat. Vnde ergo scientia? Ex his 91
nulla. At non sunt alia. Atque nec haec perfecta habere potest
iuuenis noster. Nam, (ut omittam multa recte habendi experimenti impedimenta) quot experimenta habere potest iuuenis? Sat
pauca. Quomodŏ ergo super pauca recte iudicium ferat? Nullo
modo. Plura enim vidisse oportet, ante quam recte quis iudicet:
imo omnia, ut initio dicebamus: quando & omnia se inuicem
tenent, nullumque sine alio stare possit. Quod in causa est, ut qui
hodie id opinabatur, mane aliud iudicet: imo & quod nunquam

---

[20] simplici, negatione *1581*², simplici negatione *Comparot.*

putarat, fateatur. Quis enim ante cognitum magnetem, torpedinem, echeneidem, talem illis vim tribuisset? Omnem attractionem dicebas a calido, a sicco, a vacuo, aut melius ob eius metum. Quid de illis? Quid de electro? An a quolibet horum? An putasses unquam venenum veneno additum hominem non interfecturum, imo potius liberaturum? Minime quidem, qui forsan ante experimentum asserebas, Quod unum efficit, melius idem duo. Probat autem contrarium atrox apud Ausonium uxor: quae virum veneno tollere conata, ut mortem citius acceleraret, praeparatae potioni hydrargirum admiscuit: quo a morte liber ille euasit. Teriaca etiam, & mithridatium ex venenis post experimentum composita, venenis obsistunt omnibus. Quis credidisset cicutā vino admixtam citius enecare, biliososque & calidos homines promptius quam frigidos? Videbatur enim rationabile, ut a contraria qualitate potius impediretur eius actio. At contrarium experimento apparet. Messores etiam apud Gal. pie facturos se credebant
92 si vinū / / cui praefocata vipera fuerat, bibendum darent misero elephantico, e vita ea ratione ablaturos eum existimantes: quo contra (mirum) ille a tam saeuo morbo liber euasit. Ancilla etiam elephantici domini, qui eam deperibat, initum exhorrens, ei vinum vipera infectū obtulit, ut interficeret: quod vice versa sanitatem ei conciliauit. Dixissesne tu? Minime. Multa ergo experientia & doctum & prudentem hominem facit. Inde fit ut senes doctiores sint, saltem ratione experimenti: rebusque humanis propterea gerendis accommodatiores iuuenibus: a pluribusque ea ratione gentibus maximo in honore habiti. Quibus, si etiam bonum adsit iudicium, merito committi potest reipub. administratio. Vt ergo huic obuient incommodo homines, scilicet defectui experimenti, adinuenerunt scribendi rationem: ut quae hic, illeue expertus sit tota vita, & variis locis, breui tempore alter discat. Sicque consultum est nostri saeculi hominibus, qui plurium vitas, acta, inuenta, expertaque pauca mora perlegentes, aliquid de suo insuper addunt: hisque alij: tum & de dubiis iudicium proferunt: itaque augetur ars: posterioresque hac ratione comparantur puero in collo Gigantis existenti: nec immerito. Sed ut haec via ad humanas res gerendas aliquid emolumenti videtur habere: nil tamen magis sciētias iuuat. Nam (ut omittam, libros non perpetuos esse, sicut nec & alias res,

ut qui omnino extirpentur bello, igne, incuria, nouitate aliarum
opinionum, tempore denique, & obliuione absumpti.) sequitur
statim tota difficultas, quam supra in scribentibus ostendimus.
Confusi, breues, prolixi, totque, ut si centena / / millium centum 93
viueres annorum, non sufficerent legendis omnibus: quique in
pluribus mentiantur, saepissime gloriae causa, aut fulciendae
opinionis. Statimque sequitur de intelligendis eis quaestio, & quas
nunc retulimus omnes. Ita ut dum aliquid scire quaerimus, ad
homines conuersi, & eorum scripta, naturam dimittimus, insi-
pientesque fimus. Sed ponamus experta ab illis vere referri. Quid
prodest mihi, alterum haec, aut illa expertum fuisse, nisi haec
eadem ego ipse experiar? Fidem parient mihi illa, non scientiam.
Proinde & maior literatorum numerus his temporibus fidelis quidem est, non sciens: quippe qui ex libris quidquid habent hauriant,
non adhibito iudicio, rerumque experimento, ut decet: sed creditis
his quae scripta inuenit, hisque suppositis, aliis atque aliis illatis,
male iacto fundamento. Iuuenem ergo nostrum, si aliquid scire
velit, perpetuo studere expedit, legere ea quae ab omnibus dicta
sunt, conferre experimento cum rebus usque ad extremum vitae
terminum. Quo vitae genere quid miserius? Quid infoelicius? At
quid dixi vitae genus? imo mortis genus est: ut superius dicebam.
Quem ergo vis tam calamitosae vitae se submittere? Sunt tamen
aliqui. Ex quibus sit iuuenis noster unus. Hic quidē etsi optime
cōstitutus perfecta fruatur sanitate, statim marcesset: consump-
tisque studendo corporis viribus, pluribus conflictabitur morbis,
aut morbosis affectionibus, grauedine, destilatione, arthritide,
ventriculi imbecillitate, unde cruditates, deiecta appetentia, lien-
teria, obstructiones, praecipue lienis. Quid non patitur qui studiis
incumbit? Moritur intempestiue / / tandem. Haec autem mentem 94
perturbant, affecta eius praecipua sede, cerebro scilicet: siue id per
se primo, siue ab alio accidat. Quod etsi his omnibus liberum
demus iuuenem nostrum: tamen melancholicus tandem fiet, quod
quotidiana ostendit experientia. An hi omnes recte iudicare possunt? Non videtur. Bonus enim iudex omni affectione carere debet.
Sed etsi omnibus his carere demus iuuenem nostrum nunc, & in
posterum, (quod vix fieri posse existimo) an propterea aliquid
sciet? Minime quidem. Nam et in eo continua mutatio est, quem-

admodum in omnibus aliis rebus. Illa vero praecipua, aetatis scilicet: quum multum differat iuuenis a perfecto viro, hic a sene: & in quoque horum magna sit etiā differentia principij, medij, finisque. Qui nunc iuuenis hoc iudicat, verumque credit, modicum vir reuocat reprobatque:quod idem forsan cum senex est iterum tenet, & tuetur: alias aliter, sibi nunquam constans. Nec ullus est qui si nunc opus aliquod edat, postea palinodiam non recantet, fateaturque, si probus est, se deceptum fuisse cum iuuenis esset. Qui autem hoc nollūt propter ignominiam, etsi videant falsum assseruisse, vel forsan non videntes, sui amore obfuscati, pertinaciter id defendunt, nihilque non explorant, ut se ab ignorantia, aut falsitatis nota vindicent, maximo scientiarum incommodo: praecipue si hi subtiles sint. Nec est aliquis qui, si opus emittere in lucem non velit tam cito, illius monito qui in nouem annos asseruare iubet, etsi centum annis integris corrigat, nō semper aliquid addat, demat, mutet, innouetque: sic in aeternū facturus, si in aeternū ipse quoque viueret. Vnde tāta varietas & inconstantia? / / Ab ignorātia sane. Nāque si perfecte ipsi sciremus, quae semel scribimus, nil postea esset immutandum. Qua ergo aetate melius ille iudicat? Dices, in senectute. At rationabilius videtur in statu, in quo vigent omnia, quam in senectute, in qua languent omnia, quaeque infantiae comparatur: unde illud, Maledicti pueri centum annorum. Senesque propterea delirare communi dicuntur sermone. Quid dices? Nec ipsemet scit quando verum dicat, quum modo hoc, modo illud: utrobique tamen sibi credi velit. Praeter has autem corporis mutationes, impediunt etiam veritatis cognitionem animi affectiones. Diximus iam supra in doctore. In discipulo non minus existimandum est. Amor, odium, inuidia, & reliqua quae ibi numerauimus, obstant quo minus bene iudicet. Quis autem est tam sui iuris, qui aliquo illorum non teneatur? Nullus. Quod si reliqua omnia euadat, illud minime euadet saltem, sui scilicet amorem. Quis enim est qui non credat se verum dixisse, difficultatis nodum inuenisse, imo & rem optime intelligere? Vt omittam, quod quisque reliquis doctiorem se, acutiorem, perspicatiorem, prudentiorem, sapientiorem denique existimat. An vere? Nemo, vulgus ait, rectus iudex est in propria causa. Quilibet autem propriam agit causam, dum vel verbo, vel scripto aliquid asserit. Nil ergo scimus. Sed do, (impossibile) omnibus his carere iudicem nostrum. Nil magis sciet in posterum: quanquam communi feratur sententia, perpetuo doctiores nos euadere. Contrarium enim omnino accidit iis, qui perfecte res cognoscere student. Ego antequam res considerare coepissem, doctior mihi videbar / / esse. Quae enim a praeceptoribus meis 96 acceperam, firme tenebam, perfecteque me scire credebam, nil aliud scire esse putans, quam plura vidisse, audisse, memoriaque tenuisse. Iuxta hoc dictum hunc, vel illum iudicabam, ut & alij: totum proinde me, ut & alios facere videbam, huic scientiae generi deuouebam, in hoc totus laborabam. Vt vero ad res me conuerti, tunc reiecta in totum priore fide, potius quam scientia, eas examinare coepi, ac si numquam a quopiam dictum aliquid fuisset: quamque antea scire mihi videbar, tam tunc ignorare, (contrario atque ille modo, qui usque ad virilitatem omnia se ignorare dicebat, post hanc autem omnia scire) & indies magis: eoque usque res ducta est, ut nil sciri videam, vel sciri posse sperem: quoque magis rem contemplor, magis dubito. Quid enim non dubitabo si naturas rerum percipere, nosseque non possim? a quibus vera scientia esse debet. Etenim videre magnetem facile est: sed quid is est? cur trahit ferrum? Hoc esset scire, si nosse possemus. Tamen qui magis scientes se dicunt, ab occulta proprietate id fieri respondent, idque scire esse: cum contra vere nescire sit. Quid enim differt si dicas, hoc fit mihi occulta proprietate, aut, hoc nescio a quo, aut quomodo fiat? Sic de pluribus aliis, quae minutim suo loco videbis. Quod si addas dubitationi de attractione ferri, illam, quomodo tactum ferrum ab eodem magnete secundum partem eam lapidis, quae Septentrionem respiciebat in natali solo, Septentrionem versus semper vertatur: (quod nobis parua nauicula uniuersam circuire terrram, certissimoque euentu inter medios fluctus cognoscere VBI quod occupamus, portusque / / infallibili utilitate, uti- 97 lique infallibilitate legere monstrauit) ad eamque magnetis partē, a qua tactum fuit, semper deuoluatur: contrariam autem fugiat. Quomodo non solum annulum unum, aut acum unam trahat, sed vis etiā per annulos, & acus transmissa usque ad plures diffundatur, quos omnes in aëre suspendat. Si denique, quare inunctus allio omnino langueat, trahendique vim amittat: cogeris cedere manus.

161

Quod doctissimus quidam ex recentioribus facit etiam inuitus: inscitiam nostram, non solum ubi de hoc agit magnete, sed & pluries alibi merito accusans. Iudex itaque noster quid hic agat, etsi per centenos centum viuat annos? pauca experietur, illaque male: peius iudicabit de his: nil omnino sciet. Sed etsi plura videret, non tamen omnia posset, quod necesse est vere scienti. Illaque etiam plura in dubium veniret an optime expertus esset. Si enim consulat alios de iisdem rebus authores differentes, aliud atque aliud expertos inueniet: quodque hic se expertum dicit, alter impossibile esse contendit, illumque in experientia deceptum esse pluribus rationibus hinc inde petitis ostendere conatur. Sic quomodo recte de obscuris iudicabit, iisque quae sensu nullo modo captari possunt, qui de his quae sensui obiiciūtur, aut per eum cognosci debent, dubius est? Quod si extra authores ad populum accedas, mirum quanta varietas: nusquam concordia: omnino aduersantur in pluribus iis quae in scientiis traduntur. Sed, dices, hos ignaros esse, res non perpendere, neque posse, crassos scilicet. At communiter dicitur, Vox populi, vox Dei: difficileque est 98 intelligere, totum populū decipi: Philosophum unum // verum dicere: praecipue si de rebus quae in experientia potius consistunt, quam iudicio, quaestio sit. Plura siquidem sunt in quibus illis credendum est: ut in agricultura, nauigatione, mercimoniis aliunde aduectis: cuilibet denique in arte sua excellenti. Nam & illud communi fertur voce, Doctior est quilibet, ignarus licet, in arte sua, quam sapiens in aliena. Si ergo iudicium ferre velis inter hos, Philosophosque, cum videas difficultates quae ab utrorumque opinionibus sequantur, noui quid excogitabis, (quod cōmuniter fit: nouarum enim rerum cupidi sumus) idque omnino verum esse asseres, alia omnia falsa. Alius identidem idem facit: sicque fere omnes. Quis verum dixit? Te senem iam, dices, expertumque pluries. At ut quidem fatear paucos esse qui rem attingant, sic illud quoque durum videtur, tantam multitudinem decipi, te solum verum dicere. Quid enim tu supra alios habes? Insuper, quae longo tempore a pluribus habita sunt, confirmataque, maius in veritate videntur habere fundamentum, quam quae tu nunc profers noua. Et tamen, dices, plures sunt errores qui longo durant tempore incogniti. Verum. At ego contra: plura sunt vera longo

tempore cognita, quae tandem occultantur: illis scilicet erroribus
in medium adductis, adauctisque. Quid dicemus de opinione tua
noua? Vtrumque esse potest. Quod illud? Nescimus. Quod si
dicas antiquam esse etiam opinionem tuam, eo dicto, quod Nihil
dictum quin dictum prius: ostendasque veteres aliquos ante te
idem quod tu nunc dixisse: qui errorem tuetur idem dicet. Nulla
enim est tam stulta opinio, quae fautores non habeat. Haec omnia
contra me / / etiam pugnant, qui, nil sciri, probare contendo: 99
cum nunc omnes alij aliter opinentur. Sunt tamen nihilominus
pro me: cum ex hoc manifeste colligatur, nil sciri. Scientia enim
per te certa, infallibilis, aeternaque esse debet. Quid ergo iudicabit
de his miser senex, quantumcumque eum expertum fingas? Nil
certi. Atque hucusque definitionis nostrae partes duae explanatae
videntur, res scilicet, & cognoscens. Erat autem alia, perfecte.
Nec enim quaelibet cognitio scientia est: nisi velis omnes scientes
esse, tam doctos, quam indoctos, & belluas etiam. Et quod perfecta esse debeat cognitio scientia, nulli dubium: quae autem illa
sit, ubi, & in quo, maximum. Sicut & alia, hoc etiam ignoratur.
Forsan nulibi est: & hoc magis rationale. Diximus partim supra:
Perfecta cognitio perfectum requirit cognoscentem, debiteque dis-
positam rem cognoscendam: quae duo nusquam vidi. Si vidisti tu,
scribe mihi. Nec hoc solum: sed an videris perfectum quid in
natura. Illud autem requiri vidisti iam supra, nec proinde necesse
est hic repetere. Hisque videtur exposita definitio nostra, subindeque ostensum, quod nihil scitur. Reliquas huius rei proba-
tiones latius videbis in processu operum nostrorum, ubi id semper
obiter monstrabimus: siquidem iam se extendisse plus satis videtur oratio, cui propterea finem demus. Ergo vidisti difficultates
quae scientiam nobis adimunt. Scio, plura forsan non placebunt ex
his quae hic dixi: sed nec, dices, demonstraui nil sciri. Saltem
quantum potui clare, fideliter, & vere, quid sentirem exposui. Nec
enim quod in aliis ego damno, ipse committere volui: ut rationibus a longe petitis, obscuriori- / / bus, & magis forsan quaesito 100
dubiis, intentum probarem. Mihi namque in animo est firmam, &
facilem quantum possim scientiam fundare: non vero chimaeris &
fictionibus a rei veritate alienis, quaeque ad ostendendam solum
scribentis ingenij subtilitatem, non ad docendas res comparatae

sunt, plenam. Nam nec mihi desunt subtilitates, ingeniosaque figmenta, quemadmodum & aliis: & si his contentus esset animus, plura illis habeo. Sed cum haec a rebus multum separentur, re-moueanturque, animum potius decipiunt, quam informent, & in ficta a veris transferunt. Hoc ego non scientiam voco: sed imposturam, somnium, simile his quae ab agyrtis & circulatoribus fiunt. Tuum nunc erit iudicare de his: quaeque bona videbuntur, amico corde excipere: quae secus, non hostiliter lacerare: impium enim esset prodesse conanti plagas infligere. Exerce te. Si aliquid scis, doce me: gratias enim habebo tibi plures. Interim nos ad res examinandas accingentes, an aliquid sciatur, & quomodo, libello alio praeponemus: quo methodum sciendi, quantum fragilitas humana patitur, exponemus. VALE.

Quae docentur non plus habent virium,
quam ab eo qui docetur
accipiunt.
QVID?

FINIS.

That Nothing Is Known

To the honourable and eloquent Diogo de Castro, best greetings from Francisco Sanches.[1]

My dear Diogo,

Lately, as I was going through a case of books, I came by chance on this little work, which I had produced seven years ago and put away for nine, in obedience to Horace's advice.[2] I found it so severely ravaged by worms and moths that, had I tarried two years more before I brought it to light, there would then have been reason to fear I might have to commit it to the flames rather than to the light of day; this was what made me resolve on a hurried and premature birth.[3] But just as the human foetus is capable of life not only if it has reached the term of nine months but even after seven, so too it is possible that this imperfect seven-year-old may survive.[4] And there is a further consideration: I am

---

[1] Diogo de Castro, a member of the faculty of medicine at the University of Coimbra and a respected poet and novelist, probably met Sanches in Rome. See the Introduction, section I, note 62. Sanches had previously dedicated his first published work, the *Carmen de cometa anni M.D.LXXVII*, to his friend de Castro.

[2] In the "Art of Poetry" Horace recommends that young Piso should "put the parchments in the cupboard, and let them be kept quiet till the ninth year."

[3] Sanches was possibly encouraged by Clavius, with whom he was corresponding in 1574 at the time he began working on the *Quod nihil scitur*. The Jesuit mathematician had attacked the Aristotelian dialecticians, opposing the certitude of the mathematical sciences to the contradictory opinions and doubt engendered by the dialecticians. See *Christophori Clavii, S. J., . . . Operum mathematicorum tomus primus (-quintus)* (Moguntiae: A. Hierat, 1611–12), I, Prolegomena, p. 5.

[4] A possible reference to Galen's *De septimestri partu*. There was a current medical debate on the length of the gestation period for the human foetus, Aristotle having affirmed that it extended sometimes to eleven months.

165

about to give birth presently to a few other works, which this work ought properly to precede.[5] But if it were necessary to wait until nothing remained to correct or alter, I should be like Sisyphus rolling his stone; never should I make an end of licking my bear-cub into shape, and I should never publish anything.[6]

Moreover, we often see it happen that authors who repeatedly take up the same work in order to "form" it, end by *de*forming it. So let it march off to the field – and good luck to it – like a soldier bent on storming the citadel of falsehood. If, however, it should be hard pressed by the foe, my advice to it is to withdraw to your camp, my dear Castro, since nowhere could it be safer.[7] Still, in order to guard against the danger that you may fail to recognise it, and thus shut your gates against it, I am sending it to you with instructions to bring you my greetings as soon as possible, to reaffirm our friendship, and to go forward into battle under your colours. Therefore receive it with a glad countenance and enrol it, together with myself, in the list of your devoted friends.

Toulouse.   Farewell.

FRANCISCO SANCHES TO THE READER, GREETINGS

"Mankind has an inborn desire to know"; to but a few has been granted the knowledge of how to *desire*; and to fewer still has it been granted to *know*.[8]

---

[5] Sanches evidently considered the *Quod nihil scitur* to be an introductory treatise and refers to subsequent treatises such as the *De modo sciendi, Tractatus de anima, Examen rerum, Libri de natura,* and the *Tractatus de loco* in the text of the *Quod nihil scitur.*

[6] It was a widely held belief, subscribed to by ancient authorities such as Aristotle and Pliny, and perpetuated by contemporary scholars such as Cardano in his *De subtilitate,* 10, that the mother bear brought forth an unformed cub which she licked into shape. Thomas Browne vigorously refutes this supposed truth in his *Pseudodoxia epidemica,* ed. G. Keynes (1664; London: Faber & Faber, 1964), 3, 6, p. 116.

[7] Sanches puns on his friend's name and the Latin word for camp, *castra.*

[8] This quotation from the first line of Aristotle's *Metaphysics* ironically prefaces a treatise whose entire purpose is to destroy the Aristotelian system of

My own lot has in no way differed from that of other men. From my earliest years I was devoted to the contemplation of Nature so that I looked into everything in great detail. At first my mind, hungry for knowledge, would be indiscriminately satisfied with any diet that was proffered to it; but a little later it was overtaken by indigestion, and began to spew it all forth again. Even at that period I was seeking to find some sustenance for my mind, such that my mind could grasp it completely and also enjoy it without reservations; but no one could appease my longing. I pored over the utterances of past generations of men, and picked the brains of my contemporaries. All of them gave the same answer, yet they brought me no satisfaction at all. Yes, I admit that some of them reflected a kind of shadow-image of the truth, but I found not one who gave an honest and full report of the judgments one ought to form concerning facts (*res*). Subsequently I withdrew into myself; I began to question everything, and to examine the facts themselves as though no one had ever said anything about them, which is the proper method of acquiring knowledge.[9] I broke everything down into its ultimate first principles. Beginning, as I did, my reflection at this point, the more I reflected the more I doubted. I was incapable of grasping anything in its whole nature. I was in despair, but still I persisted. I

knowledge by pointing out the inadequacies of Aristotelian scientific methodology and the failure of most ancient philosophers to formulate a theory of knowledge leading to absolute certitude. Etienne Gilson quotes the first twenty lines of Sanches's address to the reader in his historical commentary on Descartes's *Discours de la méthode* (pp. 267–8), showing the striking similarities that exist between the experiences of the two thinkers and the conclusions both draw from them.

9 Joaquim Iriarte in his *Kartesischer oder Sanchezischer Zweifel? Ein kritischer und philosophischer Vergleich zwischen dem Kartesischen "Discours de la mé-thode" und dem Sanchezischen "Quod nihil scitur"* (Bottrop: Wilhelm Postberg, 1935), which exists in manuscript in the Fonds Cazac (Boîte 5) at the Institut Catholique de Toulouse and is quoted from extensively by Carvalho in his edition of the *Quod nihil scitur* (pp. 184–7), gives the relevant quotations from the address to the reader which may have influenced Descartes. See also Joseph Moreau's "Doute et savoir chez Francisco Sanches" (pp. 26–30) for an excellent comparison of the use of doubt as philosophical method by Sanches and Descartes.

went further; I approached the doctors, in the eager expectation that I might gain the truth from them. But what do they do? Each of them maps out a scheme of knowledge, partly from someone else's speculations and partly from his own. From these they deduce other propositions, and others again from these latter, judging nothing in terms of (observed) facts until they have constructed a maze of words, without any foundation of truth; the result is that in the end one does not possess an understanding of natural phenomena, but merely learns a system of fresh notions and inventions which no intellect would be capable of understanding; for who could understand non-existent things? From this source come Democritus's Atoms, Plato's Ideas, Pythagoras's Numbers, and Aristotle's Universals, Active Intellect, and Intelligences. With these (claiming to have discovered unknown truths and the secrets of Nature) they entrap the unwary; who believe them, and readily flock to Aristotle, whom they read and pore over and commit to memory; and the more of Aristotle a person has learned to recite, the more "learned" he is. If you contradict them in the very slightest, they say nothing more except to call you a blasphemer. If you argue on the other side of the question, they call you a sophist. What can you do with them? It is a shame. Let them be deceived who wish to be deceived; it is not for them I write, and so they need not read my works. Yet among such people there will be someone who, reading me yet not understanding (for "what has the ass to do with the lyre?"), may try to bite me.[10] But "a blow on adamant the hammer breaks"; and the serpent in Aesop, thinking to chew the file, breaks its own teeth.[11] Accordingly, I would address myself to those who, "not bound by an oath of fidelity to any master's words", assess the facts for themselves, under the guidance of sense-perception and reason.[12]

[10] Sanches puns on *qui lectis nec intellectis* and follows it up by a reference to the well-known fable of Phaedrus, "The Ass and the Lyre".

[11] Ibid. "The Serpent and the File", which Phaedrus adapted from Aesop's tale.

[12] A reference here to the freedom from authority which was characteristic of the New Academy. See Cicero, *Academica*, 2, 3. Vives's definition of *lumen naturale* is very similar to Sanches's rule for guidance. See the Introduction, section III, note 26.

You, reader, whoever you may be, who share my situation and disposition, who have very often entertained private doubts concerning the nature of things – share, now, *my* doubts too. Let us together apply our intellectual gifts and our natural inclinations. Give me leave to judge freely, so long as I do not depart from rationality; and I both grant you, and wish for you, the same.

Perhaps you will say: "But, after all those great men, what fresh contribution can *you* possibly make? Was Truth waiting for *you* to come upon the scene?" No, indeed she was not; but neither was she waiting for *them* before. Nothing is new, then; but if so, why did Aristotle write? Or why are we to keep silence? Has Aristotle definitively described the whole functioning of Nature? Has he embraced the entire compass of the universe? I cannot believe this, even though certain very learned scholars of modern times,[13] who are too much under his influence, assert it, and for good measure call him "the Dictator of Truth", "the tribunal of Truth", "the commonwealth of Truth" – sobriquets worthy, no doubt, of the greatness both of him who is praised and of him who praises, but which appear (and deserve) rather to claim praise for praising another man, and also for elegance of style, than to claim the "commonwealth of Truth"; for in that commonwealth, as in Truth's "tribunal", there is nothing but Truth herself, while Aristotle contains a multitude of things that are unrelated to Truth – as we shall see in the appropriate contexts.

Furthermore, these extremely clever pupils and encomiasts of Aristotle are at odds with him in many respects (I suppose, because they were driven from that same "tribunal of Truth" – unless they prefer to explain it by the driving force of ambition and rancour). To be sure, I think Aristotle stands supreme among

---

[13] Sanches indicates in the margin that he is referring to Julius Caesar Scaliger, whose *Exotericarum exercitationum liber quintus decimus de subtilitate ad Hieronymum Cardanum* (Parisiis: apud Federicum Morellum, 1557) is one of the philosophical works constantly quoted by Sanches. Vernon Hall's "Life of Julius Caesar Scaliger (1484–1558)", *Transactions of the American Philosophical Society*, n.s. 40, part 2 (1950), pp. 85–170, gives a useful summary of Scaliger's works and influence. Scaliger was considered to be the equal of Aristotle by his contemporaries on account of his great learning.

the most gifted investigators of Nature; he is unrivalled among the wonderful intellects that the human race, in all its weakness, has produced. But I should not claim that he nowhere errs; I maintain that he was unaware of a great many things, that he was uncertain about many, and gave a confused account of not a few, and a brief and superficial account of others, while some he passed over in silence, or avoided altogether.[14] Like ourselves, he was human. Often he was obliged to reveal the sluggishness and weakness of the human mind. Regretfully, I myself, in this work, both exhibit and practise that same weakness, and drain it to the very depths, when by reflection I bring out a great many points which, though they depart widely from the doctrines of the ancients, nevertheless appear to approach the truth in proportion as they do so. It is my opinion that as generation succeeds to generation so do the different opinions of men, each of whom believes that *he* has found the truth – whereas, among a thousand who hold diverse opinions, only one can have found it.[15] So let me, among the rest (or even without them!), conduct the same investigation; it may be that I shall succeed. It is easier for several dogs to hunt the quarry than one alone. Therefore, it should not seem strange to you if – after all those great men, as you insist – I in my insignificance set my shoulder to moving this stone; for there are occasions when the mouse releases the lion from his bonds. Yet all the same I make no general promise that I shall therefore give you the Truth, for I am ignorant of her, as I am of everything else. Still, I will pursue my enquiry to the best of my powers; and you for your part shall at all events be pursuing Truth in the open, flushed from her hiding-place. Yet you are not to expect ever to capture her, or with full knowledge lay hold on her; let the chase suffice for you, as it does for myself. For me this is the aim and the end; an aim, and an end, which you too must seek.

[14] Cf. Vives's judgment of Aristotle in the *De disciplinis*. See the Introduction, section III, note 18.

[15] Cf. Descartes, *Discours de la méthode,* part I (p. 8): "et que, considérant combien il peut y avoir de diverses opinions, touchant une même matière, qui soient soutenues par des gens doctes, sans qu'il y en puisse avoir jamais plus d'une seule qui soit vraie".

This established, we shall begin with the first principles of things, and shall investigate the more important topics of philosophy, to the end that from them other questions may more easily be deduced; for it is in no way to my purpose to linger over them, since the goal of my proposed journey is the art of medicine, which I profess, and the first principles of which lie entirely within the realm of philosophical contemplation.[16] Thus we shall kill two birds with one stone. Otherwise, the whole of life would not be long enough. I come pleading for forgiveness if sometimes, while I concentrate on an enquiry into Truth, I disregard certain matters of less importance. Accordingly you are not to look in me for an elegant, polished style. Indeed, I should provide it, did I wish to do so; but Truth slips away while we substitute one word for another and employ circumlocutions – for this is verbal trickery. If that is what you want, seek it from Cicero, whose function it is; I shall speak prettily enough if I speak truly enough.[17] Elegant language is seemly for rhetoricians, poets, courtiers, lovers, harlots, pimps, flatterers, parasites, and people of that sort, for whom elegant speech is an end in itself; but for science, accurate language suffices – indeed, is indispensable; and on the other hand this cannot coexist with the former kind.[18] And you should not ask me to quote many authorities, or to treat my authorities with deference; deference is rather the mark of a

[16] Sanches affirms his belief in the intimate relationship between philosophy and medicine by the search for a common method. Descartes makes a similar statement three times in the *Discours de la méthode,* saying that he proposes to devote the rest of his life to the study of nature from which he hopes to derive laws applicable to medicine.

[17] Ciceronian eloquence was still taught in the humanities curriculum as the ideal language for discourse. Sanches recognises the unique achievement of Cicero who, as the first Roman writer to translate and summarise the works of the Greek philosophers, was instrumental in creating the language of philosophy for the Western civilised world (see the translation, p. 176). However, like Erasmus and Montaigne, he preferred a plain, unadorned style.

[18] Sanches's desire for an accurate language for science is laudable. In the sixteenth century the language of natural philosophy was basically derived from Aristotelian metaphysics, and scientific method relied heavily on Aristotelian logic. After the development of the mathematical sciences a new language for the sciences emerged.

171

servile, untrained mind than of one that is freely investigating the Truth. In my reasoning, I shall follow Nature alone. Authority bids us *believe*, whereas Reason *demonstrates*; the former is more suited to faith, the latter to the sciences.[19] Accordingly I shall establish, by rational argument, those propositions that seem to me correctly stated by others; those that seem incorrectly stated I shall disprove. And may God grant that you receive these my thoughts with open eyes, when they are worked out, in the same spirit in which I, with open eyes, am now working at them. May you judge them soundly; and when any of them seems to be untrue, pray assail it with valid reasoning (this is the way that both befits a philosopher and pleases me highly), not with feeble abuse (which is womanish, unworthy of a philosopher, and highly displeasing to me), as some do, out of rancour or ignorance. As for those that appear to be sound, pray give them your approval and support. This will be given, I trust; and so you may shortly look for more substantial works.

Toulouse, on the Calends of January, in the year of redemption 1576.

WHAT?

1   Francisco Sanches Philosopher and Doctor of Medicine

THAT NOTHING IS KNOWN

I do not *know* even this one thing, namely that I know nothing. I infer, however, that this is true both of myself and of others.[20] Let

---

[19] The revolutionary nature of Sanches's thought is revealed by his rejection of Aristotle and all other ancient authorities and his insistence on a rational method of demonstration for the natural sciences based on an examination of the facts. Nevertheless, Sanches is careful to defer to authority in the realm of faith.

[20] Sanches begins his treatise with the statement attributed to Metrodorus of Chios by Diogenes Laertius, *Lives of Eminent Philosophers*, 9, 58. Cicero in *Academica*, 2, 23, quotes also the beginning of Metrodorus's *On Nature:*

this proposition be my battle colour – it commands my allegiance – "Nothing is known". If I come to *know* how to establish this, I shall be justified in drawing the conclusion that nothing is known; whereas if I *do not know* how to establish it, then all the more so – for that was what I claimed. But you will say, "If you *know* how to establish it, this will result in a contradiction, for you already know *something*".[21] I have, however, anticipated your objection by coming to the opposite conclusion. Now I begin to upset the argument: it already follows, *from this very consideration*, that nothing is known. Perhaps you have failed to grasp my meaning and are calling me ignorant, or a quibbler. You have told the truth; but I have a better right to say this of *you*, since you have failed to understand. So we are both ignorant. This being so, you have unwittingly arrived at the conclusion I was looking for. If you have understood the ambiguity of the inference, you have clearly perceived that nothing is known; if not, then ponder, make a distinction, and untie this knot for me.[22] Sharpen your wits; I am following you closely.

"Nego ... scire nos sciamusne aliquid an nihil sciamus, ne id ipsum quidem, nescire (aut scire), scire nos, nec omnino sitne aliquid an nihil sit". Sextus Empiricus in *Against the Logicians,* 1, 88, mentions that Metrodorus abolished the criterion of truth when he said: "We know nothing, nor do we even know the very fact that we know nothing". This statement was challenged by the dogmatists on the grounds that it was an inherent contradiction. Sanches stresses the logical ambiguity of his own proposition with a marginal annotation *ambigua consequentia* and wittily proves the validity of his proposition "Nothing is known" by the success or failure of his demonstration. It should be noted that the ability to sustain both sides of an argument was characteristic of Carneades and the New Academy.

[21] André Mandouze in his preface to Andrée Comparot's French translation of the *Quod nihil scitur* (p. 5) draws attention to the problem of Sanches's imaginary partner in the eristic moot which ensues, for he is both advocate and adversary, singular and plural representing the reader/readers, Aristotle/ Aristotelians, or Sanches dialoguing with himself. The protean nature of Sanches's interlocutor poses extraordinary problems for the translator in that it is difficult to know how to punctuate the dialogue and to decide who, indeed, is speaking.

[22] Aristotle in the *Metaphysics* 995a30 speaks of untying a knot, by which he means solving a difficulty in an argument.

Let us deduce the thing from the name; for as far as I am concerned every definition, and almost every enquiry, is about names.[23] More fully: we cannot comprehend the *natures* of things; at least, I cannot. If you tell me you can easily do so, I shall not take issue with you; yet it is false – for why you, rather than myself?
2 Hence, we know nothing. But if we do not comprehend, how are we to demonstrate? There is no way of doing so. You, however, claim that there is a definition which "demonstrates the nature of a thing".[24] Show me one such; you have none; so I draw my conclusion. Furthermore, how are we to assign names to something we do not understand? I do not see how – yet names there are. Hence there is endless uncertainty concerning names, and a great deal of confusion and deceitfulness in the matter of words, perhaps even in everything I have just asserted.[25]

[23] Sanches begins his demonstration that "nothing is known" by attacking the Aristotelian theory of scientific knowledge which depended on definitions and the demonstrative syllogism. Much of his argumentation is directed against Aristotle's exposition of the problem of knowledge in the *Posterior Analytics* and the *Metaphysics*, texts Sanches had studied in the humanities curriculum prior to his medical studies. The person whom Sanches addresses could be Aristotle himself or a follower of the Nominalist school. Vives had already brilliantly censured the Parisian Nominalists in his *In pseudodialecticos*, which Sanches may have known.

[24] Aristotle declares in the *Posterior Analytics* 93b29: "Since definition is said to be the statement of a thing's nature, obviously one kind of definition will be a statement of the meaning of the name, or an equivalent nominal formula" (*The Works of Aristotle,* ed. W. D. Ross, 12 vols. [London: Oxford University Press, 1927–52], vol. I). All subsequent quotations of Aristotle are taken from this edition.

[25] Richard H. Popkin's statement that "Sanchez's *Quod nihil scitur* almost reads like a twentieth-century text of analytic philosophy" (*The History of Scepticism from Erasmus to Spinoza,* p. 41) is perfectly understandable when one realises that Sanches proceeds to refute the major Aristotelian concepts expounded in the *Posterior Analytics*. Sanches argues that the names bestowed on things do not define their essential nature, are ambiguous, and cause misunderstanding: words will always have focal meaning rather than univocal meaning. It is possible that Sanches may have had in mind Galen's treatise on language and ambiguity, *De captionibus*. See Robert Blair Edlow's excellent edition, *Galen on Language and Ambiguity. An English Translation of Galen's De captionibus (On Fallacies)* (Leiden: Brill, 1977).

It is for you to draw the conclusion. You will say that what you define by the terms "animal, rational, mortal" is a thing (namely Man), not a verbal concept. This I deny; for I have further doubts about the word "animal," the word "rational", etc.[26] You will further define these concepts by higher genera and differentiae, as you call them, until you arrive at the thing's "Being".[27] I will ask the same question about each of these names in turn. Finally, I will ask it concerning the last of them, namely Being; for you do not know what this term signifies. You will say that you will not define this Being, for it has no higher genus to which it belongs.[28] This I do not understand; nor do you. *You* do not know what Being is; much less do I. Yet you will say that we must eventually make an end of questioning. This does not resolve my doubt, nor does it satisfy my mind. *You* are obliged to reveal your ignorance, and I am glad of it; so also am *I*.

To proceed. A man is a single thing, yet you describe him by several names: Being, Substance, Body, Living, Animal, Man, and finally Socrates.[29] Are these then not words? Of course they are. If they refer to the same thing, then there are too many of them; but if they mean different things, then a man is not a single thing possessing identity. You tell me, "I am envisaging a plurality of attributes in one and the same man, attributes to which I give, severally, their appropriate names".[30] You are further confusing the enquiry. Not only do you fail to comprehend the man as a whole, who is something large, solid, and perceptible by the senses; you divide him into portions so small as to escape the senses, which are the most reliable of all means of judging – portions that have to be sought for by means of the reason, which is deceitful and obscure. This is a poor procedure; you are deceiving me, and (even more) yourself. I ask what it is in a man that you call animal, living, body, substance, or being? As before, 3

---

[26] Sanches is referring mainly to the *Posterior Analytics* 92a.
[27] See *Posterior Analytics* 96b and *Metaphysics* 1037b.
[28] Being as a primary premiss is outside definition.
[29] See *Metaphysics* 1006a–1007b.
[30] See *Posterior Analytics* 96a.

you do not know. Nor do I. This is what I was after. But I shall speak of it later.

Next, I ask what the word "quality" means, or "Nature" or "soul" or "life"? If you should say, "It is *this*", I shall have no difficulty in denying it, for it "is" something *else*. Prove it, I say. Whereupon *you* have recourse to Aristotle, but I to Cicero, whose business it is to make clear the meanings of words.[31] You will claim that Cicero's language is less exact, less choice, than Aristotle's. I shall maintain the opposite view; for this was Cicero's, not Aristotle's, trade. If you enquire further, I shall cite other artists in the Latin language (or the Greek, for it comes to the same); there is no agreement among them, no fixity or stability or set of guidelines. Each of them mutilates words as he pleases, and distorts their meaning in this way or that, adapting them to his own purpose. Hence the multitude of "tropes" and "figures" and "rules" and "mixed kinds", all of which combine to make up the art of grammar. As for rhetoric and poetry, they distort everything, and abuse every device. The practitioners of all these arts merely employ useless loquacity – but at their own pleasure; "freely", as they say. Whereas dialectic, or logic, also practises this, but in a different fashion: it arranges words in a fixed order and draws them up in line of battle, bidding them to fight not as individuals but in combination; it lays down rules, coerces, allows, or constrains. In fact, arts of the former class are like those who simulate troops of cavalry and military camps at public shows and spectacles, where a pretty effect, rather than actual strength, is called for; whereas the latter resemble men who are making genuine preparations for war and should properly be endowed with strength, rather than beauty. Now, all of these have words as their troops, and also as their objective. Which of them will you prefer to trust? It is hard to say, for each of them wishes to be trusted. And this is not enough. The meanings of

---

[31] In the *Academica*, I, 7, Cicero, whose self-appointed task it was during his retirement from public life to make Greek philosophy accessible to the ordinary reader, is obliged to invent new Latin words to convey Greek concepts such as the term "quality".

words appear to depend, for the most part or wholly, on popular usage; and here, accordingly, is where we must look for them; for who but the populace taught us how to speak?[32] It was on this principle that almost all those who have written hitherto have 4 taken as their basis for discussion the common sayings of mankind: for example, "We are said to *know* something when we comprehend its causes and its first principles";[33] and again, "But here too we must accept the universally approved principle that all men think themselves healthy when, etc".[34]

Now, is there any fixity and stability among the populace? None at all. So how can there be any point of rest in words? You have now no way of escape. Perhaps you will say that we ought to enquire what meaning was employed by the first person who bestowed a name. Enquire, then; you will not find out. But enough of this; clearly the entire investigation is about naming. I believe I have sufficiently established this, in my own opinion at any rate. Should you deny it, you will thereby support the proof of our principal enquiry, though a better proof will be given presently.

Let us, then, see what is to be understood by the word "knowledge" (*scientia*); for if no such thing exists, the consequence

[32] Vives in his treatise *In pseudodialecticos* had already made the point that Aristotle wrote in common Greek and that usage determines the meaning of words, not the grammarian or the dialectician. See Guerlac, *Jean Luis Vives against the Pseudodialecticians*, pp. 54–7, and other works *passim*.

[33] Sanches, in a marginal annotation, refers the reader to Aristotle's *Physics* [184a] and other works *passim*.

[34] Sanches refers the reader to Galen's *De differentiis morborum*, 1. In his own commentary on Galen's treatise in the 1636 edition of his *Opera medica*, pp. 686–87, Sanches writes: "Recte quidem Gal. a communi loquendi usu sanitatis et morbi significationem aucupat. Consuetudo enim et hominum voluntas sermoni vim dat. Sed hinc consurgit maxima scientiis difficultas. Populus enim verbis non apte utitur, nec res intelligit verbis designatas: sanitatem enim populus quidem nominat, quid autem ipsa sit, penitus ignorat. Doctores uero res intelligentes, aut prope accedentes, nominibus aliter uti coguntur, et ad alia significata transferre, quam populus, aut etiam ex a) Galeni, Ciceronis, aliorumque consilio, nova imponere" ([a] *Diff. simp.* 1 *Acad.* et 3 *Fin.*).

will be that nobody will derive from it the appellation "one who *knows*". Take Aristotle – for since he was the most penetrating investigator of Nature, and is in general followed by the great majority of philosophers, it will be enough to cite him as a test-case for all others. Otherwise, if I had to argue against all of them, my work would be extended to infinite length, and I should leave Nature herself out of account, just as others do.

What, then, does Aristotle say? "Knowledge is a mental disposition, acquired by demonstration".[35] I do not understand; and, what is worst of all, it is *obscurum per obscurius*. This is how philosophers mislead people. What is a "mental disposition"? I know this even less than I know what knowledge is; still less do *you* know. If you tell me that it is "an established quality", still less do I understand you. The further you advance, the less progress you make; the more words you use, the greater becomes the confusion. You are attempting to force me into a linear series of categorical propositions, and from these continually onwards, to Being – and what *that* is, you do not know. But are not all issues to be reduced to categorical propositions? Yes, indeed. What follows? They must all be brought into a labyrinth. What *are* categorical propositions?[36] A long series of words. Remarkable;
5 but what did I mean? I will explain. Some words are quite everyday: "Being", "Truth", "Goodness", if you like. Others are less familiar: "Substance", "Body". Others again are proper names: "Socrates", "Plato". Words of the first class have a general meaning; of the second, a multiple reference; of the last, an individual reference. It follows that when they say "Socrates is a man", and imply that by this is meant "animal, etc.", the object I am pointing to, namely Socrates, is in this way being referred to by his individual (proper) name, but in company with other beings who resemble him in shape he is called by a common name, Man; in company with the horse and other creatures that move but have

---

[35] See *Categories* 8b 25–35, *Posterior Analytics* 71b9–23, and *Nicomachean Ethics* 1139b15–35.
[36] The discussion centres on Aristotle's *Categories,* a required text in the Renaissance university arts course.

not a shape like his, he is called Animal; and in company with all things he is called by the most common name of all, Being. Similarly with the rest of the categorical propositions. This is not enough. Not content with straightforward words, in order to make the business more difficult they employ common terms with some differentia added: as, for Man, "Animal, rational, mortal", any one of which is harder than the first term. For whenever there is a multitude, there is confusion; and the more numerous words are, the more confused and obscure they are. This is the least of it; on top of this they build extraordinary structures.

There are many arguments concerning this series of words, which they call "categorical propositions": arguments about their order, number, status; about their differentia and their properties, and about the method of reducing everything to them (some things directly, some by indirect means; some by themselves, others in terms of their contraries; while some are common to two propositions, whereas others can hardly be reduced to the first, and others again have none at all to which they can be reduced). So even if the sky should exist, it at once ceases to be anything at all if it has not found a place in some categorical proposition! In short, this leads those philosophers into endless quibbles. Manufacturing still more words to explain words, they plunge themselves and their unfortunate audience utterly into a deep abyss of chaotic folly. Aristotle's works on logic are quite full of such things; and much more the systems of dialectic written by later philosophers after him. Those names that are more widely shared they call "genera", others "species" or "differentiae" or "propria" or "in- 6 dividua". If you should ask what this means, I would answer as follows: it is something universal, abstracted by the rational intelligence; and it is an invention of Aristotle's, not unlike the "Ideas" [of Plato]. I shall deal at once with "abstraction": it comes from the "active intellect" (a new notion), which "abstracts" or illuminates (or rather, obscures!), and from the *intellegens*, the product being a "universal", namely "Animal"; they go so far that "ass" designates the mind of those logicians, a mind that cannot grasp any but a "universal" ass – nay cannot depict one, even though

179

each one of them is an ass "in particular".[37] What will you say? Are these arguments not verbiage and foolishness? Yes, it is true – and true of the simple terms alone, which they call "predicables". Moreover, concerning these, still one must ask, how many? which? or what? Nothing – mere quibbling. Again, they call some of them "equivocal", others "univocal", "analogous", "denominative", "terms", "expressions", "words", "utterances", either simple or composite; "complex" or "non-complex"; "mental", "vocal", "written"; arising from rational choice, or from Nature; of first or second *intentio; categoremata; syncategoremata;* "vague", "confused"; and countless other denominations of words, and others again of these; and they surround them with exceedingly subtle arguments, so subtle indeed that you can annihilate them with the very lightest blow.

Do you call this *knowledge*? I call it ignorance. But now we are only at the beginning. If you join word to word, "this the work is, and this the painful toil"; they establish subject, predicate, copula, proposition, definition, distribution, and proof by inference; and, again, numberless other "species," "differentiae", and "conditions" of these. In short, even while they allege that the mind is made perfect by knowledge, they become totally mindless; and whereas they ought to investigate the natures of things and their causes, and do in fact claim to do so, they invent *new* things; and the more things one of them invents (and the more obscure these are), the more learned he; hence Aristotle even applied the word "science" to sophisms.[38] Thus invention undoes invention, and "a nail drives out a nail"; and *they* seem to me to resemble those who deal with necromancy and spells, among whom anyone who is especially skilful – as they put it – frustrates the actions and the attempts of another, bringing them to naught, undoing and obstructing them. Long ago, certain impious men made the same reproach to the divine Moses concerning the serpent that devoured

---

[37] Cf. Vives's criticism of the sophists and statements such as "Socrates and this donkey are brothers" (Guerlac, *Jean Luis Vives against the Pseudodialecticians*, p. 59).

[38] A reference to Aristotle's *Elenchi* [170a25–40].

the other serpents belonging to the magicians.[39] Even so do these sorcerers of ours, trusting in words and *knowing* nothing, nevertheless claim to know many things, lest they be convicted of ignorance. I, on the other hand, freely confess my own ignorance, and thus am all the more willing to explore yours. I know nothing; less still do they know. Why, therefore, do they muddy our minds with obscure terms? So much for "mental disposition". What, now, is this thing called a "demonstration"? You will define it afresh as follows: "a syllogism that gives birth to knowledge". You have been guilty of a circular argument, and have deceived me just as you have deceived yourself. But – what is a syllogism? This is marvellous – prick up your ears! strain your imagination (*phantasia*)! – for perhaps it will not be large enough to contain so many words. How subtle, how long, and how difficult is the science of syllogisms! In fact it is *futile*, long, and difficult, and there is *no* science of syllogisms. Ah, I have spoken blasphemy! Aye, truly – because I spoke the truth; and now I deserve to be stoned. On the contrary, it is you who merit a cudgelling, as a deceiver; for ignorance deserves to be pardoned, whereas deceitfulness deserves to be punished.

Listen to me. Prove that a man is a Being. You say, "A man is a substance; now substance is Being; therefore a man is a Being". I doubt the first premiss, also the second. If your proof runs thus: "A man is a body; body is a substance; therefore a man is a substance", I again doubt both premisses. Suppose you say, "A man is a living creature; a living creature is a body; therefore a man is a body", and draw from those proofs of yours another proof to this effect, "A man is an animal; an animal is a living creature; therefore a man is a living creature" – God Almighty, what a chain of proofs! what a hodge-podge! all to prove that a man is a Being! The proof is more obscure than the problem itself. If I still deny that a man is an animal, what will you say? There are no more 8 genera; where will you go to escape? You will go to the definition of "animal", which is, "a living creature, able to move and to feel. Such is a human being". Both of these I deny; so proceed. "A

[39] See Exodus 7:12.

living creature is a body that receives nourishment. Such is an animal. Therefore..." Prove these statements. "A body is a three-dimensional substance. Such is a living creature. Therefore ..." Both statements are false. "A substance is Being *per se.* Such is a body. Therefore ..." This too I should like to see proved. But you can go no farther. In the end, what is Being? As before, you do not know.

What have you achieved by means of these syllogisms? You have not proved that a man is a Being, which is what in the first place I asked you to do. On the contrary, by going now up, now down, on that line of reasoning you employ, in order that that exalted "Being" should be brought close to me, you have brought upon yourself a great deal of danger, and upon me a fear lest you should fall and shatter yourself completely, and me along with you if you were to grab me from below.[40] And in the end you have left the question as unresolved as it was before, or perhaps more so. Yet you always thought you had proved only the first propositions; you never so much as made a start on the second. But if you *had* proved the first propositions, and we had come to the second, you would have more trouble with these. Why, then, are you hoodwinking me with those word–chains of yours? My own reasoning is simpler: "Being" signifies everything (man, horse, ass, and so on). Therefore, a man is a Being (and so are a horse and an ass). Should you deny the first statement, I will not prove it, for I could not. It is for you to prove it to me, if you can. But you too are unable to do this. Therefore, we know nothing.

I now return to syllogisms, the "very subtle" science of which has totally collapsed. As I have already remarked above, some terms are perfectly general, like Being or truth; others less so, like substance or quality; while others again are individual, like Plato or Mithridates. In between these, there are a great many terms that denote neither as many objects as the former class, nor as few as the latter, for example, body, living creature, animal. Hence it is easy for anyone who asks if a man is a substance to point to the
9 answer with one word, in this way. "Substance" designates

---

[40] Sanches refers humorously to the *Posterior Analytics* [82a20.]

everything that exists by itself; hence it designates a man, also a stone, and also a piece of wood; therefore a man is a substance. But those who hunt for circumlocutions in order to prevent their knowledge from being despised, if it should be easy, are making it hard, and painful to acquire, by wrapping it up in a tissue of words, boasting that they have scientifically demonstrated that a man is a substance. This is how it goes in *Barbara*, that impregnable fortress: "Every animal is a substance; but every man is an animal; therefore every man is a substance".[41]

You have told the truth, but without *knowing* it, and in a more obscure way than one who *knew* could have told it. For it is exactly as if you said: " 'Substance' denotes living as well as non-living things; now, 'living' denotes a man and also a cherry; therefore, proceeding from the first premiss to the conclusion, 'substance' denotes a man". But the intellect is confused by all those intermediate steps, or rather is inclined now and then to doubt concerning each intermediate step. Is not this what the same author (Aristotle) wrote in another place: "What is said of the predicate is also said of the subject"?[42] Now, these are the ways in which we apply terms. Similarly, "That which is, is expressed in many modes. If it is the name of a person, it refers to a single object".[43] Another kind of term is called a "first principle", but in another mode we speak of a "cause", in another we speak of "nature", and again we speak of a "necessary property". To sum up, everything in Aristotle's *Metaphysics* and his other works is a definition of terms. Hence, almost every enquiry is about a name, for example the enquiry whether substance can be predicated of a man, and similarly with other enquiries. And inasmuch as no one can know this for sure, there is no knowledge, either of things or of words. Very well then, let us assign names afresh; you have my permission. We shall then know that this word has *this* meaning.

---

[41] The term "Barbara" designates mnemonically the first figure of the perfect syllogism.

[42] See *Posterior Analytics* 83a18–21.

[43] Sanches states that this definition is found throughout Aristotle's *Physics* and *Metaphysics*.

But this is false. You do not know what "word" is, what "this" is, what "meaning" is; therefore, you do not know that *this* word has *this* meaning. I can show that this follows; for when the parts are
10   unknown, the whole is unknown. But both you and I are ignorant of the parts, and of the whole; so we know nothing. Why, then, do you, being yourself ignorant, completely lacking knowledge of words, call me – and yourself – ignorant, yet call knowledge itself "subtle," and bury it in a hodge-podge of obscurities and in still greater ignorance? You will say: "To make myself appear knowledgeable". But the result is the opposite; for while you are reciting your false and absurd propositions, yet at the same time boasting of the extent of your knowledge, I conclude that you are totally ignorant, insofar as you do not know that you know nothing. Were you aware of this, I should infer that you were a cheat and a liar in claiming, as you do, to know a great deal.

Now, what I have always most earnestly looked for in anyone is what I am doing, namely that he should truly say whether he knew anything completely. But such a person I have nowhere found, save for that wise and honest man Socrates (though the Pyrrhonians, and the Academic school, and the so-called sceptics, and Favorinus too, made the same assertion), who knew only this, that he knew nothing.[44] For this saying alone he earns in my opinion the supreme place among mankind for wisdom; yet even so, he has not fully satisfied my mind, since he was ignorant even of that one fact, just as he was of others. But it was in order the more positively to assert that he knew nothing, that he said he knew that one fact. Accordingly, since he knew nothing, he decided not to write anything down for us moderns to read. The same thought has often occurred to me. For what can I say that is not under sus-

[44] In a marginal note Sanches refers the reader to Galen's *De optimo docendi genere*, Diogenes Laertius's *Lives of Eminent Philosophers*, 9, and Plutarch's *Adversus Colotem*. All three texts contain useful information on Academic scepticism and Pyrrhonism; book 9 of Diogenes Laertius's *Lives of Eminent Philosophers* gives one of the longest and most detailed accounts of Pyrrhonism and is Sanches's major source of information on scepticism. The exposition of Socratic ignorance is undoubtedly culled from Cicero's *Academica*, I, 4: "nihil se scire dicat nisi id ipsum ... ipse se nihil scire, id unum sciat."

picion of falsehood? To me, at least, all human activities are suspect, including the very words I am writing at the moment. Yet I
shall not hold my peace; at the least I will freely utter the statement
that I know nothing, in case you should labour fruitlessly over an
"enquiry into Truth", in the hope that some day you may clearly
understand it. But if, like the rest of mankind, I subsequently
proceed on the strength of this to attack one of the questions that
lie in the realm of Nature, on this hypothesis; then believe, if you
like – I still do not care, for that "all is vanity" was the saying of
that very wise man Solomon, the most learned of all men whom 11
past history has recorded, as is clearly shown by his works, supreme among which is that golden little book entitled *Ecclesiastes*,
or *The Preacher*.

But let us return to *knowledge*. Later, when we come to the
method of knowing, I shall explain what impelled Aristotle to
indulge in so many lengthy discussions of the arrangement of
words and to invent his celebrated "universals"; and also, whether
we can know anything without the help of all these. For the
present, we can gain no knowledge from this source. Consider
this statement: "Knowledge is gained by demonstration". What is
demonstration? It is a fantasy-ideal of Aristotle's, not unlike
Plato's "Republic" or Cicero's "Orator" or Horace's "Poet". It
does not exist at all, or in any place. Aristotle himself certainly
described it, and at very great length; but never did he give a single
demonstration, nor did any of his successors; or if he did, then you
must give it yourself: send it to me! But I know you have none to
give. But he did not even construct a syllogism at any point except
when he was teaching others how to construct one – and even
then, not out of terms that possessed meaning, but out of the
letters A, B, and C – and with some difficulty as well.[45] (But if he
had used terms possessing meaning, he would never have brought
his work to a conclusion!)

Of what use then, are syllogisms? Why did Aristotle devote so
much effort to the business of teaching them? And why, following
him, do the others still expend so much effort upon them? We do

[45] See *Prior Analytics* 25a–26b.

185

not use them in our writing; neither did he. No science has ever been created by means of them; on the contrary, many sciences have been brought to ruin and confusion because of them. In the conduct of an argument, and in the course of a debate, we are satisfied with a direct relation of antecedent and consequent, and so we use them still less; for otherwise debate would be never-ending, and we should have to struggle endlessly at reducing the syllogism to "mode" and "figure", at "converting" it, and at countless other frivolous exercises.[46] Nay, even today some foolish philosophers concern themselves with this, and reject any argument that is not formulated according to "mode" and "figure". So stupid are they, and so "clever and so useful" is the science of syllogisms, that they completely forget realities and turn to shadows. For this reason, one is prompted to marvel that

12 Averröes, in other respects an acute thinker, and many others after him, tried to reduce to syllogisms, with enormous and futile effort, things Aristotle said informally – aye, and they made it their aim to show at all points that these syllogisms were infallible, completely certain, and probative; whereas, as I shall later show, nothing is farther from the truth. *Per contra,* it is not surprising that Saint Augustine, that brilliant luminary of the Christian church, learnt all the sciences by his own efforts without any teacher, excepting only this "science" of syllogisms. For other sciences are based on facts, whereas this one is a subtle invention, and quite useless – or rather most harmful, inasmuch as it distracts me from the observation of facts and keeps me engaged in the study of itself – as you will be able to see more clearly from what I shall say in my works. But this is very different from the claim made by the members of that school, namely that there is a "method of knowing", and a first rule of procedure without which there is no science. They speak truth, but they speak without *knowledge.* In fact, their *knowledge* amounts to this: the only thing they know is

[46] Evidently Sanches did not enjoy the study of Aristotelian logic with its four figures and different modes for each figure of the syllogism. Ernest Kapp has pointed out that syllogistical games were played as mental exercises for beginners in philosophy. See *Greek Foundations of Traditional Logic* (New York: Columbia University Press, 1942), p. 64.

how to construct a syllogism from nothing, that is, from A and B and C. If it had to be constructed from *something,* they would fall dumb, inasmuch as they possess no understanding of even the most trivial statement of fact.

But to return to my theme. Take, then, the case of a person who teaches how to build a house, yet has never built one himself, nor knows how, nor has pupils who know how to do it. Why should I believe that a house ought to be built in the way he teaches? But "if there is no demonstration, there is for this reason no knowledge". Rather, the other statement is equally false: "Demonstration is what produces the acquired disposition of knowledge". For knowledge emerges from one who does not know yet is ready and eager to learn; all demonstration does is to point to the thing that has to be known; indeed, this is indicated by the very word "de-monstration" [from *monstrare,* "to show"]. Furthermore, I have never once been led to understand the very smallest fact, or proposition, by Aristotle and the rest; but I was stimulated by their remarks into preparing myself to examine any and every *thing;* and when I observed their contradictions and difficulties, in 13 order to avoid falling into these myself I dismissed those authors and fled for refuge to the facts, with the intention of seeking in them a basis for judgment. And Aristotle became for me, what Aristotle himself says Timotheus was to his fellow singers: that is to say, if someone of Aristotle's sort (and Plato's, and others too) had not come into the world, I myself would not perhaps have become such as I am.[47] Consequently, it is easy to see how foolish are those who look to the authorities for a complete and single system of knowledge, without making any investigation in the realm of facts. Therefore the man who with his finger points out

---

[47] In the *Metaphysics* 993b, Aristotle writes: "It is just that we should be grateful, not only to those with whose views we may agree, but also to those who have expressed more superficial views; for these also contributed something, by developing before us the powers of thought. It is true that if there had been no Timotheus we should have been without much of our lyric poetry; but if there had been no Phrynis there would have been no Timotheus" (*Works,* vol. VIII). In Plutarch's apocryphal dialogue *De musica,* Poetry describes Timotheus as "murder, mayhem and outrage".

to me something that is to be seen is not producing in me an act of *seeing,* but stimulating in me a *potential* capacity of seeing, so that it may be converted into actuality. For this reason I also find remarkably foolish the additional claim made by some, namely that "demonstration draws conclusions and makes proofs, with inevitability and on the basis of eternal and inviolable principles" – whereas perhaps none such exist; or if any do exist, they are entirely unknown, as such, to us men, who are in the highest degree subject to decay in the first place, and extremely vulnerable in a very short span of time.[48]

True knowledge, therefore, if it existed, would – on the contrary – be free, and would proceed from a free intellect; and if such an intellect does not by itself perceive a fact, then no "demonstrations" will make it perceive. Accordingly, "demonstration" constrains only the ignorant, for whom belief alone is sufficient.[49] Why, then, do you ignorantly amass quantities of propositions from here and there in Aristotle, and finally construct from them a "Barbarous" syllogism without understanding any single one of those propositions?[50] My advice to you would be better: give up philosophy, for you are quite unfitted for it, while you might be an excellent architect or tailor or cobbler, if you prefer. Such men arrange wood, stone, cloth, and leather into a "shape" or "figure" which is not "Barbarous," like the one you make, but elegant;[51] not asking what wood or stone or cloth *is,* but how to make out of them a house, a suit of clothes, or a pair of shoes for the Emperor (*Caesar*), just as you – using the "Caesarean" power – construct a labyrinth in which you can entrap yourself and the unfortunates who resemble you and who lack the guiding thread of reason.[52] But on the one hand you do

14

---

[48] Sanches is arguing against the existence of primary premisses, as outlined in the *Posterior Analytics* 72b–73a.

[49] Sanches contests belief in basic truths which are indemonstrable and are the required grounds of the Aristotelian theory of knowledge. Thus Aristotle begins the *Posterior Analytics* with the statement: "All instruction given or received by way of argument proceeds from pre-existent knowledge".

[50] Sanches puns on the syllogism in *Barbara*.

[51] Another pun on the *figurae* of the syllogism.

[52] Yet another pun on the syllogism in *Caesar*.

not *know* anything, yet you claim to instruct others; whereas I myself, like you, do not (on the other hand) know anything, but that is the very fact of which I am endeavouring to convince you. Hence, inasmuch as you do not know these things, this too you will not be able to grasp; while I for my part, since I am ignorant of everything, will be unable to demonstrate it to you. Therefore, we know nothing, as I have up to now been pointing out.

I am pursuing a definition of *knowledge*. They explain this as an acquired disposition which is an accumulation of many syllogistic inferences. It is strange how they always dismiss the facts completely and return to their own fantasies, like the cat in Aesop who was changed into a girl but even after her change of shape still continued to catch mice.[53] But really, for them this is what knowledge *is* like. They know nothing but a multitude of syllogistic inferences – no facts at all. For who ever defined *seeing* in terms of "an accumulation of images"? Yet knowledge is nothing but inward seeing. But if knowledge is an accumulation of syllogistic inferences then this book contains a great deal of knowledge. You are impudent: you will perhaps claim to possess *written* knowledge, on the principle that there is a distinction between oral and written and mental terms. I do not understand this; yet I grant it. What follows? It follows that neither you know anything, nor do I. This has the support of Aesop, who when he was put up for sale between two of his fellow slaves, a grammarian and a rhetorician, being asked after them what he knew, replied, "Nothing". "How so?" they asked him. "Because", he replied, "the grammarian and the rhetorician have left nothing for me to know" (since when they were previously asked what they knew, they had answered "Everything").[54] So now, according to you this book "knows" many things, another in the same way "knows" more things, and similarly with all other books; therefore nothing is left for us to know.

---

[53] See Aesop's fable "Venus and the Cat".

[54] This story is derived from a life of Aesop, prefixed to a book of fables collected by Maximus Planudes, a monk of the fourteenth century. About 1480 the collection of Planudes was published in Milan by Accursius with Ranuzio's Latin translation. This edition was reprinted by Estienne in Paris in 1546.

To continue: had they said in their definition of knowledge that it was "an accumulation of several things in the mind", that might have been a better way of putting it, yet it is not completely true, for knowledge can be knowledge of one thing only, or rather knowledge is only of each individual thing, taken by itself, not of 15 many things at once, just as a single act of seeing relates only to one particular object; for as it is not possible to focus perfectly on two objects at once, so too it is impossible to have complete understanding of two things at once, but only of one after the other. Hence the jingle:

> He that to many things attends
> On each the less attention spends.

Now just as all of mankind, taken together, amount to a single concept, "Man", whether its unity lies in species ["shape"], or (better) in name, so we speak of "seeing" in the singular, even though it may be a seeing of several different things and there may be several (numerically distinct) acts of seeing. In the same way, Philosophy is referred to as one science, even if it consists in the contemplation of several objects each of which is contemplated separately, and the knowledge of each of them after the act of contemplation is single and separate likewise. Nor is the saying true that knowledge is the accumulation of many things in the mind, as some people foolishly suppose, citing as examples of "learning" those who have seen and heard many things and can repeat them from time to time, both in the same science and in different sciences. Whereas rather "he who would encompass everything, loses everything". For a single science is large enough for the whole world, and yet the whole world is not large enough for it. For me, even the smallest thing in the world is enough and more than enough to engage me in studying it all my life long, yet even so I do not expect in the end to be capable of knowing it; how then could a single human being be capable of knowing so many things?[55] Nay, believe me, "many are called, but few are chosen".

---

[55] Sanches states in a marginal note that everything is incomprehensible according to the Academics, Pyrrhonians, and Xenophanes, and refers the reader to Diogenes Laertius's *Lives of Eminent Philosophers*, 9, and Plutarch's *Lucullus* and the *Adversus Colotem*.

Try it on yourself: study some *thing,* a worm if you like, its living soul; you could not grasp anything.

I do indeed admit that these things must *exist* in someone's mind in order to be known by him; this, however, is not knowledge but memory, just as seeing is not an accumulation of visual present-ations within the eye (suppose that this is how seeing occurs), even though seeing cannot occur *without* those visual presentations.[56] For we notice that those who form a fixed opinion concerning anything that presents itself to the senses still do not *perceive* anything, even though at that moment images are being im-pressed upon both eyes and ears.[57] It was on the same principle 16 that certain philosophers used to claim that everything was in everything. For how, they ask, are we to recognise things that are external to ourselves? (Thus all things *were* in us, but we find them out by bringing them to light, and this is knowledge.) But they are gravely mistaken; first because what they are claiming is that in us there is a donkey (perhaps in them there is!), a lion, and so forth. For how is it possible that I should be in a lion, and a lion in me? You are inventing a chimera. And I very much wish they would prove that we know something, for in that case we should allow them to reason as follows: "Nothing can be known unless it exists within ourselves; but all things are known; therefore all things exist within us". But in this instance the major premiss is doubtful, the minor, false. How, then, are you to infer the conclusion? Again, they reason unsoundly if they believe that for us to know it is enough that the objects of our knowledge should be within us. For although this might perhaps he relevant if it

---

[56] The primacy of the sense of sight, the noblest of the senses with respect to cognition, had been upheld by most mediaeval and Renaissance philosophers from Albertus Magnus and Duns Scotus to Leonardo da Vinci and Jacob Zabarella. See the essay by David C. Lindberg and Nicholas H. Steneck, "The Sense of Vision and the Origins of Modern Science", in *Science, Medicine and Society in the Renaissance,* ed. Allen C. Debus (New York: Neale Watson, 1972), I, pp. 29–45. Aristotle in the beginning of the *Metaphysics* states that sight is loved above all the senses since it "makes us know and brings to light many differences between things" (980a26–7). The act of seeing becomes cognition.

[57] In the *De sensu* 437a Aristotle stresses that the two most important senses for those animals that have intelligence are sight and hearing.

were possible, yet the inference does not follow that *all* things are in us; quite the contrary, since clearly there are in us many things (body, soul, understanding, faculties, imagination, etc.) which nevertheless we by no means know perfectly. But I shall systematically discuss this question – that is, whether all things are in us – in my books on Nature; for the present, let it suffice to have touched on those aspects that are relevant to the discussion before us.

It is not, therefore, things or images of them existing within us that produce or constitute knowledge; rather, the memory is filled up by them and the intellect subsequently reflects on them. Hence I can now draw the inference that it is quite wrong for knowledge to be described as an "acquired disposition"; for an "acquired disposition" is a *quality*, and cannot easily be transferred, whereas knowledge is not a quality, unless you were willing to describe seeing as a quality; rather it is a single action of the mind, which can be entirely perfect even at the first glance and lasts no longer than the mind is engaged in it – and this is also true of seeing. Of this observation and recognition (*cognitio*), which comes about through the mind's action, an image is committed to the memory and retained there. If this image is securely settled in the memory, it will be called an "acquired disposition" (*habitus*); but if not, it will be called simply a "disposition". But these images will then belong to the memory, not to knowledge. If the subject recalls them subsequently, he will be said to "remember" things known, not to "know" them, except when he contemplates them; just as a person who is relating the things he has seen is not engaged in the act of seeing. Yet one who retains in this way in his memory what he knows is said to "know" many things because he both knew all of them before and can "know" them whenever he pleases; for it costs him very little effort to understand them by a backward 17 glance, inasmuch as he understood them already beforehand. From which it is clear that the "possession" (*habitus*) of many things in the memory is not called "knowledge" unless these same things had previously been grasped by the understanding.

But still another philosopher strangely asserted that our knowledge was nothing but remembering; that is, before we are

born our soul knows everything, but once it is incarnate within us
it forgets everything, and a little later, as if reawakened after a
descent to oblivion, it remembers.[58] But with apologies to this
otherwise brilliant thinker, this is a quite baseless fiction, not supported either by experience or by rational argument – like many
other dreams he dreamed up concerning the soul, as I shall demonstrate in my *Treatise on the Soul*. Now, Aristotle has in many
places refuted this error, but I shall not repeat his arguments, since
anyone may read them in his works.[59] Let us examine Plato's mistake so far as concerns my purpose. If Plato had said that he himself had perceived that his soul, before its incarnation in the body,
knew everything, I might perhaps have believed him. In that event
he would not have been a human being, but a ghost or apparition.
Surely I have no knowledge of events that took place before my
time; I find it hard to believe in what I *do* see; how, then, am I to
believe in your dreams? Tell me: either the soul possessed knowledge before it entered the body, or it did not. You will not opt for
the second of these. Well, then: either that "knowledge" was
merely the soul's recollection, or not. If it was, then it came from
another soul that was in the soul itself, and which knew everything
before it entered the soul. Then, concerning this other soul, we
pose once again the same question: "Is its knowledge recollection?"
I am leading you into an infinite regress.   18

But if it does not recollect with the help of another soul but by
itself, then it had previously "forgotten". Why? And if it had
"forgotten" before this happened, was its "knowledge" a further
instance of recollection? Once more we are faced with an infinite
regress. If the soul's knowledge was *not* recollection, does the
soul, once incarnated in body, lose that knowledge? If not, then
it continues to know, as it did before. Yet previously, by your
account, its knowledge was *not* recollection. But if, as you

[58] A reference to Plato's theory of recollection in the *Meno* [81c5–e1].

[59] In the following marginal annotation Sanches indicates that Aristotle refutes
Plato's theories in the *Posterior Analytics, Metaphysics,* and his treatise *On the
Soul.* Much of Sanches's subsequent argumentation is derived from Aris-
totle's critique of Plato in the *De memoria et reminiscentia* 449b–451b.

maintain, the soul, by its incarnation in body, through the shock of exchanging its place of abode (so to speak), remains for a time forgetful of itself, though it will certainly remember afterwards the things it had forgotten, nevertheless it will not know them afresh; just as we too, though we forget things we knew before, in the end remember them – yet this remembering is not knowing. But if the soul loses this knowledge, it will not afterwards remember. For we remember those things that are indeed still in the memory or imagination but do not present themselves to conscious thought; hence, when they are stimulated by encountering either a similar thing or another example of the same thing, as a result of the encounter they turn into a mental presentation, but are accompanied by the recollection that they were in the same situation before.

But if they had been blotted out altogether, it would be an instance not of memory but of a fresh impression, as happens to those who on account of sickness come to forget completely even their own names. If they happen to learn them afterwards, you will not speak of them as "remembering", for even popular belief maintains the contrary, namely that they have fallen into total forgetfulness and must subsequently learn afresh, just as if they were children; and they themselves say that they never knew before the things that they are now being taught.[60] Therefore, knowledge is not recollection. Moreover, whenever we recollect we say, "Surely I had forgotten this before, since I now remember that it happened in this or that way". But if what happened to the soul was merely that it remembered, then even a child could say, while he was being taught, "I too knew these things before, and now I remember them". But does anyone in fact say this? Similarly, if the soul knew before it was incarnated in body, then it will be the soul, not the man, that will subsequently possess know-

[60] A marginal note refers the reader to Galen's *De symptomatum differentiis* and the *De symptomatum causis* (see Sanches's commentaries on these works in his *Opera medica*, pp. 741–54, 755–807); also to Pliny's *Natural History*, 7, 24, and to Valerius Maximus's *Factorum et dictorum memorabilium* (probably book 1, 8, 12, ext. 2). The reference to Thucydides is possibly to *History of the Peloponnesian War*, 1, 20.

ledge. Moreover, is it not foolish to say that the soul "knows"? Let us proceed to clarify the point, for our enquiry is about a name.

Either knowledge and recollection mean the same thing, or not. Not the same; for why do we not use one word indifferently in place of the other? Indeed, I have no doubt that even dogs remember; for not so long ago, I deliberately struck one, and now every time he sees me he barks at me, doubtless remembering my blows. But who will maintain that dogs "know"? Perhaps, on account of Aristotle, you will not allow that dogs remember; but more of this later.[61] Women and children at least remember, yet they know nothing; or rather *all* of us remember, yet we know nothing.

But if these terms do not mean the same thing, why did Plato take them to be the same? If one of the two is of a wider application, why did he not add some specifying term (*differentia*) to limit that application? For Man is "animal", but not the only instance of "animal", for so is a horse; therefore we add "four-footed" to the latter, "two-footed" to the former. Consequently they do not mean the same; so knowledge and memory are different things. But for the moment I will not comment on this, but will turn to something else.

What, I repeat, is "knowing"? We are told that it is "understanding something by means of its causes".[62] This is still not quite satisfactory; the definition is obscure. For it immediately raises the problem of *causes,* which is harder to solve than the first question. In order to understand something, must we understand *all* its causes? Certainly not its *efficient* cause; for what does my father contribute to an understanding of *me?*[63] What, then, of the *final* cause? Then again, if you would like to gain complete under-

---

[61] In Aristotle's *De memoria et reminiscentia* [453a5–10], to which the marginal note refers, only man has the faculty of recollection since it is a mode of inference.

[62] Sanches refers the reader to Aristotle's *Posterior Analytics,* 1, *Physics,* 2, and *Metaphysics passim.*

[63] Aristotle in the *Physics* 194b30–1 gives as an example of efficient cause: "The father is the cause of the child".

standing of the thing that is caused, you ought also to understand its causes completely. What follows? That nothing can be known, if you should wish to have complete understanding of its efficient and final causes. I shall now demonstrate this. In order to understand me completely, you ought to understand my father 20 completely; and in order to understand him, you must first understand *his* father, and after him another father, and so on *ad infinitum*. Similarly with other objects; and the same may be said of the final cause.

You will maintain that you are not considering particular things, which as such are not objects of knowledge, but universals such as "man", "horse", and so on. But in fact, as I said before, your "knowledge" is knowledge not of the real man but of the "man" whom you invent for yourself; accordingly, you *know* nothing. So be it, then; consider that invented "man" of yours. You will not know him, unless you first know his causes. Has he not an efficient cause? You will not deny that he has. If you wish to know this efficient cause in turn, you must ponder *its* efficient cause. There will be no end to this; hence it will not result in your coming to know what that "man" of yours is. Nor did you previously know what the *real* man was. Therefore, you know nothing. Perhaps you will have recourse to Almighty God, as both the first cause and the final end of all things, and will assert that *there* you must stop, and not proceed to infinity. More of this later; but I would now say: what follows from this? That you know nothing. In avoiding the infinite you fall into what is both infinite and measureless, incomprehensible, ineffable, and beyond the reach of the understanding.[64] Can this Being be known? Certainly not. Yet, by your account, He is the cause of everything; and therefore, according to your definition, understanding of Him is necessary for the understanding of His works. Therefore, you know nothing.

If you do not believe that the efficient cause *and* the final cause

---

[64] Sanches's fideistic conception of God shows a close affinity with Montaigne's thought in the closing paragraphs of the "Apologie de Raimond Sebond", which is heavily influenced by Plutarch's treatise "On the E at Delphi".

are necessary for understanding a thing, why do you not distinguish between causes in your definition?[65] For my part, I supposed that when you said, without reservation, "understand a thing by means of its causes", this meant *all* its causes. (But elsewhere, too, Aristotle comprehensively lists and enumerates all the causes – efficient, material, formal, and final – although he has said that we believe we understand a thing only when we grasp its "first" cause.) Yet suppose I concede to you, even though it neither need be nor could rightly be conceded, that the efficient and the final cause are not necessary; there remain two causes, the material and the formal, which – as I believe you understand the matter – must be comprehended, but this is still less correct. 21 On your definition, should you wish to know the *form,* you ought to know it by its causes; not by the efficient and the final cause, as before; therefore, by the material and the formal cause. But these it does not possess. Therefore you will not know it. But if you do not know this [i.e. the form], you will not know that of which it is the form; for when the parts are unknown, the whole is unknown. I may say the same of the *matter,* which is simpler still, and less of an entity; and it may be that it has no cause – at least, efficient, material, and formal cause, according to Aristotle. As to the final cause, a doubt may be entertained about it. What are you saying? "Any understanding of causes whatever, albeit imperfect, is enough for acquiring knowledge of a thing". This is nonsense.

"It is impossible fully to understand a whole without fully understanding its parts".[66] But if I were to grant that also – I ask whether one can have knowledge of form and matter? You will allow this, inasmuch as you profess to know everything. I ask once more: can one acquire knowledge by means of causes? If you

---

[65] See Aristotle *Metaphysics* 1013a–1014a. The following quotation refers to the argument in book 3 of the *Metaphysics.*

[66] Sanches refers here to the opening paragraph of Aristotle's *Physics* [184a]: "When the objects of an inquiry, in any department, have principles, conditions, or elements, it is through acquaintance with these that knowledge, that is to say scientific knowledge, is attained. For we do not think that we know a thing until we are acquainted with its primary conditions or first principles, and have carried our analysis as far as its simplest elements".

answer no, then your definition is no definition. If yes, I ask again
concerning these causes: can they be known? Not less than the other
things; nay, more than they; for, by your account, simpler things
are by nature more familiarly known, and consequently more
knowable in themselves. Knowable by causes, then? – We are
entering an infinite regress. Thus, you have no definition. Nay,
rather, for these same reasons also, you know nothing. And
Aristotle elsewhere raises this very same objection against himself:
"If the only knowledge is, in fact, that which is acquired by
demonstration, while its first principles are incapable of being
demonstrated, then there will be no knowledge of the first
principles, and hence there will be no knowledge".[67] But he did
not give a satisfactory answer to this objection when he said that
not *all* knowledge is demonstrative, but knowledge of those
things that have no intermediate terms cannot be demonstrated.[68]
For it follows from this that the statement "Knowledge is
understanding a thing by means of its causes" is not true in an
unqualified sense, nor is that other statement, "Knowledge is an
acquired disposition (*habitus*), gained by demonstration", if there
22 is some knowledge that is *not* gained by demonstration. Now,
Aristotle had expressed it better elsewhere, and could have been
excused if he had always spoken in the same way, and had once for
all given a full account of knowledge. As it is, however, since at all
points he is vague, confused, and inconsistent, he has left himself
no grounds to be excused. Further, he had said that "knowledge
of things depends on understanding their first principles, causes,
and elements, where these exist".[69] It is absurd how Aristotle's
followers enlarge upon this statement; for, perverting realities into
words and syllogisms (lulled to sleep by an ancient mistake, and

---

[67] Aristotle makes the same point in the *Posterior Analytics* 72b5–6 when he tries
to refute the school of thought (to which Sanches belongs) which maintains
that "owing to the necessity of knowing the primary premisses, there is no
scientific knowledge".

[68] Ibid. 72b18–20. "Our own doctrine is that not all knowledge is demonstrative: on the contrary, knowledge of the immediate premisses is independent of
demonstration".

[69] See note 66.

stagnating under its influence), they identify "first principles" with the primary, familiar, and underlying propositions of each particular science, which they themselves refer to as "first principles" and "axioms"; whereas they identify "causes" with the *intermediate* propositions between the first principles and the fact that is to be proved. As for "elements", these they interpret as subject and predicate, copula, middle term, major and minor "extreme terms". Is not this a clever invention – or rather, delusion? In this way, while their leader is *slightly* mistaken, they – since they do not understand him or follow his thought – do worse than this, to the extent that finally they slip into a multitude of foolish fancies, gradually falling away from the truth. But let us return to Aristotle. In an earlier context he argued that there *was* knowledge of first principles but it could not be demonstrated. Elsewhere he calls a grasp of first principles "understanding" (*intellectus*), not "knowledge"; but this is a misnomer, since if first principles, like other things, were fully understood then perfect knowledge would exist. As it is, however, since we do not possess understanding of first principles, we do not possess it either in respect of things of which they are first principles. From which it follows that nothing is known. Again, what else is knowledge but understanding an object? For it is only when we understand something that we say we "know" it. But on the other hand it is not true that there are two kinds of knowledge. For knowledge, if any existed, would be one, and single in nature, just as there is only one faculty of seeing, but it would be *acquired* in two ways: 23 one way would be simple, when we comprehended a simple thing (such as matter, form, and spirit, if you like); the other would be complex, so to speak, when we comprehended a complex thing, which it would be necessary first to break down into its parts and comprehend them individually, and then finally to comprehend the whole. Now, this last method is always *preceded* by the first; however, it does not invariably follow it. In all these matters, demonstration is useful only perhaps for pointing out the thing that is to be known. But enough of this, for I have said more than might have appeared suitable to one who knows nothing!

But my remarks were not unreasonable, for up to this point I have occasionally pointed out the ignorance of others in relation to the definition of knowledge and the nature of understanding; I shall now exhibit my own ignorance, just in case it seems that I am alone in knowing *something*. From this you will be able to see how completely we lack knowledge. Now, the doctrines that have hitherto been accepted by the majority appear to me false, as I have already shown, whereas those I am about to formulate appear to me true. Perhaps you will take the opposite view, and it may be that this will be the true one – from which results the confirmation of the proposition that "nothing is known". Accordingly let us now see what "knowing" is, in order that it may as a result become clearer whether anything is known. KNOWLEDGE IS PERFECT UNDERSTANDING OF A THING.[70] There you have an easy, yet true, explanation of the term "knowledge." If you ask me what are its genus and differentia, I will not provide you with these, for these two words are more obscure than the thing that is defined. What is "understanding"? Certainly I could not explain it in any other way; and if I were to define it in any other way, you could again ask the same question about this definition and the parts thereof. Thus there would be no end, and the doubt about names would go on for ever.

24 Consequently, the sources of our knowledge are both extended to infinity and also completely insecure; for we attempt to demonstrate the natures of things in words, and these words again in other words, which is both hard and impossible. We know nothing. You say that we must come to a halt somewhere in our questioning. True – because we can do nothing else. But I do not know what "understanding" is; define it for me. I should call it comprehension or perception or "intellection" of a thing, and anything else that means what these words mean. If you are still in

---

[70] In the text Sanches capitalises this statement: "SCIENTIA EST REI PERFECTA COGNITIO". Popkin analyses the meaning thus: "Genuine knowledge is immediate, intuitive apprehension of all the real qualities of an object. Thus, science will deal with particulars, each somehow to be individually understood" (*The History of Scepticism from Erasmus to Spinoza*, p. 38).

doubt about this, I will be silent; but I shall ask you for another definition, and if you reply to my request I will raise a doubt about your statement. Thus we are always in difficulties because of our ignorance. What course remains to us? The final remedy: you must think for yourself. You *have* thought, and it may be that you have acquired understanding; but nothing could be less true. I, too, believe that I have comprehended. What follows? When, afterwards, I discuss understanding with you, *I* suppose it to be such as I have grasped, while *you* suppose it to be such as you have grasped. *I* assert that it is *this,* while *you,* on the other hand, assert that it is *that.* Who is to arbitrate our dispute? Why, one who recognises what understanding *truly* is. But who is he? He does not exist. Everyone believes himself to be extremely learned; to me, all men seem ignorant. It may be that I am the *only* ignorant man alive; but I should like to *know this* at least, and this I cannot do. What, therefore, can I go on to say that is free of the suspicion of ignorance? Nothing. Why, then, do I write? What do I know? With fools you will be foolish. I am a human being – what am I to do? It is the same thing exactly. Now I return to my theme.

We know nothing. So, in order that our discussion may proceed, please assume the explanation of the word "knowledge" which I set down; and let us infer from it that nothing can be known – for to assume a supposition is not to know but to invent; consequently it is invention, not knowledge, that will emerge from assumptions. Observe the point to which our discussion has now brought us: all knowledge is invention. This is evident. "Knowledge is acquired by demonstration"; this in turn assumes a definition. Now, definitions cannot be *proved,* but have to be *believed;* therefore demonstration based on assumptions (*ex suppositis*) will produce knowledge of a suppositious kind, not sound and exact knowledge. (All these conclusions are based on statements of your own.) Again, according to you, first principles 25 must be assumed in every branch of knowledge, and Aristotle has no right to challenge these. So the conclusions to be drawn from these first principles will be things assumed, not things known.

What could be more pitiable than our situation? In order to know, we have to be ignorant! For what is making an assumption

201

but admitting things we do not know? Would it not be better to know the first principles beforehand? Say that I deny, to you, the first principles of your science; now prove them. You say that "you need not argue against people who deny your first principles".[71] You do not know how to prove them; then you are an ignorant person, not one who knows. But "it belongs to a higher, or generalised, kind of science to test the first principles of other sciences". So then, he who possesses this generalised science will perhaps know everything, while you know nothing; for he who is ignorant of the first principles is also ignorant of the subject itself. But what *is* that generalised science? It is strange how *your* experts divide their functions among themselves; they draw boundaries between one another, just as the commonalty of fools appropriates and shares out the land. Nay, rather, they have erected an empire of sciences, among which the queen and supreme arbitrator is the "generalised" science; to it disputes are, in the last instance, referred. It lays down rules for the others, rules which they must accept as binding; and to none of the others is it allowed with impunity to encroach on *its* preserves, nor upon one another's either. Thus they quarrel, all their lives long, about the subject-matter of each science, and nobody can adjudicate this suit – or rather this ignorance. Hence if in the realm of physical science anyone argues about the stars, they say he does this either in the capacity of a physical scientist or of an astrologer; and of another, "He borrows this from Arithmetic"; but still another "purloins that from Mathematics". What does this mean?

Surely all of this is childish nonsense. For it is children who in a public place – the square, the forum, or the Campus – build their "gardens" and enclose them with tiles; and each of them forbids anyone else to set foot on his little plot. I can see what this means: since each one could not possibly embrace everything, one man chose *this* part for himself, another seized another part. Hence 26 nothing is known. For since all things that are in this world unite

---

[71] The "you" in question is Aristotle who, in the *Posterior Analytics* 72a–72b, does not refute the objections of his opponents very convincingly, since first principles are a matter of belief.

to make up a single collective whole, some of them cannot exist without others, while again some cannot continue in existence along with others; each thing performs its own function, separate and differing from another's function, yet all things contribute to a single whole. Some are the cause of others; and some are caused by the action of others. The links between all of them are inexpressibly complicated. It is not, therefore, surprising if, one of them being unknown, the rest are also unknown. The reason for this may be the following: one who is interested in studying the stars, in considering their motions, and the causes of those motions, takes as proved the statements of a physicist on the questions what a star is, and what motion is; he then has only to study the variety and the multiplicity of motion in stars. Similarly with the other sciences. But this is not knowledge.

For true knowledge is to understand, in the first place the nature of a thing, in the second place its accidents, where it has any.[72] From which it follows that a "demonstration" is not a "syllogism resulting in knowledge"; rather, it is nothing, insofar as it merely demonstrates that the accident inheres in the thing, according to you (since for me, so far is it from demonstrating anything that it rather conceals something, and manages only to confuse the intellect), but takes for granted the definition of the thing itself. Consequently all those who rely on demonstrations, and look for knowledge as a result of them, in fact know nothing; as for those who condemn demonstrations, they too know nothing, as you yourself maintain and as I shall presently prove. Therefore, we all alike know nothing. Accordingly, if you grant my definition, there are three factors in knowledge: the thing that is to be known; understanding (*cognitio*); and the perfection of knowledge. We

---

[72] Aristotle argues in the *Posterior Analytics* 74b that there is no demonstrative knowledge of *accidents,* since they are not necessary attributes. Furthermore, in the *Metaphysics* 1026b1 – 5, he states that there can be no scientific treatment of the *accidental,* since "no science – practical, productive, or theoretical – troubles itself about it". Sanches, on the other hand, argues that the natural philosopher should seek total "perfect knowledge" of things, dealing with the particulars, i.e. *accidents,* as well as the universals. Knowledge of universals is, therefore, knowledge of nothing, if science does not deal with the particulars.

shall have to consider each of them singly, in order that we may deduce that nothing is known.

First of all, how many *things* are there? Perhaps they are infinite in number, not only as individuals but even in species. You will deny that they are infinite in number; yet you will not prove that they are finite, for you have not been able to count even the least part of them; for myself, I have barely come to identify "man" and "horse" and "dog".[73] Therefore, on this point we already know nothing; for *you* have not seen the finite limit of all things,

27 yet you say they are finite, whereas *I* have not seen their *infinity*, yet I conjecture that they are infinite. Can anything be more certain? You must decide for yourself, but so far as I am concerned *nothing* is more certain. But how, you will say, can their infinity hamper us in respect to the understanding of one single thing? A very great deal, in your view; for in order to understand the thing, one must understand first principles (matter and form, perhaps), but in the infinite state it may be that infinite quantities of matter are distinct in outward form (and yet *you* would not have matter be distinguished in terms of outward form, inasmuch as you deprive it of form altogether; more of this later).[74] Concerning forms, there is no doubt; but concerning the infinite, there is no knowledge. But, you will say, even infinite numbers of things may share the same matter. This is indeed true, but it is also possible that their matter may not be the same, and so it may be of various kinds.

For it may be that other things exist, totally different from those that are familiar to us – things with which none of us is acquainted. But as to what may either exist or not exist, it is hard

[73] According to Sanches, Aristotle's demonstrative science with its reliance on definitions which embrace universal terms, as outlined in the *Prior Analytics*, cannot produce scientific knowledge. Aristotle argues against an infinite series of intermediate terms in the *Posterior Analytics* 82a–84b and, again, in the *Physics* 187a, where he refutes the theory of Anaxagoras that the principles are infinite in number.

[74] Much of Sanches's argument concerning matter and form (the essential nature of a thing) is directed against Aristotle's definitions in the *Physics* 193a–194b and *Metaphysics* 1028b– 1033b. Sanches takes up the topic again on p. 229.

to tell whether it belongs to that class. By your own account, however, knowledge is of what *is* (and may not be otherwise). Nor is it necessary that things should be infinite in number in order that matter should be of diverse kinds; for even to you, who believe things to be finite, it is not clear (and never – though I may be mistaken – will be clear) whether the matter of the sky is the same as that of these lower realms.[75] Nay, is not there a special matter appertaining to the spirits, although they are said to be of a single substance? Assuredly. *You* maintain that there are several genera of these, and therefore several differentiae. Accordingly, they agree in having some common component, which in your view is their *matter,* and they differ in another component, namely their *form.* But do not the "accidents" likewise possess a matter of their own? You call their matter genus, while you call their form differentia. Is the matter of the stars the same as that of the sky? You do not know, but it appears not to be the same.[76] Therefore, what the first principles are, and how many of them there are, is unknown, even should things be finite in number. And you will never come to an end of the first principles; but the first principles of Man are elements; of these elements the matter is such-and-such, the form again such-and-such; and of this matter and this 28 form there are other elements, of more unitary structure. It is the same with lion and ass and bear, and so on *ad infinitum*. And there is no doubt concerning the forms, because in infinity these will be infinite. But we ought to grasp the first principles in advance. You will say the elements are not first principles; I shall discuss this later.[77] Rather, there will be *no* first principles, for of the infinite

---

[75] In the Aristotelian theory of matter, "local matter" is independent of the sublunary world and exists only in the heavenly spheres. The intelligences that move the spheres are pure substances, of which the highest is God.

[76] Sanches refers the reader to a different opinion given by Julius Caesar Scaliger in his *Exercitationes,* 61: "Non enim esse in Caelo variam substantiam, colligere licet ex secundo libro De Caelo: ubi Stellarum, Caelique eandem esse substantiam, scriptum est. Quemadmodum et apud Averrois in tertia disputatione legibus, negantem in Caelo Heterogeneitatem" (p. 93v.)

[77] Since the elements are subject to change and limited in number, they cannot be first principles.

there *is* no first principle. But even suppose things are finite, you will not be any more in possession of knowledge, for you are not acquainted with the first principle, the most necessary of all things, and therefore also fail to understand the rest, which derive from it. Therefore, we know nothing.

Again, of things, some exist only from themselves, out of themselves, in themselves, by means of themselves, and on account of themselves; such, if I may be permitted to say so, is our God, who is Aristotle's First Cause; whereas all other things derive from Him, not from themselves or out of themselves, or in themselves, or by means of themselves, or for themselves alone, or on account of themselves, but some from others, and others again from these; some in others, and some on account of others.[78] But we have to understand both kinds of things. Yet who has complete understanding of God? "There shall no man see me and live". So Moses alone was permitted to see "the hinder parts of God", that is, God through His works.[79] Hence the Apostle wrote, "The invisible things of God are clearly seen, being understood by the things that are made".[80] In addition to this we should also understand what things are the causes of what others and how they cause them, in order that we may know something completely. For all things are linked together in such a way that no single thing is detached from the function of hindering or helping another. Nay, one and the same thing was made by Nature to harm many others, and to help many others. Therefore, in order to understand any one thing perfectly we must understand everything; and who is capable of this? Such a person I have nowhere seen. And, for the same reason, certain sciences assist

[78] In the *Metaphysics*, book 1, Aristotle defines wisdom as being not only *scientia* or knowledge of causes (the material, formal, efficient, and final) but also knowledge of the first and universal causes. Thus he seeks comprehensive knowledge of all things. Aristotle found it necessary to assert that there was an eternal unmovable substance which was the First Cause. The incorporation of Aristotelian science into Christianity was largely due to the influence of Thomas Aquinas

[79] Exodus, 33.

[80] Romans 1:20.

certain others, and one science contributes to the understanding of another. Nay, what is more, one science cannot be completely known in isolation from others; and accordingly they are obliged to borrow, one from another. For the subject-matters of the sciences are such that they mutually depend on one another, and 29 one subject-matter makes up another, turn and turn about.[81] From which it once again follows that nothing is known. For who understands *all* sciences?

I will add a brief example, lest these statements remain unsupported by proof. Let an example from mankind suffice. Now, man dislikes the basilisk; indeed, it is said that the basilisk is killed by the saliva of a fasting human being.[82] The basilisk dislikes man and also the weasel – the only creatures that, it is said, are able to kill it. The weasel dislikes the basilisk and the mouse; the mouse, the weasel and the cat; the cat, the mouse and the dog; the dog, the cat and the hare; the hare, the dog and the ferret. And let this suffice concerning *antipathy*.[83] In the same way, the human being does not eat and enjoy just any food, but the flesh of ox, ram, and so forth. These latter do not eat anything offered to them but hay, oats, chaff – and these again do not grow in any ground,

---

[81] In the *Metaphysics* 1025b–1026a Aristotle divides the sciences into the theoretical, the practical, and the productive: all are interrelated, since they depend on common first principles and a common method. In book 3 of the *Metaphysics*, Aristotle discusses the contribution of all of the sciences to the pursuit of knowledge of first principles and concludes that "it would seem to belong to different sciences to investigate these causes severally" (996b24–6).

[82] The source for Sanches's remark on the basilisk was probably Scaliger's *Exercitationes*. Sir Thomas Browne in the *Pseudodoxia epidemica*, 3, 7, mentions that the basilisk is found in Dioscorides, Galen, Pliny, and many more ancient authors. Ferdinando Ponzetti in his treatise on poisons, *Libellus de venenis* (Rome: J. Mazochii, 1521), describes how snake charmers protected themselves by spitting on the heads of snakes, since human saliva had a special property.

[83] In the *History of Animals* 608a–610a, Aristotle describes the enmity (antipathy) that exists between animals that dwell in the same localities or subsist on the same food. However, the philosophy of antipathy and sympathy was based on the Aristotelian doctrine of the continuity of nature, of the attraction of like for like and the mutual opposition of contraries.

but only in this or that kind of ground. This ground, again, does not produce everything, but one particular crop or another; and a great deal is also contributed by a particular climate. So much for *sympathy*. How does all of this come about? You must understand the nature of each of these before you come to have a satisfactory understanding of man. In the same way, since a man is nourished, grows, lives, reproduces, deteriorates, and reasons, we have at once to ask questions about the soul and its faculties. And on the analogy of man, we must enquire, about plants, by what "soul" they live; also about animals, and inanimate things too; for the science of contraries is the same science.[84] Take coming-to-be and passing-away: whence do they arise? From contrary qualities. I shall forthwith proceed to discuss these qualities and elements and pre-existent bodies (for it is the sun and a human being that combine to bring a human being into existence); we must also discuss the incarnation of soul in body, and the introduction of forms, and doing and suffering, and quality and quantity, place and relation, because man sits, reproduces, grows warm. But again, because one action is performed at rest, another in an instant, another in time, we must see what *time* is, and this leads at once to the heavens 30 and the celestial movements, for time, as Aristotle remarks (though he puts it badly, as we shall notice at the appropriate place), is "the number of motions according to 'before' and 'after'".[85] Because the motion of the world is in a vertical and downward direction, we have at once to ask what is "up" and "down", and discuss the world's centre, its poles, and its parts.[86] Because man sees, and

---

[84] Sanches reviews the problems concerning the soul which are dealt with by Aristotle in the *De anima*. If soul is the form or actuality of all living things, then it must be considered in all its manifestations, both in the animal and in the plant world, and in all its faculties – nutritive, sensitive, cognitive, and motive. Moreover, Sanches states that the science of contraries, as expounded in the *Metaphysics,* is the fundamental concept governing Aristotle's writings.

[85] Sanches refers the reader to Aristotle's definition of time in the *Physics* [219a22−5]: "But we apprehend time only when we have marked motion, marking it by 'before' and 'after'; and it is only when we have perceived 'before' and 'after' in motion that we say that time has elapsed".

[86] See the *De caelo* 285b and 300a.

does so with the aid of light, we have at once to ask about colours, atmospheric conditions, shapes, light and the luminous, the sun and the stars.[87] Since man is body, and exists in space, we must enquire concerning body, substance, space, and the void. Because space is said to be finite, we must enquire about the finite and the infinite.[88] Because human beings bring others into being, and are themselves brought into being, we have immediately to enquire concerning the totality of causes, up to the very first cause.[89] Because man reasons, we must enquire concerning the "understanding soul" (*anima intellectiva*) and its faculties; concerning knowledge and the knowable; concerning practical wisdom and the other so-called acquired dispositions.[90] Because he kills; because he never lives in contentment; because for his country's sake he places his life in mortal peril; because he relieves the sick and the needy, we must enquire concerning good and evil, and concerning the ultimate and supreme good, and virtue and vice, and the immortality of the rational soul (*animus*).[91] Now, any one of these brings with it all other things, and it would be tiresome to go through the list.[92] One might say the same about anything whatever, even the smallest. This you can understand from the wholly familiar example of an ordinary clock. For if you should wish to know how it strikes the hours you must make a comprehensive inspection of all its wheel-movements, from the

---

[87] See the *De anima* 418b.

[88] See the *Physics* 200b–224a.

[89] Sanches refers in general to the *De generatione et corruptione*.

[90] See *De anima* 427a–432a.

[91] Sanches, of course, is referring to the *Nicomachean Ethics*, which is a work of Aristotle he rarely cites.

[92] In his enumeration of the major writings of Aristotle it is evident that Sanches had spent many years (1574–81) examining the basic suppositions of Aristotle's enquiry into the problem of knowledge, scientific method, and the organisation of the sciences. In fact, the first part of the *Quod nihil scitur* is a sustained commentary in the Scholastic tradition, using Aristotelian terminology, on the *Posterior Analytics*, the *Physics*, the *De caelo*, the *De anima*, and the *Metaphysics*. To follow Sanches's arguments the reader must possess a detailed knowledge of these texts, which played such an important role in the humanities curriculum of the universities in the Renaissance.

first to the last, and so determine what moves the first wheel, how this moves another, and this again two more, and so on to the very last wheel. But if the clock, besides striking the hours, should also indicate them externally by means of a hand on a dial, and if, moreover, it should show the movement of the moon – its waxing and waning – and likewise the whole passage of the sun through the zodiac, in an alignment reflecting that which it follows in the sky (all of which, and much more, I have seen for myself, exhibited on a portable clock according to the true course of the 31 stars), then certainly you will have a more difficult feat to achieve – nor will you be able to perceive how even the least of these things is done without taking apart the whole machinery from the beginning, and examining it and coming to understand its in-dividual parts and their functions.[93] You can find an illustration of this very point in the glass sphere that was constructed, with amazing skill, by the celebrated Archimedes of Syracuse, in which there moved and were visible all the spheres and planets, exactly as in the mechanism of our actual world; air, blown through a number of pipes and conduits, propelled the whole apparatus in symmetrical movement. Should anyone wish to discover how this worked, would it not be necessary for him to possess a complete mastery of the entire machinery and its parts, down to the very smallest, together with their functioning? We must believe that the same thing occurs in this world of ours. For what could you find in it that does not both cause and suffer movement and change – movement alone, or change alone, or both movement *and* change? But in proportion as the ideal world

---

[93] As Alex Keller has pointed out, the technological achievements at the end of the Middle Ages and during the Renaissance were symbolised by automata such as planetaria resembling that of Archimedes and the magnificent mechanical clocks. See Alex Keller, "Mathematical Technologies and the Growth of the Idea of Technical Progress in the Sixteenth Century", in *Science, Medicine and Society in the Renaissance*, ed. Debus, I, pp. 16–17. The revival of interest in Archimedes was stimulated by Niccolò Tartaglia's Latin edition of Archimedes in 1543. Sanches does not subscribe to the mechanist hypothesis that it is possible to comprehend the universe by the laws of mechanics.

contains more things that exist and happen than does Archimedes' glass sphere, so much the more difficult is it for the former to be comprehended in its entirety than the latter – yet not less necessary, for anyone who wishes to possess knowledge.

Observe the stage we have now reached in our discussion. In the natural universe there is but one kind of knowledge, not several kinds (or would be, if it could be obtained), by which all things might be fully understood; for one thing cannot be fully understood apart from all other things. The "sciences" we do possess are trivialities – farragos – fragments consisting of but few, and ill-digested, observations. The rest consists of imagination, invention, fiction, mere opinion. Hence it was not altogether absurd for the Apostle to remark, "The wisdom of mankind is foolishness with God". But let us go back to the point at which we digressed: you are to deduce from this that there is one science embracing all things. For whenever we happen to speak of something, we need – à propos of that thing – to discuss some other thing, and then again something else because of this, and thirdly something else because of *that*. In this way we should proceed to an infinite regress, unless we were to draw back in the midst of 32 our progression – and this we could not do without the loss of our knowledge. Consequently a principle has gained ground in the sciences, namely, "not all things in all things". For thinkers saw that all things followed from all things; but lest the knowledge of them should be extended to infinity they tried to establish limits; yet they cannot keep to those limits (for how are they going to preserve limits which Nature does not tolerate?); hence it is necessary to repeat the same statements a thousand times in one and the same work, and in different works as well – as I could easily demonstrate from any philosopher, but it would take too long.[94] Did not Aristotle say in the *Physics* all that he had said in

---

[94] The problem of infinite regress is examined in the *Metaphysics* 994a–994b, Aristotle reaching the conclusion that first principles and final causes cannot form an endless series. However, Sanches makes the witty observation that philosophers did not apply this principle to their own writings, Aristotle and Galen being notorious for their prolixity and repetition.

the *Categories*, and repeat it in the *Metaphysics*? – and repeat everywhere else in his work what he had written in these? And how wordy our own Galen is! You can hardly find in him a chapter where you do not read, "And though we have spoken on these topics at greater length elsewhere, it will do no harm if we briefly repeat once again what bears on my present subject"; or, "This is enough as touching my present purpose, since you can find the rest in such-and-such a book", or in fine, some other expression of the kind.

Which clearly shows that, in order to understand any one thing, it is necessary to understand other things as well, since even for the production, preservation, or destruction of the one, a combination of all the others is indispensable, as I shall prove at greater length in the course of my *Enquiry into Things*. This is also supported by those who undertake a discussion of some topic or other; for if they set out to prove that a man is an animal, so far are they from managing to do this that on the contrary they simply rush about from one to another of a mass of syllogisms, and finally reach either heaven or hell, according to the middle terms employed by the author of the proof, and to the propositions which are denied by another thinker. For what the inventor of the method of demonstration lays down concerning demonstrations, namely that by means of them one can arrive at the very first principles and there make an end, is itself an invention; just as 33 are other pronouncements on the same topic. For there *are no* middle terms of such a sort – fixed, counted, and arranged in order – that by means of them we may freely proceed; nor *are* there any first principles upon which the intellect may rest secure, in peace and contentment.[95] But if you, for your part, possess any such, you will oblige me if you send them to me.

Do you look for still further proof of the fact that we know nothing? Then I shall provide it. You have already observed the

---

[95] According to Aristotle in the *Posterior Analytics* 90a35–6, all questions are a search for a "middle." Thus the middle term of the demonstrative syllogism reveals the nature of the thing and the reason of the fact. Sanches denies both the existence of universals and their intermediate terms.

difficulty that resides in "species".[96] Now, as far as individual things are concerned, you admit that there is no science of these, since they are infinite in number. But "species" either are nothing, or (failing that) they are a kind of image-making.[97] Individuals alone exist, and can be perceived; it is only of individuals that knowledge can be possessed, and only from individuals that it can be sought. If this is not so, show me where those "universals" you speak of occur in nature; you will admit that they occur in the particulars themselves. Yet in those particulars I cannot see anything that is "universal"; everything in them is particular.[98] And what enormous variety is to be seen in them! – a marvellous degree of variety.[99] One human being is nothing but a thief; another, a murderer; one is born for nothing but Grammar; another is quite unsuited for the sciences; one is cruel and aggressive from his very cradle; one cannot by any amount of skill be kept away from wine, another from lust, another from gambling; another faints away at the sight or even the smell of a

---

[96] W. D. Ross in his masterly study, *Aristotle* (1923; rpt. London: Methuen, 1953), p. 57, comments: "The place of species in Aristotle's account is not as one of the predicables but as the subject". Porphyry had confused the issue by assigning species as a fifth predicable.

[97] Sanches is using "species" in the sense of "kinds" and "appearances".

[98] Sanches refutes the idea that it is possible to understand *scientia* as deduction from indemonstrable first principles. As A. C. Crombie points out in his study of science from the thirteenth to the seventeenth centuries, *Augustine to Galileo* (1952; rpt. London: Mercury Books, 1964), II, p. 9, it was the medical empiricists with their experiential knowledge of individual facts who had resisted Aristotelian scientific method by pointing out its inadequacies. William of Ockham had already attacked Aristotelian physics and metaphysics by affirming: "It was impossible to be certain about any particular causal connections, for experience gave evident knowledge only of individual objects or events and never of the relation between them as cause and effect" (ibid., pp. 32–3).

[99] The sceptical argument from variety was stated by Aenesidemus in the first and second modes of the *Pyrrhonics*. Sanches was familiar with this argument from the lengthy exposition of Pyrrhonic doctrine given by Diogenes Laertius in his life of Pyrrho. Girolamo Cardano devoted seventeen books in his *De rerum varietate* to describing the infinite variety of things in the universe, and this work was read fairly extensively by Sanches.

cat.[100] One man has never tasted a piece of fruit, and cannot endure the sight of anyone else tasting one; so is another with meat, another with cheese, another with fish – everyone knows some people of all these different types. Another person can devour and digest indifferently coins, glass, feathers, bricks, wool – in fact anything and everything.[101] One man falls into a swoon at the scent, or the sight, of a rose. Yon fellow dislikes women. This woman feeds on hemlock.[102] This man snores by day and by night. For my part, I have on many occasions thrown books away in a fit of temper, and I have run away from my little study; but in the public square, or on the Campus, I am never thinking of nothing, and I am "never less alone than when I am alone", nor less idle than when I am idle. I have an enemy with me; him I

34 cannot escape; and, as Horace says, "I avoid myself like a runaway and vagabond, / seeking to beguile Care, now by sociability and now by sleep, / in vain; for my gloomy companion [Care] is hard on my heels, and follows me as I try to flee".[103] Finally, there are some people concerning whom you would be hard put to it to know whether you ought to call them reasonable beings or, more

---

[100] The reference is to Petrus Andreas Matthiolus's commentaries on the six books of Dioscorides in which he describes the medicinal properties of plants, and brought his contemporaries up to date on the use of medicinal herbs. The usefulness of the book, with its beautiful illustrations of herbs, flowers, and animals, is borne out by the fact that a French translation appeared at Lyons in 1572. The anecdote appears in book 6, chapter 25, where Matthiolus speaks of his travels in Germany and states he saw several people swoon with fear at the sight of a cat, and related that another man began to sweat, tremble, and grow pale when he smelled a cat by a stove, even though it was hidden in a box.

[101] The references are to the last book of Fallopio's *De humani corporis anatome compendium* and to the *Curationum medicinalium centuria secunda*, cura 69, of the famous Portuguese-Jewish physician, Amatus Lusitanus, who relates: "Alius numismata, vitrum, pennas, lateres, lanam, omnia denique *vorat* et *coquit* indifferenter". Amatus Lusitanus retired to Salonika, where there was a colony of Sephardic Jews. He dedicated his great *Curationum medicinalium centuriae septem* (1561) to his Turkish protector, Ghedalia Ebn Iahya.

[102] More anecdotes from Amatus Lusitanus, *Centuria* II, cura 36, 76, and from Galen's *De simplicium medicamentorum temperamentis et facultatibus*, 3.

[103] See Horace, *Satires*, 2, 7.

properly, devoid of reason. On the other hand, you may see brute beasts that you could, with greater reason, call "reasonable" than certain members of the human race.[104] You will reply that one swallow does not make a summer, and that the "universal" is not destroyed by a single particular instance. Against this, I urge that the "universal" is wholly false unless it both includes and affirms all the things contained in it, according to their true nature. For how could it be true to say that every human being is reasonable if several – or only one – were unreasonable? If you should say that in *this* man there is a defect, not in his mind but in the body which is that mind's instrument, then perhaps you will speak the truth, but you will speak it in support of *my* view. For a man is not mind alone, or body alone, but both at once; therefore, should one of these two be defective, the man will be defective. For this reason, he is not *purely and simply* a man – for his body belongs to his essence, as does his mind; and not *merely* his body, but a body of such-and-such a kind.[105] From which it follows that what some philosophers say is absurd, namely that a man's soul can be of a spherical shape, or any shape other than that which all of us have, and that *that* would constitute a man.[106] I rather think those philosophers never themselves saw a "man" of this shape. If they did, then they are arguing for *my* view. For *I* would not believe that *that* "man" was constituted on our own lines – yet *they* assert that he is a human being, and a true one, all the same. Who knows? No one at all.

If they have not seen any such person, why do they invent an

---

[104] Sanches refers to Galen's *Oratio suasoria ad artes* and to Plutarch's treatise *Bruta animalia ratione uti, sive Gryllus*.

[105] Ross explains that in Aristotle's view the soul "requires a body with a certain kind of chemical constitution and a certain shape, and it cannot exist embodied in another kind of body. To speak of transmigration of human souls into animal bodies is like supposing that carpentry could embody itself in flutes instead of chisels" (*Aristotle*, p. 132).

[106] Sanches is probably referring to Aristotle's scornful refutation of Democritus's theory that spherical atoms constitute the soul and owing to their ceaseless movements draw the whole body after them, thus producing its movements (*De anima* 406b15–25).

imaginary "man" of a kind that, it may be, Nature cannot produce? And if Nature *can* do so, how will the following statement be of permanent validity: "The soul is the actualisation 35 of a natural body which has organs", etc.?[107] This is what their "science" amounts to! Yes, and that other statement is still more absurd by far, namely that even if no human beings existed it would still be true to say, "Man is an animal". For they assume an impossible notion in order to derive from it a false inference. For if you are speaking in the language of philosophy, human beings will never be non-existent, since the world is eternal; whereas if you are speaking in the language of faith, will Our Lord Christ cease to exist? You can see how in either case you are making an impossible assumption. But do you not know from your teacher that if the *possible* is assumed to exist, no inconsistent results follow, whereas if the *im*possible is admitted, a great many inconsistent results follow?[108] But suppose we grant that it *is* possible: if man does not exist, how can man be an animal? They maintain that in the above statement they are applying the word "is" to signify essence, not existence, and that it is merely a copula.[109] Accordingly they maintain that the proposition in question has permanent validity, and that in the sciences it is always taken in the sense they indicate; nay, that even before Man was created that proposition was true, and that all the essences of things existed in the mind of God. Hence the strange things they write concerning Being and essence. Could anything be more unsound?

In this way they distort words from their commonly accepted meanings, and corrupt them in order to have another language of their own, quite different from their mother-tongue, yet the same. And when you go to them in order to learn something, they change the meanings of the words you had hitherto employed, in such a way that these no longer denote the same objects – that is, objects in the natural world – but instead the objects that they

---

[107] In the *De anima* 412b5−6, Aristotle describes the soul "as the first grade of actuality of a natural organized body".

[108] See *De interpretatione* 21b−23b.

[109] See *Metaphysics* 1049a and *Categories* 2a−4b.

themselves have invented, in order that you, being eager for knowledge and totally ignorant of this revolutionary change, may hearken to them when they are arguing and discoursing about them in a subtle way and recalling – with marvellous technical skill – how they appeared to them in their hours of sleeplessness; and so may regard them with admiration and with reverence, and stand in awe of their brilliance as investigators of nature. How amazingly crude they are! Is anything simpler, clearer, and more familiar than the word "is"? Yet what a vast amount of argument 36 is devoted to it! Children are better scholars than philosophers. If you ask them whether papa is at home, then (if he should in fact be there) they answer, "He is". If you ask whether he is wicked, they say, "No, he is not". Yet the philosopher maintains, *à propos* of a "man" who does not exist, "He is an animal"! Equally absurd is the corollary that some thinkers endeavour to add, namely that philosophy can be taught in no language but Greek or Latin; because, they claim, there are no words available for us to translate a great many expressions that are in those tongues, as for example Aristotle's *entelecheia* (ἐντελέχεια), about which there has been a fruitless debate, down to the present time, on how it ought to be rendered in Latin. Among users of Latin we find *essentia, quidditas, corporeitas*, and similarly artificial creations of the philosophers, which, having no meaning at all, can be neither understood nor explained by anyone – much less rendered into everyday speech, which is accustomed to assign only to *real* things (but not to invented things) names of their own. To this we must add the worthless opinion of some others, who would attribute some kind of special efficacy to words in themselves, claiming as the consequence that names were assigned to things in accordance with the nature of the things.[110] Following this lead, others again no

[110] Sanches's long and interesting discussion on language is designed to demonstrate that there are no universals, for a word does not represent the essential nature of a thing. Each language uses different words, different sounds to convey the same meaning. Citing Genesis 2, Sanches remarks that Adam was the first man to assign names to the animals and birds in conformity with their nature. But all languages, even Greek and Latin, the languages of philosophy, have changed over the centuries and, therefore, cannot express the nature of things.

less foolishly attempt to derive the meanings of all words from some particular quality, for example "a stone" (*la-pis*) inasmuch as it hurts (*laedat*) the foot (*pes*); and "earth" (*humus*) from moisture (*humiditas*) – or so they say. And what is the derivation of "ass" (*asinus*)? From you, since you are "without sense" (for in Greek, and often in Latin, the prefix *a* has a privative force, while *sinus* is more or less *sensus*; therefore, *a-sinus* is the same as *sine sensu*, "without sense", and this is exactly what you are). Is not this a good etymology?

They pursue the same enquiry in relation to all other words, with more enthusiasm than truth or usefulness; and in this way they regard all words as being either derivative or composite – none of them as simple or primary; and who could fail to see the foolish and ignorant character of this procedure? If the expression "stone" (*lapis*) has been assigned in accordance with the nature of the thing signified, as you maintain, *is* it in fact the nature of a stone to hurt the foot (*ut laedat pedem*)? I think not. But suppose it
37 to be so, how does *laedo* stand for the "nature" of the injury to which it refers? How does *pes* indicate the "nature" of a foot? We are proceeding to an infinite regress. Again, *humus* (earth) is not so named after *humiditas*; for on the contrary earth is the driest of all the elements, by your own account. But even suppose it should be very damp, and hence be called *humus*, what will be the source of the word *humiditas*? If you should offer me something else from which *humiditas* can take its name, I will ask the same question again. Once more we proceed to an infinite regress. If you should finally come to a stop with some particular word, it will in any event have no means of indicating the nature of the thing it signifies. For the reason why intermediate names, preceding it in the series, *seemed* to represent the nature of the object, was simply that they were derived from others which in turn signified something else, up to the very last in the series of them, which – by your account – is derived from no other term at all; otherwise I should ask the same question again concerning it. Now, how many names are simple? Almost all of them are. Furthermore, if the word *panis* (bread) has been assigned in accordance with the nature of the thing it signifies, what of ἄρτος (bread) in Greek, or *Bara*

218

in Breton, or *Ouguia* in Basque? – words so different in sound, spelling, and accentuation that you would say that they have nothing in common.

If you were to maintain that only *one* language was assigned in conformity with the nature of things, why not others similarly? Or which language *was* that? If you were to say that the first language to be laid down was that of Adam, of course this is true, for he was capable of it inasmuch as he knew the nature of things – the author of the Pentateuch bears witness to this; and in that case it were much to be desired that Adam had committed to writing either his own philosophy or a version, in his own language, of the philosophy we have. And if you had told me that at that period philosophy could not be taught or explained in any other language than that of Adam, this I would not deny either; but what you are saying is that it could not be done except in the Greek or Latin language, and these languages were not laid down in conformity with the nature of the object.

What of the fact that words are continually corrupted, and that there exist French and Spanish books in which you may find a great many words of which the meanings are quite unknown? Moreover, in the realm of Latin are there not a great many words 38 that are obsolete, while others are invented afresh every day? In the spoken language the same phenomenon occurs as in other departments: there is change through continual use, and finally so much change occurs that the language degenerates completely and becomes a different language; hence it is that the ancient spoken Latin has now died out altogether, having been transformed into the Italian vernacular of today. Similarly with Greek. And such books as preserve and keep alive both Greek and Latin are so different from the glorious language of antiquity that if Demosthenes or Cicero were to be present while we spoke their language they would perhaps laugh us to scorn. Not only this, but one person borrows a great many expressions from another, and he from a third; and in this way I believe no wholly regular and uncorrupted language remains to us today. Therefore there lies in words no power to explain the nature of things, except that which they derive from the arbitrary decision of him who applies them;

and the same word, *canis* (dog), may mean "bread" (*panis*) just as much as "dog", if he so pleases. There are, of course, some words that are applied to things on account of some result of circumstances, or accident, but not one arising from the *nature* of the things. For who is there who understands the natures of things sufficiently to be able to allot names to the things in accordance with those natures? Or what, indeed, do names have in common with things? There are, certainly, some terms which we call "proper", as if you should call a human being "laughable" or "fit for weeping"; yet in these epithets the primary words, that is to say "laughter" and "weeping", have no force beyond what they have acquired from our own arbitrary decision.

Thus we have phrases like "Mercury with wingèd feet", and "the bearer of arms", and similar compound expressions. There are other words too which by resemblance of sound imitate the voices of the creatures they refer to, and hence are called *onomatopoeic*, as for example "to crow" of cocks, "to caw" of rooks, "to roar" of lions, "to bleat" of sheep, "to bark" of dogs, "to neigh" of horses, "to low" of oxen, "to grunt" of pigs, "to 39 snore" of sleepers; also the "murmuring" of waters, and "whistling" and "ringing"; "drum-beats" and "clangorous noises" and the verse: " 'Tis a mark of cowardice / to be affrighted at a *howling* dog"; also the other line: "And the trumpet spoke, with terrible sound, *taratantara*"; and another: *Quadrupedante putrem sonitu quatit ungula campum* ("The hoof, with galloping sound, shakes the dry dust of the plain").[111] But even in these, there is no revelation of the *nature* of the things they signify, but merely a resemblance in the sound. Much less should we look in all words for their derivation; for did we not avoid doing this we should enter an infinite regress.

But we have spent more time on this enquiry than I had supposed. I now return to my subject. What a degree of variety there is among human beings themselves, even in respect of outward appearance! In some regions all the human beings are of very

---

[111] The source of the first quotation is unknown; the second quotation is from Ennius, *Annales*, 451 S; the last quotation is from Virgil's *Aeneid*, 8. 596.

short stature – the so-called pygmies; in other regions all of them are very tall, and these are called giants.[112] Some walk about entirely naked. Some are shaggy, with long hair covering the entire body. Some, indeed, have no power of articulate speech at all, and live like wild beasts in the forests, or hide themselves in caves, or even perch in trees like birds – yet these also are delighted to eat human beings of our own sort, whenever they happen to catch any. Some, caring nothing for God and religion, possess all things in common, including sons and wives; they wander about, having no settled abode. Others on the contrary are devoted to God and religion, and are ready to shed their blood fearlessly for their sake. Each man wishes to have his own community, his own house, his own wife and family; and when he has this, defends it to the death. Some, when they die, are cremated together with living friends, wives, and household goods; others, caring nothing for these things, remain unburied; one allows himself, and indeed tries, to be torn and cut to pieces while still alive, whereas another believes one ought to flee from death at all costs. I should never end if I set out to catalogue all the customs of the entire human race. Would you for your part suppose that those I have just described were creatures of the same pattern as ourselves? To me it seems unlikely; yet neither you nor I know anything. Perhaps you will deny that any such human beings exist. I will not take issue with you; this is simply what I have heard from others. There are an- 40 cient and modern books full of accounts of them, and it does not seem impossible that they should exist. Nay, perhaps there are (or have been, or will be) some others still more unlike us than they are, in some part of the world not yet discovered by us. For who can state anything with certainty about all that was, is, or will be? Yesterday you said in the light of your complete scientific knowledge – or rather, knowledge that was complete even long

---

[112] Both Paracelsus in the *Liber de Pigmaeis, Nymphis, etc.* and Cardano in *De rerum varietate*, 8, 43, speak of pygmies and giants. Traveller's tales were full of accounts of strange customs and beliefs. Ancient authorities such as Aristotle, Galen, Herodotus, Strabo, and Pliny lent authenticity to the new accounts.

ages ago – that the entire earth was surrounded by the Ocean; and you divided it into three all-embracing parts, namely Asia, Africa, and Europe. But what are you to say today? A new world has been discovered – new realities – in New Spain or in the West and East Indies. Moreover, you used to say that the southern zone, situated below the equator, was uninhabitable on account of heat, but that close to the poles, and the extreme polar zones, the same thing was true because of the cold. Experience has now shown both these statements to be false. Construct another "science", then, for your first is now false. So how can you maintain that your propositions are eternally valid, incorruptible, infallible, and incapable of being otherwise – you miserable worm, who scarcely know, and are scarcely even capable of knowing, what you are and whence you come and whither you are going?

The same may be said of other species, both of animals and of plants, according to their differing situation in the world, inasmuch as in different zones the lack of resemblance in the same "species", as it is called, is so great that you have to admit that they are different "species" – as indeed they are. Yet neither of us knows anything, inasmuch as we do not comprehend the distinguishing forms of each of the two species in question. Moreover, our ignorance is increased by the fact that access to some things is barred to us because of their remoteness from us in space or in time; and such things are in the majority.

Hence there is a great deal of doubt concerning those things that come into being, and exist, in the sea, or the inward parts of the earth, or the highest regions of the air, or (finally) in the celestial 41 bodies. And with reason too; for all our information is derived from sense-perception, and since those objects cannot be perceived by the senses it follows that they cannot be *known* either – nay, they are much less capable of being known than things that are familiar to us. For we do not doubt that these latter *exist*, whereas concerning the former category of things a great many statements are made of which – as to their reality – there is no proof; nay, sometimes the opposite, as I shall remark in the appropriate context. To this is also relevant the enquiry concerning the plurality of worlds, and concerning what lies beyond the sky, and similar questions. Not only this, but in the separate parts of the world, which no single individual can traverse in their entirety (yet traversed they must be on account of the variety of phenomena to which I have just referred), men's opinions differ, and there is no *knowledge*. But concerning those events which occurred long before our time – and concerning those which will occur after it – who can express any reliable opinion? This is what has occasioned so much debate among philosophers regarding the beginning of the world, or its eternity; its duration, and its end; and no one (so far as I know) has brought this debate to a close, or perhaps ever will, on a basis of *knowledge*. For how should a corruptible being pass judgment on that which is incorruptible, or a finite being judge that which is infinite? In a word, how is one who lives only for an instant (as though he did not really live at all), and who exists as though he did not really exist at all – how is he to be capable of proving anything about that which is everlasting? The enquiry into this question, the question whether he exists, like the enquiry into the other questions, is the foundation of other enquiries; and he himself has absolutely no understanding of it, nor can he have. But concerning all these matters there are certain higher philosophic doubts which are very necessary to the understanding of all other things, and ignorance of these leads immediately to lack of knowledge in respect to other enquiries. But that nothing can be perfectly known in human terms appears from the fact that the Peripatetic philosopher and the rest of his school try by countless methods to show that the world is eternal, never had a beginning, and will never end; and 42 this is the received opinion among philosophers. Hence the Roman writer [Pliny] began his *Natural History* with this dictum. And assuredly, if you are guided by human reason, you would be inclined to this opinion; for you came into a world already made, and so did your father and your forebears; they have departed this world, and you too will depart from it, and you see others born and dying while you yourself remain. Nor would anyone on earth maintain, either orally or in writing, that he either has seen the world's beginning or has seen another person who either saw it or else heard from a third person that *he* saw it.

And, as the Man of Wisdom says, "One generation passeth away and another generation cometh; but the earth abideth forever. The sun also ariseth, and the sun goeth down, and hasteth to his place where he arose. The wind goeth toward the south, and turneth about unto the north; it whirleth about continually, and the wind returneth again according to his circuits. All the rivers run into the sea; yet the sea is not full; unto the place from whence the rivers come, thither they return to flow again. All things are full of labour; man cannot utter it".[113]

You have heard the opinion of the philosophers; yet you see that the truth stands contrary to them all, according to the Faith, and that the world both was created and will have an end, at least in respect of the qualities it now possesses. For it will not be totally destroyed, according to that saying of the royal prophet, "And as a vesture shalt thou change them [sc. earth and heaven], and they shall be changed", etc.[114] Now, all these facts are known by divine revelation, not by human reasoning, for this is not possible. Hence Moses, the divine law-giver, begins his divine narrative divinely, under the inspiration of the Divine Spirit, with the creation of the world – exactly the opposite of what Pliny did. So there is some excuse for the philosophers' opinion, but none for persistence in disbelief, and contumacy directed against the Faith. But let us 43 return to the argument.

There is yet another reason for our ignorance, namely that the substance of certain things is so vast that it cannot be perceived by us at all. Such is the philosophers' "infinite", if there *is* such a thing, and – in our own realm – God, of whom there can be no measure or limit, and hence no comprehension by the intellect. And rightly so; for there should be a certain proportion in size between the comprehending subject and the comprehended object, so that he who comprehends is either greater than the thing comprehended or at least equal to it (though it may seem scarcely possible that an equal should literally "comprehend", or embrace

[113] Ecclesiastes 1.
[114] Sanches quotes Psalm 101 and follows tradition in attributing the Pentateuch to Moses.

some other thing equal to itself, as we shall see in my treatise on Space – but let us allow this for the moment); to us, however, there is no proportion in relation to God, since there can be no proportion between the finite and the infinite, or the corruptible and the eternal; in a word, compared to Him we are nothing, rather than something. On the same principle, God knows everything, inasmuch as He is greater, higher, and more excellent than all else – or, better (lest I should seem to compare Him with His creatures), He is greatest, highest, and most excellent of all. Whatever things approach more closely to this Supreme Artificer are for that very reason also unknown to us.

There is another kind of thing, quite opposite to the former kind. Of these things the substance is so *small* that it can scarcely be comprehended by the intellect. They are exceedingly numerous; it is absolutely necessary to be familiar with them in order to possess knowledge, yet we have virtually no knowledge of them at all. In this kind, it may be, are all the "accidents" which are nearly non-existent, to such an extent that never to this day has there been anyone who could give a full explanation of their nature (any more than the nature of all other things; for we know nothing, so how are we going to explain anything?). Nor is it surprising if some thinkers have opined that "accidents" are nothing in themselves, but only a number of appearances presented to our view, which show themselves in diverse ways according to the variations in our own situation and disposition; as, for example, one who has a fever judges that everything is hot, 44 while to one whose tongue is coated with yellow bile everything tastes bitter.[115]

Besides these, one more reason for our ignorance remains, in the realm of things, namely the everlasting permanence of some of them and *per contra* the endless coming-to-be and passing-away, or endless change, of some others; so that you could give an account neither of the former class, since you do not live for ever, nor of

[115] Sanches directs the reader to Diogenes Laertius's life of Pyrrho and Plutarch's *Adversus Colotem*. Democritus, according to Colotes, had abolished the criterion of sensation.

225

the latter class, since they are never wholly the same, and moreover sometimes exist and sometimes do not.[116] This is the reason why the debate about coming-to-be and passing-away is still unresolved; I shall give my opinion about this elsewhere. How many different ways there are of coming into being and of passing away! The former may come about from seed, eggs, ordure, decaying matter, dew, dust, mud, the exhalation of breath, rotting flesh, and several other sources; the latter, from heat, cold, breakage, disintegration, or crushing; and perhaps there *is* no fixed number of ways for them to happen. If the tale about the phoenix is true, from the ashes of its parent's funeral pyre there arises a worm, out of which emerges another phoenix.[117] The worms that make silk for us dry up completely; after a long time other worms come to life once again and are regenerated out of certain small granules, as though from seed. It is said that the ostrich fertilises its eggs by fixing them with its

---

[116] The question of coming into being is mentioned by Diogenes Laertius in his life of Pyrrho in the following terms: "Nor, say they, is there any coming into being. For that which is does not come into being, since it *is*; nor yet that which is not, for it has no substantial existence, and that which is neither substantial nor existent cannot have had the chance of coming into being" (*Lives of Eminent Philosophers*, II, pp. 511–12). Sanches develops the contradiction inherent in Aristotelian doctrine, as expounded in the *De generatione et corruptione*, along the sceptical outlines given by Diogenes Laertius. His examples are culled from Cardano's *De subtilitate*, 9, entitled "De animalibus, quae ex putredine generantur", and Julius Caesar Scaliger's commentary on the *De subtilitate* in his *Exercitationes*. For contemporary theories on generation see Linda Allen Deer, "Academic Theories of Generation in the Renaissance: The Contemporaries and Successors of Jean Fernel (1497–1558)" (Ph.D. thesis, University of London [Warburg Institute], 1980).

[117] See Pliny, *Natural History*, 10, 2. In Diogenes Laertius's life of Pyrrho the commentary on the first mode of Aenesidemus points out the differences in generation between creatures: "For some creatures multiply without intercourse, for example, creatures that live in fire, the Arabian phoenix and worms; others by union, such as man and the rest" (*Lives of Eminent Philosophers*, II, p. 493). The salamander and phoenix were often quoted as examples of miraculous generation through fire.

gaze, and that the bear shapes its cub by licking it.[118] Figs and walnuts and the woody parts of fruit pass into worms and become petrified. The leaves of certain trees that hang over a river in Ireland assume the nature of fish if they happen to fall into the stream. There are many other trees of which the foliage, when it falls to earth, is turned into flying creatures.[119] Gall-nuts, wheat, the pods of the mastic and follicles of the poplar, the pith of fuller's thistle, cheese, meat, and the turpentine-tree – all of these turn into worms and small winged insects.

More remarkable still, if our author's [Scaliger's] tale is true, is this: in the ocean off Brittany a bird of duck-like shape hangs by its beak from the rotting remains of shipwrecked vessels, until it is detached, and begins to seek for its own food by pursuing fish.[120]

[118] See note 6. Contrary to Sanches's marginal annotation, which refers the reader to Aristotle's *De generatione animalium*, 5, it is in book 4, 6 (774b13–15), that Aristotle states that the young of the bear is produced in an imperfect shape. Both Matthiolus in his commentaries on Dioscorides and Scaliger in his *Exercitationes*, 15 (not 7 as stated by Sanches), refute this error, which was still perpetuated by Cardano in the *De subtilitate*.

[119] Most of the information on the generation of plants and fishes is taken from Scaliger's *Exercitationes*, 59, 2. Scaliger's critical sense, as well as that of Sanches, was entirely absent when recounting miraculous examples of generation and alteration of species as follows: "De Iuvernae vero fluvio non silebo. In eum, quae arboris unius imminentis collapsae frondes fuerint, piscium formam induunt. Pisces vivunt deinceps ... Nam quae frondes in terram cadunt, animalia volucria effecta avolant" (p. 89r.).

[120] Wightman in *Science and the Renaissance* (pp. 181–4) uses the legend of the generation of the barnacle goose to illustrate that Renaissance naturalists still unquestioningly accepted ancient beliefs. In the biological sciences little original research was being carried out. Sanches quotes Scaliger's tale in its entirety: "In Oceano Britannico magis mireris ignotam vobis avem, Anatis facie, rostro pendere de reliquiis putridis naufragiorum, quoad absolvatur, atque abeat quaesitum sibi pisces, unde alatur. Hanc quoque vidimus nos. Vascones Oceani accolae Crabans vocant illas: a Britonibus Bernachiae appellantur: recepto etiam in proverbium vocabulo, cum ignaviam cuipiam exprobare volunt: quasi neque caro sit, neque piscis. Singularis nunc miraculi subtexenda historia est: ubi de aquis agimus. Allata est Francisco Regi optimo maximo concha non admodum magna cum avicula intus pene perfecta, alarum fastigiis, rostro, pedibus, haerente extremis oris ostraci" (*Exercitationes*, 59, p. 89v.).

45 This bird is called *craban* by the Basques who dwell beside the ocean, and *bernache* (barnacle goose) by the Bretons. Scaliger adds that once a shell was brought to King Francis [I] of France; inside it was an almost perfectly formed small bird, attached by its wing-tips, beak, and feet to the extremities of the shell. At Cairo in Egypt, eggs are incubated in ovens, the heat of the fire being kept low; elsewhere, this occurs even in piles of ordure.[121] I have no doubt that there are several methods of generation among fishes and birds, and just as many again among lifeless things – and equally numerous methods of destruction.

Between coming into existence and perishing, how many changes take place? Countless. Among living things, the endless process of nourishment; timely growth; maturity and decline; reproduction; births, in their various kinds; alteration, dwindling, increase; full development of character; actions, and work of different sorts – very often in contrary senses within the same individual; in a word, no point of *rest* anywhere.[122] And it is not strange if some philosophers have maintained the opinion that it cannot be said of any one man, after an interval of one hour, that he is the same person he was an hour ago. This opinion should not be wholly derided; rather, it may perhaps be true. For so indivisible is *identity* that if, to any given thing whatsoever, you were to add a single jot (or took it away), it would no longer, from that moment, be entirely the *same thing* as before; while as for the "accidents" of a particular thing, they belong to its nature, and since they vary endlessly the result is that the particular thing itself also varies from time to time. "*I* know", you say, "that the individual thing is always the same so long as its form remains the

---

[121] Cf. Scaliger, *Exercitationes*, 23, p. 46: "Quod vero de ovis cinere exceptis negas, falsum est. In Aegypto nanque ad Cairum furnos construunt, alii alio multiplici fornice imposito: in quorum tholi supremi medio foramen est: per quod caloris vis, quae immodica posset officere subit, atque exhalat".

[122] Sanches argues, contrary to Aristotelian doctrine that taught the eternity of form in the *Metaphysics*, that the individual form is always in a state of constant change. Therefore form or identity can never be entirely the same. Ross points out, however, that for Aristotle, "Form is eternal only by virtue of the never-failing succession of its embodiments" (*Aristotle*, p. 175).

same; for it is from that [i.e. the form] that the individual thing takes its name – and that the minutiae of these 'accidents' do not change the thing's identity".[123] But what *I* maintained was that nothing must be changed in respect to a thing's identity; otherwise the thing will not be completely the same.

"One form makes one thing". It may be that the same form always "in-forms" – but *what* it "in-forms" is not always the same thing; for in the thing itself there is an endless process of change, as there is in my own body. But I am a composite of both soul and body – principally of soul, a little less of body – and if one of these suffers change, then I too am changed. However, I shall speak of this elsewhere, at greater length and in a more appropriate context.[124] So much, then, for animals, considered in their entirety. But if you consider their parts, there is much *greater* cause 46 for doubt. Why are some parts arranged thus, and others thus? Would a different arrangement have been better, or worse? Why were there not more of them; why just *so* many? Why were they of such a large (or small) size? One goes on for ever. Similarly with lifeless things. What, then, is fixed, when things are so changeable? What is determinate when they are so various? What is certain, when *things* are so uncertain? Nothing, indeed. Hence there has arisen such a quantity of argument concerning the introduction, and first principle, of forms as no one shall ever bring to an end. In addition, one might wish to mention all the many different kinds of monstrosities that come into existence every day, in Man above all – the hermaphrodite sex, both in certain species and in a number of individuals of other species; the mixed species, as for example the mule from a donkey and a mare, or the hinny from a stallion and a she-ass; the wolf-dog, from a wolf and a dog, the "small hinny" from bull and mare, which are common examples from our own experience, though there ought to be a third species produced by the coupling of dog with fox, tiger, hyena, wolf, with all of which the dog is *said* to unite; just as

---

[123] Sanches is contesting the arguments advanced by Aristotle in the *Metaphysics* 1031a15–1032a.
[124] Sanches is referring to his projected *Tractatus de anima*.

also from camel and mare, from barnyard fowl and partridge, and (if it be true what they say about the osprey) from vulture and eagle.[125]

We can see the same kind of mixing in trees and other plants, as for example in kohlrabi, in peaches and almonds, and several others, in which by means of grafting the plant acquires a nature intermediate between that of the graft and that of the root-stock, on to which it is grafted. If, again, you add changes in species, as darnel often comes from wheat and sometimes wheat from darnel, and wild-oats from rye; or if you add to this list the alteration of sex in certain human beings, from a girl to a man (as some authorities have recorded); you will be performing an exceedingly difficult task, and yet you will still not know *what* a given phenomenon is, or *how* it occurs, or from what source it comes, or *why* it happens.[126] Still less do I know. And there is an even greater amount of change in lifeless things, and greater diversity in
47 their coming into existence and passing away. We are deprived of the opportunity of knowing more by the various and many – but also contradictory – effects of a single thing, and, *per contra*, of the various and many – but also contradictory – causes of a single effect. Let me give you just one example (lest I be too diffuse, since these matters will have to be discussed at greater length in my *Enquiry into Things*), namely heat, which brings into being, and also destroys; removes whiteness, and also blackness; warms, and also cools; thins, and also thickens; separates, and mixes; liquefies, and solidifies; dries out, and moistens; rarefies, and compresses; extends, and contracts; widens, and narrows; sweetens, and makes bitter; renders heavier, and also lighter; softens, and hardens; pulls, and pushes; moves, and checks movement; makes happy, and also depresses. In short, what cannot heat do?[127] It is a

---

[125] Sanches derives most of his examples from Aristotle's *De generatione animalium* 746a–746b. Hermaphrodites and other monstrous births are related by Pliny in his *Natural History*, 7, 3.

[126] See Hippocrates, *Epid.*, 6, Pliny, *Natural History*, 7, 4, and Amatus Lusitanus, *Centuria* II, cura 39.

[127] The encomium of heat, one of the elementary qualities, fire being a simple sublunary body, is not surprising, since in the Aristotelian and Galenic theory

sublunary deity, Nature's right hand, the agent of agents, the mover of movers, the first principle of first principles, the cause of causes (in the sublunar realms), the instrument of instruments, the soul of the world. And not undeservedly did a multitude of ancient thinkers, in their "First Philosophy", consider fire to be the first primary principle.[128] Rightly did [Hermes] Trismegistus call fire a god.[129] With very good reason, Aristotle was capable of calling God "the fire of heaven", though he did not believe that the fire of heaven was in fact God; and accordingly he is severely criticised for this by Cicero.[130] For what word better than "fire" could suggest to us the power and the goodness combined – together with some notion of the ineffable divinity – of Almighty God? God Himself suggested this when He first revealed Himself in the burning bush to His faithful servant, and when in the column of fire He led the chosen people through the desert, and also when He descended in tongues of fire upon the assembly of the Elect.[131] You see what mighty things heat can accomplish; yet it is a simple "accident", the rational explanation of which, like that of other things, is not understood. How can it, alone, perform so many different functions? It is hard to understand and harder still to describe; both of these are most difficult, perhaps

of matter all things are composed of the four elements of fire, air, earth, and water, having as qualities heat, coldness, dryness, and moisture respectively. Galen had affirmed that the substance of the soul was heat, a kind of inborn heat in man (see Temkin, *Galenism*, pp. 87–8, 142–7). Heat was considered to be essential in maintaining the life processes. Aristotle examines in the *Meteorologica* 4, the primary effect of heat in generation and concoction, describing the characteristics associated with passive qualities such as hardness and softness, solidification and liquefaction, dryness and moisture, etc.

[128] Sanches refers the reader to Diogenes Laertius, *Lives of Eminent Philosophers,* 8, in which the Pythagorean doctrine of vital heat is expounded: "The sun, the moon, and the other stars are gods; for in them is a preponderance of heat, and heat is the cause of life" (vol. II, p. 343).

[129] Ibid., books 10 and 8 for references to Epicurus and Pythagoras.

[130] " . . . tum caeli ardorem deum dicit esse, non intellegere caelum mundi esse partem quem alio loco ipse designarit deum" (Cicero, *De natura deorum*, 1, 13).

[131] Exodus, 3 and 14, and Acts, 1.

even impossible. Yet philosophers distinguish what exists *per se*
48 from what occurs *ex accidenti,* and they offer as an *ob*jection the
variation in the "subject", the sense-datum – and any single one of
these phenomena is more difficult to explain than the original
notion.[132] Who has attained an exact understanding of all this
variety? Nobody at all. All *they* are doing is to express a number of
probabilities; there is nothing that they *know* for sure. Concerning
these matters, however, I shall argue later; for the present, let it
suffice to understand that we understand nothing completely.

In the same way, an identical effect, produced by contrary
causes, occasions in us the greatest ambiguity. Take coolness: it
may be produced by motion, as in the rapid movement of the
heart, chest, arteries – and also by the bubbling of hot water; or by
rest, as when a person who is heated as the result of exercise takes
a rest. In the same manner, warmth may come from movement,
in running; or from rest, if the heart grows still, or you refrain
from moving water that is boiling. Blackness may result from
heat, as with the Ethiopians; or from cold, as in a gangrened limb,
or one that has been tied up for too long; particularly if the passage
of breath through the arteries is prevented. Decay may result from
any and every quality, when things are not kept dry. Not only
this, but one of two opposites is produced by the other: heat from
cold, when lime is slaked in cold water, and also in our own
bodies (and in springs of water, and in the earth) in the *winter*
season (hence the saying: "men's bellies are warmest in winter and
spring");[133] cold from heat, when hot bodies are consumed by
fire, and also in the Ethiopians, who are cold inside (and so are
we, in *summer*). How these things happen I completely fail to
understand; so must this not be true of others likewise? I do not
regard this as an inescapable conclusion, but it does seem
probable. I am told what they themselves have to say on these
topics, yet I do not therefore understand the problem any better. I
used to have the very same notion as they do, but it did not satisfy

---

[132] Sanches uses the argument from contraries in Aristotle's *De generatione et corruptione* 329a–330a to prove that nothing is known for sure.

[133] See Hippocrates, *Aphorisms* 15: "Ventres hyeme et vere natura calidissimi sunt".

my mind. For had I understood anything completely, I should not have denied the fact – nay, I should have shouted aloud for happiness, since no better stroke of luck than this could possibly come my way. But as it is, I am tortured incessantly by grief, in despair of being able to know anything completely. Therefore, either I am alone among mankind in my state of utter ignorance, or else everyone else shares my situation. Both of these alternatives are true, I believe. Yet I should still know something if 49 others in fact know something; for it is unlikely that Nature should have turned her back on me, and on no single person else. But I know nothing whatsoever; nor do you. There are in us many other reasons for ignorance in the domain of facts, reasons which it would be both tedious and unprofitable to introduce *en masse* into this enquiry, since you may examine them in the separate treatises devoted to each, and I shall everywhere indicate where the discussion refers to them. I will merely append one or two of the most important. The variety in things, their diversities of form, shape, bulk, modes of acting, and their numerous very different uses, so beset – or, better, distract – the mind that it cannot with equanimity either express or feel anything without being besieged from another side and obliged to give way to [the contrary] belief – and thus, vacillating this way and that, it can never come to rest. Should it maintain that whiteness (if I may assume that it will be enough to cite an example from colours) is caused by heat, then snow and ice and the colouring of Germans refute this; if it maintains that it is caused by cold, this will be refuted by ashes, lime, plaster of Paris, and bone, all of which are *burned*. If humidity be the cause, one set of facts is relevant; if dryness, another. And just as many doubts arise in connection with blackness.

But what would you say about intermediate objects? What mixture will you assign to them? Moreover, the limiting cases seem to have an obvious cause, as snow has cold, ashes have heat – since each of these two is detected by the senses. But what would you say of spotted animals – the panther, leopard, dog, and so forth?[134] Or of herbs and grasses such as tarragon, silver thistle,

---

[134] Aristotle explained variegation in the *De generatione animalium* 785b as being a

and spotted trefoil? Or of the variegated flowers of the fleshy
betony and violet? Or of the Turkish kidney-bean? Or of birds
such as the peacock and the parrot? Will you assign different
constitutive qualities to the peacock, to particoloured flowers, to
the leopard, whose feathers or flower or coat are the same? And
these colours are *lasting*. What will you say of the rainbow; of the
variegated dove; of a glass full of water, and another with no
50 water in it – all of which, on being exposed to sunlight at different
angles, or else because of a change of viewpoint on the observer's
part, present such diverse colours? Rightly, you will not have
anything to say; nor shall I. Much more so, in the instances of all
else that I have recounted above. And it will go on for ever: the
more we investigate, the more numerous are the confusions that
present themselves, the more *we* are confused, and the harder it is
for us to extricate ourselves. For where there is a multitude there is
confusion. Thus we may quite properly compare our philosophy
to the labyrinth of Minos: if we once enter it, we cannot go back,
or get ourselves free of its mazes. If we go on, we encounter the
Minotaur, who deprives us of life. *This* is the end of our studies,
this the reward of fruitless and useless toil, of endless vigils: namely
distress, anxiety, worry, solitude, and the loss of all life's pleasures
– a life like unto death, a life to be spent in the company of the
dead and in struggling, talking, thinking; to shun the living and
lay aside the care of one's private interests; to destroy the bodily
physique by training the mind. From this cause come diseases,
often madness, and always death. Nor does "unflinching toil all
problems overcome" – except in the sense that it takes life away
and hastens death, which frees a man from *everything*. In this
sense, the dying man conquers all, and what Horace says is so far
from being true that on the contrary exactly the opposite happens.
Now, what he says is this:

> To sum up, the Wise Man is inferior only to Jove; he is rich,
> Free, full of honours, handsome, in fact king of kings,

natural attribute of the whole class not to have one single colour. Sceptics, on
the other hand, used the argument from variety (in Aenesidemus's first trope)
to advocate the suspension of judgment.

And pre-eminently *sound* – unless he is bothered by a bad cold.[135]

Notice how he disclosed the "cold" at the very end! But elsewhere the opposite is said, and with greater truth:

> Homer, even though you arrive escorted by the Muses,
> You shall be thrown out, Homer, if you come empty-handed![136]

And it is Horace, too, who writes further on (and better):

> 'Tis true that Money's the queen who gives you a wife with a
>   dowry, and credit, and friends – and high birth, and beauty as
>   well;
> Aye, and the man with a well-filled wallet is full of persuasion;   51
>   and *most* attractive to boot.

But indeed there is still truth in what Ovid, too, says elsewhere:

The Senate is closed to the poor, and place is the gift of your – *fortune;*
Money gives weight to the Judge; money, respect to the Knight.[137]

Nowadays, *value*'s what's valued, and place is the gift of your – *fortune;*
Friendship's the gift of your purse; poor men lie crushed everywhere.[138]

Learning is reckoned as worthless, and in fact togas give way to arms, tongues yield place to the laurel. Men of letters are held in contempt. Why, then, do we wear ourselves out? I do not know. 'Tis our destiny. "God has given to the sons of men this worst of occupations, that they might be occupied therewith. ... He made all things good in His own time; and He has handed over the world to their debating, so that no man may find out the work that God has performed, from the beginning to the end".[139] And (to return to the point from which I had digressed) this same philosophy seems also to be not dissimilar to the Lernean Hydra,

[135] Horace, *Epistles,* 1, 1.
[136] Ibid., 1, 6.
[137] Ovid, *Amores*, 3, 8, 55–6.
[138] Ovid, *Fasti*, 1, 217–18.
[139] Ecclesiastes, 1.

which Hercules vanquished. But there is no one to vanquish *our* Hydra. When you cut off one of its heads, a hundred more appear, ever fiercer. For the mind's *fire* is wanting – that fire which, in fully understanding one thing, deprives the remaining difficulties of a chance to increase. Let us come to our conclusion. All understanding is derived from the senses, and beyond this kind of understanding, all is confusion, doubt, perplexity, guesswork; nothing is certain.

The sense perceives only the outward appearance of things, and does not attain understanding (I am for the moment applying the word "sense" to the *eye*). It is the mind that receives images from the sense, and considers them. If the sense was deceived, so is the mind; but if not, what follows next? The mind regards only the images of things, which the eye has taken in; it studies them from this side and from that, and turns them about, putting the questions "What is this?" and "Whence comes its nature?" and "Why" – and no more than this, for it too sees nothing that is 52 certain. Surely this is the meaning of Aesop's fable, in which the crane, inviting the fox to dinner, put before him a beaker full of meal, with a narrow neck. The fox applied his tongue and mouth to the beaker, attempting to take some of the dish which he saw, but failed in his attempt, and so paid his penalty to the crane, who had previously been the butt of a similar joke played on him by that same fox.[140] In like manner, the celebrated painter Zeuxis deceived birds by means of his picture of a bunch of grapes: when the birds pecked at them on purpose to eat them, they smote their beaks on the painting.[141] Another artist, again, deceived Zeuxis himself with a drapery so cleverly depicted that it appeared to be genuine. When Zeuxis, full of conceit as though he had already won the contest, rushed forward in eagerness to see his rival's painting, thinking it to be covered with a cloth he put forth his

---

[140] Aesop's fable of "The Fox and the Stork" concerns deception, and the deceiver is paid back in his own coin.

[141] Sanches refers the reader to Pliny's *Natural History*, 35, 10 [36, 62–5]. Zeuxis (c. 420–390 B.C.) had introduced light and shadow into the art of painting, thus achieving a strong degree of realism.

hand in order to remove the "drapery" from the "canvas", and struck – bare "canvas"![142]

Now, this is how Nature presents things to our under-standing.[143] And, in another place, Aristotle has observed that our intellect is disposed towards the natures of things just as the eye of the night-raven is towards the light of the sun: it makes judgments about things *by means of images*.[144] Can its judgment then be correct? That would be a reasonable inference, if from our senses we received images of all the things we wish to know. But in fact it is the opposite situation: we have no images of particular things in themselves, only of their "accidents"; and these, as we are told, contribute nothing to the *essence* of a thing, which is the source of true *knowledge;* and in fact "accidents" are the most commonplace of all existents. We have to use them in order to make inferences about everything else. So it is the things that can be perceived by the senses, and are solid and crude (these comprise the "accidents", and also compound bodies), that are familiar to us in any event; while *per contra* the things that are immaterial, subtle in texture, and exalted in nature (these comprise the first principles of compound bodies, and also the heavenly bodies) are by no means so.[145] Yet the latter are more intelligible in terms of their own

---

[142] Ibid. Pliny recounts how Zeuxis was deceived by his rival, Parrhasius, one of the greatest painters of Greece, who produced such a realistic picture of a curtain that Zeuxis requested that it be drawn to display the picture.

[143] Aristotle, in the *Posterior Analytics* 81b, had pointed out that sense-perception was adequate for grasping particulars but did not operate on the same level as demonstration. However, from sense particulars one may proceed to universal concepts. Sanches argues on the other hand that even the primary sense, vision, created illusions: presentations do not conform to reality. Many are the favourite sceptical arguments concerning vision, such as the broken oar, the pigeon's neck, and the size of the sun.

[144] A reference to *Metaphysics* 993b10. Aristotle states: "For as the eyes of bats are to the blaze of day, so is the reason in our soul to the things which are by nature most evident of all". Sight for Aristotle was the noblest of the senses (see note 56).

[145] According to Aristotle in the *Metaphysics* 1039b27–31, "There is neither definition of nor demonstration about sensible individual substances, because they have matter whose nature is such that they are capable both of being and

nature, inasmuch as they are more perfect, more endowed with *Being,* and less complex; and these three qualities produce perfect understanding of a thing. Less so for us, insofar as they are more remote from the senses. But those things that are closer to the senses are more readily understood by us, for the simple reason that the *better* part of our understanding depends on the senses. Yet in terms of their own nature such things are only in the very

53 smallest degree accessible to the understanding; inasmuch as they are highly imperfect, almost nothing can be understood at all.

Now, Being is the object, subject, and first principle of all understanding – nay, rather, of all acts and motions. (You observe the great opportunity that is presented to us for ignorance in the realm of *things,* and you will see this more clearly when we come to explain things themselves.) For suppose these concepts are formulated only in terms of universals; in themselves they do not demonstrate that nothing is known. And I myself have not proposed to demonstrate the truth of that proposition (using the word "demonstration" in your sense), nor could I. For nothing *is* known. It is enough if I point out difficulties to you; should you succeed in overcoming these difficulties, you will then know something. But in fact you will not succeed in this, unless another and a fresh spirit is secretly sent down to you from above. It is possible that this might happen, but I have never yet beheld it. As things stand, however, we are discussing not what *can* be but what *is.* And the impediments to knowledge that reside in *things* (as objects) are very slight in comparison with those that reside in the subject who seeks understanding. For a person endowed with a perfect, and very acute, intellect, coupled with faultless sense-perception, might possibly overcome all of them (to make you a present of this admission, though in fact he could not do so, even if he had wholly perfect objects to consider). But as it is, the

of not being; for which reason all the individual instances of them are destructible". Sanches maintains that the senses can only make us aware of the concrete individual things that are subject to generation and destruction. The quintessence, or ether, is the purest substance, source of vital heat, and is a region occupied by the stars.

contrary is evident. Well then, the second point in the definition of knowledge was understanding (*cognitio*), in which three things can be observed: the object that is apprehended (*res cognita*); the apprehending subject, of whom I shall speak later; and apprehension itself, which is the action of the subject directed towards the object. This last I shall now discuss – but briefly, for it has its proper context in my *Treatise on the Soul*. And indeed to contemplate the soul, its faculties, and its actions, is indeed very difficult and full of perplexity; as difficult as any study that there is. But this is especially so in relation to the kind of understanding with which our present enquiry is concerned. Since there is nothing of higher worth than the soul, there is accordingly nothing more excellent than this supreme kind of understanding. Anyone who possessed this in perfection would be God–like, or rather he would be God Himself; for no one can perfectly 54 understand things he has not himself created. Even God could not have created, nor (having created) control, things He had not perfectly understood beforehand. Only He, being Himself perfect wisdom and understanding, and perfect intelligence, enters into all things, is wise in relation to all things, comprehends everything and understands everything, because He Himself *is* all things and is in all things, while all things *are* God Himself and are in Him. But how shall little Man, imperfect and wretched as he is, comprehend other things, he who is incapable of comprehending the self that is *in* him and *with* him?[146] How is he to comprehend the most abstruse secrets of Nature, among which are included spiritual things (and among these latter, our own human soul), when he completely fails to understand the clearest and most obvious things, things which he eats and drinks, touches, sees, and hears?

As for the thoughts I am now thinking, the words I am writing on this page, assuredly neither do I understand them, nor will you have understood them once you have read them. Yet you will, perhaps, judge them to be fine and true utterances. And I, for my

---

[146] Sanches refers to the Delphic inscription "Know Thyself" in Plutarch's *Adversus Colotem*.

part, believe them to be such. Yet neither of us knows anything. In this light it is wrong of Scaliger, great scholar though he is, to call Vives "absurd" because he says that a close investigation of the nature of mind is full of obscurity.[147] Nay, if Vives' opinion is absurd, then I myself am inclined to be the most absurd of all, for I consider it not merely full of obscurity but also murky, stony, abstruse, trackless, attempted by many and mastered by none – and not of a sort to be mastered at all.[148] It may be that Scaliger, with his outstandingly keen intelligence, thought it easy. And indeed his investigation of the soul, like that of almost every topic he discussed, was characterised by great brilliance and skill; yet it was not quite exhaustive or methodical or complete. He produced a great many arguments that beguile the mind with superficial and wordy rhetoric, and when consumed in great quantities appear to blunt the edge of hunger, but which, if one examines them more closely, in the end reveal their artificial colouring and leave the question in as perplexing a state as before; this I shall show, at the appropriate place. But for the present, so far as concerns the
55 business in hand, let us propose for discussion the question "What is understanding?" It is the apprehension of an object. And what is apprehension? Apprehend this for yourself, from your own resources, for I cannot suggest everything to you. If you persist in asking, I shall say "intellectual grasp, penetrating vision, or intuition". If you ask further about *these* concepts, I shall hold my tongue. This is beyond my powers; I do not know. But you must distinguish "apprehension" (grasping) from "reception" (taking in). For a dog "takes in" an image of a man, or a stone – its size, that is; yet he does not "understand". Nay, more; our human eye

---

[147] See Scaliger's *Exercitationes,* 308, 2, p. 388r. Vives had stated: "intricatum, ac plenum obscuritatis negotium, mentis naturam perscrutari".

[148] Sanches refers here to the judgment passed on Heraclitus by the satirical poet Scythinas: "Do not be in too great a hurry to get to the end of Heraclitus the Ephesian's book: the path is hard to travel. Gloom is there and darkness devoid of light. But if an initiate be your guide, the path shines brighter than sunlight" (Diogenes Laertius, *Lives of Eminent Philosophers,* 9). See also Plutarch's *Adversus Colotem* in which Heraclitus is quoted as saying "as of some great and lofty achievement 'I searched myself out'..."

"takes in", but does not "understand". Often the soul "takes in" without "understanding", as for example when it entertains false impressions, or when obscure images are presented to a sluggish intelligence. You must also distinguish "understanding" (*cognitio*), properly so called, which we have just described but nevertheless do not understand, from another kind of *cognitio*, improperly named, by which a person is said to "cognise" (recognise) things he has seen at another time, and retains in his memory, furnished with their appropriate signs. For this is the kind of "cognition" by which a child is said to "know" (by recognition) his father and his brother, and a dog his master and the road he has taken. In a word, you must divide all "cognition" into two kinds. One kind is perfect, the kind by which a thing examined from all sides, both inside and outside, is understood. And this is scientific knowledge (*scientia*). such as we should now like to acquire for Man – but science itself wishes otherwise! The other kind is imperfect, the kind by which a thing is apprehended by any means at all and after any fashion whatever. This is the kind with which we are familiar. But it is greater or less, brighter or more obscure, and – lastly – distributed in varying degrees according to the varying abilities of men. It is divided into two sorts: one of these is external, and comes about through the senses (hence it is called "sensory knowledge"); the other is internal, and originates in the mind alone, but is just as fully "knowledge". These matters have to be viewed in a different light. The human being, who is the "cognitive" subject, is *one* thing. In all cases, "cognition" (understanding) is *one*. For it is the same mind that "cognises" external and internal objects. The senses "cognise" nothing, inasmuch as they make no judgment; they merely absorb impressions, so that they may present them to the mind which is to perform the act of cognition, just as the air does not *see* colours or light, although it absorbs them so that they may be presented to the sight. However, there are three 56 kinds of objects that are cognised by the mind in different ways. Some objects are wholly external, requiring no action on the part of the mind. Others are wholly internal, and some of these are devoid of action by the mind, while others are not wholly devoid of it. Others again are partly external, partly internal. Then again

241

the first class make their presence known through the senses; the second class, in no way through the senses but by themselves directly; the last class, partly through the senses and partly by themselves.

Let me elaborate on these remarks. Colour and sound and heat cannot be presented to the mind by themselves, so that the mind may "cognise" (understand) them, unless they imprint an image of themselves (let us for the moment assume that sensory perception occurs through the reception of images) on an organ adapted to receive that image; and the same image, or another like it, is presented to the mind so that it can "cognise" it, or (through it) the object of which it is an image. But the objects which originate wholly in the understanding (*intellectus*) itself, and of which the understanding is the parent, and which lie deep within ourselves – these disclose and show themselves to the understanding, not by other images but by themselves alone. Such are the majority among those which the understanding invents for itself; as also when, after a great deal of cogitation, it thinks out and brings to completion some new idea, and when it grasps for itself the nature of its own intellectual processes, and when it creates within itself conjunctions, divisions, comparisons, categorical assertions, and notions, and, considering these, understands them in terms of themselves. Now, to the second class belong all internal objects that are similarly accompanied by the understanding, which nevertheless come to be, or are, without its agency: as, for example, the will, memory, inclination, anger, fear, and the rest of the emotions; also anything else that is internal, and directly "cognised" by the understanding through itself. Lastly, there are a great many objects that partly reach the understanding by way of the senses and partly come into being by way of the understanding itself.

Take the *nature* of a dog, or of a magnet. This can by no means be grasped by the senses. Therefore, it is invested with colour, size, and shape by the senses, and is thus presented by them to the 57 mind. The mind strips it of these "accidents," and considers what is left, looking at it from different angles and making comparisons. Finally, as best it can, it constructs out of that, for its own use, a kind of "nature" expressed in general terms. Philosophers of your school try to impress on me the view that there are "intelligences" in the sky.[149] I listen to what they say, but do not understand it. Yet I *can* invent something that will give me a notion of "intelligence". I can, under all circumstances, identify air by touch, but it has no image in my mind, except a *sort* of image, which I have invented for myself, of a *kind* of "body" which is (as it were) bodiless – I know not *what*. I think of empty space in the same way. I can grasp "infinity" without ever comprehending an end (*finis*), but it the midst of my reflections about it I am forced to pause when I reflect that "infinity" is an object that I shall never succeed in finally grasping, even if I add and add for ever, and make mental pictures, extended for ever. In this way I imagine a shape which is indeed bounded, but of which *neither* extremity is bounded and complete, but (as it were) defective; together with the idea that it is *not* bounded, nor can be, since we might go on for ever adding infinite parts at both ends. What can one do?

How unhappy our situation is! We are blind in the midst of light. I have often reflected about light, but have always given up without thinking it through or understanding or comprehending it. It is the same if you should reflect on the will and the intellect and other objects that are not perceived by means of the senses. Of this I am sure, that I am at this moment thinking of the words I am writing, and that I wish to write them, and long for them both to be true and to win your approval, yet do not set too much store by this last; when I try to reflect on what this thinking is, and this wishing, and this longing, and this indifference, then my thinking quite fails me, my wishing is frustrated, and my yearning grows ever greater, while my concern increases also. I see nothing that I could seek to lay hold on, or might possibly grasp. And indeed the kind of understanding (*cognitio*) that has to do with inward ideas, and does not depend on the senses, is in this respect inferior to the kind that is concerned with external objects and operates through the senses; for in the latter kind the understanding has something it 58 can grasp, namely the *shape* of a man or a rock or a tree, which it

[149] These are the intelligences which move the planetary spheres.

243

has derived from the senses – and, as it believes, it comprehends the man by means of his image. But in the former kind, which has to do with inward notions, the understanding finds nothing which it can grasp, and dashes this way and that, groping like a blind man to find if it can lay hold on anything; and no more than this. *Per contra,* however, the understanding of external objects, acquired by means of the senses, is outdone in *certainty* by the kind of understanding that is drawn from internal objects that either exist, or originate, *within* ourselves. For I am *more* sure that I possess both inclination and will, and that I am at one moment contemplating *this* idea, at another moment shunning and abominating *that* idea, than I am that I can see a temple, or Socrates.

I have said that we are certain about the real existence of those things that either exist, or else originate, within ourselves. As for the opinions we form about things by means of argumentation and reasoning and by inferring that they were in fact *thus,* such opinions are, as I personally believe, attended by very great uncertainty. And to me it is much more certain that this paper, on which I am writing, both exists and is white, than that same paper is made of the four elements, and that these elements are "actively" in it, and that it has a different *form* from theirs. Again, if you take away the things that exist in us, or originate in us, then the most trustworthy of all kinds of understanding is the kind that occurs by means of the senses, and the least trustworthy is that which occurs as a result of argumentation. For the latter kind is not really understanding, but merely groping, doubt, supposition, and conjecture. From which, once again, follows the result that scientific knowledge (*scientia*) is *not* that which is gained by syllogisms and divisions and categories and other mental operations of a similar sort; but if it were possible that, in the same way as we can perceive the external qualities of things in some manner by means of sensation, so we could grasp the internal principles of each and every object, then we could truly be said to *know*. But no one, so far as I know, has ever been able to achieve this. Hence, we know nothing.

Further, concerning the kind of understanding that has to do with inward things, and the other kind, which I call not

"understanding" but "opinion", and which results from conjunc- 59
tions, negations, comparisons, divisions, and other mental operations, I shall treat of this at the appropriate place, where the *lack*
of knowledge, inherent in both kinds, will be made clear. For the
present, let it suffice to say something concerning only the kind of
understanding of external objects that we acquire by means of the
senses. In this kind, there are two intermediate terms (sometimes
three or four, but always two at least) by way of which sensory
experience occurs (no matter whether such experience occurs
internally or as the result of a process of transmission, for this
question will not delay us for the present). One of these two terms
is something internal, viz. the eye; the other is something external,
viz. the air.[150] Can any object be understood completely by means
of them? Certainly not. For anything that is to be understood
completely must be understood not in terms of *another* thing
but in terms of itself, and directly (without mediation) by the
"cognising" subject *him*self. As things stand, however, the
substance of things either reveals itself by means of "accidents"
perceived *by* the senses or, *per contra*, conceals itself *from* the
senses. Either the mind receives information about the substance
of things, or (on other occasions) it is misinformed about that
substance, from senses which are deceptive in any case. How
then could we *know* anything perfectly? And yet, according
to you, there ought to be scientific knowledge concerning the
substances of things. As for the "accidents", can there be perfect
knowledge of these? Less than in the case of substance; for whereas
one factor could be helpful, namely that "accidents" are perceived
by the senses, yet there are several disadvantageous factors: that
they *are* virtually nothing; that not they themselves, but only their
images, reach the mind; and lastly, that they very frequently deceive the senses. This occurs because of the variety in substance,
location, and arrangement of the external, as well as internal,
medium. Let it suffice to mention one or two of the senses. Take

---

[150] See Rudolph E. Siegel, *Galen on Sense Perception* (Basel: S. Karger, 1970), pp.
10–126, for an excellent historical survey of ancient doctrines of vision.

eyesight. Even though this sense operates through the most perfect of all organs, and is the most reliable and the most refined among all the senses, yet it is very often deceived. The external medium may vary, and it affects the sense in various ways accordingly. The common element, air, seems to give a more accurate 60 report of things, inasmuch as it appears totally colourless, whereas water distorts the image. So much for natural media. A great many media are artificial, such as glass, thin sheets of horn, crystal, and suchlike. Which of all these can one trust? It is by sight that we distinguish, not colours only, but size, number, shape, movement, distance, roughness, and brightness, and also the qualities that have reference to these, such as equality, likeness, speed, and their opposites. Water makes bodies seem dark or appear double; now larger, now smaller; or of another shape; or thicker; or moving; or smooth – and not always to the same effect, but in different ways at different times. As for air, it sometimes makes objects appear thick (in the south wind), or dark, or large in extent, or double (as in the echo, in the sun, in the moon), and sometimes the opposite. Why, even pictures sometimes appear to be three-dimensional and alive; and sculptures, too, very often appear to be alive. Glass, horn, and crystal can at will make larger objects appear smaller, thick objects appear thin, and objects of one solid hue appear particoloured – in brief, they do just what the craftsman desires. Hence the enormous variety of mirrors and hand-mirrors, large and small. Which of these media reflects a better and truer likeness of the object? Surely you could not know. If you were to say "air", and I deny this, you cannot prove it. But given that I agree, still it sometimes shows objects as larger, sometimes as smaller. As to its colour, this is attended by much more doubt. When can you be sure of it? Why, when it is closer to its own nature and less influenced by external factors. But who has ever gained an understanding of its nature? Who has ever seen it in its pure state? It undergoes ceaseless alteration from the sun, the moon, and other celestial bodies; and among terrestrial influences, from earth, water, and mixed substances. We are bound to come to the same judgment concerning glass and water – or rather, the difficulty is even harder to resolve. For *two* external media are involved in seeing something through glass or water, namely the air and the water (or glass) itself.

Place a coin in a small, wide vessel. Cause the vessel to rest on the ground. Withdraw to a distance from which you can no longer see the coin. Then require the vessel to be filled with water. At once you will see the coin, and see it as larger than before. Why could you not previously see it through the air, since according to you this [air] is the best medium of all?[151] Why does the coin now appear larger? We do not know. One can only attempt some kind 61 of conjecture; and I shall give my own conjecture when I come to my *Enquiry into Things*. So much, then, for the substance of the external medium, to which also are referred thickness or thinness, greatness or smallness, and this or that shape of the medium through which any object is seen. For although not all of these characteristics are to be found in the air, yet in the artificial media they cause great alterations in the appearance of the object. A thick pane of glass shows the object differently from thin glass; a square or round pane shows it differently from a triangular pane; and a large pane shows it differently from a small one. The same phenomenon appears in various manufactured patterns of crystal and of glass: through these, one can see things either the right way up, or upside down; in this, or that, colour and shape – in a word, otherwise than as they are. The sea, where it is deep, is it itself perceived as dark blue in colour, and tints with the same hue the things that are beneath it; at small depths, however, it is perceived as clear white in colour.[152] How does this happen? You do not know; nor do I. Altering the position of an object has a way of altering at the same time the perception of that object by the

---

[151] Aristotle in the *De anima* 418b describes the medium as "transparent"; it is the influence of this substance, ether, of which light is the activity that gives rise to colour.

[152] Aristotle's doctrine of vision is set out in the *De anima* and in the *De sensu*. However, in the *De generatione animalium* 779b24−6, he considers the eye as the organ of sight and posits, as in the previous treatises, that sight consists of water, the difference in the colour of the eyes being explained, as in the example of the varying colours of the sea which Sanches uses, by the amount of fluid in the eye.

senses. Similarly in regard to the medium. This is evident in the case of mirrors; if you move them towards the eye they reflect a different image from that which they show if you move them slightly further away. This is equally true of air. A lamp, seen close up, appears symmetrical, oblong in shape, steady, small, and yellowish in colour; but from a distance it appears round, producing rays in all directions, and also unsymmetrical, twinkling, and moving (from which fact, Aristotle has borrowed the demonstration he employs to prove that the planets are close to us – because they do not twinkle), large, bright, and colourless. Objects that are far away *appear* dark and small; those that are too close either cannot be seen, or are seen otherwise than as they are. What is one to do? Keep hold of the "middle" distance? Where is that "middle"? Is it measured at two paces, or any other fixed number? A man far off from us may be running very fast, yet he

62 seems to move with extreme slowness, especially if *you* are looking down at *him* from a height, or *vice versa*. Events that happen gradually, such as the movement of the hand in a clock, are unperceived by the senses. How are you to judge for sure? You do not know; still less do I. Nor is it a matter of only slight importance that we should understand this, for it is the source of endless doubts concerning the size of the stars, not to mention their distance from us, their speed of movement, and their position, all of which can clearly be seen to depend on it. As for the objects we have available close at hand, we may investigate them again and again, just as we please, using different organs of sense – if it *should* be that they are open to several senses at once – and obtain a more exact understanding of them at very close quarters. But who can do this with the former class of objects? And not *only* those: if *from a distance* we see a stick half submerged in water, it will appear twisted or bent. You will say that the stick *is* nevertheless unbroken, because on another occasion you found out by experience that it was so. But suppose that it is in fact broken: it will *nonetheless* appear broken.[153] For the Law of

---

[153] The stick which appears bent in water (or the oar) is a common example of sensory deception quoted by sceptics. See Diogenes Laertius, *Lives of Eminent*

Contraries does not apply in this situation. On the basis of your previous argument. you will maintain that it is unbroken; yet this is false. What are you going to do, if you are not in a position to withdraw it from the water? Why, you will remain in doubt.

As for colours, the difference made in respect to them by *position* is proved by the rainbow, by a glass jar full of water, by the variegated hues of the dove's plumage, by silken webs woven out of diverse colours, and by the proximity, to an object, of a luminous body of a different colour (so too if you set upon a plane surface a sheet of gold or silver, set perpendicularly to the plane, and much more pronouncedly if you tilt it downwards). All these objects, when they are moved this way or that, reflect a very different colour; but in which position are you going to claim to be showing their *true* colour? On the *same* side it is now red, now yellowish, and then again dark blue; which of them is it more properly said to be? You can only remain in doubt. That numbers, shape, movement, and size are altered by alteration of position – by which I mean, altered not in themselves but in terms of our sense-perception of them – there is no need for me to demonstrate at great length, since you can test this in everyday experience. And so I need say no more on the subject of position.

It is inevitable that alteration in the arrangement of the external medium should cause alteration in the images conveyed through 63 it. Some of this I have already stated. In thick air, all objects appear dark and small; in a thin atmosphere, the opposite. In a meadow, everything assumes a green coloration. In the vicinity of red or yellow objects, bodies are marked with these colours. Under excessive light it is impossible to see, especially to see white or (above all) very bright bodies. Still less is it possible to see in darkness. In the vicinity of the latter (sc. darkness) and the former (sc. bright light), one can have only doubtful and erroneous vision. What is the "middle distance"? You must define it for

Philosophers, 9, 85, where the seventh mode of Aenesidemus regarding distance, position, and place is discussed. Cicero in the *Academica*, 2, 7 and at greater length in 25 and 26 examines optical illusions. Sanches's main arguments, however, are drawn from Plutarch's *Adversus Colotem,* 1121.

yourself. But even in the air, when it is illuminated by a display of fireworks, many different colours, and shapes too, can be seen, corresponding to differences in the material out of which the firework is made. Should the medium be glass or crystal, objects are exhibited in very different aspects in accordance with the different colours and varying shapes and consistency of the media. These are the "means" (*media*) through the middle (medium) of which things are seen; other media reveal things only superficially – in them, there is no stability. How many monstrous, absurd, multiple, inverted, and truncated shapes there are among them! What cannot mirrors invent? What is one to say about them? Do you see yonder shape? It does not exist; how could you see it? Yet you do; how so? Not unreasonably, you do not know.

Let us now pass to the internal medium, where so many difficulties are to be met with. When a single eye acquires an upward or sideways cast, things appear double (Aristotle's contrary opinion notwithstanding). Hence it is strange that those who suffer from a squint do not see everything double. (But I shall give an account of this in my *Enquiry into Things*.) The same phenomenon occurs if, lying on your side, you have in front of you some body that blocks the view of the lower eye; for then the upper eye will see all objects that are below the body in question, but the other eye will see only the body itself, and that not distinctly but in a shadowy fashion. Thus, when one eye looks at objects located behind the body, while the other looks at the body itself, we appear to see two bodies at the same time, of which one is superimposed upon the other. And you can more easily test this
64 by experiment if you move one eye to the outer corner and examine in order the things on that side; for then, when one of the eyes moves in that direction, the nose enters the field of vision and seems to cover, like a shadow, everything that the other eye beholds. Similarly, if you hold a finger in front of your eyes, not looking at it but observing the objects that are either behind or beside it, it will nonetheless appear double. The same thing will happen if you turn both eyes towards your nose; everything will then appear double. If you move one eye, the objects you see appear to move – or rather, of two things that appear, one moves

while the other stays at rest. But also the left-hand object moves to the right and the right-hand object to the left if, when you study a book, you keep moving the eyes by themselves without the help of a finger, merely looking at the lines without reading. To these is added the position of an eye which, by nature or accident, is either deep-set or prominent; these differ greatly in their mode of seeing, and much more if, with one eye deep-set, the other is prominent. Also if one eye should be set higher, the other lower – but in this case the distortion is obvious. Where, however, *both* eyes are either deep-set or prominent, there is no distortion. Related to position, also, is the greater or smaller closing or opening of the eyelid. If you look at a lamp with half-closed eyes, it will seem as if a multitude of rays extend forward towards your eyes, and these rays move in response to the movement of the eyelids. If you open your eyes wide, the rays then cease to move and their length diminishes. Let these suffice as examples; from them you will be able to think out, and experiment with, a great many others for yourself.

Colours change according to the varied position of the eye no less than that of the object of vision and also of the medium. But I have already made my point. Perhaps you attach very little importance to all of this, and do not believe that it can stand in the way of scientific knowledge. But the reality is very different; for these phenomena have prompted certain thinkers to entertain doubts about everything that appears to the senses, and to hold that colours are not permanent constituents of things, but come 65 into being, and change, on account of light.[154] As you shall see, I have elsewhere expressed my view about this. But now let us proceed to discuss "substance".

Five "internal" media are listed by philosophers, viz. sight, touch, taste, hearing, and smell. All of these have differing "substances". Accordingly, different things too are perceived by them, though they have certain things in common, which I have

---

[154] Sanches refers the reader to Diogenes Laertius, *Lives of Eminent Philosophers,* 9 and 10 and Plutarch's *Adversus Colotem* for the opinions of the Pyrrhonians, Democritus, and Epicurus on colour and light.

touched on above: size, number, shape, and so on. The eye perceives a *single* act of striking, but the ear hears a *double* blow; if the eye had not seen, you would undoubtedly have opined that there had been two blows. Now suppose you are blind: I shall strike two blows – or only one myself, but another blow is struck by someone at a distance from me, and immediately after me, like an echo. If you have never been endowed with sight you will say – informed by someone else – that it *is* an echo, and you will be wrong. Now suppose on the other hand that you can see. I ask someone to strike a blow after me, out of sight. You will say *this* is an echo, but it is not. Very frequently, when only a single horse is running, the ear judges that there are two horses; or, if there are two, but moving at a uniform steady pace, the ear judges them to be one; and even the eye does so, if it is far distant. If several things are in movement, both ear and eye are even more readily deceived. This is equally true in judgments about size, where that which the eye judges to be small, the ear judges to be large, or *vice versa*. In the matter of shape, the eye is more easily deceived than is the sense of touch, just as the latter sense is likewise less easily deceived than the former in the matter of size.

Things close at hand sometimes appear to sight and hearing to be very far distant – but more to hearing than to sight; at other times it is the other way round. Touch is no less deceptive in the matter of distance: if a large, hot object is in the vicinity, even some way off, the sense of touch still deems it to be close at hand, on account of the powerful impression it produces. The nose, too, is very often deceived. There is no need for me to cite many instances; nothing is more reliable, or again more deceptive, than the senses. Which of them can you trust? The ear, or the eye? Then "you have a wolf by the ears". Let us proceed. We have to face a very important further consideration, namely that it is the varying arrangements of all these sense-organs that more than anything 66 else cause us to go astray. The different colours of eyes; the different "temperaments"; the consistency, substance, quantity, situation, and transparency of the vapours and humours contained in the eyes – surely these combine to produce the greatest differences in seeing. But if the discussion is couched in more technical medical terms, the substance of the membranes and of the optic nerve and the quantity of the vapours and humours – all these, taken together with the eye's transparency, usually cause great variations in the sight. Often, from an external cause, we appear to see flies, particles of fluff, spiders' webs, and similar objects, when in fact they are not present. When the eye is inflamed, everything appears red; when it is suffused with bile, everything appears yellow. If moisture is pressing on the pupil of the eye, things appear to be full of holes, or covered with a veil, or large or small or double or dim. These particular defects accompany sickness; but even if people are well, some of them are long-sighted, some are short-sighted; one sees more brightly, another more dimly; one sees objects as large, another sees them as small; one sees them as red, another sees them as yellow. In short, no one sees either perfectly, or in the same way as others. What, then, prevents us from seeing objects (which are various and indeterminate and unstable), not as they are, but *differently,* considering that we do so through the medium of an eye that is subject to so many kinds of change (that is, indeed, so changeable in itself) and also through air, which is not less – nay, more – fluid and unreliable than the eye itself? What is to prevent us from being continually deceived? or from being unable ever to lay hold on anything that is certain, or (consequently) to make any reliable statement? Yet the eye is the finest of all organs of sense, and the most reliable of them all; and if you turn from it to the other sense-organs you will encounter much greater dubiety. How is that which is always *hot* to judge aright concerning hot and cold? Now, we humans are always hot. Thus it comes about that people in hot-water bathing establishments (*thermae*), or in artificially constructed baths, judge both urine and warm water to be cold, which (by your own account) is false. Is it not true that all the things we touch are exposed to the air and affected by it? Are we not ourselves continually affected by that same air? And is not air, 67 in its turn, affected by water, earth, and the stars? What therefore, obliges men to speak of water as "cold" or of air as "warm"? To beings that are very hot, things that are less hot seem cold. Such creatures, perhaps, are we. Therefore, water is *hot*. In winter,

because we are greatly affected by external cold, water freshly drawn from a spring or well seems warm, because it is less cold; in summer, however hot it is, the air seems cool if you run, or stir the air with a fan – even though (by your own account) it is warm, and much more so at that season. What, then, *is* heat or cold? Reason can do nothing, here, to let us see what things are hot, or what things are cold. Who understands their rational principle? No one, We have to submit our judgment to the senses. But even if sense-perception functioned perfectly, and could distinguish their qualities, it would not for that cause *know*, but merely "(re)cognise", just as a peasant can tell his donkey apart from a neighbour's (or his own) ox. As things stand, however, sense-perception cannot offer even as much as this. What, then, do we *know?* Nothing. Run through the other senses: less still can they offer. Yet this kind of understanding is better than any other we have. What can the mind do, when it is deceived by the senses? It can only fall further into deception. When one assumption proves false, it introduces a great many more; hence come others (for a small mistake at the beginning turns into a great mistake in the end). At length, when the mind sees the error (for there is but a *single* truth, which is self-consistent), it retraces its steps and looks for the point in the argument that caused the failure. Not finding this, it regards one or another of the media as suspect. Concerning this latter it once again puts the question whether it is true or false. It is incapable of determining this, since it is above sense. It then proceeds to argue on the basis of probability; and so on, *ad infinitum*. There is no conclusion, no end to doubt. Come, try it for yourself; I am not forcing it upon you. If I were in your company, I could easily prove to you, by oral argument, that everything is doubtful; but my written page has no room for so long a discussion, and we are hastening towards the *Enquiry into Things*, in the course of which I shall illustrate this from
68 experience. You have succeeded in gaining some kind of insight into this from what I have written above, and presently you will have a more adequate view of it. I now continue my explanation.

We have already spoken of the *object (res)*, and also of the media, having regard to understanding (*cognitio*); now to speak of the understanding *subject* (*cognoscens*). In him, there are countless opportunities for ignorance. Life is short, but the "art" is long, yea, endless – or rather the things that underlie the "art" or which the "art" underlies. But opportunity is treacherous ground, experiment is full of risks, and judgment is hard. Yet "not only must one vouch for *oneself* doing the right thing at the right time, but also one's neighbours, and external circumstances as well".[155] One would say that this aphorism was admirably suited to my purposes, in a work in which are propounded the difficulties faced by him who has to *know* something. Some of these difficulties you have already perceived; others you are about to perceive. So let us begin with the human being, at the moment when his life commences; for *he* is what we understand in the aphorism by "one who does the right things at the right time". At the moment of birth he is but a lump of wax capable of assuming virtually any shape both in body and in soul, but particularly in soul. Thus though he is not unaptly compared to a *tabula rasa* on which nothing has yet been drawn, still it is not quite correct to maintain that anything and everything can be drawn on it.[156] For not all men are suited to Letters, even though they are provided with everything necessary for the purpose. And can the nature of things be depicted on the soul? or the nature of infinity? or of empty space? Evidently not. And, as things now stand, it is not in fact so. The newly-born human being, then, possesses two characteristics: no capability has been stamped upon him *in actuality*, but several capabilities, of this or that kind, are there *in potentiality* – either many of them, or only a few.[157] (But no one possesses *all* capabilities.) This is merely a passive potential capacity, the

---

[155] Sanches refers to the first aphorism of Hippocrates: "Vita brevis, ars vero longa, occasio autem praeceps: experimentum periculosum, iudicium difficile. Nec solum seipsum praestare oportet opportuna facientem, sed et aegrum, et assidentes, et exteriora".

[156] See Aristotle *De anima* 430a.

[157] Sanches in his discussion of Aristotle's doctrine of potentiality and actuality (*Metaphysics, 8*) subscribes to the view that all individual things in the world vary according to the extent they are imbued with potentiality, which would explain differences in capacity.

opposite of which is the other passive, namely potential *incapacity*, by which a person is unfitted for many, or a few, functions of one kind or another. These two are shared by mankind with other animals also. For by virtue of the former, namely potential capacity, the parrot can mimic human speech; which by virtue of the latter, namely potential incapacity, the ape cannot do. *Per contra,* the ape can by virtue of the former [potential capacity] perform many actions in imitation of a human being which the parrot, on account of the latter [potential incapacity] cannot perform. In the same way, among human beings one person is totally unfitted for Grammar; he is best fitted to be a sailor, while with another person it is just the reverse. Now, mankind possesses an *active* "potential capacity", which the brute beasts lack, and by which sciences and arts are discovered.[158] But I shall discuss this at greater length when I come to speak of the Soul. For the present let it suffice to have adduced these arguments in order that what follows may be understood.

How few, then, of all the many thousands of human beings are suited to the sciences – even to such sciences as we have. Persons of this sort are the merest handful; and as for *perfect* science, there is not one who is suited to that. I can prove this. Anyone who has to *know* something perfectly ought himself to be perfect. Does any such person exist? Yet observe that he *must* be so. You yourself maintain – being ignorant of the soul's nature, as I shall elsewhere demonstrate – that the soul is equally perfect in all men, but that the body is the cause why one man is more learned, and another less learned, and another not learned at all. Very well, I grant this. Is our human soul perfect enough for a man to be able to know anything perfectly? No; but suppose it is. Then the person with a less perfect body will have less perfect knowledge, he who has a more perfect body will have more perfect knowledge, and he who has the most perfect body will have the most perfect knowledge. For this seems a more reasonable deduction from your argument than its contrary would be. To whom has a perfect body been given? To no one (even if a physician loudly denies this); nor, if it

---

[158] The reference by Sanches is to the opening paragraphs of the *Metaphysics*.

were given, would it remain perfect for more than an instant.[159] If you deny this, I will not prove it now, since I intend to prove it elsewhere. I shall, however, request something of you – and I know you will not grant my request, for you are devoid of knowledge, as I myself am. Now, like Galen I describe as a "most perfect" body one that is most evenly balanced in its elements and most beautiful. And Galen maintains that only the most evenly balanced body (though he ought to have remembered the components in the mixture, on account of their actions in the role of instruments) performs the most perfect operations. Among these actions, intellectual understanding, on which science depends, stands highest.[160] But that, too, is supported by the reason. 70 Some medical men have maintained that in order to be perfect a physician must first suffer from all diseases, before he should be perfectly capable of passing judgment concerning them.[161] And this opinion does not seem altogether foolish, though if that were so it would be better not to be a physician! For how can someone who has never felt pain form a correct opinion about pain? And we shall better diagnose and treat, in others, the pains and diseases that we have experienced in ourselves. In the same way, how is a blind or one-eyed man to make a correct judgment about colours, or a partly deaf man about sounds, or a paralysed person about qualities related to the sense of touch? Therefore, anyone who would judge with perfect correctness about colours must have perfect eyesight; about sounds, perfect hearing; about tactile qualities, a perfect sense of touch; about things possessing flavour, a perfect sense of taste; about motion, a perfect power of movement; about digestion, perfect digestive powers; about pain, perfect sensitivity to pain; about imagination, perfect imagination; about memory, perfect memory; and about the intellectual understand-

---

[159] The physician in question is Galen, whose famous treatise *De usu partium corporis humani* praises Nature for having fashioned the human body to such a degree of perfection.

[160] In the *Adhortatio ad artes addiscendas* Galen stresses that man possesses mind in common with the gods and that he alone of all the animals is capable of cultivating the sciences.

[161] A marginal annotation refers to Plato's *Republic* [III, 408].

ing, perfect intelligence. Otherwise, as Galen observes, he will be like the sailor in the book, who, sitting unconcernedly on a bench, gives an excellent description of harbours, rocks, promontories, Scyllas and Charybdises – in a word, navigates his ship superbly through the kitchen, or across the table – but who, if he were to go aboard a ship and you were to put the helm of a trireme in his care, would dash you on those very rocks, that very Scylla and Charybdis, with which he was previously so well acquainted. Or, again, he will be like the man who announces in the market-place the loss of a donkey or of a dog, describing it by means of its peculiar markings, yet would fail to recognise it if he had it before him. And it is for this reason that Our Lord Christ is said to have wished to undergo the sufferings of humanity: namely that, having experienced our misfortunes, He might pity us the more. For one who has once been poor sympathises more genuinely with the poor, one who has been a captive, with the captive, and finally one who has been wretched, with the wretched, than one who has never been poor or captive or wretched can sympathise 71 with those so afflicted. Therefore, the most perfect understanding requires the most perfect body. Let this be the final argument: all perfect things rejoice in what is perfect, and are produced (a) by perfect agents and (b) through perfect means. Now, what is more perfect than the work of Creation? It is performed by the only perfect being, God, who is perfection itself. By what means? By means of His wholly perfect power; which alone is utterly perfect, because it is the only *infinite* power, and because it is God Himself. All other things are becoming *more* perfect, being made so by agents that are themselves becoming more perfect. The actions of the heavenly bodies could not be performed by any body that was more *im*perfect. Of all this, the principle is the following: the active agent, whenever it meets a passive, passes over into it; for any given thing desires to change another thing into itself, which it cannot do unless it gives a part of itself to the other. While it is doing this, it receives influence from the other in return, while the latter, attempting to preserve itself in its own being (which is also a characteristic bestowed on every entity; hence the further consequence follows, that it wishes to absorb another thing into itself, lest its own extinction should at some time come about), partly resists, and partly, wishing again to convert another thing into itself, extends and exercises its own power, and impresses its own force, as far as it is able, towards the active agent; but since it is inferior to the agent in strength, it is defeated in the struggle, and is forced to follow the other's lead and abandon its original state and sink itself in the other. Therefore, if the active agent is perfect, then its action must be perfect too; so must the means to completion of the action; and so must the passive agent that receives the action, insofar as it receives it, even though it should be imperfect in other respects. But if the action should not result in the absorption of the passive object into the agent, at all events the work that is accomplished as a result of such action is perfect if done by a perfect agent, imperfect if done by an imperfect one. For, as the physicians say, consequences bear witness to their beginnings. What anything is, that it does; and such as a thing is, even such is what it does, whenever suitable means are available. Such means are those that resemble the agent; for when this is so, the two will combine better against the passive object. Therefore a perfect agent, if it is aided by perfect instruments and means, will 72 act better on the passive object, and achieve its purpose better, than if those instruments and means are imperfect. You can observe this in all actions, both natural and voluntary. The sun, which is the most perfect of all bodies – for which reason a great many people have believed it to be a god – what action does it perform?[162] Why, the most perfect action possible, an action resembling that of God; for whereas God *creates* all things, the sun *generates* all things, and generation is but one step below creation.

Yet there is a difference. For God creates out of Himself, alone, from nothing, and without a medium or instrument; the sun, which takes its power from God, generates man with man's help, from seed, and by means of heat; though sometimes the sun by itself alone even generates a large number of things without a

[162] A marginal annotation refers to the beliefs of Pythagoras and the Egyptians, as recounted in Diogenes Laertius, *Lives of Eminent Philosophers*, 8, and Plutarch's *De amore*.

second partner in generation, as for example the mouse from dung, the frog from dust after rain, the locust, the flea, the gnat, the lizard, the dung-beetle, the louse, and a great many other living creatures; and among plants, hart's tongue fern, scaly spleenwort [fern], goldenhair [moss], maidenhair fern, lichen, lungwort, mistletoe, mushroom; also all inanimate things – gold, silver, stones, and gems of all kinds; and the elements of these things in their turn.[163] But perhaps you will object that the sun also spoils things, which is a very *bad* action, and *not* perfect, if generating be a perfect act. Yet it is not so. For it does not spoil things; while it is generating them, corruption inevitably follows, for it is clear that it *first* generates them, since being is prior to non-being, and action is prior to the deprivation of action, in terms of its worth, its excellence, and its nature.[164] Now, corruption is not an entity. It is the deprivation or destruction of a given entity; it is nothing, therefore. Accordingly, generation is prior to corruption; so the latter follows the former, not the other way about. Therefore, the sun first generates; and when it corrupts it does so subsequently, and as a result. This is clear also from the following consideration: no entity acts for *nothing,* or intends *nothing.* (Hence it is also true that evil too does not exist *per se;* for evil is the 73 deprivation of good, which is as much as to say that it is nothing.)[165] All entities, then, act for the sake of an end. But it is not possible for *nothing* to be an end for that which *is.* For an end is perfection, and perfection has the first place among *entities.* Deprivation, destruction, disappearance, are merely the negation of an entity: they are *nothing.* How else am I to describe nothing

---

[163] This section on generation and putrefaction from the sun's heat is largely drawn from Julius Caesar Scaliger's *Exercitationes,* 26, pp 50v.–51r.

[164] Sanches is using the arguments advanced by Aristotle in the *Metaphysics* 1049[b]–1051[b] to defeat his adversary, presumably Scaliger.

[165] Sanches is here paraphrasing Aristotle's doctrine of the priority of actuality, which leads to the conclusion that there is no evil principle in the world: "Clearly, then, the bad does not exist apart from bad things; for the bad is in its nature posterior to the potency. And therefore we may also say that in the things which are from the beginning, i.e. in eternal things, there is nothing bad, nothing defective, nothing perverted (for perversion is something bad)" (*Metaphysics* 1051a17–21).

itself, save by the highly invidious term "nothing"? It is absolutely opposite, and hostile, to perfection and to Being (*ens*). In the end, it is nothing. And who will intend or seek *that?* Everything naturally avoids it. Nothing terrifies or depresses me, or prostrates my mind, except this same "nothing", when I reflect that one day I shall visit the court of Nothing (were it not that Faith, accompanied by Hope and Charity, destroyed this fear, together with its cause, Nothing, and comforted me by promising me an indissoluble union with Almighty God after the dissolution of this present compound of body and soul). Is the sun, the most perfect of all bodies, to intend and accomplish corruption? It generates, then. By what means? By means of heat, the most perfect and excellent and active of all qualities. This you will see in my *Enquiry into Things.* You add *light,* besides; but I do not agree. Still, it supports my argument. Light is the brightest of things, the friendliest, and the kindliest. Men compare life to it, as they compare death to darkness. It cheers us. By means of it, we become acquainted with the most beautiful objects – a great many of them. God describes Himself as light. Without light we should be blind, we should fall asleep and fall silent, and wander about like dead men, not only not seeing ourselves but not even discerning the natures of things. Do you observe what a profound silence there is on a dark and cloudy night? It seems almost like a return of chaos, or like death. Assuredly I should not wish to live without light. The sun, which is the parent of both heat and light, uses both of them for generating things, as you 74 yourself would have it; but the same facts show that it does not use them for corruption. When the sun is coming closer to us, everything revives and is reborn, burgeons, germinates, puts forth leaves, breaks into flower, and becomes fruitful. Animals, numbed by the cold and half-perished – animals that would have perished utterly if the celestial body had stayed away any longer – emerge from their lairs, are livelier in their movements, show signs of gladness, run about, leap up, rejoice and sing, and become ready for the generative function on the arrival of the generative star; and to this function they happily betake themselves. In a word, spring and summer mean procreation and life. For myself,

261

it is only then that I am alive. But when God's right eye (for I have a fancy so to call the sun) departs from us, everything becomes faint and sluggish, enters into a decline, and perishes. What are autumn and winter but continual death? The poets call death "cold", "frozen", "stiff", "grim," and "pale"; and they are right to do so. Life, on the other hand, they describe as "flowery", "green", and "full of vigour". Death results from cold, life from heat, and heat from the sun. Therefore the sun is the most perfect of all bodies, by virtue of the most perfect quality of all, namely heat; and it performs the most perfect of all natural actions, namely generation. So much for natural actions. As for voluntary actions, surely the painter or sculptor or lyre-player will paint or sculpt or play better, if these artists use more perfect, rather than less perfect, means and instruments? Will a man who is hoarse sing well? Or a lame one dance well? Or one with a clumsy hand write well? Yet what more perfect organ could have been devised by nature than this same hand? Surely none, as our authority, Galen, insists: see his *On the Use of the Parts,* Book I. Now, man, the most perfect of all animals, needed also the most perfect instrument of all, in order to perform the most perfect works in the whole 75 animal realm. If that instrument had been less perfect, could he have perfectly discharged the numerous functions that in fact he does discharge? I do not think so. But to what result does all this lead? To this: that we are proving that every perfect being produces a perfect result, and, in order to produce that result, employs a perfect instrument.

What follows? This: the human soul, the most perfect of all things created by God, needs a wholly perfect body in order to perform the most perfect of all the actions of which it is capable, namely perfect understanding (*cognitio*). "What!" you will say. "Understanding does not depend on the body, nor is it in any way helped by it, but it is produced by the mind alone". This, as I have elsewhere proved, is false. It is futile to say that the mind understands, just as it is to say that the mind hears. It is the *human being* who does both, using body *and* mind in both instances, and performing any other action whatsoever with the aid of both of these at once – and performing no action at all without the support and co-operation and activity of both of them. But if you stand by your own remarks, that very point is proved. Why is one man more learned and another less? The *mind* is equally perfect in both. Therefore, as *you* said, the defect lies in the body. Accordingly, the more learned man owns a more perfect body, however he uses it, whether for imagination or for understanding. Therefore, the most learned man has the most perfect body; and he is the one who truly *knows*. Now, I have already explained of what sort a perfect body is; and since such a body is nowhere to be found, then nowhere can one find perfect understanding (*cognitio*), and consequently not scientific knowledge (*scientia*) either – which is *the same thing*. But perhaps you will say that, for the purpose of understanding, we do not need arms and legs, and that, accordingly, it is enough if only our brain be in good condition, even if arms and legs should be defective. But you are deceived. If the limbs of a person are badly formed from the very first stage of his engendering, the defect lay either (a) in the material from which 76 they were made or (b) in the power that gave them shape. In either case it is inevitable that one, or several, of the principal members should be defective. But (a) concerning the material there can be no doubt, for all the members are made from the same seed. As to (b), the formative power, this is not in the first instance weak *per se,* but only because it is lacking in the vital breath, or else the proper mixture of elements, these being its principal instruments. And if either of these be defective, there is a defect in the inward parts also. But even if the defect were only in the external parts, it would be shared by them with the internal parts. For weak extremities do not attract, retain, digest, or excrete with perfect efficiency; consequently the blood is infected with the body's refuse, and from it the vital breath and the internal organs too. If a deformity occurs after the body is completely formed and is born, this comes about either from an internal or an external cause. However it happens, it still alters the inward parts, and mars their perfection, in the same way as if it happened from the very beginnings of life. Lastly, either a perfect body exists nowhere, or it will last only for a moment. Therefore, no one possesses scientific knowledge, and nothing is known.

But perhaps you will say that even an imperfect body is fitted for the sciences; for it seems difficult to believe that among all mankind *no* one is suited to undertake them. For my part, I gladly grant this, as I allow several other points; but I do not grant anything and everything, for you yourself do not wish this – and you will never succeed in proving it. Therefore, that body must be endowed with a determinate kind of "temperament". *What* kind of temperament? (Perhaps you will not grant this; but let us suppose that you *have* granted it.) How many changes this newborn babe undergoes as a result of air, place, motion, food, education! Reflect on this for yourself. If he is rich, he is spoiled, grows fat, and becomes entirely gross in physique and unfitted for study; for the soul and the body have in any case opposite aims, by your own account, as I shall remark in my *Treatise on the soul.*
77 Why, even the child's parents will not allow him to be exhausted by the toil of studying, but arrange everything with a view to the cultivation of the body; only about his morals are they somewhat concerned (and would that they really were!). And – as most of mankind does, and wisely, at Nature's bidding – they teach him to pay attention to health, wealth, and the other things that can make life happy, the result being that so few people devote themselves to the study of Letters. But let us suppose that the parents both allow it and desire it, while the youth himself refuses. For the body always looks for ease; to all of us, hard toil is the enemy. Riches distract the mind, luxury upsets it, and worldly values allure it. To me, indeed, that man seems to be a very Lord Apollo who, when he is in a position to enjoy the good things of this life, pays no heed to them, but devotes himself to the contemplative study of the universe, thereby exchanging his station in life for the most wretched of all. But he is a "rare bird on earth". Everyone is ready to embrace science for the sake of fame or rank or wealth; scarcely one man will do so for its own sake. Thus each man toils just hard enough to reach the goal – not of science, but of his personal ambition. But as for the needy persons, who flock to study in the greatest numbers, their *début* is depressing, their mid-career a struggle, their end far from creditable. For gloomy poverty is what drives them, and also hinders them: once it has a full

264

belly, it puts an end to the poor man's science. For they study only so long as to be able to escape from it. Hence the sayings, "The mind flies high, but poortith drags it down"; "A full purse makes a talent divine"; and "Money should first be sought. And virtue? Why, *after* the cash". And just as "Venus (i.e. physical love) is cold without Ceres (food) and Bacchus (wine)", so it is with Pallas [Athena: goddess of the intellect and the arts]. Consequently, parrots chatter, and learn, better after drinking wine; and so do some human beings. Hence the verses, "What man ever was *not* made eloquent by generous cups?" and "What does hunger not drive man to attempt?"

Need I cite more? If I did, I should go on for ever. Let me draw my conclusion as follows. A student ought to have no end in view 78 but *knowledge*. Now, a needy person either does not have this end in view, or keeps it in view only so far as he can avoid poverty. Therefore he who was studying merely for his belly's sake goes to sleep once his belly is filled, and puts the sciences behind him; he takes no delight in them, because he is unfitted for them. But if he *is* fit for them and *does* delight in them, poverty gets in his way – and this is a pitiable state of affairs. If, however, you should still maintain that both rich and poor alike possess everything necessary for knowledge, and that the will does not fail them, let us suppose this to be so: observe what difficulties then follow. Each of them, at the outset, needs to be instructed; for who is so well endowed that he can turn into a scholar all by himself? And what unhappy experiences people have while receiving instruction! How few students obtain good teachers! This class of men, whether on account of the meagreness of their pay, or idleness, or poor health, or poverty (in coping with which they cannot find time for study), or ill-will, or fear, or arrogance, or the passion of love – or of hatred – or the incapacity of their pupils (if they have come to believe this of them), or (and this is worst of all, and very common) on account of ignorance – this class of men, I repeat, for all or most of the above reasons either conceal the truth (if they ever did acquire it at all) or teach falsehoods. Can anything more disastrous happen to a beginner? For he believes his teacher, as is both proper and also necessary for a beginner; and scarcely can he

265

ever rid himself of an error he has once absorbed, however one may try to do so, so powerfully receptive and retentive are the years of childhood, especially if the instructor has exercised a very strong influence over his pupil. Hence the saying, "The jug will keep for long / the fragrance of the scent that filled it first". Hence their dictum *autos epha* (Αὐτὸς ἔφα, "The Master himself said it"), which is so slavish and unworthy of a philosopher.[166] It was on this principle that the celebrated teacher of music, Timotheus,
79 contracted with the beginner for a single fee, but a *double* fee for one who had learnt under another teacher, since the instructor must labour twice over – in the first place, to eradicate the faulty method which the pupil had already absorbed, and in the second place to sow the seeds of a right method.[167] From this source have arisen sects among philosophers – and the phrase "to swear to the formulas of a master". It is for this reason that they pour forth so many – and such voluminous – tracts: X in defence of Y, and *per contra* Z seeking to demolish Y. They fill up whole volumes on the theme "How to understand your teacher"; they invent new and endless "explanations", "understandings", and "distinctions", which the Master himself never dreamt of. Indeed, so foolish are some of them that they boast that they are capable of defending all of the views expressed by this or that authority; and they equip themselves for the task by surrounding themselves with such an armoury of quibbling and trickery that you would suppose each one of them to be a hunter, attempting to go a-fowling for thrushes with nets and a bird-whistle. But they become entangled in their own nets, unable to free themselves; and thus they fall into the pit-trap which they were preparing for others, and, like the fowler in Aesop's fable, while laying snares

[166] The recourse to the authority of Aristotle, invoked by the Schoolmen to justify any statement, is, according to Sanches, a denial of freedom of thought and hampers the enquiry into the true nature of things.
[167] Timotheus of Miletus, a dithyrambic poet who lived from the fifth to the fourth centuries B.C., is mentioned several times in Plutarch's treatise *De musica,* now considered apocryphal, but which was included by Planudes in his edition of Plutarch. The original source of the anecdote for Sanches is Vives's *In pseudodialecticos.*

for a dove they fall victim to the snake.[168] And just as those who use the warlike fire-arms called "arquebuses" or "muskets" (when in order to kill someone else they bring the piece close to one eye so that the bullet may travel in a straight line, and then set fire to the powder) experience the opposite of what they intended, if the bore of the piece is excessively choked – in which event the piece recoils and shatters their skull – just so, these persons I speak of, while they are inventing false contrivances against others, are themselves entrapped in falsehoods.[169] Some of them make collections of leading points, and compose epitomes. Others arrange, in tables and chapters and books, matters that have been set out in a disorderly fashion by other writers; others, again, amplify and extend, write "commentaries", – and commit a great many "commendacities" in doing so. Others, out of a pedantic and foolish loyalty, endeavour to reconcile dissenting parties and to bring quarrelling factions into a state of complete harmony. Some, on the other hand, make enemies of their own supporters 80 when they claim that they do not *mean* what they write. Some maintain that such-and-such a work was written by X, whereas others say, "No, it was written by Y".

But, in proving all these things, what arguments do they *not* use? What evidence do they not invent, or tamper with, or distort? Should statements that are false, but probable, not suffice, they make use of statements that are true, but deplorable: that is to say, insults, invectives, defamatory libels, and abuse. Finally, not content with these, they have recourse to arms, so that violence may compel what reason could not, in the fashion of soldiers. Thus those who bear the name of "men of science" turn into brutes. Is this not madness and insanity? Men who are said to "study Nature" do nothing *less* than study it, whereas they fight to the death about what X or Y *meant* to say, not what this or that *is* in Nature, and spend their entire lives on such questions, like the dog that abandoned the piece of meat it was carrying and

[168] The reference is probably to Aesop's fable "The Ant and the Dove".

[169] The arquebus played an important part in the French wars in Italy and was displaced by the musket only around 1570.

foolishly and uselessly attempted to pursue its reflection in the water, or the bull which, while it was chasing a man, found his coat and vented its anger upon that, forgetting the man and caring no more about him. Just so, in their search for Nature these men turn aside to follow human beings and thus abandon Nature completely. Accordingly they know nothing but how to repeat, in parrot-like fashion, what they have found written in the works of others, knowing nothing at all about the material they cite. And in the sciences there is a vast horde of such persons, while of those who would investigate Nature herself, *in* herself, there is scarce one, or at least very few indeed, and these are considered unlearned both by those I have mentioned and by the public at large. And this is not strange, for each person judges all others in terms of his own nature. Thus, the scholar properly judges, and praises, the scholar, because he understands what he says; the unscholârly person despises him because he does not understand him, whereas he highly esteems the dullard, since he shares his

81 opinions. For like rejoices in like, and rejects what is *un*like. Now, no matter which of those persons it may be, under whom the unlucky youth has his first taste of Letters, if he tastes often (and very fortunate is he – and also very rare – who has had a proper introduction to Letters under an experienced and truly learned master), all is over with his knowledge – unless, driven by some star of destiny, he comes to his senses later.

And if he should continually study under the same teacher (which can happen but rarely), then if he has erred once he will always be in error – nay, his error will steadily increase; for a small mistake at the outset becomes a large one in the end, and if one absurdity is conceded, a great many follow. For who is there who does not make *one* mistake? Or rather, who is there who makes *only* one? I am not sure whether we are not always in error. But if the youth be taught by several teachers, then "This the work is, and this the painful toil".[170] A few, "whom kindly Jove hath loved", or whom the fire of their own genius has borne aloft to the heavens, sons of the gods, have been able to free themselves from

[170] Virgil, *Aeneid*, 6.129.

errors; but "all the middle ground is filled by forests" – very obstructive ones too. While they, in everlasting argument, drive themselves this way and that, they tear apart and maul to pieces the unfortunate tyro's mind. When one of them imposes some notion upon him, another endeavours to convince him of its opposite. For who has ever seen two people agree in everything? Yet agreement between scholars is the greatest evidence for the reliability of truth – and accordingly of any kind of scientific *knowledge*. For truth is always consistent with itself, whereas on the other hand nothing proves the *un*reliability of scientific knowledge more clearly than divergent opinions among the experts in that science. This is common to all teachers of each and every science; from which you may further infer how little reliability there is in the sciences we have. In this fashion, opposing teachers drag the poor, weak little tyro into confusion and ambiguity. He, accordingly, does not know which way he should turn, but attaches himself either to teacher A or to teacher B, just as he thinks best. And he is usually disappointed in his instructor, for the latter *talks* a great deal, as is the way of those who erect a heap of falsehoods, and so draws on to his side the poor little youth, who considers that the winner in the contest was 82 the person who made more noise than his opponent. There's the "man of science" for you! So the pupil is caught in the midst of storms like these for a very long time: more often than not, all his life long.

But if we come now to the *method* of teaching, the difficulty will be no less here – nay, greater – whether you consider those who teach by oral methods or by writing. For in both instances the method is the same. Further, from this point of view the learner benefits greatly if the teacher uses a sound method, but suffers impediment and harm if the method is unsound. For in teaching, *nothing* possesses such importance as method.[171] Men's methods

---

[171] See Gilbert, *Renaissance Concepts of Method*, pp. 17–18, for a description of the seven factors in the acquisition of knowledge. Method allows the student to distinguish truth from falsehood, the final criteria of judgment being reason and experience.

are continually subject to great changes. To know how to use method is no less arduous, and demands no less talent, than it is useful – and it is no less *rare* than necessary. There is, therefore, no teacher who does not devote to it a great amount of study and effort, and very few or almost none who either have attained the goal, or are thought to have done so. For since the "art" is (perhaps infinitely) long, as I have already observed, while life is the shortest of all things – and life is the measure to which the aspiring teacher or student must apportion the "art" – it places on us a very grave responsibility, inasmuch as we are attempting to measure the infinite by the finite and, what is more, to include the infinite *within* the finite. Hence the enormous differences among writers on this subject; some of whom, endeavouring to abbreviate the "art" (since they are unable to lengthen life, which would be better, and necessary too), make the road longer and harder by their very brevity and occasional obscurity (for "when I try hard to be brief I become obscure"), and take up our time – time that ought to be spent on understanding things, not on their own texts. This sort give us merely summary headings of topics, which we must gobble down. Another sort, communicating the art in a lengthy fashion (for lengthy it is indeed), grow old and tired over its very "first principles" – and we along with them. The latter are censured by those who are impatient of drudgery and possess quicker minds, because they teach, in a great many words, things that they themselves could grasp in a few; but they are praised by sullen and boorish wits for whom no explanation is ever full enough. With the former class, the opposite happens. Anyone who writes at a moderate length – assuming that such a person should happen to exist! – is blamed by *all* of these: he is blamed both for not being brief enough, and also for being briefer than is right. For the middle way is always contrary to both extremes; it is praised only by those who also have a liking for the middle way, and who in fact are themselves moderate in character. Such people are extremely rare, like all fine things, and men do not know of their existence.

Again, some are considered learned by one group, but it is the other way about with another group. Some speak in a cultured and elegant manner; others, harshly and boorishly. Some steal the works of others and peddle them as their own; others repeat whole pages of their own writings, forgetting who was the author of them. One kind of person mixes up and confuses everything in every place; another leaves every topic bare, without examining it. One kind of person is talkative and apt to quibble, while another is austere and serious. One is a clever inventor of novelties; another defends the ancients even to the point of foolishness. In short, what can I say? Did anyone ever please all of mankind? Not even Nature herself did so; some people have had the audacity to condemn and reproach *her.* There is such variety in *things,* that in this department Nature can be clearly seen to have played a trick and indulged her personal whim by promoting our confusion, so that she – albeit standing plainly in our view – might make fools of us, and laugh at us, as we seek her in this place or that. Nor is variety to be seen only in the variousness of *things.* One and the same person now is willing and now refuses; now defends some proposition, and in the end himself condemns it; or else makes a declaration at this moment, but if you ask him about it next morning neither remembers it nor is willing to remember. Yet, again, Letters may flourish in a particular part of the world at a certain time, but the end, there, may be barbarity of all kinds; whereas in another part of the world, once the domain of the sword and of war, one can now find nothing but books. And, what is more significant, where today a certain view is accepted by all, and a certain great doctor is highly esteemed, tomorrow it will be entirely different. You will find examples of all these phenomena if you read history; I shall, however, cite one or two 84 more.

Was any part of the ancient world more brilliantly distinguished in the field of Letters than Egypt or Greece? Or any more fertile in idol-worship? Where were there men of greater distinction, not only in each and every branch of science, but also in warlike achievements? Yet nowadays one will not find there any Museum, or any idol, or any distinguished man. Now, in Italy and France and Spain at that time no teacher was even dreamt of; Mercury and Jupiter were all in all; but nowadays the Muses have their abode here, and here Christ has His dwelling. Again, how great is the ignorance that has hitherto held sway in India! But now its people are gradually becoming more clever, pious, and learned than ourselves. Let these examples suffice.

What then is the unfortunate youth to do, when there is so much variety in things? Whom is he to follow, whom to believe? This one; that other; or no one. Under these circumstances, he chooses for himself, if he should chance to be free to do so. If not, then either he must attach himself wholly to this one or wholly to that one or wholly to none. Which of these courses is best? In all of them lies disappointment and sorrow. Should he totally devote himself to anyone, he becomes a slave, and not a scholar; and to the utmost of his powers he defends the teachings of his master, right or wrong. In this way he turns into a soldier, who follows his commander wherever he may drag him, in order to fight for *him,* no longer mindful of himself; and with *him* he perishes. Just so our youth perishes – and his knowledge perishes too – whenever he ties himself resolutely to another; for it is impossible that anyone should "swear by a Master's words" except at the expense of the truth. But if he puts equal trust in all or in none, so that he may select from all of them whatever he approves of, this is indeed a freer course, but it is also more difficult; for enormous powers of judgment are needed by the person who attempts to resolve their differences. Each of them has his own good reasons on his side, together with what seem to him irrefutable proofs. Yet even to come to a judgment, as between these teachers, is not without peril for the person who judges: no matter in whose favour he decides, he should also bear in mind that he has a duty to
85 stand by him. But if he makes a bad decision, he will pay a price for his judgment, inasmuch as he will be just as ignorant of the truth as that other person in favour of whom he cast his faulty vote – and this is disastrous. But also, no matter for whom he votes he will always have to take up the cudgels for him against another, inasmuch as there is always someone else who is creating trouble for both of them and forging new weapons which must be repelled. And it often happens that just as in war, though a person may be superior to his enemy in the justice of his cause *and* in

272

armed might, he may yet perish outwitted by skill and trickery, so too one who grasps and defends the truth may be overwhelmed by opposing arguments which he cannot resist, and thus lose heart and abandon the truth, so that he places himself in the enemy's hands. This not only happens frequently but also puts the truth in the shade; while he who constructs a heap of falsehoods is both clever and subtle. And Aristotle furthered this tendency with his "science" of syllogisms, in which a true conclusion sometimes follows from a false premiss with complete logical rigour. Thus truth is not distinguished as such when it is sometimes mixed with truth, sometimes with falsehood; but sometimes truth appears as falsehood, and sometimes falsehood as truth. And so the person who is unusually skilful in spreading out the nets of syllogisms can make such additions as he pleases to the construction. And whereas the ignorant should be taught the truth, and rigorous precautions should be taken to see that they are not deceived, especially inasmuch as they do not posses the power to find it out for themselves, Aristotle, on the contrary, has shown how to lay snares for them, by means of which they may be forced to abandon the truth, if they have somehow laid hold on it: truth, to which they would otherwise adhere were they not outwitted by the devices I have mentioned. In this way, I have sometimes seen a verbose quibbler attempting to persuade some ignorant person or other that white was black; to which the latter replied, "I do not understand your reasoning, since I have not studied as much as you have; yet I honestly believe that white differs from black. But pray go on refuting me for just as long as you like".

And indeed I remember that when, scarcely past boyhood, I 86 was being initiated into dialectics, I was often challenged to debate by my seniors in age and in study, so that they might test my ability. From time to time they confronted me with fallacious syllogisms; and I, not seeing that they were fallacious, used sometimes to be crushed by their weight and admitted false – but not *obviously* false – propositions; but when obviously false conclusions followed from these, I suffered extreme torments in cases where I had not at once pointed to the logical defect, and I could not rest until I had discovered this. Would it not have been better to spend the time I wasted in looking for the defect in a syllogism, in gaining an understanding of some natural cause or other? In short, among those dealers in syllogisms, the better a person chatters, the more learned he is; the one who has discovered the truth is he who has, by very cleverly constructing a snare, beaten his associate or adversary, and obliged him either to concede that what they call "infallible consequences" will follow (i.e. consequences, to deny which would be both absurd and morally wrong, yet which are full of pitfalls and snares; and anyone who fails to see these is by them captured and forced to surrender, and to grant what his opponent wanted, false though it should be); or else, seeing himself to be a prisoner, yet not seeing the trick, he would in general fall silent. This is what they call "scientific instruction in syllogisms", and nothing is more *harmful* to the sciences than this. Seeing this for himself, Aristotle wrote another work on "Sophistical Quibbles", so that we might be rescued from their deceptions. In this way he has given us poison to drink and later tries to cure it with an antidote which itself is poisonous; but the first poison is the more potent, and so in most instances it overcomes and slays the truth. In order to resist this poison, Aristotle's successors have invented a great many "conditions", and other deceitful tricks, and book after book of *suppositiones, indissolubilia, exponibilia, obligationes, reflexiones,* and *modalia.* See what an amount of subtlety there is here; and as for "scientific knowledge" – what a "power" of that there is too! Aye, and dialectic is a second Circe: she converts her followers into asses. Nothing is more certain than this; for in the midst of their "science" they have built a bridge, which they call the Bridge of Asses. Do they not deserve some oats on account of this brilliant discovery? Near the bridge, in the picture, lie asses, drinking the waters of Circe. Drunk on these, they bray for ever around the bridge. And almost the same thing would have happened to me, had it not been that, aided by Ulysses' spells , I avoided the bewitching songs of the Circean mistresses of the bridge, that is, the figures of syllogisms. What tortures those poor asses suffer in order to prop up their ancient dwelling! How they

87

honour, defend, praise, and portray their own mistress Circe, namely dialectics! – like Aeneas, who (forgetting himself, and quite oblivious towards Italy, for which he had been making), effeminate and out of his mind, clothed in the mantle of wantonness, became Dido's mere slave, devoting himself wholly to her and worshipping her alone; until at Mercury's warning he blushed for shame, his eyes were opened, and he realised that he had been disgracefully ensnared; and forthwith he put away his effeminacy and took manhood upon himself, and thereafter became the ruler of a great part of the world, with Virtue to guide him and Fortune to accompany him.

And I would that I might be a Mercury to our modern Aeneases, so that they might abandon the weakness of Dialectic, with her bewitching spells, and turn to Nature; then many of them might perhaps become rulers of the world. But as it is, they are still blinded, and entangle themselves ever more by their own doing – setting so many snares for themselves that one could go on reading them for ever, just as they themselves never stop writing them, revealing new collapses every day, like some ancient building that keeps threatening to fall down, or else one built on sand and on an unstable site, with foundations made of fragile materials; a building that must be continually shored up with wooden props, or reinforced with stone, mortar, and so forth, since cracks keep continually opening in its structure on this side or that. Just so, as the syllogistic discipline continually crumbles (for, being superficial and hollow, it can by no means stand firm), its inhabitants and craftsmen continually struggle to 88 prevent it from collapsing. And these are the things they teach to young men who come to them; with these, they first of all confuse their wits, and in these they practise them! As for *facts,* anyone who wishes may search for them. And so this plague is passed on by infection from one to another, with the result that all your life long you know nothing. But perhaps you will say, "What? Do you then, like an emperor, desire that anything you say should become law, without discussion or proof – which everyone considers distasteful?" This is not my purpose either; but later on I

275

will show how you can employ another and a better method than this one of syllogisms.[172] So then, our young man, whom we were impelling in the direction of science – what is he to do amid all these difficulties? He must plunge into the middle of them, as his teachers also did before him, and as they are teaching him to do; and he trusts them. For surely the artist ought to be believed by the pupil when he comes to him to learn the art. So the latter will be such as the former is: ignorant the master, and ignorant the pupil also. And it is hard to spew forth error, once it is swallowed.

But suppose instead that this youth has relied on his own judgment, and that, after he has sat under these men for a long time and learnt their science and observed the disagreements among their opinions, he wishes to pass judgment on the matter – an attitude that is very hard to find, but at the same time most useful, and indeed quite indispensable, for anyone who wishes to *know*. I have shown above how perilous this is. But what enormous difficulties arise at this point! If he himself is to judge correctly, he must examine very carefully the matters about which they are in disagreement, which few people do; the result being that there are few who understand the opinions they cite, yet in spite of this they fill up whole volumes with the labours of other men. They bring together authorities whom they themselves do not understand, and for this reason often their very compilation is badly done. They pass judgment on the controversies among these authorities – and this too they do badly; for, concentrating 89 *only* on authorities who disagree, and borrowing help from other writers on this side or on that, as for example when they use evidence from Aristotle and others, drawing some conclusions from the doctrines of these authors and some from the doctrines of others, in this way they deliver judgment against X or Y, not by showing that the *facts* are thus or thus, but that "such is the opinion of Aristotle, such of X or Y; such is the inference to be drawn from this or that [untested] assumption". It may be that all these propositions are more doubtful than the very one at issue! Thus, while they foolishly attempt to pass judgment on others, they ex-

---

[172] A reference to his projected treatise *De modo sciendi*. See the Bibliography.

pose themselves to judgment; nay, even to condemnation. For what bearing has it on the matter, that something was said by X or Y? Is it for *that* reason true? This is impossible; for if so, the first principles of all things would be atoms, air, water, earth, matter, form, deprivation of form, chaos, strife and amity, the great and the small, ether, the One, and Number – all of which are designated as the first principles of things by different philosophers! Consequently the truth was told, not by him who merely reported what someone else has said, but by him who stated that which is the fact. (Why, then, do they so persistently confront us with this or that authority, as one to contradict whom is, as they themselves put it, "disloyal" and "heretical"?) And even the Master himself said (those foolish authority-quoters do not notice this, or at any rate pretend not to have noticed it): "A proposition is true or false not because someone has affirmed or denied it, but because *in fact* it is thus or thus". Once, when he was opposing Plato, he had the same experience with fools of that kind as I have had with those I speak of, when I was opposing Aristotle himself and others. He thought it sufficient reply to them to say that "Plato was his friend, but Truth was a better friend still". And elsewhere he remarks: "Authority is something external, and possesses very little importance".[173] But I can see what makes these ignoramuses so obsequious towards their teacher. They know nothing outside him: all they know is in and from him, while in *facts* they cannot see anything. Consequently it is not surprising if, having nothing with which they can express the thought in *their* mind, or bring to naught the thought in *your* mind – it is not surprising, I repeat, if they are annoyed at being defeated 90 by a straightforward denial. And since men of learning have facts at their command which the ignorant cannot deny, unless they wish to experiment and *see* whether fire is hot, they have no want of authorities if they should deny the fact. Therefore anyone who wishes to *know* something – hence, our young man – must study *facts*. But is this easy? Alas, no! At no point is so much difficulty to be met with, and such ambiguity; at no point is scientific know-

---

[173] Sanches makes an obscure reference to Aristotle's *Topics*.

ledge so hard to come by. You have already seen what diversity there is in *things,* and how much change – in a word, how much difficulty they create for the person who desires to *know;* and you will see this elusiveness more clearly when I commence my enquiry into Things themselves. For the present, however, let us rehearse these obstacles from the student's point of view; in this way we shall make an end of this short treatise.

For luckless humanity, there are two means of discovering truth, since men cannot *know* things in themselves. If they could acquire intellectual understanding of them as they should be able to do, then they would need no other means; but since they cannot do this, they have found additional ways of coming to the aid of their own ignorance. Consequently, although they have no more *knowledge* because of these aids (at least in the sense of perfect knowledge) yet they do perceive something, and learn something. Those methods consist of experience and judgment. Neither of these two can properly retain validity without the other. I shall explain at greater length how each of them is to be acquired, and how applied, in my next treatise after this one (I am daily bringing it to birth). For the present, observe how it follows, from the following consideration, that "nothing is known". Experience is in every instance deceitful and difficult. Even if it is possessed perfectly, it only reveals the external aspect of events; in no way does it reveal the natures of *things.* As for judgment, it is applied to what is found out by experience; and it, likewise, can in any case not only be applied solely to externals, but even this is done badly. In respect to the natures of things, it reveals them only by speculation; and since it has not ascertained them by means of experience, not only does it too fail to reach the thing itself, but 91 sometimes it forms an opinion in exactly the wrong sense. So where is scientific knowledge to come from (since none emerges from these procedures)? But there are no others; and even these cannot be completely acquired by our young man. For – to say nothing of numerous obstacles in the way of conducting an experiment properly – how *many* experiences can a mere youth command? Few enough. How, then, is he to judge aright on the basis of only a few? In no way can he do so. For before anyone can form a right judgment he ought to have observed many things – nay, everything, as I said at the outset – since all things are linked one with another, and none can stand secure independently of another.[174] This is the reason why a person who held such-and-such an opinion today expresses a different view next morning – nay, even admits to an opinion he had never previously entertained. Who indeed, before the magnet and the electric ray-fish and the remora were familarly understood, would have attributed to them a power of that kind? It used to be said that all attraction was derived from heat or dryness or a vacuum (or, better, from the fear of *causing* a vacuum). What of these? And what of amber? Does *its* power come from any one of these sources?[175] Would you

---

[174] A marginal annotation refers to Empedocles' remark to Xenophanes that it is impossible to find a wise man (Diogenes Laertius, *Lives* of *Eminent Philosophers*, 9,20).

[175] The magnet's power of attraction had been discussed by many ancient writers. The main sources of information on the magnet for Sanches were Galen, Plutarch, Lucretius, and Pliny. Contemporary discussion of the nature of magnetism was to be found in Cardano's *De subtilitate* and Scaliger's comments on the work. Galen devotes a chapter in the *De facultatibus naturalibus*, 1, 14, to the lodestone, in an attempt to disprove Epicurus's absurd hypothesis that the particles which flow from the lodestone collide with the iron and then rebound back, thus the iron becomes suspended. The examples of rings and needles Sanches mentions later (translation, p. 286) are found in Galen. Plutarch, in the *Platonicae quaestiones*, 7.7.1005 B–D, stated in similar terms that the lodestone emitted strong exhalations which strike adjacent particles of iron, impelling them towards the magnet. Lucretius said that the magnet sends off particles which create a vacuum into which the atoms of iron are drawn (*De natura rerum*, 6.998–1008). Pliny, in his *Natural History*, 34, 42, and 36, 126, speaks of the natural sympathy between iron and the lodestone. "Magnetic virtue" and "electric effluvium" (the attractive power of rubbed amber) were discussed by Cardano in the *De subtilitate* and their relative powers distinguished thus: "Neque enim lapidis Magnetis, et succini eadem trahendi ratio: nam succinum omne leve trahit, Magnes ferrum solum. Succinum interposito corpore non movet paleam, Magnes ferrum. Succinum non trahitur vicissim a palea, Magnes trahitur a ferro; etiam palea a succino in nullam partem dirigitur, ferrum modo ad Boream, modo ad Austrum contactu Magnetis tendit, denique succini attractio calido et frictione iuvatur multum, Magnetis eo solum quod purior pars lapidis redditur" (3.444a). It was not until William Gilbert published his *De magnete*

ever have supposed that one poison added to another would not kill a man but, on the contrary, would instead deliver him from death? Certainly you would by no means have supposed this; it may be that before making the experiment you used to claim that "what one does, two will do better". Now, the contrary of this is proved by that sinister wife in Ausonius, who, having tried to make away with her husband by means of poison, in order to hasten his death mixed quicksilver in the potion she had prepared – whereby he escaped the clutches of death. Also, snake serum ("Venice treacle") and *mithridatium*, compounded from poisonous substances on the basis of experiment, resist all kinds of poison.[176] Who would have thought that hemlock kills more rapidly if it is mixed with wine, and kills bilious and hot-blooded ("sanguine") persons more speedily than cold ("lymphatic") ones? For it would have appeared reasonable to suppose that its action should, rather, be *impeded* by the opposite quality; yet experiment shows the con-

in 1600 that the theory of magnetism and electricity was to be demonstrated scientifically. His study of electrified bodies (*electrica*) showed that the attractive power of rubbed amber was common to other substances.

Sanches was familiar with the story of the electric ray-fish (torpedo) and the remora from Scaliger's comments on Cardano's *De subtilitate* in his *Exercitatio*, 59, 2. Sir Thomas Browne in the *Pseudodoxia epidemica* (p. 262) mentions that "the Torpedo, which alive hath a power to stupifie at a distance, hath none upon contaction being dead, as Galen and Rondeletius particularly experimented". Pliny, in 9, 41 of his *Natural History*, related that a small fish called the sucking fish (remora) was believed to make ships go more slowly by sticking to their hulls.

[176] Sanches was greatly interested in the use of drugs, and his *Pharmacopoeia* occupies an important part of his medical works. The *Materia medica* of Dioscorides, together with Matthiolus's *Commentaries,* and Galen's *Simples,* had furnished the basic information on the preparation of herbal remedies. Compound drugs, such as theriac (known as "Venice treacle"), became popular in the sixteenth century. Venice was an important centre of research into medical botany and chemical therapies. Richard Palmer describes in his article "Pharmacy in the Republic of Venice in the Sixteenth Century" (*The Medical Renaissance of the Sixteenth Century*, pp. 100– 17) the importance of Venetian exports of theriac and mithridatium, the most prestigious drugs on the market. Mithridates VI, king of Pontus, was supposed to have slowly saturated his body with poisons so that no one would harm him.

trary to be true.[177] Also, in Galen's writings, some harvesters 92
believed that they would do a good deed if they gave to a person
who suffered from acute elephantiasis a drink of wine in which an
adder had been smothered, thinking by this method to remove
him from life; but on the contrary (astonishingly) he was delivered
by it from that dreadful disease.[178] Moreover, it was a maidservant
of his who, terrified at the approach of her master, the victim of
elephantiasis – he was desperately enamoured of her – offered him
the wine tainted with viper's venom in order to cause his death;
yet it was the other way about – she restored him to health![179]
Would you have predicted this? Certainly not.

Much experience, then, makes a man both learned and wise.
Hence it comes about that old men are more learned, at least in
terms of experience, and better adapted, therefore, for the conduct
of human affairs than the young; and for this reason they are, by
many nations, held in the greatest honour. If they possess good
judgment as well, the administration of the state can fittingly be
entrusted to them. In order, therefore, to deal with this disadvantage – namely lack of experience – men have made the additional
discovery of the art of writing, so that what one or another person
has learnt by experience, through an entire lifetime and in different
places, another may learn in a short time. And in this way our
ancestors served the interests of the men of our own generation,
who by reading through the lives, the deeds, the discoveries, and
the experiences of many men, without great expenditure of time,
are adding something from their own resources to the total, as
others in turn will do for them. Besides, they pass judgment also
on doubtful questions, and so the body of transmitted lore (*ars*)
receives increase; and for this reason, posterity is compared (and
rightly) to a boy standing on the shoulders of a giant. But
although this method clearly possesses some advantages for the

---

[177] Sanches refers the reader to Galen's *De simplicium medicamentorum temperamentis et facultatibus*, 3, and Plutarch's "Quomodo amicum ab adulatore discernas".
[178] See Galen, *De subfiguratione empirica*.
[179] Ibid. Galen criticized the empiricists for relying on experiential data due to chance.

conduct of human affairs, yet in no way does it further assist the sciences.

For (not to mention the fact that books, like other things, do not last for ever – they are totally destroyed by war, fire, neglect, or the appearance of new and different opinions, and finally consumed by time and oblivion) there follows at once the entire difficulty which I indicated above in my discussion of writers. They are confused, too short or too wordy, and so numerous that if one lived a hundred times a hundred thousand years one would not have years enough to read them all; and they have a way of being repeatedly untruthful, most commonly from vainglory or in order to prop up their reputations. And at once there follows the question about comprehending their meaning, together with all the questions I have just mentioned; to such an extent that, when we seek to *know* something by turning to human beings and their writings, we forsake Nature and wisdom. But let us suppose that they [i.e. writers] give a true report of their experiences; what good does it do *me* that another person has had a particular set of experiences, unless I should have the same experiences for myself? They [i.e. other men's experiences] will produce belief, not scientific *knowledge,* in me. For just this reason, the majority of educated men in our day are indeed characterised by belief, not knowledge, insofar as they derive all they possess from books. They do not apply judgment and an experimental grasp of facts, as they should, but on the contrary, believing the statements they find set down in writing, and using these as their hypotheses, deduce more and more propositions in turn from them, thereby laying their foundations insecurely. Therefore it is in the interest of our young man, if he wishes to learn anything, to study continually, to read what has been written by everyone, and to compare this information experimentally with *facts*, up to the very end of his life. What kind of life could be more unhappy or more unfortunate than this? Why did I say "kind of life"? Rather, it is a kind of death – as I previously remarked. Well then, would you wish anyone to submit himself to such a disastrous way of living? Yet there are some who do so. Suppose our young man to be one of these. Then, even though he should possess an excellent constitution and perfect health, he will at once fall into a decline. When he has wasted his bodily strength by studying, he will have to battle with a host of diseases, or morbid conditions: cold in the head, catarrh, arthritis, weakness of the bowels, and hence bouts of indigestion, loss of appetite, diarrhoea, and obstructions, especially those of the spleen; he who devotes himself to his studies suffers from every kind of ailment. In the end, he dies prematurely. Again, these things disturb the mind, affecting its 94 principal seat, namely the brain, whether initially this happens of itself, or is transmitted from another. But even if we suppose our young man to be free from all these troubles, yet finally he will become melancholic, as everyday experience proves. Can people of all these kinds judge aright? I think not, for a good judge must be free of every emotion.

Yet even suppose we grant that this young man of ours is free of all these afflictions both now and in the future (which I think scarcely possible), will he therefore *know* anything? Not in the least. For in him there is the same process of ceaseless change as there is in all other things. But chief among these, of course, is change of age, since there is a great difference between a youth and a man, and between the latter and an old man; and within each of these ages there is again a great difference between beginning, middle, and end. He who today, as a youth, makes a given judgment and believes it to be true, once he is fairly well on in his mature years, gives that judgment up and disapproves of it – and then, it may be, in his old age embraces it and defends it once more. He does one thing at one time, another at another, and is never consistent with himself. And there is no one who, if he publishes some work today, will not compose his recantation afterwards and admit, if he is honest, that he was mistaken when he was young. But those who, through shame, are unwilling to do this, even though they can see that they have stated something that was false – or perhaps failing to see this because blinded by self-love – continue stubbornly to defend what they have said, and try every avenue in order to clear themselves of the charge of ignorance, or the infamy attached to falsehood – greatly to the disadvantage of the sciences, particularly if they are subtle thinkers.

And there is no one who, if he should *not* wish to publish his work so quickly, on the advice of the author who bids one lay it away for nine years [Horace], would not be for ever adding, subtracting, changing, and renewing something, even if he should go on correcting it for a full hundred years, and would do it for ever, if he himself also were to live for ever!

95   Where does all this variety and inconsistency come from? Undoubtedly it comes from ignorance; for if we ourselves were to possess perfect *knowledge,* none of the things we have once written would ever need to be altered. At what age, then, does our friend possess better judgment than at others? "In old age", you will reply. But it appears more reasonable to say "in the state in which all of a man's powers are vigorous", rather than in old age, when all of them are weakened, the age that is compared to infancy; hence the saying "Cursed are the *children* who are a hundred years old". And it is for this reason that, in common parlance, old men are said to "wander" in their wits. What will you say? Even he himself does not know when he is telling the truth, saying (as he does) now this, now that; yet he wants to be believed in *both* instances. And besides these physical changes, morbid states of the mind also get in the way of understanding the truth. I have mentioned this already, above, in speaking of the teacher, but it must be equally reckoned with in the case of the pupil. Affection, dislike, ill-will, and the other emotions we there enumerated, interfere with the soundness of a person's judgment. For who is so completely master of himself as not to be under the influence of one of these? No one at all. But if he should escape all the other emotions, he will at least by no means escape one of them, namely self-love. For is there anyone who does not believe that he has uttered the truth, that he has discovered the knotty point of a problem – nay, even that he understands some matter extremely well? – not to mention the fact that each one considers himself more learned, more keen-witted, more perspicacious, more judicious, and finally wiser, than all the rest. Is he right to do so? Nobody – so the popular saying goes – is a good judge in his own cause; and anyone at all is pleading his own cause, so long as he *defends* any proposition, whether he does so orally or in writing.

So, we know nothing. But let me grant (what is impossible) that our "judge" is free from all these emotions: he will possess no more knowledge, for the future, even though the general opinion of mankind will have it that we keep continually improving our scholarship. For the very opposite happens to those who endeavour to obtain a perfect understanding of things: I myself thought I was becoming more learned, until I began to fix my attention on things; for I firmly retained what I had received from 96 my instructors, and so I thought I possessed perfect scientific knowledge – believing that "knowledge" meant only to have seen, heard, and remembered a great deal. It was in accordance with this formula that I judged this person or that, as others also did. I devoted myself wholeheartedly, as I observed others also to do, to this kind of "science"; I put all my energies into it. But as soon as I turned my attention to *things,* I completely abandoned my former *belief* (rather than scientific "knowledge"), and began to examine those things as if no proposition had ever been laid down by anyone; and I was now just as fully convinced that I possessed *no* knowledge, as I had previously appeared to myself to *possess* knowledge (in the opposite fashion from the philosopher who used to say that until he grew to manhood he was ignorant of everything, but after that he *knew* everything).[180] And this I felt more and more from day to day; in the end it has come to a point when I can neither see that anything is scientifically known, nor even expect that anything *can* be so known, and the more I ponder the matter, the more I doubt.

For how am I to avoid doubt if I cannot grasp the natures of *things,* from which true scientific knowledge has to come? For it is easy to *see* a magnet, but what is its nature? Why does it attract iron? It *would* be scientific knowledge (*scientia*) if we were able to gain cognitive understanding (*cognitio*) of this phenomenon. And yet those who claim to be superior in scientific knowledge reply

---

[180] A marginal annotation informs the reader that the philosopher is Heraclitus who, in Diogenes Laertius, *Lives of Eminent Philosophers,* 9, 5, said that as a boy he knew nothing but when he was grown he claimed to know everything.

that it happens by "a hidden property", and that *that* answer constitutes "science," when on the contrary it really constitutes ignorance. For what difference does it make whether one says "this results from a property hidden from my observation" or "I do not *know* from what cause, or in what way, this happens"? Similarly in the case of many other things which you will see discussed in detail in the appropriate context. But if to the problem of the attraction of iron you add the other problem, namely how iron touched by that same magnet always turns towards the north, conforming to the part of the stone that – in its original site – faced the north (and this has shown us how to circumnavigate the earth in a little ship, and, in the midst of ocean
97 waves, how to determine our WHEREABOUTS, and with infallible usefulness, and useful infallibility, to pick up harbours), and moreover always turns towards the part of the magnet by which it was touched and moves away from the other end; and if you ask how it is that it does not merely attract a *single* ring or needle, but its force can also be transmitted through a series (and even diffused through considerable numbers) of rings and needles, all of which it will suspend in the air; and finally if you ask why, on being rubbed with garlic, it becomes totally inactive and loses its power of attraction – then you will be obliged to give up! Which is in fact what was done, albeit unwillingly, by a great scholar of modern times; and in doing so he rightly indicted us for ignorance, not only in the question of this phenomenon of the magnet, but in several other contexts also.[181] So what is our "judge" to do here,

[181] Sanches indicates in the margin that the scholar is Scaliger who, in his *Exercitationes,* 131, "Quae de Magnete", writes: "De Magnete multas, maximasque proponis quaestiones. Quarum prima est. Quare Magnes trahit ferrum. Quia, inquis, Magnes vivit. Ferrum eius pabulum est. Idcirco in ferri scobe optime servatur. Levissime esse argumentum, et supra ostendimus, et hic demonstramus [p. 185v.] ... Nos in luce rerum tenui caligare, in mediocri caecutire, in maiore caecos esse, in maxima insanire. Quid aliud, quam me *nescire?* Nanque ad Iluae montes ipsae cum applicant naves, cum in anchoris sunt, cum discedunt: nullam sentiunt in pyxide mutationem. Ferrum tamen ab illius loci Sidentide tactum ad polum vertitur, non ad ipsam insulam. Respondent: in sua fodina, atque matrice Iluanum Magnetem non habere vim: exemptum habere. Ego contra: nativam cuiusque Naturae sedem,

286

even if he should live for ten thousand years? He will have experience of only a few things, and faulty experience at that; still worse will be the *judgments* he makes concerning these things; and he will *know* nothing at all. But even if he were to observe a huge number of facts, yet even so he would not be able to observe *all* the facts, as anyone possessing true scientific knowledge must do. And it would be open to doubt whether he had fully adequate experience of them, huge though their number was. For if he should consult treatises on these same topics by other authorities, he will find that they have had totally divergent experimental findings; and what one of them reports as *his* result, another man holds to be impossible, and tries to show, by a number of arguments drawn from this or that source, that the former has made errors in his experimentation. So how will he be able to judge aright on obscure questions, and on problems that can by no means be investigated by means of the senses, if he is doubtful about such as *are* presented to the senses, or have to be "cognised" (cognitively understood) by means of the senses? But if you appeal over the heads of authorities to popular opinions, you will find that their variety is astonishing. There is no agreement anywhere. In most questions, such opinions are totally at variance with what is taught in the sciences. But you will say that these are ignorant people, who do not reflect on things and cannot do so – dolts, in fact. Yet there is a common saying: "The voice of the people is the voice of God", and it is hard to understand how an entire population can be mistaken, while just one philosopher is speaking the truth – 98 especially if the enquiry is concerned with matters that depend on experience rather than on judgment. For there are several departments in which we have to trust them (i.e. the general opinion of mankind), as in agriculture, navigation, and commerce; in a word, we must trust anyone at all who is highly proficient in his art. For

cuiusvis peregrino situi anteferendam iudico" (p. 186v.). Sir Thomas Browne in his *Pseudodoxia epidemica*, 2, 3, devotes many pages to the lodestone and mentions that experiments have proved false the statement that garlic deactivates the power of attraction, as reported in Pliny and Plutarch and many other writers. Magnetism was a topic that intrigued scientists througout the centuries.

this too is a common saying: "Any man at all, ignorant person though he be, is more skilled at his own trade than even a wise man at someone else's".

If, therefore, you wish to decide between men of the common sort and philosophers, in view of the difficulties that follow from the opinions of persons in these two categories, then you will think of a new solution (which is what usually happens, for we are eager for novelties), and you would claim that *that* is wholly true and all else is error. Someone else does the same thing, over and over again; and so does almost all of mankind. Who then spoke the truth? You will say – yourself; for you are already old, and have had a greater number of experiences. But although I would indeed admit that there are few who grasp a subject, yet the other possibility does for its part too seem hard to credit, namely that so many people should be mistaken while you alone speak the truth. For what do you have, above and beyond what they have? Furthermore, ideas that have been held and corroborated by many people over a long period of time appear more solidly based on truth than the new ideas you are now producing. "And yet", you will say, "there are a great many errors that last, unrecognised as such, for a long time". True. But I reply: "There are a great many truths, familiar throughout a long period, that are finally blotted out from view; this happens when errors like these are introduced and grow". What shall we say about that new opinion of yours? It could be either of these. What, then, is it? We do not know. But if you were to say that your opinion is an ancient one (citing the adage "Nothing has ever been said that was not said before"), and if you were to show that some old writers before you said just what you are now saying – why, one who is defending an error will say the same. For there is no opinion so foolish that it does not have some to support it. All these considerations tell against me too, as I endeavour to prove that nothing is *known,* whereas (as things now stand) everyone has an *opinion,* different from those of his neighbours. Yet they *support* me just as much, since from this very fact of their diversity it can clearly be deduced that nothing is known. For, by your own account, scientific knowledge ought to be certain, infallible, and everlasting. What judgment about

99

these matters, then, will be passed by an unhappy old man, however great be the amount of experience you imagine him to possess? No reliable judgment at all. And up to this point the two parts of my own definition seem to have been clearly explained, namely the fact, and the "cognising" subject (*cognoscens*). But there was another part of my definition: the word "perfectly". For not any and every cognitive understanding (*cognitio*) is scientific knowledge (*scientia*), unless you would have it that everyone possesses knowledge, the learned as well as the unlearned, and even brute beasts too. And no one doubts that scientific knowledge ought to be a perfect form of "cognition"; but *what* that is, and where and *in* what it is – about this there is the greatest doubt. This too, like other things, is unknown. Perhaps it does not exist anywhere, and this is the more reasonable supposition. Some of this I have said above: perfect cognitive understanding (*cognitio*) demands a perfect "cognising" subject (*cognoscens*), and an object to be "cognised", which is duly arranged – and these two things I have not anywhere beheld. If you have seen them, write to me. And not only this, but tell me if you have seen anything in Nature that is *perfect*.

Now, you have already seen – above – that this additional point needed to be considered, and accordingly it is not necessary to repeat it here. And with these remarks I believe that I have fully explained my definition, and subsequently shown that nothing is known. There remain some additional proofs of this, which you will see more fully expounded as my works progress. In these works, I shall at all times continue to demonstrate this truth in passing; for my present discourse appears to me to have been drawn out to a more than sufficient length, for which reason therefore let me now bring it to a close.

You have, then, observed the difficulties that place scientific knowledge beyond our reach. I am aware that perhaps much of what I have said will not find favour; but on the other hand, you will say, neither have I *demonstrated* that nothing is known. At least, I have expounded my own opinion as clearly, accurately, and truthfully as I could; for I was not anxious myself to perpetrate the fault I condemn in others, namely to prove my

100 assertion with arguments that were far-fetched, excessively obscure, and perhaps more doubtful than the very problem under investigation. For my purpose is to establish, as far as I am able, a kind of scientific knowledge that is both sound and as easy as possible to attain; but *not* a science that is full of those chimeras and fictions, unconnected with factual truth, which are put together, not to teach facts, but solely to show off the writer's intellectual subtlety. For, like others, I am not devoid of subtleties and clever fictions – and, if my intellect were content with these, I have *more* than they have! But since these notions are far removed from facts, they tend to deceive rather than to instruct the mind, and divert it from truth to fictions. To this I do not give the name of science but of imposture; of a dream, like those made up by wandering charlatans and mountebanks. It will now be for you to judge of these, and to receive in a friendly spirit whatever things seem good to you, but not to pull to pieces, with hostile intent, those that shall seem otherwise; for it would be a far from brotherly act to inflict blows on someone who is trying to be of service. To work, then; and if you know something, then teach me; I shall be extremely grateful to you. In the meantime, as I prepare to examine *Things,* I shall raise the question whether anything is *known,* and if so, how, in the introductory passages of another book, a book in which I will expound, as far as human frailty allows, the *method of knowing.* Farewell.

WHAT IS TAUGHT HAS NO MORE STRENGTH THAN IT DERIVES FROM HIM WHO IS TAUGHT.[182]
WHAT?[183]

---

[182] Sanches ends the *Carmen de cometa anni M.D.LXXVII* with the identical phrase.

[183] The famous *"Quid?"* of Sanches appears for the first time and was the usual interrogative ending for most of his philosophical and medical treatises. Sanches thereby challenges his philosophical and medical opponents to refute his arguments.

Bibliography

Editions of the works of Sanches (Sanchez)

Sanchez, Franciscus. *Carmen de cometa anni M.D.LXXVII*. Lugduni: apud Antonium Gryphium, 1578.
    Quod nihil scitur. Lugduni: apud Antonium Gryphium, 1581. *Editio princeps*. 100 pp.
    Quod nihil scitur. Lugduni: apud Antonium Gryphium, 1581. 100 pp. + *Errata*.
    De multum nobili et prima universali scientia Quod nihil scitur. Francofurti: sumptibus Ioannis Berneri bibliopolae, 1618.
    Opera medica. His iuncti sunt tractatus quidam philosophici non insubtiles. Tolosae tectosagum: apud Petrum Bosc, 1636.
    Tractatus philosophici. Quod nihil scitur. De divinatione per somnum, ad Aristotelem. In lib. Aristotelis Physiognomicon commentarius. De longitudine et brevitate vitae. Roterodami: ex officina Arnoldi Leers, 1649.
    I.N.I. Sanchez aliquid sciens, h.e. in Francisci Sanchez ... tractatum Quod nihil scitur. Notae aliquot et animadversiones Danielis Hartnaccii. Stetini: apud Jeremiam Mamphrasium, 1665.
    O Cometa do ano de 1577 (Carmen de cometa anni M.D.LXXVII). Ludguni, 1578. Trans. G. Manuppella. Introdução e notas do Doutor Artur Moreira de Sá. Lisbon, 1950.
    Opera philosophica. Nova Edição, introdução por Joaquim de Carvalho. Coimbra: Separata da *Revista da Universidade de Coimbra*, vol. XVIII, Imprensa de Coimbra, 1955.
    Opera philosophica. Posfácio por Joaquim de Carvalho. Coimbra: Separata da *Revista da Universidade de Coimbra*, vol. XVIII, Imprensa de Coimbra, 1957.

TRANSLATIONS

1. Portuguese Translations

Que Nada Se Sabe. Trans. Basílio de Vasconcelos. In *Revista de História*, vols. 2–5 (1913–16). Reprinted in Artur Moreira de Sá. *Francisco Sanches. Prefácio e Selecção*. Lisbon: SNI, 1948.
Carta Consulta Ao P. Cristóvão Clavío. In *Revista Portuguesa de Filosofia*, I (1945), pp. 294–305. Reprinted in Artur Moreira de Sá. *Francisco Sanches, filósofo e matemático*. 2 vols. Lisbon, 1947.

Bibliography

Tratados Filosóficos. Trans. Basílio de Vasconcelos e Miguel Pinto de Meneses. Prefácio e Notas A. Moreira de Sá. Lisbon: Gaspar Pinto de Sousa, 1955.

2. Spanish Translations

Que Nada Se Sabe por el Doctor Francisco Sánchez, Médico e Filósófo. Primera traducción en lengua castellana con un prólogo de Menéndez y Pelayo. Trans. Jaime Torrubiano. Madrid: Gil-Blas Renacimiento, n.d. Reprinted Buenos Aires: Editorial Nova, 1944.
Que Nada Se Sabe. Madrid: Espasa-Calpe, 1972.

3. French Translations

"Qu'on ne sait rien". Trans. Henri Pierre Cazac. Fonds Cazac, Institut Catholique de Toulouse.
"Francisco Sanchez et le *Quod Nihil Scitur* Que l'on ne sait rien". Introduction, traduction et notes par Jean Cobos. Diss. Université de Toulouse Le Mirail, 1976.
Il n'est science de rien. Edition critique Latin-Français. Trans. Andrée Comparot. Paris: Klincksieck, 1984.

UNPUBLISHED, LOST, OR PROJECTED WORKS

Commentarius in libros Metheorum. (Sanches refers to this commentary in his *In lib. Aristotelis Physiognomicon* [see *Opera medica*, 1636, p. 34; Carvalho edition, p. 83, line 17].)
De modo sciendi or *Methodus sciendi*. (Sanches refers to this work in the *Quod nihil scitur*. According to Guy Patin [see *Naudaeana et Patiniana*, pp. 72–3] and Moreri [see *Dictionnaire historique*, vol. IX, p. 129], the work appeared in Spanish under the title *Método universal de las ciencias*.)
Erotemata super geometricas Euclidis demonstrationes ad Christophorum Clavium. (Barbosa Machado in his *Biblioteca Lusitana*, vol. II. Lisbon: Na officina de Ignacio Rodrigues, 1747, p. 257, gives the date of publication as 1627. Carvalho believes this work to be contained in Sanches's first letter to Clavius.)
Examen rerum. (Sanches refers to this work in both the *Quod nihil scitur* and the *De longitudine et brevitate vitae*.)
Libri de natura. (Sanches refers to this work in the *Quod nihil scitur*.)
Tractatus de anima. (Sanches refers to this treatise in both the *Quod nihil scitur* and the *De longitudine et brevitate vitae*.)
Tractatus de elementis. (Sanches refers to this treatise in his *In librum Galeni de causis morborum commentarius* [*Opera medica*, pp. 729 and 732].)

Bibliography

Tractatus de loco. (Sanches refers to this treatise in the *Quod nihil scitur.*)

Tractatus de semine. (See Nicolau António, *Bibliotheca Hispana Nova*, I, p. 475, col. I.)

Tractatus de vita. (Sanches refers to this treatise in the *De longitudine et brevitate vitae.*)

Traicté des os, de l'usage, substance, différence et nombre des os. (The original manuscript was lost in a fire at the Departmental Archives of Toulouse.)

SANCHES: STUDIES AND GENERAL REFERENCE WORKS

António, Nicolau. *Bibliotheca Hispana Nova.* Vol. I. Romae: ex officina Nicolai Tinassi, 1672.

Barbosa Machado, Diogo. *Biblioteca Lusitana.* Vol. II. Lisbon: na officina de Ignacio Rodrigues, 1747.

Bayle, Pierre. *Dictionnaire historique et critique par Mr. Pierre Bayle.* Troisième édition. Rotterdam: Michel Bohm, 1720.

Braga, Theophilo. *Renascença.* Vol. II of *História da Litteratura Portugueza.* Porto: Livraria Chardron, de Lello & Irmão, 1914.

Bullón, Eloy. *De los Orígenes de la Filosofía Moderna. Los precursores españoles de Bacon y Descartes.* Salamanca, 1905.

Calmette, Joseph. *Quatre Thèses de 1574 conservées aux archives de la Faculté de Médecine de Montpellier.* Montpellier, 1907.

Un Concours professionel à la Faculté de Médecine de Montpellier au XVIe siècle. Toulouse: Imprimerie Privat, 1909.

Carvalho, Joaquim de. "Vulto e Pensamento de Francisco Sanches". *Revista Filosófica*, 3 (December 1951), pp. 229–66.

Francisco Sanches, filósofo. Braga: Edições Bracera, 1952.

Cazac, Henri Pierre. "Le Fonds Cazac". Institut Catholique de Toulouse.

"L'Espagnol Francisco Sanchez dit le Sceptique". *Bulletin du Comité des Travaux Historiques*, 1903, pp. 179ff.

"Le lieu d'origine et les dates de naissance et de mort du philosophe Francisco Sanchez". *Bulletin Hispanique*, 5 (1903), pp. 326–49.

"Voyages du philosophe Francisco Sanchez en Italie et à Rome ... Arrivée à l'université de Montpellier, persécutions des Huguenots contre Ciro". *Journal officiel de la République Française*, 1903, p. 2476.

"Le Philosophe Francisco Sanchez le sceptique (1550–1623) et les Maisons Galiciennes de Castro". *Bulletin de l'Académie Royale de l'Histoire*, 53 (July, September 1908).

Coelho, Eduardo. *O Cepticismo de Francisco Sanches, médico e filósofo de Quinhentos.* Lisbon, 1938.

Copleston, Frederick. *Late Mediaeval and Renaissance Philosophy.* vol. III, part 2 of

Bibliography

A History of Philosophy. 1946–75. Rpt. New York: Doubleday [Image Books]. 1963.

Coralnik, A. "Zur Geschichte der Skepsis". *Archiv für Geschichte der Philosophie*, 27, n.s. 20 (1941), pp. 188–222.

Costa, Avelino de Jesus. "O célebre Médico e Filósofo Francisco Sanches é Português ou Espanhol?" *Diário do Minho*, August 21, 22, 1942.

Costa, João Cruz. "Ensaio sobre a vida e a obra do Filósofo Francisco Sanches". *Boletim da Faculdade de Filosofia Ciências e Letras da Universidade de S. Paulo*, 1942.

Craveiro da Silva, Lúcio. "Sanches, Filósofo". *Revista Portuguesa de Filosofia*, 7, fasc. 2 (1951), pp. 124–43.

"Francisco Sanches e o pensamento escolástico da época". *Studium Generale*, 8, part 1 (1961), pp. 63–77.

Crescini, Angelo. "Le origini del metodo analitico – Il Cinquente". In *Pubblicazioni dell'Instituto di Filosofia dell'Università di Trieste*, pp. 243–70. Udine: Edizioni Del Bianco, 1965.

Il problema metodologica alle origini della scienza moderna. Rome: Edizioni Dell'Anteneo, 1972.

Descartes, René. *Correspondance*. Vol. III of *Oeuvres de Descartes*. Ed. Charles Adam and Paul Tannery. Paris: Vrin, 1971.

Dizionario dei Filosofi. Florence: G. C. Sansoni Nuova S. P. A., 1976.

Félix, Jean. *Deux médecins-philosophes à l'Université de Toulouse: Raymond Sebon (. . . 1432) Francisco Sanches (1550–1623)*. Toulouse, 1920.

Du Scepticisme en Médecine: Essai sur la Méthode. Toulouse, 1921.

Formey, Jean-Henri Samuel. *Histoire abrégée de la philosophie*. Amsterdam: H. Schneider, 1760.

Gerkrath, Ludwig. *Franz Sanchez. Ein Beitrag zur Geschichte der philosophischen Bewegungen im Anfänge der neueren Zeit*. Vienna: Wilhelm Braumüller, 1860.

Giarratano, Cesare. *Il Pensiero di Francesco Sanchez*. Naples, 1903.

Grande Enciclopédia Portuguesa e Brasileira. Lisbon-Rio de Janeiro: Editorial Enciclopédia, 1936–60.

Hartnack, Daniel. *Sanchez aliquid sciens, h.e. in Francisci Sanchez* . . . Stetini: apud Jeremiam Mamphrasium, 1665.

Iriarte, Joaquim. *Kartesischer oder Sanchezischer Zweifel?* Bottrop: Wilhelm Postberg, 1935.

"Francisco Sánchez, el autor de Quod nihil scitur (Que nada se sabe) a la luz de muy recientes estudios". *Razón y Fé*, 1936, pp. 23–43 and 157–81.

"Francisco Sánchez el Escéptico disfrazado de Carneadas en discusión epistolar con Cristóbal Clavio". *Gregorianum*, 21 (1940), pp. 413–51.

Ishigami-Iagolnitzer, Mitchiko. "Le *Quod nihil scitur* de Sanchez et l'essai 'De l'expérience' de Montaigne". *Bulletin de la Société des Amis de Montaigne*, 5th ser., no. 9 (1974), pp. 11–19.

Joly, L'Abbé Philippe Louis. *Remarques critiques sur le dictionnaire de Bayle*. Vol. II.

294

Paris: Hyppolite Louis Guérin, 1748.

Limbrick, Elaine. "Ce dernier tour d'escrime". *Cahiers de l'Association Internationale des Etudes Françaises*, no. 33 (May 1981), in pp. 53–64.

"Franciscus Sanchez 'Scepticus': un médecin philosophe précurseur de Descartes (1550–1623)". *Renaissance and Reformation*, n.s. 6, no. 4 (1982), pp. 264–72.

Lopes, José da Mota. "Nova Tese: Francisco Sanchez é valenciano". *O Minhoto*, June 3, 1945.

Machado, José. "Francisco Sanches". *Boletim da Biblioteca Pública e Arquivo Distrital de Braga*, 1920, pp. 127–32.

Matos, Luis de. *Les Portugais en France au XVIe siècle*. Coimbra: Nas Officinas Da Atlãntida R. Fernandes Tomás, 1952.

Mellizo, Carlos. "La Preoccupación pedagogica de Francisco Sánchez". *Cuardernos Salamantinos de Filosofia*, 2 (1975), pp. 217–29.

Menéndez y Pelayo, M. "De los Orígenes del Criticismo y del Escepticismo". *Ensayos de Crítica Filosófica*. Vol. XLIII of *Edición nacional de las obras completas de Menéndez y Pelayo*. Santander: Aldus, S. A. de Artes Gráficas, 1948.

Mesnard, Pierre. "L'Aristotélisme critique de Fr. Sanches et la comète de 1577". *Aufsätze zur portugiesischen Kulturgeschichte*, 2 (1961), pp. 60–9.

Miccolis, Salvatore. *Francesco Sanchez*. Bari: Tipografia Levante, 1965.

Michaud, L. G. *Biographie Universelle*. Vol. XIV. Paris: Mme C. Desplaces & Michaud, 1856.

Moraes Filho, Evaristo de. *Francisco Sanches Na Renascença Portuguesa*. Lisbon: Ministério da Educação e Saúde, 1953.

Moreau, Joseph. "Doute et savoir chez Francisco Sanches". *Portugiesische Forschungen des Görresgesellschaft*, 1st ser., *Aufsätze zur Portugiesischen Kulturgesischte*, 1 (1960), pp. 24–50.

"Sanchez précartésien". *Revue philosophique*, 2 (1966), pp. 264–70.

"Un Ecolier bordelais oublié: Francisco Sanchez, médecin philosophe de la Renaissance". *Actes de l'Académie Nationale des Sciences, Belles-Lettres et Arts de Bordeaux*, 4th ser., 22 (1967), pp. 65–71.

"Penseurs Portugais dans l'Europe des Nations". *Arquivos Do Centro Cultural Portugues*, VII. Paris: Fundação Calouste Gulbenkian, 1974.

Moreira de Sá, Artur. *Os Precursores de Descartes*. Lisbon: Na Tipografia Couto Martins, 1944.

Francisco Sanches, Filósofo e matemático. 2 vols. Lisbon, 1947.

Francisco Sanches Prefácio e Selecção. Lisbon: Edições SNI, 1948.

"Francisco Sanches em Montpellier e Toulouse". *Rumo*, 6 (1949), pp. 247ff.

Francisco Sanches Tratados Filosóficos. Lisbon: Gaspar Pinto de Sousa, 1955.

"Raízes e Projecção do Pensamento de Francisco Sanches". *Revista Portuguesa de Filosofia*, .Vol. XI, part 2 (1955), pp. 739–55.

Moreri, Louis. *Le Grand Dictionnaire historique ou le mélange curieux de l'histoire de Paris*. Vol IX. Paris: Libraires Associés, 1759.

Owen, John. *The Skeptics of the French Renaissance*. London: Swan Sonnenschein, 1893.

Passos, Carlos de. "Francisco Sanches: a dúvida metódica". *Revista de Guimarães*, 1922, pp. 386ff.

Patin, Guy. *Naudaeana et Patiniana ou Singularitez remarquables prises des conversations de Mess, Naudé et Patin*. Paris: Florentin & Pierre Delaulne, 1701.

Pimenta, Alfredo. "O Filósofo Francisco Sanches". *Estudos Filosóficos e Críticos*, 1930, pp. 83ff.

"Ainda Francisco Sanches". *Correio do Minho*, August 8, 1942, and in the *Diário do Minho*, August 21, 1942.

"Outra vez Francisco Sanches". *Correio do Minho*, August 19, 1945.

"O caso de Francisco Sanches". *Correio do Minho*, January 23, 1946.

"A Naturalidade de Francisco Sanches". *Sete Cores*. Lisbon: Organizações Bloco, 1950.

Pina, A. Ambrósio de. "Será Tuido, a terra natal do filósofo Francisco Sanches?" *Diário do Minho*, May 11, 1945.

Pina, Luís de. *Os portugueses Francisco Sanches e Zacuto Lusitano na História da Anatómia*. Lisbon, 1944.

"Francisco Sanches, Médico". *Revista Portuguesa de Filosofia*, 7 (1951), pp. 156–91.

Pinto, Sérgio da Silva. "Uma vez mais Francisco Sanches". *Correio do Minho*, August 15, 1942.

"A Naturalidade de Francisco Sanches". *Correio do Minho*, September 18, 19, 1942.

"Filósofos de Braga". *Correio do Minho*, December 3, 1942.

"Ainda a naturalidade de Francisco Sanches". *Correio do Minho*, May 16, 1945.

"A Naturalidade de Francisco Sanches. Crítica duma resposta". *Diário do Minho*, September 18, 19, 1945.

"A Naturalidade de Francisco Sanches". *Diário do Minho*, August 15, 1946.

"No quarto centenário de Francisco Sanches. A primeira educação do filósofo bracarense". *Correio do Minho*, May 5, 1951.

Popkin, Richard H. *The History of Scepticism from Erasmus to Spinoza*. Berkeley: University of California Press, 1979.

Poudou, Fernand. *Deux Médecins-philosophes de l'ancienne Faculté de Médecine de Toulouse: Raymond de Sebonde et François Sanchez*. Toulouse: Imprimerie Toulousaine, 1939.

Revista Portuguesa de Filosofia, 7, fasc. 1 (1951), pp. 113–210 (special issue devoted to Sanches).

Ribeiro, Aquilino. "O filósofo Francisco Sanches". *Anais das Bibliotecas e Arquivos*, 3, no. 1 (1922), pp. 40–1.

Rocha Brito, Alberto Monteiro da. "O Português Francisco Sanches, Prof. de Filosofia e de Medicina na Universidade de Montpellier e Tolosa". *Bulletin des études portugaises de l'Institut français au Portugal*, 7 (1940), pp. 47–8.

Bibliography

"Francisco Sanches, médico, professor e pedagogo". *Bracara Augusta*, 3, nos. 3–4 (1952), pp. 343‑4.

Schoock, Martin (Schoockius, Martinus). *De scepticismo pars prior, sive libri quatuor.* Groningae: ex officina Henrici Lussindi, 1562.

Senchet, Emilien. *Essai sur la méthode de Francisco Sanchez.* Paris: V. Giard and E. Briere, 1904.

Sendrail, Marcel. *Le Serpent et le miroir.* Paris: Plon, 1954.

"Les Années d'apprentissage de F. Sanchez". *Montpeliensis Hippocratis*, no. 29 1955), pp. 3–12.

Spruzzola, Ada Ciribini. "Francesco Sanchez alla luce delle ultime ricerche". *Rivista di Filosofia Neo-Scolastica*, 28 (1936), pp. 372–91.

"Il problema del Metodo e l'empirismo pseudo scettico nel pensiero di Fr. Sanchez". *Rivista di Filosofia Neo-Scolastica*, 35 (1943), pp. 71–91.

Stäudlin, Carl Friedrich. *Geschichte und Geist des Skepticismus.* 2 vols. Leipzig: S. L. Crusius, 1794.

Strowski, Fortunat. *Montaigne.* Paris: Félix Alcan, 1906.

Tavares, Severiano. "Francisco Sanches e o problema da sua nacionalidade." *Revista Portuguesa de Filosofia*, 1 (1945), pp. 63ff.

"Ainda a naturalidade de Francisco Sanches". *Revista Portuguesa de Filosofia*, 1 (1945), pp. 150ff.

"A data da publicação do *Quod nihil scitur*". *Revista Portuguesa de Filosofia*, 1 (1945), pp. 386ff.

"Sanches ou Sanchez?" *Revista Portuguesa de Filosofia*, 1 (1945), pp. 392ff.

"A Naturalidade de Francisco Sanches: Resposta a uma critica". *Revista Portuguesa de Filosofia*, 2 (1946), pp. 81–6.

"Francisco Sanches e a Crítica". *Revista Portuguesa de Filosofia*, 2 (1946), pp. 163–76.

"Francisco Sanches, Filósofo e Matemático: nótulas a um livro". *Revista Portuguesa de Filosofia*, 4 (1948), pp. 72ff.

"Francisco Sanches e o problema da certeza". *Actas del primer Congreso Nacional de Filosofia* (Mendoza), 3 (1950) pp. 205ff.

"Francisco Sanches, Humanista". *Revista Portuguesa de Filosofia*, 7, fasc. 1 (1951), pp. 192–204.

"Francisco Sanches. Vida e Obra". *Revista Portuguesa de Filosofia*, 7, fasc. 1 (1951), pp. 114–23.

"Bibliografia Sanchesiana". *Revista Portuguesa de Filosofia*, 7, fasc. 1 (1951), pp. 205–10.

"Francisco Sanches. O homem", *Revista Portuguesa de Filosofia*, 7, fasc. 1 (1951), pp. 118–19.

Veríssimo Serrão, Joaquim. "Francisco Sanches e a querela do Reitorado tolosano". *Revista Filosófica*, 3 (1951), p. 218.

Présence du Portugal à Toulouse. Toulouse: Imprimerie Fournié, 1956.

Les Portugais à l'Université de Toulouse. (XIII–XVII siècles). Trans. Mme

Chauveau-Biberfeld. Paris: Fundação Calouste Gulbenkian, 1970.

Villey, Pierre. *Les Sources et l'évolution des Essais de Montaigne.* 2 vols. 1908. Rpt. New York: Burt Franklin, 1968.

Wedderkopff, Gabriel. *Dissertationes duae quarum prior de Scepticismo profano et sacro praecipue remonstrantium, posterior de Atheismo praeprimis Socinianorum.* Argentorati: ex officina Josiae Staedelii, 1665.

Wild, Johann Ulrich (Wildtius). *Dissertationes quinque quod aliquid scitur.* Lipsiae: 1664.

GENERAL WORKS: RENAISSANCE PHILOSOPHY AND MEDICINE

Agrippa, Henricus Cornelius. *De incertitudine et vanitate scientiarum et artium atque excellentia verbi Dei declamatio.* Parisiis: apud. J. Petrum, 1531.

Déclamation sur l'Incertitude, Vanité et Abus des Sciences. Trans. Louis de Mayerne-Turquet. Paris: Jean Durand, 1582.

Of the Vanitie and Uncertaintie of Artes and Sciences. Trans. James Sanford. Ed. Catherine M. Dunn. Northridge: California State University, 1974.

Antonioli, Roland. *Rabelais et la médecine.* Geneva: Droz, 1976.

Aristotle. *The Works of Aristotle.* 12 vols. Ed. W. D. Ross. London: Oxford University Press, 1927–52.

De sensu and De memoria. Trans. G. R. T. Ross. New York: Arno Press, 1977.

Generation of Animals. Trans. A. L. Peck. London: William Heinemann, 1943.

Minor Works. Trans. W. S. Hett. London: William Heinemann, 1936.

On the Heavens. Trans. W. K. C. Guthrie. London: William Heinemann, 1939.

Parva naturalia. Ed. Sir David Ross. Oxford: Clarendon Press, 1955.

Arnauld and Nicole. *La Logique ou l'Art de penser.* 1662. Rpt. Paris: Flammarion, 1970.

Barbosa Machado, Diogo. *Memorias para a historia de Portugal que comprehendem o governo del rey D. Sebastião, unico em o nome, a decimo sexto entre os monarcas portuguezes, do anno de 1554 até o anno de 1561 ...* 4 vols. Lisboa Occidental: na officina de J. A. da Sylva. 1736–51.

Boase, Alan M. *The Fortunes of Montaigne: A History of the Essays in France, 1580–1669.* 1935. Rpt. New York: Octagon Books, 1970.

Boucher, Jean. *Les Triomphes de la Religion Chrestienne.* Paris: L. Sonnius, 1628.

Bouillier, Francisque. *Histoire de la Philosophie Cartésienne.* Vol. I. 3rd ed. Paris: Ch. Delagrave, 1868.

Brochard, Victor. *Les Sceptiques Grecs.* Paris: Imprimerie Nationale, 1887.

Browne, Sir Thomas. *Pseudodoxia epidemica books I–VII* (1664). Vol. II of *The Works of Sir Thomas Browne.* Ed. Geoffrey Keynes. London: Faber & Faber, 1964.

Brués, Guy de. *The Dialogues of Guy de Brués. A Critical Edition with a Study in*

Bibliography

Renaissance Scepticism and Relativism. Ed. Panos Paul Morphos. Baltimore: Johns Hopkins University Press, 1953.

Brush, Craig B. *Montaigne and Bayle. Variations on the Theme of Skepticism.* The Hague: Martinus Nijhoff, 1966.

Burnyeat, M. F. "Idealism and Greek Philosophy: What Descartes Saw and Berkeley Missed". *Philosophical Review,* 91 (1982), pp. 3–40.

Bylebyl, Jerome J. "The School of Padua: Humanistic Medicine in the Sixteenth Century". In *Health, Medicine and Mortality in the Sixteenth Century.* Ed. Charles Webster. Cambridge: Cambridge University Press, 1979.

Byrne, Edmund F. *Probability and Opinion: A Study in the Medieval Presuppositions of Post-Medieval Theories of Probability.* The Hague: Martinus Nijhoff, 1968.

Callot, Emile. *La Renaissance des Sciences de la Vie au XVIᵉ siècle.* Paris: Presses Universitaires Françaises, 1950.

Cardano, Girolamo. *Hieronymi Cardani ... Opera Omnia.* 10 vols. Lugduni: sumptibus Joannis Antonii Huguetan & Marcii Antonii Ravaud, 1663. Rpt. New York: Johnson Reprint, 1967.

In C. Ptolemaei Pelusiensis IIII de astrorum iudiciis ... Basileae: excudebat H. Petri, 1554.

Metoposcopia libris tredecim. Lutetiae Parisiorum: apud T. Jolly, 1558.

De rerum varietate libri XVII. Basileae: per H. Petri, 1557.

De subtilitate libri XXI. Norimbergae: apud J. Petreium, 1550.

Les Livres de Hierome Cardanus ... intitulez de la subtilité, et subtiles inventions, ensemble les causes occultes, et raisons d'icelles. traduis de latin en françoys, par Richard le Blanc ... Paris: G. Le Noir, 1556.

Carmaly, E. *Histoire des Médecins Juifs Anciens et Modernes.* Vol. I. Brussels: Société Encyclographique des Sciences Médicales, 1844.

Carvalho, Joaquim de. *António de Gouveia e Pedro Ramo.* Vol. 1 of *António de Gouveia e o Aristotelismo da Renascença.* Coimbra, 1916.

Cass, Myrtle Marguerite. *The First Book of Jerome Cardan's De Subtilitate.* Williamsport: Bayard Press, 1934.

Castro, Américo. *The Structure of Spanish History.* Trans. Edmund L. King. Princeton, N.J.: Princeton University Press, 1954.

Céard, Jean. *La Nature et les Prodiges.* Geneva: Droz, 1977.

Chomel, Louis. *Essai Historique sur la Médecine en France.* Paris: Lottin l'Aîné, 1762.

Cicero. *De natura deorum. Academica.* Trans. H. Rackham. London: William Heinemann, 1933.

Clavius, Christophorus. *(Christophori Clavii, S. J. ... Operum mathematicorum tomus primus (-quintus).* Moguntiae: A. Hierat, 1611–12.

Euclidis elementorum lib. XV. Accessit XVI de solidorum regularium comparatione. n.p., 1574.

Comparot, Andrée. *Amour et Vérité. Sebon, Vivès et Montaigne.* Paris: Klincksieck, 1983.

299

Bibliography

Crombie, A. C. *Augustine to Galileo*. Vol. II of *Science in the Later Middle Ages and Early Modern Times 13th–17 Century*. 1952. Rpt. London: Mercury Books, 1964.

Cumston, Charles Greene. *An Introduction to the History of Medicine*. New York: Knopf, 1927.

Daremberg, Charles. *La Médecine: histoire et doctrines*. Paris, 1865. Rpt. New York: Arno Press, 1976.

Debus, Allen G., ed. *Science, Medicine and Society in the Renaissance. Essays to honor Walter Pagel*. Vol. I. New York: Neale Watson, 1972.

Man and Nature in the Renaissance. Cambridge: Cambridge University Press, 1978.

Deer, Linda Allen. "Academic Theories of Generation in the Renaissance: The Contemporaries and Successors of Jean Fernel (1497–1558)". Ph.D. diss. University of London (Warburg Institute), 1980.

Descartes, René. *Discours de la méthode*. Ed. Etienne Gilson. 4th ed. Paris: Vrin, 1967.

Detcheverry, Arnaud. *Histoire des Israélites de Bordeaux*. Bordeaux: Imprimerie de Balàrac Jeune, 1850.

Dibon, Paul. *L'Enseignement philosophique dans les universités à l'époque précarté-sienne*. Vol. I of *La Philosophie Néerlandaise au siècle d'or*. Paris: Elsevier, 1954.

Dictionnaire des Sciences Philosophiques. Ed. A. Franck. Paris: 1875.

Diogenes Laertius. *Lives of Eminent Philosophers*. 2 vols. Trans. R. D. Hicks. London: William Heinemann, 1925.

Duhem, Pierre M. M. *Le Système du monde*. Vol. X. Paris: Hermann, 1959.

Dulieu, Louis. *La Médecine à Montpellier*. 2 vols. Avignon: Les Presses Universelles, 1975.

Durling, Richard J. "A Chronological Census of Renaissance Editions and Translations of Galen". *Journal of the Warburg and Courtauld Institutes*, 24 (1961), pp. 230–305.

"Linacre and Medical Humanism". In *Linacre Studies: Essays on the Life and Work of Thomas Linacre c. 1460–1524*. Ed. Francis Maddison, Margaret Pelling, and Charles Webster. Oxford: Clarendon Press, 1977.

Eckman, James. *Jerome Cardan*. Baltimore: Johns Hopkins University Press, 1946.

Edwards, William F. "Niccolò Leoniceno and the Origins of Humanist Discussion of Method". In *Philosophy and Humanism*, ed. Edward P. Mahoney, pp. 283–305. Leiden: Brill, 1976.

Fallopio, Gabriello. *Observationes anatomicae*. Parisiis: apud Jacobium Kerver, 1562.

De humani corporis anatome compendium. Venetiis: apud Paulum et Antonium Meietos Fratres, 1571.

Opera genuina omnia. 3 vols. Venetiis: apud Ie. Antonium et Jacobum de Franciscis, 1606.

Bibliography

Febvre, Lucien. *Le Problème de l'incroyance au 16ᵉ siècle.* 1942. Rpt. Paris: Albin Michel, 1968.

Fernel, Jean. *Ioannis Fernelii Ambiani de abditis rerum causis libri duo.* Venetiis: apud Andream Arrivabenum, 1550.

Universa medicina. Francofurti: apud Andream Wechelum, 1584.

Ferrier, Auger. *Liber de diebus decretoriis secundum pythagoricam doctrinam et astronomicam observationem.* Lugduni: J. Tornaesius, 1549.

Fox Morcillo, Sebastian. *De demonstratione eiusque necessitate ac vi.* Basileae: per Ioannem Oporinum, 1556.

De naturae philosophia seu de Platonis et Aristotelis consensione libri V. Parisiis: ex officina Iacobi Puteani, 1560.

French, R. K. "Berengario da Carpi and the Use of Commentary in Anatomical Teaching". In *The Medical Renaissance of the Sixteenth Century.* Ed. Andrew Wear, R. K. French, and I. M. Lonie. Cambridge: Cambridge University Press, 1985.

Fuchs, Leonhart. *Compendiaria ac succinta admodum in medendi artem introductio.* Haganoae: per J. Secerium, 1531.

Methodus seu ratio compendiaria cognoscendi veram solidamque medicinam ad Hippocratis et Galeni scripta recte intelligenda mire utilis ... Parisiis: apud J. Dupuys, 1550.

Institutionum medicinae, sive methodi ad Hippocratis, Galeni, aliorumque veterum scripta recte intelligenda mire utiles libri quinque ... Editio secunda. Lugduni, 1560.

Galenus, Claudius. *Commentariorum in Claudii Galeni opera, medicorum principis.* Authore Thoma A'Veiga Eborensi. Antwerpiae: Plantin, 1564.

De Hippocratis et Platonis placitis. Trans. Joanne Guinterio Audermaeo. Parisiis: apud Simonem Colinaeum, 1534.

De optimo docendi genere liber. In quo adversus veteres Academicos Pyrrhoniosque disputat. In Sextus Empiricus, *Adversus mathematicos.* Paris: Martinum Invenem, 1569.

Galen on Language and Ambiguity: an English translation of Galen's De captionibus (On Fallacies). Trans. Robert Blair Edlow. Leiden: Brill, 1977.

Galeni methodus medendi, vel de morbis curandis, T. Linacro ... *interprete, libri quatuordecim.* Lutetiae, 1519.

Institutio logica. Trans. John Spangler Kieffer. Baltimore: Johns Hopkins University Press, 1964.

Oeuvres Anatomiques, Physiologiques et Médicales. 2 vols. Trans. Ch. Daremberg. Paris: J. B. Baillière, 1854–6.

On the Natural Faculties. Trans. Arthur John Brock. London: William Heinemann, 1916.

On the Usefulness of the Parts of the Body. De usu partium. 2 vols. Trans. Margaret Tallmadge May. New York: Cornell University Press, 1968.

Garasse, Le P. François. *La Doctrine curieuse des beaux esprits de ce temps, ou*

Bibliography

prétendus tels ... Paris: S. Chappelet, 1623.

Apologie du père François Garasse, de la Compagnie de Jesus, pour son livre contre les athéistes et libertins de nostre siècle, et response aux censures et calomnies de l'autheur anonyme. Paris: S. Chappelet, 1624.

La Somme théologique des véritez capitales de la Religion chrestienne. Paris: S. Chappelet, 1625.

Garin, Eugenio. *Astrology in the Renaissance.* London: Routledge & Kegan Paul, 1983.

Gaullieur, Ernest. *Histoire du Collège de Guyenne.* Paris: Sandoz & Fischbacher, 1874.

Gilbert, Neal Ward. *Renaissance Concepts of Method.* New York: Columbia University Press, 1960.

Gouhier, Henri. "Doute méthodique ou négation méthodique? *Les Etudes Philosophiques*, n.s., 9, no. 1 (1954), pp. 135–62.

Les Premières Pensées de Descartes. Paris: Vrin, 1958.

Gouveia, António de. *Commentário sobre as conclusões e em defesa de Aristóteles contra as calúnias de Pedro Ramo.* Trans. Miguel Pinto de Meneses. Introdução de Artur Moreira de Sá. Lisbon: Instituto de Alta Cultura, 1966.

Goux, Jean-Joseph. "Descartes et la perspective." *L'Esprit Créateur*, 25, no. 1 (1985), pp. 10–20.

Grouchy, Nicolas de. *Aristotelis logica.* Coimbra, 1549.

Praeceptiones dialecticae. n.p., 1555.

Guérente, Guillaume. *Aristotelis logica.* Parisisiis: ex typographia T. Richardi, 1559.

Guerlac, Rita. *Jean Luis Vives against the Pseudodialecticians. A Humanist Attack on Medieval Logic.* Dordrecht: Reidel, 1979

Guy, Alain. *Vivès ou l'Humanisme engagé.* Paris: Seghers, 1972.

Hall, A. R. *The Scientific Revolution 1500–1800.* London: Longmans, Green, 1954.

Hall, Vernon, Jr. "Life of Julius Caesar Scaliger (1484–1558)". *Transactions of the American Philosophical Society*, n.s. 40, part 2 (1950), pp. 85–170.

Haskins, Charles H. *The Rise of Universities.* New York: Henry Holt, 1923.

Haydn, Hiram. *The Counter-Renaissance.* New York: Charles Scribner's Sons, 1950.

Hellman, C. Doris. *The Comet of 1577: Its Place in the History of Astronomy.* 1944. Rpt. New York: AMS Press, 1971.

Hippocrates. *Aphorismorum Hippocratis sectiones septem.* Ex. Franc. Rabelaesi recognitione. Lugduni: apud. Seb. Gryphium, 1532.

Les Aphorismes d'Hippocrates avec le commentaire de Galien sur le premier livre. Traduits du Grec en François par M. I. Breche. Lyon: Jean Ant. Huguetan, 1605.

Ingegno, Alfonso. *Saggio sulla filosofia di Cardano.* Florence: La Nuova Italia Editrice, 1980.

Kapp, Ernest. *Greek Foundations of Traditional Logic.* New York: Columbia

University Press, 1942.

Kearney, Hugh. *Science and Change 1500–1700*. London: Weidenfeld & Nicolson, 1971.

Keller, Alex. "Mathematical Technologies and the Growth of the Idea of Technical Progress". In *Science, Medicine and Society in the Renaissance*. Vol. I. Ed. Allen G. Debus. New York: Neale Watson, 1972.

Laguna, Andres de. *Aristotelis Stagiritae de physiognomicis liber unus*. Parisiis: apud Ludovicum Cyaneum, 1535.

Launoy, Jean de. *De scholis celebrioribus*. Vol. IV of *Opera omnia*. Lutetiae Parisiorum: typis-viduae E. Martini, 1672.

Lehoux, Françoise. *Le Cadre de vie des médecins parisiens au XVIe et XVIIe siècles*. Paris: A. et J. Picard, 1976.

Leoniceno, Niccolò. *De Plinii et plurium aliorum medicorum in medicina erroribus opus primum*. Ferrariae: per Ioannem Maciochium, 1509.

De tribus doctrinis ordinatis secundum Galeni sententiam. Venetiis, 1523.

Lichtenthaeler, Charles. *Histoire de la médecine*. Trans. Denise Meunier. Paris: Fayard, 1978.

Limbrick, Elaine. "Was Montaigne Really a Pyrrhonian?" *Bibliothèque d'Humanisme et Renaissance*, 39 (1977), pp. 67–80.

"Le Pyrrhonisme est le vrai." In *Mélanges sur la littérature de la Renaissance à la mémoire de V.-L. Saulnier*, pp. 439–48. Geneva: Droz, 1984.

Linacre, Thomas. *Galeni methodus medendi, vel de morbis curandis, T. Linacro . . . interprete, libri quatuordecim*. Lutetiae, 1519.

Lindberg, David C., and Steneck, Nicolas H. "The Sense of Vision and the Origins of Modern Science". In *Science, Medicine and Society in the Renaissance*. Vol. I. Ed. Allen C. Debus. New York: Neale Watson, 1972.

Lusitanus, Amatus. *Amati Lusitani medici praestantissimi curationum medicinalium centuria secunda*. Venetiis: ex officina Erasmiana Vincenti Valgrisii, 1552.

Martini, Maria Cristina. *Piante medicamentose e rituali magico-religiosi in Plinio*. Rome: Bulzoni editore, 1977.

Matthiolus, Petrus Andreas. *Commentaires de M. P. André Matthiolus Medecin Senois sur les six livres de Pedacius Dioscoride Anazarbeen de la matiere medicinale*. Trans. Antoine de Pinet. Lyon: A l'escu de Milan par la veuve du feu Gabriel Cotier, 1572.

Mersenne, Marin. *La Vérité des sciences contre les septiques ou pyrrhoniens*. Paris: T. Du Bray, 1625.

Michel, Francisque. *Histoire du commerce à Bordeaux*. 2 vols. Bordeaux: Imprimerie J. Delmas, 1866.

Montaigne, Michel de. *Essais de Montaigne*. Paris: Gallimard, 1950.

Nauert, Charles. *Agrippa and the Crisis of Renaissance Thought*. Urbana: University of Illinois Press, 1965.

Noreña, Carlos G. *Juan Luis Vives*. The Hague: Martinus Nijhoff, 1970.

Nutton, Vivian. *Karl Gottlob Kühn and his Edition of the Works of Galen*. Oxford:

Oxford Microform Publications, 1976.

"Humanist Surgery". In *The Medical Renaissance of the Sixteenth Century*. Ed. Andrew Wear, R. K. French and I. M. Lonie. Cambridge: Cambridge University Press, 1985.

O'Malley, Charles D. *English Medical Humanists. T. Linacre and J. Caius.* Lawrence: University of Kansas Press, 1965.

Andreas Vesalius of Brussels 1514–1564. Berkeley: University of California Press, 1965.

Ong, Walter J. *Ramus: Method and the Decay of Dialogue.* Cambridge, Mass.: Harvard University Press, 1958.

Pagel, Walter. *Paracelse. Introduction à la médecine philosophique de la Renaissance.* Trans. Michel Deutsch. Paris: Arthaud, 1963.

Palmer, Richard. "Pharmacy in the Republic of Venice in the Sixteenth Century". In *The Medical Renaissance of the Sixteenth Century*. Ed. Andrew Wear, R. K. French, and I. M. Lonie. Cambridge: Cambridge University Press, 1985.

Paré, Ambroise. *Oeuvres d'Ambroise Paré.* Paris: G. Buon, 1579.

Platter, Félix. *Félix et Thomas Platter à Montpellier, 1552–1559, 1595–1599. Notes de voyage de deux étudiants bâlois.* Montpellier: C. Coulet, 1892.

Pliny. *Natural History.* 10 vols. Trans. H. Rackham. London: William Heinemann, 1952.

Plutarch. *Plutarch's Moralia.* 15 vols. Trans. F. C. Babbitt et al. London: William Heinemann, 1927–76.

Ponzetti, Cardinal Ferdinando. *Libellus de venenis.* Romae: J. Mazochii, 1521.

Quicherat, J. *Histoire de Sainte Barbe.* 3 vols. Paris: Hachette, 1860.

Ramus, Petrus. *Animadversionum Aristotelicarum libri XX.* Lutetiae Parisiorum: apud Ioañem Roigny, 1548.

Randall, John Herman. *The School of Padua and the Emergence of Modern Science.* Padua: Antenore, 1956.

Renazzi, Filippo Maria. *Storia dell'Università degli Studi di Roma detta communemente. La Sapienza.* 2 vols. Rome: Nella Stamperia Pagliarini, 1803–6.

Rescher, Nicholas. *Galen and the Syllogism.* Pittsburgh, Pa.: University of Pittsburgh Press, 1966.

Scepticism. Oxford: Blackwell, 1980.

Reulos, Michel. "L'Enseignement d'Aristote dans les collèges au XVIᵉ siècle". In *Platon et Aristote à la Renaissance.* Ed. J.-C. Margolin, pp. 147–54. Paris: Vrin, 1976.

Riccoboni, Antonio. *De gymnasio patavino.* Patavii: apud Franciscum Bolzetam, 1598.

Roger, Jacques. "Jean Fernel et les problèmes de la médecine de la Renaissance". *Les Conférences du Palais de la Découverte.* Series D, no. 51. Paris: Edition du Palais de la Découverte, 1960.

Les Sciences de la vie dans la pensée française du XVIIIᵉ siècle. Paris: Armand

Bibliography

Colin, 1963.

Rose, Paul L. *The Italian Renaissance of Mathematics*. Geneva: Droz, 1975.

Ross, W. D. *Aristotle*. 1923. Rpt. London: Methuen, 1953.

Sarton, George. *Galen of Pergamon*. Lawrence: University of Kansas Press, 1954.

Scaliger, Julius Caesar. *Exotericarum exercitationum liber quintus decimus de subtilitate ad Hieronymum Cardanum*. Parisiis: apud Federicum Morellum, 1557.

Schmitt, Charles B. *A Critical Survey and Bibliography of Studies on Renaissance Aristotelianism 1958–1969*. Padua: Antenore, 1971.

Cicero Scepticus: A Study of the Influence of the Academica in the Renaissance. The Hague: Martinus Nijhoff, 1972.

Aristotle and the Renaissance. Cambridge, Mass.: Harvard University Press, 1983.

"Aristotle among the Physicians". In *The Medical Renaissance of the Sixteenth Century*. Ed. Andrew Wear, R. K. French, and I. M. Lonie. Cambridge: Cambridge University Press, 1985.

Schofield, Malcolm, Myles Burnyeat, and Jonathan Barnes, eds. *Doubt and Dogmatism*. Oxford: Clarendon Press, 1980.

Schoockius, Martinus, and Gisbert Voetius. *Admiranda methodus novae philosophiae Renati Des Cartes*. Ultraiecti: ex officina J. Van Waesbergae, 1643.

Sextus Empiricus. *Sexti Philosophi Pyrrhoniarum Hypotypωsewn libri III . . . latine nunc primum editi interprete Henrico Stephano*. Parisiis: Henricus Stephanus, 1562.

Adversus Mathematicos . . . Graece nunquam, Latine nunc primum editum, Gentiano Herveto Aurelio interprete. Eiusdem Sexti Pyrrhoniarum HYPOTYPΩSEΩN libri tres . . . interprete Henrico Stephano. Parisiis: Martinum Iuvenem, 1569.

[Works]. 4 vols. Trans. R. G. Bury. London, 1933–49. Rpt. Cambridge, Mass.: Harvard University Press, 1961.

Oeuvres choisies de Sextus Empiricus. Trans. Jean Grenier and Geneviève Goron. Paris: Aubier, 1948.

Siegel, Rudolph E. *Galen's System of Physiology and Medicine*. Basel: S. Karger, 1968.

Galen on Sense Perception. Basel: S. Karger, 1970.

Galen on Psychology, Psychopathology, and Function and Diseases of the Nervous System. Basel: S. Karger, 1973.

Singer, Charles. *A Short History of Anatomy and Physiology from the Greeks to Harvey*. New York: Dover, 1957.

Stough, Charlotte. *Greek Skepticism. A Study in Epistemology*. Berkeley: University of California Press, 1969.

Talaeus, Audomarus (Omer Talon). *Academia. Eiusdem in Academicum Ciceronis fragmentum explicatio*. Lutetiae: M. David, 1547.

Temkin. Owsei. *Galenism: Rise and Decline of a Medical Philosophy*. Ithaca: Cornell University Press, 1973.

Thorndike, Lynn. *The Sixteenth Century*. Vol. V of *A History of Magic and*

305

Bibliography

Experimental Science. New York: Columbia University Press, 1941.

Thou, Jacques de. *Historiarum sui temporis ab anno 1543 usque ad annum 1607, libri CXXXVIIII*. Geneva: Pierre de la Rouiere, 1626.

Traverso, Edilia. *Montaigne e Aristotele*. Florence: Felice Le Monnier, 1974.

Trinquet, Roger. *La Jeunesse de Montaigne*. Paris: Nizet, 1972.

Van Leeuwen, Henry G. *The Problem of Certainty in English Thought*. The Hague: Martinus Nijhoff, 1963.

Vinet, Elie. *Schola Aquitanica*. Trans. Louis Massebieau. Paris: Le Musée pédagogique, 1886.

Vives, Ioannes Lodovicus. *De disciplinis libri XX*. Antwerpiae: excudebat M. Hillenius, 1531.

Opera Omnia. 8 vols. Ed. Gregorio Mayano y Siscar. Valencia, 1782–90. Rpt. London: Gregg Press, 1964.

Wear, A., R. K. French, and I. M. Lonie, eds. *The Medical Renaissance of the Sixteenth Century*. Cambridge: Cambridge University Press, 1985.

"Explorations in Renaissance Writings on the Practice of Medicine". In *The Medical Renaissance of the Sixteenth Century*. Cambridge: Cambridge University Press, 1985.

Wightman, William P. D. *The Growth of Scientific Ideas*. New Haven, Conn.: Yale University Press, 1953.

Science and the Renaissance. Vol. I. Edinburgh: Oliver & Boyd, 1962.

"Quid sit methodus? 'Method' in Sixteenth Century Medical Teaching and 'Discovery'. *Journal of the History of Medicine*, 19 (1964), pp. 360–76.

Winther von Andernach, Johann (Guinterius). *Methodus medendi*. Parisiis, 1528.

Woodward, William Harrison. *Studies in Education in the Age of the Renaissance*. Cambridge, 1906. Rpt. New York: Russell & Russell, 1965.

Index Nominum

In the present index are primarily listed the proper names found in the text and footnotes of the book. Not listed, however, are frequently occurring names such as Sanches and Aristotle. All references to works of Sanches other than the *Quod nihil scitur* have been indexed. References to the works of Aristotle are too numerous to be included.

Index Nominum

Index Nominum

Matthiolus, Petrus Andreas, 214 *n*100, 227 *n*118, 280 *n*176

Menéndez y Pelayo, M., 2 *n*4

Mersenne, Marin, 82 *n*44, 83

Metrodorus of Chios, 172 *n*20

Miccolis, Salvatore, 11 *n*28, 20 *n*62

Mithridates, 100, 182

Montaigne, Michel de, 2, 6, 8, 25, 28, 42, 67, 69, 79–81, 82 *n*44, 84, 171 *n*17, 196 *n*64

Montanus, 61

Moraes Filho, Evaristo de, 4 *n*1

Moreau, Joseph, 82 *n*45, 167 *n*9

Moreira de Sá, Artur, 3 *n*4, 20 *n*62, 38

Moses, 99, 124, 180, 206

Muret, Marc-Antoine, 7

Nauert, Charles, 73 *n*19

New Academy, 30, 35, 48, 70, 71, 72, 75, 77, 78, 168 *n*12, 173 *n*20

Nominalism (Parisian), 24, 25 *n*1, 27

Noreña, Carlos G., 31, 32 *n*29, 36 *n*40

Nutton, Vivian, 62 *n*55

Ong, Walter J., 27, 28 *n*10, 36 *n*41

Ovid, 235

Owen, John, 2 *n*4, 67 *n*1

Pagés, Bermond, 17, 18

Pascal, Blaise, 2, 68

Patin, Guy, 5, 24

Paul of Aegina, 18, 60

Peter of Spain, 27, 30

Phaedrus, 168 *n*10

Philip I, king of Spain, 35 *n*39

Piccolomini, Arcangelo, 13

Planudes, Maximus, 189 *n*54, 266 *n*167

Plato, 12, 34 *n*34, 61, 64, 92, 100, 102, 103, 156, 168, 178, 182, 185, 187, 193 *n*58 & *n*59, 257 *n*161

Platter, Félix, 7 *n*11, 16

Platter, Thomas, 6, 7 *n*11, 16

Pliny, *Natural History*, 12, 124, 166 *n*6, 194 *n*60, 226 *n*117, 230 *n*125 & *n*126, 236 *n*141, 237 *n*142, 279 *n*175

Plutarch, *Adversus Colotem*, 78, 79, 184 *n*44, 190 *n*55, 225 *n*115, 239 *n*146, 240 *n*148, 249 *n*153, 251 *n*154; *De amore*, 259 *n*162; *De musica*, 187 *n*47, 266 *n*167; *Gryllus*, 215 *n*104; *Lucullus*, 190 *n*55; *Platonicae quaestiones*, 279 *n*175; *Quomodo amicum ab adultaore discernas*, 281 *n*177

Popkin, Richard H., 3, 24, 25, 68 *n*5, 71, 74 *n*19, 77 *n*32, 82 *n*44, 174 *n*25, 200 *n*70

Porphyry, 10 *n*23

Pythagoras, 92, 168, 231 *n*128

Queyrats, Jean, 23

Ramus, Petrus, 27, 36, 37, 75

Randall, John Herman, Jr., 26 *n*4

Renazzi, Filippo Maria, 12, 13, 14 *n*36

Rescher, Nicholas, 70 *n*13, 78 *n*35

Reulos, Michel, 26, 27 *n*7

Rhazes, 18, 33

Rose, Paul L., 48 *n*1

Ross, W.D., 213 *n*96, 215 *n*105, 228 *n*122

Ruellius, Johannes, 34

Sanches, Adám-Francisco, 5, 10 *n*25

Sanches, António, 4 *n*1, 5, 10 *n*25

Sanches, Denys, 4 *n*1

Sanches, Francisco (Sanchez, Franciscus): *Carmen de cometa anni M.D. LXXVII*, 20, 37–40, 57, 290 *n*182; *De divinatione per somnum, ad Aristotelem*, 13, 14, 40 –4; *De longitudine et brevitate vitae liber*, 11 *n*29, 40, 44–5, 62, 81 *n*42; *De modo sciendi*, 166 *n*5, 276 *n*172, 290; *Examen rerum (Enquiry into things)*, 139, 141, 145, 166 *n*5, 212, 230, 247, 250, 254, 261, 290; *In lib. Aristotelis physiognomicon commentarius*, 40, 45–6, 47 *n*75; *Libri de natura*, 166 *n*5; *Objectiones et erotemata super geometricas Euclidis demonstrationes*, 20, 47–50; *Tractatus de anima*, 148, 166 *n*5, 193, 229, 239, 264; *Tractatus de loco*, 166 *n*5; *Tractatus philosophici*, 41; *Opera medica*, 3, 14, 15 *n*40, 18, 40, 56 *n*32, 68, *et passim; De pulsibus*, 79 *n*38; *De theriaca ad pharmacopoeos liber*, 14 *n*39; *In librum Galeni de differentiis morborum commentarius*, 79 *n*39; *Observationes in Praxi*, 10; *Pharmacopoeia*, 14 *n*39; *Summa Anatomica libris quatuor*, 14, 15 *n*40

Sanches, Guillaume, 4 *n*1

Saporta, Antoine, 17

Saporta, Jean, 17, 18

Sarton, George, 62 *n*54

Scaliger, Julius Caesar, 169 *n*13, 205 *n*76, 207 *n*82, 226 *n*116, 227 *n*118–20, 228 *n*121, 240 *n*147, 260 *n*163, 280 *n*175, 286 *n*181

Scepticism: Academic, 24 *n*1, 64, 67–72, 74–80, 83 *n*48, 88, 101, 184, 190 *n*55; Pyrrhonian, 1 *n*1, 2, 24 *n*1, 35, 64–9, 70–3, 76–82, 84–7, 101, 184, 190 *n*55, 251 *n*154